LABOR'S SEARCH FOR MORE

By

MALCOLM KEIR

PROFESSOR OF ECONOMICS, DARTMOUTH COLLEGE

THE RONALD PRESS COMPANY
NEW YORK

To

EDITH WARREN PECK

Who first showed me the pleasures in the
reading and the writing of books.

PREFACE

More security, more wages, more leisure, and, for farmers, more income are the objects of labor's search. In this country the search for these blessings has been, and now is, by democratic means. The European methods of fascism or communism need not be thrust upon Americans if our leaders strive to make our democracy really effective.

Democracies are notorious for their tendency to allow problems to drift toward a muddled solution. Our system now faces important decisions which cannot be made in a happy-go-lucky manner. The choices made in the present decade are likely to influence the rest of the century.

Wisdom seldom is intuitive but is based upon experience. Since our immediate national problems mostly are social, the experience of our business executives in production is inadequate; they therefore must supplement their own experience with broader studies. Unfortunately, many business men are so immersed in their daily affairs that they have slight information about the feelings and aspirations of the wage earners who constitute the bulk of our population. In the long run it will be the workers and farmers who will attempt to put their hopes into realities. Wise executives will try to learn in advance what the majority of our people want.

Therefore, it is essential to know something of the recent record of the struggles of ordinary persons to improve their lot. *That record is the guide to what they hope to achieve.* No executive or student can evaluate current labor crises unless judgments are based on knowledge of labor experiences in the past generation. This book endeavors to fill this need.

Regardless of what labor or any one else wants in the way of economic improvements, the only source of gains is in enlarged production. In turn, production is the result of the joint efforts of land, capital, management and labor. Therefore, preliminary examination of the bases of production becomes the first task before the story of labor's search for more can be told.

Since radicalism is a barometer which reveals the weight of economic pressures and thus directs attention to zones of stress, this book includes reviews of the radicalism of American farmers and wage earners. Any effective radicalism would need to unite these two groups.

Southern white and colored workers during the generation that ended in 1929 were the most laggard in the contest for more comfortable living. Consequently their misery threatened to overwhelm northern workers who had advanced further toward comfort. An account of southern workers is doubly important, first to reveal their own status, and secondly to show the influence of their drag upon other workers.

Since unions directly affected only a minority of workers, to unions we devote a minority of space.

After 1929 farmers and wage earners emerged as contenders for political power in order to bolster their economic power. Despite varying opinions there may be about the desirability of this action the effort itself was a logical sequence to the experiences of labor between 1896 and 1929.

Business executives, students, and even modern labor leaders and laborers ought to know something of what these experiences were. This book is submitted so that an insight may be gained as to why workers then—as now—sought "more."

MALCOLM KEIR

Hanover, N. H.,
    January, 1937.

CONTENTS

CHAPTER 1

PAGE

LAND: Uncrowded America. LABOR: Immigration. Changed Attitude Toward Immigration Since World War. Exploitation of Immigrants. Women as Wage Earners up to 1918. Effect of World War on Employment of Women. Women as Competitors with Men. Child Labor Laws. Where Child Labor Is Worst. Why Child Labor Exists. Effects of Regulation of Child Labor. CAPITAL: Growth of Capitalism. Concentration of Wealth and Income. Capital vs. Labor. Business Management. Salaried Experts. Cooperation of Wage Earners Sought. The Capitalist and the Hired Manager. Why Labor Sought "More".

CHAPTER 2

Where Unions Are Strong. Where Unions Failed. Variations in Degree of Unionization. Explanation of the Tardy Growth of Unionism. Why Unionism Declined after 1920. Neglect of Unskilled. Wages and Hours—Did Unionism Raise Wages? Shorter Work Day—By Law. Arguments for Shorter Work Day. Against Shorter Hours. Unionism in Relation to Shorter Hours.

CHAPTER 3

The Number of Strikes—Relation to Corporate Business. Industries Most Often Affected by Strikes: Building Trades. Clothing Trades. Miners' Strikes. Textile Industry. Summary.

CHAPTER 4

Anthracite Strike of 1902: Colorado Fuel and Iron Co. Strike 1913-14—Importance of This Strike. Lawrence, Massachusetts, Textile Strike 1912. The Record Year of 1919. Noteworthy Strikes of 1919—Seattle Strike. The General Strike at Seattle. No Disorder. Mayor Hanson's Acts. Original Strike Loses.

CHAPTER 5

The Boston Police Strike 1919. The Steel Strike of 1919. Soft Coal Strike of 1919: Shopmen's Strike of 1922—Daugherty Injunction. Southern Textile Strikes 1929-30. Results of Strikes.

CHAPTER 6

CHAPTER 7

CHAPTER 8

CHAPTER 9

CHAPTER 10

Chapter 17

FOREWORD

"More," replied Samuel Gompers when in 1914 the U. S. Commission on Industrial Relations asked him what it was that American labor sought.

Not only was organized labor fittingly characterized by that word but the word "More" also was applicable to nearly all Americans in the generation from McKinley to Hoover. Capitalists strove to create larger business units which returned more generous dividends. Engineers tried to produce these results by devising methods of greater output per man. Communities cheered the boosters who sought greater numbers in the towns. The nation itself although still relatively sparsely inhabited was induced to support a program of imperialism by which the lands of distant colonies were brought under the American flag; some national officers even dreamed of widening our boundaries to include the whole North American continent. "Bigger and better" was the slogan of both farmers and factory owners as well as of both financier and politician. Nor were consumers laggard in demanding more goods in greater varieties and in new forms; the living standards of parents were scorned by children so that "keeping up with the Joneses" became an almost universal struggle.

If the passion for "more" always has been a trait of mankind, few generations have been able to satisfy this zeal to the extent of the Americans who lived in the days when the gold standard was immutable and unique. Men and women not only bent all their energies to get "more" but honored most those who succeeded best in this pursuit. Morals were shaped by possessions; he who had most was held guiltless even if in the process of getting he had departed from conventional standards, while he who had nothing was both scorned and held to strict accountability. In all of the industrial countries the avid pursuit of "more" was for a generation a common trait; in none was it so true as of the United States that a sizable proportion of the population for a while really got "more."

In the last five years of the generation the quick attainment of "more" became outright gambling indulged by people in all walks of life, from the widow over a washtub to the banker-custodian of bulging vaults. Inevitably the reaction to a "more," the pursuit of which had become a disease, was severe and prolonged; so that at the worst, in the six years after 1929, thirteen million men and women were made jobless; and there was hardly a person in the whole nation who did not lose considerable of his accumulated "more." The generation had begun in 1896 after a time when children had wailed with hunger and it ended in 1929 when for a time the piling up of too much left nearly every one with too little and many with nothing.

LABOR'S SEARCH
FOR MORE

CHAPTER 1

PRODUCTION

"Production is the result of the cooperation of land, labor, capital, and business management." If this definition of the economists is correct, labor is only one of four factors in the creation of wealth; labor uses the other three and in turn is used by the other three. Therefore, whatever changes after 1896 occurred in land, capital, or business management had a bearing upon labor's search for "more." If labor was backed by more soil or resources, more capital, or more effective management there could be more product; in turn any enlargement of product made it possible for each of the four cooperators to get "more." The ability of labor to attain "more" was not dependent solely upon the quantity and quality of labor.

Land

The Frontier Spirit.—It is not necessary to linger in the discussion of "land," a word which as used by economists includes in addition to soil, all natural resources. Concerning land as a factor in production two facts were most important; the generation after 1896 saw the disappearance of an abundance of *free* land, and yet land in relation to the other three factors of production was not scarce.

As the Census of 1890 pointed out, by that year there was no continuous frontier left in the United States. In just 100 years after the first Census our continental boundaries were occupied, and the "West" as a refuge for the desirous, discontented, disinherited, or defeated was gone. The opportunity to acquire land cheaply or with no payment save personal labor, which had been an American birthright for nearly 300 years, vanished. To be sure, tracts of public land aside from forest reserves still existed; but most of these on account of their soil,

their slope, or their aridity were of slight economic significance, except as unknown methods of utilization might later
give them value, or as expensive public works for irrigation or
drainage made them useful. These public lands were mostly
important as potential playgrounds, and a preservation of the
romantic "great open spaces" so intimately a part of American
tradition. However, the hardihood required of frontiersmen
was still a requisite for life in many parts of the United States,
and immigrants had to possess a modicum of it to transplant
themselves to a new land and often to new occupations. Hence,
the frontier spirit lingered.

As long as the frontier lasted it had a liberalizing influence
on wages and working conditions; for although relatively few
wage earners sought the frontier as an escape from intolerable
or irksome working conditions the fact that some did, and all
could, mitigated the power of employers. After 1890 labor
was apt to be shut within its industry with escape only to another
employer.

Before the disappearance of the frontier and especially in
the previous generation, immigrants tended to seek the land,
not wage-paying occupations. After 1890 the immigrants
crowded into colonies of their own nationality, first in the cities
and then in smaller towns and mining camps. Most of the
later immigrants became unskilled wage-earners who not only
tended to depress the wages of their own and other labor groups
but greatly increased the difficulties of organization of labor
into unions. By making a drastic separation between the alien
unskilled, and skilled Americans, the immigrants blunted any
tendency toward working class consciousness. The former immigrants who had gone to the frontier had set up demands for
the products of workers behind the frontier; these demands
were for plows, farm machines, harness, wagons, lumber, nails,
wire, stoves, beds, tables—in short, everything needed to start
a new farm. These demands after 1890 no longer were subject
to sudden great increases. Nor was this tendency offset by
different demands of the later unskilled immigrants; for one
reason because their standards of living were the lowest of any
aliens in our history, and for another, because many were single

men who sent the bulk of their earnings back to their original homelands where its only benefit to American labor was in helping to balance our foreign trade. Aliens whose presence in earlier years mostly was felt as consumers became competitive producers.

Imperialism.—When the passing of the frontier closed our long career as imperialists on our own continent, we followed the example of constricted European nations in search for imperialism over distant places. The war with Spain in 1898 enabled our imperialists to acquire islands in the Caribbean Sea and the Pacific, possessions which were supplemented by control of Hawaii (1898), Guam (1899), American Samoa (1900), Panama Canal Zone (1904), and the Virgin Islands (1917). The new empire was no substitute for the vanished continental frontier. It was American capital not American labor that found outlets in the Caribbean and Pacific. Any gain to labor from increased overseas trade was offset by taxes to pay the costs of colonies and potential or actual migration from them to our mainland. The capital invested in colonies was lost as to giving employment to Americans at home and there was no compensatory increased demand for American goods and labor from the colonies.

Uncrowded America.—Despite the disappearance of our continental frontier and the absence of migration to colonies the United States was by no means overcrowded. Experts in population matters have said that granting our known techniques the optimum population for this country was about 150 million. At this figure the nation's resources could best be utilized so as to maintain the highest average standard of living. Measured against this standard the nation in 1896 was not half-way toward the optimum, for it numbered only 63 million. Even in 1929 there were only 123 million men, women, and children in the United States. Looked at from the viewpoint of population per square mile, the United States in 1890 had only 21 and in 1930 had but 41 whereas in the latter year Belgium had 698 and the United Kingdom 504. This is to say that despite the virtual disappearance of free land after 1890, and the disregard of colonies, there was still plenty of room within the nation to furnish opportunities for more people without a sacrifice of standards of living.

American Resources.—The absence of a land frontier was somewhat compensated by discovery and exploitation of resources in the lands already acquired. This was especially true in respect to minerals; soft coal and petroleum being cases in point. Forests in the South and Far West likewise were transferred from scenic to economic values. Large-scale water powers were developed, sometimes in connection with irrigation that turned waste lands into production. Inventions were less the haphazard inspirations of genius than the studied experiments of hired researchers. Science was harnessed to capital. When a soil chemist or metallurgist discovered methods of turning wastes into commodities he did as much for labor as the pathfinders who had opened new lands to settlement. Moreover, when the frontier vanished, there arose a movement to conserve the land and its products; a conservation that did not mean *withdrawal* from use, but *wise* use of resources. If it is admitted that the economic concept of "land" included resources other than soil, then the generation after 1896 did not lack for "land."

Labor

Immigration.—Labor as a factor in production was recruited in the United States as in other countries from nativeborn men, women, and children. Immigration, however, as a source of labor was much more important than in European nations. Moreover, the American population contained millions of Negroes who were native-born but of a distinctly different race from the majority of the population. Hence, our labor force had certain aspects that were largely peculiar to America.

Most of the American population in 1896 as well as in 1929 was composed of wage earners and their families. On the one hand, the population was the source of labor supply, so that quantitatively and qualitatively the competition of worker with worker depended upon the size, increase, and kind of population in the nation; on the other hand, the population was the principal market for workers' products, so its size and purchasing power were largely the determinants for the demand for labor.

Retardation in Rate of Growth.—To say that our population increased from nearly 63 million in 1890 (76 million in 1900) to 123 million in 1930 leaves untold the significant features. Of these the first was the *rate* of growth each decade. Up to 1910 the rate of increase while smaller than earlier decades (which had been 30% or more) still was greater than 20%; but in the decade of the World War the rate shrank to about 15%. This fall in the rate would not have been significant if it had not been repeated in the next decade (rate 16%) thus continuing and magnifying a tendency toward slackened growth that had begun to be noticeable by 1900. For 30 years then the nation while still expanding was doing so at a slower pace. This can be interpreted as a sign that the United States was passing from a period of youth to one of maturity.

For the generation we have under examination, the approach of national maturity meant that the old heedless expansion of productive facilities no longer so easily could be requited by the customary surge of seekers of consumption goods. Management had to learn to manage; so when Frederick W. Taylor in 1903 began to teach Scientific Management he found the most farseeing heads of businesses eager to learn and practice the new ways of operation. For labor the maturity meant easement from the competition of thousands of new yearly recruits, a competition from which labor had suffered ever since the Civil War. When the flush 1920's arrived labor's real wages and standards of living could, and did, rise. For the country as a whole the custom of ruthless scrapping of the middle-aged and old began to be questioned because the supply of native and imported vigorous youths had begun to shrink. Few people before 1920 were definitely conscious of our passage from national youth to national maturity; after that year many of the leaders took it into consideration in shaping their plans, and some, in urging legal restraints upon immigration or agitating for removal of the legal bars to dissemination of information concerning birth control, quite deliberately were hastening the arrival of a stage of national maturity.

The retardation in the rate of growth was due partly to a decline in the birth rate and partly to reduced immigration. As to the birth rate, that had been falling for native Americans throughout the generation prior to 1896, but had been offset by the fecundity of recently arrived aliens. After 1910 the check to immigration, the adoption of the American code by longer established immigrants and especially by the second generation of that stock, the greater urbanization of both Americans and aliens, and the migration of many Negroes to northern cities all acted together to limit the number of children to a family. Along with these and materially augmenting them were the campaigns of Margaret Sanger and others for spreading information about birth control. They tried also to persuade legislatures to modify the laws that forbade this task. For the poor and aliens there were founded many birth control clinics; for the well-to-do and Americans the information was passed along by word of mouth, by the reading of books available to those who knew of their existence and the manner of obtaining them, and from persons whose advice was respected. Doctors as a class gave very little assistance. The removal of the taboo on sex by this generation made everything pertaining to it the subject of eager examination.

Underneath all the factors that tended toward a smaller birth rate were economic compulsions. Children, with the passing of the frontier, no longer were compelled to be producers and so for most families were a burden. The greatly increased expenses of maternity, the costs of feeding, clothing, and taking proper medical care of children, and the charges incurred for a much prolonged education became large items in family budgets. Therefore, if the family standard of living was not to be sacrificed and if children were to be granted full opportunities for healthy bodies and trained minds or hands, the number of children per family had to be restricted.

By 1915, all of these things, economic and otherwise, had made their impress upon the majority of people within the country so that after that date the birth rate fell much more rapidly than it had hitherto. By 1929 the rate was 18.9 per thousand for the entire country; it was considerably below that figure on the Pacific Coast and in New England, New York, and New Jersey, and above it chiefly in those southern states that had a large rural Negro population. The normal family in the United States by 1930 had shrunk to two children.

Peaks of Immigration.—Not births, however, but immigration since 1840 had been the principal reason for the numerical increase of the nation. Although until 1931 there was no year without a net increase in population by the arrivals and departures of aliens, there had been four periods when the net increase was unusually large. Three of these were before the generation of "More," one beginning in 1851 (to 1854), the second started in 1865 (to 1875) while the third was more intimately related to this generation, the wave beginning in 1882 and running highest between 1889 and 1892. Within the generation between 1903 and 1914, one of the largest of all crests of immigration swept into the country. Again, in 1921 to all appearances a new surge was starting; but this was dammed by rigid restrictive legislation.

The swell that began in 1889 carried into the country about half a million persons a year. The next tide which commenced in 1902 lifted above the half-million mark and in six of the years (1905, 1906, 1907, 1910, 1913, 1914) more than a million immigrants passed inward through our gates. In 1921 the million mark was almost reached when 805,000 were admitted. It should be recognized, of course, that not every immigrant became a permanent resident; but inasmuch as 60% to 70% did remain in the country the net increase from immigration ranged from a hundred thousand to half a million a year up to 1915. In 1921 and 1924 the net increase passed the half-million figure.

The "New" Immigration.—The numerical proportions of the immigration were not only record-breaking, but until 1915 sustained at high figures; nevertheless these totals were not so significant as the shifts in origins of the immigrants. Up to 1871 immigrants almost exclusively came from northwestern Europe with the United Kingdom and Germany by far the leading contributors. These immigrants literally were akin to the types which had founded and developed this country. After 1882 persons departing from southeastern Europe constituted increasing proportions of the total immigrants and the year 1896 was a landmark in population history; then for the first time the arrivals from southeastern Europe surpassed those coming from the northwestern countries. After that important year, southeastern Europe dominated immigration into America in every year save 1919 when less than 25,000 persons came here from all of Europe. Throughout most of the generation after 1896, therefore, this nation not only was accepting unusually large numbers of immigrants but from sources with social cultures and economic standards quite different from those we had called "American."

The new immigrants tended to colonize in the towns and cities within close reach either of the Atlantic or the Great Lakes. The immigration zone was primarily limited to the six states of New York, New Jersey, Pennsylvania, Michigan, Ohio and Illinois. From New York and Pennsylvania thousands of immigrants spilled over into Connecticut, Rhode Island, and Massachusetts, while all the New England states received thousands of French-Canadians. In these areas the immigrants performed all kinds of unskilled labor but crowded particularly into coal mining, iron and steel manufacture, textile and clothing factories.

Effects of Immigration.—To American labor the immigration after 1896 had several significances. The very volume of it acted as a depressor of wages, a factor that well nigh excluded Americans from unskilled jobs. Americans thus were forced into occupations demanding some kind of skill, and tended to overcrowd these jobs with a consequent adverse effect on wages, hours, and working conditions. The natural influence of volume was heightened by the relatively lower standards of living of the immigrants; the lower standard enabled them to flourish on wages that Americans deemed below a subsistence level.   Hence, in industries such as coal mining, textile and clothing manufacture in which immigrants predominated, Americans could not maintain themselves and would not enter as young people.   Again, the usurpation of unskilled jobs by immigrants split the wage-earning class into two groups—unskilled and skilled—differing in nationality, social customs, economic standards, and dwelling areas.   The ordinary American craftsman regarded immigrants much as the suburbanite looked upon a neighboring farmer's bullocks—sometimes picturesque but dumb brutes with no discernible connection with himself. Unions therefore gave scant attention to the unskilled and by the limitations of unions to the skilled, widened the ordinary wage differential between the two classes of labor.   The belief current in America that wage levels were conspicuously high was true only to a partial extent of that minority of skilled men who belonged to trade unions.   For the majority of the skilled and still more for nearly all of the unskilled, American wages were quite low when put against an American standard of living.

In the industries in which immigrants were the rule, organization of unions was a herculean task on account partly of the diversity of tongues, partly on national antipathies that were not cleansed at Quarantine, and partly on the fact that most of the immigrants were peasants suddenly thrust into an industrial arena with little understanding of their wrongs to say nothing of their rights.   Because of immigrants, therefore, Americans made slow headway in the organization of labor, and no appreciable development of class consciousness.   A minor but interesting result of immigration was the extent to which labor leaders of the generation were Irish.   For several years after 1896 the Irish were close to the bottom of the economic ladder, but did possess both the knowledge of English and the ability to use it eloquently; moreover, they were reckless fighters and so had the traits necessary to bellwether the bewildered flock.   As leaders they were much more successful in the United States than in the British Isles, including Ireland.

Changed Attitude Toward Immigration Since World War.—Toward the end of the generation of "More," an epochal change occurred in the attitude of most Americans toward unlimited immigration. Until 1862 that attitude generally had been one of cordial welcome to any and all mentally, physically, and morally fit persons who sought entrance; for America not only needed a larger population but our citizens deemed this country a refuge against all varieties of oppression. Between 1862 and 1921 timid gestures toward qualitative selection were made; these denied admission only to the most obviously undesirable such as the incurably diseased, the mentally deficient, and the morally depraved including non-political convicts. Somewhat more rigorous qualitative selection was sought in 1917 by a law that required a literacy test. Indicative of the persistence of the refuge idea was the fact that three Presidents in succession vetoed bills incorporating this literacy test and finally it was made law by a two-thirds Congressional vote overriding a second veto by President Wilson.

Reasons for Changed Attitude.—The experience of the World War and its aftermath changed public opinion in favor of more rigid *qualitative* selection, and in addition for the first time in favor of *numerical* limitation.

In the first place, during the war there was ample evidence that our previous policy had not produced the assimilation we believed we had gotten in the "melting pot" despite the warnings we had received from an investigating commission appointed by President Theodore Roosevelt in 1907 and reporting in 1910. Thousands of recent aliens among us during the war revealed that they did not put American interests on as high a plane as they did the interests of their former nationality, so that our original position as a neutral and later as a combatant both were seriously hampered by former foreign nationals among our population. Hence, many people were made anxious to restrict the numbers of our immigrants to those we might most easily mould into a homogeneous American citizenry. Army tests had revealed that one-half of the aliens examined at recruiting stations were classifiable as "inferior" or "very inferior" in intelligence.

Despite the chagrin that these same tests had shown that even the native-born were seldom classifiable above "average," the natives generally were above the recently arrived foreigners.

Secondly, the radicalism rampant in Russia and only a little less extravagant in Germany, Austria, Hungary and Italy—from all of which sources before the war we had drawn hundreds of thousands of immigrants—made many Americans anxious about our own security; indeed this fear condoned an inhuman housecleaning of foreign-born radicals already within our boundaries. Considerable force in 1919 was given to this terror by an unprecedented number both of strikes and strikers, many in reputedly peaceable groups such as public servants (Boston police). Violence in strikes at Seattle, Lawrence, and New York City, and radicalism among workers in steel, the railroads, needle trades, and coal mining all gave rise to foreboding. Headed in 1919 by no less an official than the Attorney General, A. Mitchell Palmer, a campaign for the arrest and deportation of aliens was brutally carried on for two years. Between February 1919, when 54 were seized and 42 sent to their foreign homes, to June 1920, some 2,635 arrests had taken place throughout the nation and these suspected persons shipped to New York for deportation. After the middle of the year, due to protests from labor organizations, ministers' associations, and individuals of national repute, the hue and cry quieted; by the next spring deportations were about normal in number and the degree or kind of turpitude involved. A sufficient residual fear of radicalism remained to bring many citizens to the support of a policy of restricted immigration.

In the third place, there was a spectre of hungry hordes alike in Europe and America. For the former, confirmation was apparent in the 800,000 milling immigrants who in 1921 taxed every ship line to America and overflowed all of our immigrant stations. For the latter, verification seemed ample the same year in the reports from all of our industrial centers of such alarming unemployment that the War Food Administrator, Herbert Hoover, was called upon to conduct at Washington in October a National Unemployment Conference. Many people connected swollen immigration with unemployment.

Finally, a group of bellicose employers in 1921 started against unions a nation-wide drive which the employers labeled the "American Plan" or "Open Shop Campaign." Because unlimited immigration would help employers in this effort, the unions, in keeping with an old policy, solidly lobbied for restriction of immigration.

Quota System of Immigration.—Importuned from so many directions and from a variety of motives, Congress had to give heed to the voices of the people. An act passed in 1921 inaugurated the quota system of immigration. By the act, aliens were admitted in a quota which was 3% of the nationality resident in the nation according to the Census of 1910. The purpose was to reduce the numbers and at the same time shift the source from southeast to northwest Europe. Before the law expired on June 30, 1924, two opposed sets of objectors sought its change; the first wanted the "standard" census date set back so as to insure greater restraints upon southeastern Europeans, while the other—composed of naturalized southeastern Europeans in the United States and certain officials in the countries from which they came—pleaded for a greater liberality toward southeastern Europe. The law as modified in 1924 satisfied the first group of objectors; for the quota was reduced to 2%, and the Census of 1890 taken as the standard. This law also applied to all other nations excepting those of the American continents and in the Orient, the latter already having been excluded.

For political and practical reasons this act was termed an emergency measure to be reconsidered in 1927; meanwhile a Commission was appointed to study and report on the origins of the existing American people. Because the Commission was unprepared for final report in 1927, the law as administered was continued until 1929. The 1924 Act had provided that after a study of origins had been made a new basis for quotas should be established. This was that the total of all immigrants from quota nations should be 150,000 per year, and that each nation's quota would be that percentage of 150,000 that its nationals bore to all the other nationals composing the American population. The Commission's report on national origins was received and accepted in 1929 and on July 1 of that year, President Hoover declared the new basis for quotas to be in effect. Although experts questioned the accuracy of the determination of national origins the law obtained consistent popular support.

Unforeseen Effects of Immigration Laws.—The quota laws were pleasing to labor leaders for the acts had an effect for which the leaders long had been fighting. The domestic market was preserved to American labor with a consequent buttressing of the wages, hours, and working conditions won by American labor. Yet there were effects not foreseen. One was the fuller utilization of machinery not only to do the tasks formerly allotted to unskilled labor but also to supersede skilled labor. This proceeded at such an unprecedented rate between 1920 and 1930 that the process has been called the "Technological Revolution"; it was one of the causes of collapse in 1929. Another unforeseen effect was the draft upon female labor reserves to fill the gap left by declining immigration. Again, the laws not being applicable to our nearest neighbors nor to our colonial possessions there was an influx of Canadians and Porto Ricans in the Northeast, of Mexicans in the Southwest, and of Filipinos on the Pacific Coast and on railways in all sections. The fourth result was a shifting of Negro population from the South to northern industrial and mining centers. Fuller discussion of these effects is reserved until later portions of this book.[1]

---

[1] The special action in respect to Chinese and Japanese immigration merits separate discussion. The earlier exclusion of the Chinese had resulted in a dwindling of Chinese among our population; many Chinese had returned home in order to be buried with their ancestors and the relative scarcity of women among Chinese immigrants prevented natural increase. Consequently, there were only half as many Chinese in the United States in 1921 as there had been in 1890. But the gates barred against Chinese swung freely for the Japanese.

Before 1900 the number of Japanese immigrants was not noticeable; beginning in that year with 12,000 the arrivals were at such continuously high annual totals that by 1905 the states on the Pacific slope and especially California were seriously alarmed at the large actual and relative numbers already within their borders. Two facts forcibly struck their minds; one was that Japan proper in an area smaller than California had a population more than half as great as the whole United States, or a density about fifteen times as great as either California or the United States; the other was that unlike the Chinese the Japanese immigration contained almost a normal proportion

Exploitation of Immigrants.—Before turning from this subject, it should not be overlooked that the immigrants often had been lured on ships by false claims; on board they frequently had been overcrowded, subjected to physical or moral assaults, and served less in proportion to their fares than any

of women whose fecundity after settling here was two and a half times as great as the white women living in the same territory. Those who were most pessimistic foresaw a Japanese dependency teeming in population occupying our whole Pacific slope. Some Japanese thought so too, for articles in certain Japanese magazines urging the virtues of California as a place to live referred to that state as "New Japan." In defense against this prospect California took action that soon involved the diplomacy of both Japan and our federal government.

First, the Japanese in California were denied citizenship on the grounds that our naturalization laws extended this privilege only to free white aliens or aliens of African nativity or descent and that the Japanese were neither whites nor Africans. California's own constitution of 1849 limited naturalization to free white aliens and the revised constitution of 1879 specifically barred Mongolians from citizenship.

Next, the action of San Francisco in 1906, insisting that both young and old Japanese attend schools segregated from whites, was deemed insulting by the Japanese residing in California and by their home government. Be it remembered that Japan had just won her war with Russia and so felt herself strong enough to resent any slight put upon her by any western nation. Because our State Department was at the time laying the foundations for a Far Eastern policy that required the cooperation of Japan, the federal administration was embarrassed by the racial feelings aroused in California. President Theodore Roosevelt reminded America in a message to Congress that it was the federal government, not states, that had the constitutional right to involve the nation in foreign affairs. Soon afterwards when the great fleet which Roosevelt had sent for a "cruise" in Pacific waters visited Japan it was received with cordial politeness, one of the amenities being a parade of a Japanese fleet that matched identically ship for ship with the American vessels.

In the latter part of November 1908 the Root-Takahira "agreement" was announced to the world. In this exchange of published notes the sole topic was the relationship of Japan and America to China, but in the negotiations that led to this major diplomatic achievement the minor problem of the Japanese in California was settled by an "understanding" that Japan herself would place an embargo on the emigration of Japanese laborers to the United States. The Immigration Act of 1907 had blocked admission indirectly by way of Canada, Mexico, or our island possessions.

In carrying out this arrangement Japan did not construe farmers as laborers nor did she deny passports to exceedingly numerous "picture brides." Added to these cases were the Japanese ship crews that deserted in our ports, and the many otherwise barred individuals who were smuggled across our borders chiefly from Mexico; so the Pacific states continued to receive more Japanese immigrants than they wanted. Again California took the matter in her own hands by passing in 1912 the Heney-Webb Land Act by which persons not eligible to citizenship were barred from owning land in the state. Since American-born children of Japanese parents were eligible to citizenship by "the law of the soil" the Land Act was circumvented by putting Japanese land holdings in California in the names of the children. Not only

other class of passengers. Upon arrival on our soil, the immigrants sometimes had been shockingly cheated and most of all by acclimated members of their own nationality. After they got employment their ignorance was exploited to the limit. Unions ignored them, native Americans ridiculed them, and

California but Oregon and Idaho in 1917 prepared legislative bills to close this loophole in the land laws.

Once more the local action disturbed delicate international negotiations that were in progress. There was first the effect of the World War upon American-Japanese policy in respect to China; secondly there was the matter of more active participation by Japan especially her navy in the prosecution of the War, and finally there was the dissipation of a fog of mutual distrust and fear raised by German agents who spread the rumor in both countries that each was preparing armed attack upon the other. Because of the threat to all these uncertainties, the federal administration implored Congress to omit all special reference to the Japanese in the Immigration Act of 1917, in that section that defined an Asiatic Barred Zone so as to exclude Hindus. The success of these pleas however stirred the Pacific Coast states to action for their own protection. In the summer of 1917 Japan sent Viscount Ishii as head of a special diplomatic mission to the United States to discuss all the perplexities that had arisen between the two nations. On November 2 the Lansing-Ishii agreement was placed before the world. The two identical notes that comprised the agreement dealt solely with a policy relative to China, but since the talks had covered all the issues at ferment between the two powers, private agreements were reached as to Japan's share in the burdens of War, and Japan promised to limit her passports to emigrants to one hundred and fifty per year.

In 1919 another attempt by California to amend her land laws was checked in deference to a request from the federal administration not to stir troubled waters while negotiation of the Versailles Treaty was in progress. Although the petition was heeded, an anti-Japanese movement became a dominant element in political alignments in the Coast states particularly in California. An Exclusion League let loose a barrage of propaganda and the question in the summer of 1920 greatly overshadowed in the state the national political issue of membership in the League of Nations. One special piece of informative material, a report of 225 pages issued June 19, 1920, by the California State Board of Control had a considerable influence in the state political campaign. Likewise, the hearings in Pacific Coast states of the federal House Committee on Immigration and Naturalization elicited much information that swayed voters. The question put to the ballot was: Should California amend its land laws so as to restrict the administration of land by "guardians," and should it prohibit even the leasing of land by those ineligible to citizenship. The yea vote was three times the nay.

At the beginning of the anti-Japanese agitation in 1906, labor, as it had been in regard to Chinese exclusion, was actively in support of restriction. As time went on, labor as well as town business men either were lukewarm exclusionists or else tacitly supported the Japanese. The anti group mostly was composed of farmers and their political spokesmen. The division was a natural result of the economic interest of the Japanese settlers. They sought for and clung to the soil. Besides converting barren deserts into gardens, the Japanese invaded some of the older developed valleys and soon by purchase or by superior economic management of the soil got control of the major proportion of the land. Some crops were almost entirely pro-

they lived apart from our social organization.   Nevertheless, it was cheap immigrant labor that yielded large profits to many stockholders or landlords.   As young males they saved America all the expense of producing adult common labor.   Scorned by the native-born, the naturalized aliens easily were manipulated by friendly albeit crooked politicians.   The abused immigrants profoundly influenced American history first in the economic sphere, but quickly in many other phases of national life.

Women as Wage Earners up to 1918.—In addition to immigrants—and to some extent in place of them—the American labor market after 1896 was swollen by the advent of female wage earners.   Of course, women always had worked; and after 1800 an increasing number had been employed in wage occupations.   The new features after 1896 were the growing *numbers* of girls and women who took money-making jobs, the

---

duced by the Japanese and the fishing industry was just about monopolized by them.   Of course, under these circumstances, the white farmers and fishermen most affected and their kind who feared similar competition were solidly arrayed against the Japanese.   On the other hand, Japanese domestic and farm servants did not undercut American wages and Japanese who employed any kind of white labor paid it the going rate and gave it more consideration than many white employers.   These facts toned down the white labor opposition to the Japanese; moreover, the whites feared that if the Japanese were driven from the soil they would have to crowd into the crafts where white labor was then dominant.   Although the Japanese did much of their business with each other the town merchants liked the buying market furnished by the farm Japanese as well as the low prices of produce brought into town by them.   The merchants also were afraid that if the Japanese were denied access to the soil many of them would flock into towns where they might become public charges and the rest would set up small merchant enterprises in competition with the whites already in business.   For these reasons, in the final vote in 1920, although the Japanese themselves kept curiously silent, a count of 222 thousand was registered in their favor; that is, against the amendment.   As we have said the majority was three times this number but it was astonishing that the negative vote was so large.

In 1924, when Congress had under consideration the Immigration Act later known as the National Origins Quota Law, the Representatives and Senators from the Pacific slope states injected a discussion of complete restriction of the Japanese.   Despite energetic opposition to the provision by the federal administration, and by powerful lobbyists, Congress adopted a clause which denied admission to aliens ineligible to become naturalized citizens except those admissible under existing Treaty stipulations.   The exceptions referred to students, travellers and others allowed entrance on temporary permits.   From that time the Japanese like the Chinese were not admissible immigrants.

Somewhat the same kind of anti-Asiatic agitation flared up against the Filipinos in the later 1920's.

expanding numbers of *occupations* opened to women, and the startling advances in the proportions of *married* women who worked for wages outside their homes.

In 1896, only 1 woman out of 6 over 15 years of age had a wage-paying job; in 1900 the ratio was 1 in 5, and from 1910 to 1929 the proportion fluctuated around 1 to 4. In gross numbers, there were 4 million working women in 1890 and 10.7 million in 1930. In contrast, the males in 1890 who worked for wages were 4 out of every 5 and this ratio held steadily until 1920; after that date the ratio dropped slightly to 3¾ workers for every 5 boys and men. There were 19 million male wage earners in 1890 and 38 million in 1930. Concerning these figures two things are noticeable; first, that women wage earners had many more *potential* women competitors than male workers had *potential* male competitors; secondly, that female wage earners tended to increase in proportion to the total of both sexes.

Women's Wages.—The large potential competition of their own sex was the principal reason why women's wages were low: the increase of women workers among all wage earners made them a problem for male workers and most of all for those men who were unionized. Inasmuch as the principal opposition to women as wage earners was the fear that their low wages would undermine the male wage standards the matter of women's wages merits more extended comment.

Between 1896 and the World War, any woman who earned more than $6 a week was unusual. In those years most men were paid from $10-$20 a week. After 1920, the money wages for women rarely were greater than $15 per week while at the same time the average male wages were between $25-$30 per week. Although these figures were averages which meant very little, they nevertheless did show that women's wages were in themselves low and in comparison with men's wages were discriminatory. The most authoritative sources for the history of women's wages were first the 19 volumes "Report on Condition of Woman and Child Wage Earners in the United States" for which the studies were made in 1907-8 the "Reports" being issued from 1910-1913. Secondly, the Women's Bureau of the United States Department of Labor in the 1920's made many special studies concerning women's wages. From these two sets of investigations it was learned that the wages paid to women almost invariably were lower than those paid to men even in the relatively rare instances when they did equivalent work; as a matter of fact, the average wage for women frequently fell below the average of the *lowest* paid group of men when both were engaged in the same industry. Two other facts were validated by the special studies; first, that women's wages declined as the location of the work went southward, and secondly, that for the same jobs white women were paid from a third to a half more than female Negroes.

Reasons for Low Wages of Women.—The basic cause for the sorry showing of women's wage rates was that the *potential* supply of female workers was 4 times the demand represented by women who were hired. Moreover, the women who had jobs were crowded into a limited number of occupations. There were more women in domestic and personal service, teaching, and agriculture than in any other occupations. As a group, manufacturing stood second to domestic service in respect to giving employment to women; however, only about a dozen types of manufacturing hired any great numbers and these were almost exclusively for semi-skilled or unskilled operations. There were 30 occupations each employing 50,000 or more women and these together accounted for about 85% of all those gainfully employed. Another cause for low wages was that about two-thirds of the younger women—daughters—turned over to their parents the girls' entire earnings; since the daughters themselves did not have the use of their own earnings they were not always interested in their amount.

While the essential economic reasons for the low wages of women were the three just cited, nevertheless there were a great many special individual excuses given for the situation. Among these were: the relative immobility of women workers—they had to stay in the towns where their parents or husbands lived; the belief that women's wages were solely for themselves whereas men's wages supported families; the supposition that women were partly subsidized by parents, male kin or admirers; and the myth that women lived more cheaply than men because they ate less and did many personal services for themselves such as laundry and mending.   There was just enough truth in these excuses to obscure their general absurdity.

Women's Jobs.—Inasmuch as two of the most important causes for the paltry wages of women were the redundant number in a few occupations, and a youthfulness that allowed parents to sequester earnings, the two tendencies after 1900— one toward diversification of occupation, the other for women over 21 years of age and married women to stay in industry— were remedial.   Traditionally, the manufacturing industries that employed the most women were the textiles, clothing (and other sewing trades), food and beverage, tobacco, paper, and printing.   After 1900, continuously more females were engaged in the manufacture of metals, wood, clay, glass and chemicals.   Outside of the manufacturing group the number of women greatly expanded in trade and transportation.   Clerical work in all these categories more and more fell into the hands of women.   Although most people did not know, or would not admit, that there was scarcely any job done by men that some women could not do equally well, the findings of the Census in 1910, 1920, and 1930 gave conclusive proof of the fact.   Of the more than 500 occupations listed women were found in every one except 35 (30 in 1929); the excepted occupations were not impossible for some women to perform but they were kept out of them by custom (steam engineers), law (underground miners), or union rules (molders).

Effect of World War on Employment of Women.—The World War opened many new opportunities to women.   In May 1918 the Judge Advocate General issued a "Work or Fight" order to men of the draft ages.   Since the order classed as unessential occupations the operation of passenger elevators, ushering in theatres, clerking in stores, and the jobs of waiters, doormen, or attendants, the men in these positions were replaced by women.   The first (American) official call for women war-workers was in September 1918.   A month later the United States Employment Service started a campaign to replace men by women.   Women were taken into banks, laboratories, draughting rooms, factories making war supplies for the Quartermaster and Ordnance Corps, and all kinds of clerical work—the Navy even enlisted and uniformed female Yeomen. The most spectacular new work for women was in transportation; they were used not only in ticket offices but as freight loaders, in section gangs on track work, and in repair shops. The street railways employed "conductorettes" in New York City, Newark, Cleveland, and Detroit.

By no means all the women war-workers were wage-rookies. About 100,000 school teachers left their desks for the dirtier but more lucrative work-benches in shops.   Likewise domestic servants, waitresses, and laundry workers—especially Negresses in these occupations—got out of these low paid jobs for better ones in factories and on railroads; there were 40,000 new openings for women in the railroad industry alone.   In clothing and food manufacturing the 1¼ million workers simply shifted from peace products to war supplies.   Munition manufacture, however, created 100,000 new jobs for women; automobile plants also put many women in machine shops and assembly units.

At first many employers and a few state legislatures (e.g., New York, Massachusetts, New Hampshire) tried to use the war as a reason for abandonment of some or all the legislative safeguards on women's work.   A vigorous disapproval from President Wilson and a backdown by the Council of National Defense quickly stopped the tendency toward laxity.   Soon an active federal committee concerned with women's war-work used the opportunity of the war to strengthen the controls over women's work.

The Armistice came before the women-workers were acclimated to their new work.   Public opinion would not tolerate women freight loaders or section gang hands.   The Amalgamated Association of Street and Electric Railway Employees raised test cases against "conductorettes" in Cleveland and

Detroit. In other instances there was a drift of women back to their pre-war jobs. Nevertheless, a considerable nucleus of women stayed with their new-won occupations and became precedents for still more in later years; this applied especially to machine work on metals.

The broadening occupational bases for women's work was beneficial to the incomes of women who pioneered, and by lessening the supply in the traditional jobs tended toward an improvement in them.

Age and Marital Status of Women Workers.—The trend toward the greater employment of women over 21 years of age had a direct relationship to wages. Rates usually improved with years from 16 to 19 or 20; at 21-25 there was a plateau without much variation and then the added years up to 35 were accompanied by higher earnings. The age groups over 21 were not only related to wages but to marital status; the continuously more numerous wage earners in the older age groups were made up of constantly increased numbers and percentages of married women.

In 1890 the half-million married women workers were 13.9% of all female wage earners and 4.6% of all females over 10 years of age. In 1910 the number of married women at wage work was 3 times the earlier figure; the percentage of all female workers married was 24.7; and was 10.7% of all females over 10 years old. In 1929 there were 3½ million married women at work for wages; these were 30% of all women at work, and 11.7% of all females over 10 years. Of the 29 million American families in 1929, the mothers in 3.9 million families were breadwinners.

Why Married Women Seek Jobs.—The greatly added numbers of married women workers were due to opposite causes. Wherever the male earnings were not enough to support a family at a subsistence level, the wives and mothers were forced to seek jobs so that the family might live. For more than half the married women at work this was the reason, and their employment really was an indictment of our social-economic system.   The women were overworked because they had all their housework to do after the wage day was over; their children were neglected.   On the other hand, a large number of married women worked partly because factories had taken over the traditional household tasks, and partly on account of knowledge of birth control which limited offspring to two or less.   Often the earnings of these married women lifted the family income above the subsistence and even the comfort levels.   This increased income either gave rise to direct effective demands that added to the employment of both men and women, or provided the means of greater security through savings or insurance and indirectly created demands for labor.

Women as Competitors with Men.—From the viewpoint of some male workers the rise in the employment of women was a menacing competition because the women's low wages threatened to pull down the wages of men; and also because at times women "scabbed" on men's strikes.   While there was some truth in these fears, the women as a rule did not do exactly the same kinds of work as men.   When engaged in the same industry the women were restricted to the light and unskilled tasks.   Only at one point in the ordinary evolution of a job did both sexes compete.   This evolution began with a task that was highly skilled at which point only men were hired.   The skilled task was subdivided and if any skill remained in any of the parts the men got preference on these while women were given the unskilled operations.   However, if the subdivision *eliminated* skill there was likely to be competition between the sexes; and if the new tasks were light or repetitive the women generally by their cheapness gained at the expense of men.   At this stage, therefore, there might be sex competition.   The last stage was the installation of more or less automatic machinery at which time both men and women were ousted; if any labor was required it was likely to be very highly skilled male technicians or very low skilled attendants, e.g., oilers.

From the viewpoint of womankind some kind of useful occupation was necessary for their mental and physical health. Throughout history, the sexes had worked either shoulder to shoulder or at complementary tasks. Modern changes on the one hand took away from women the compulsion to bear and rear numerous children and on the other removed from the home most of women's arts and crafts, the ones that remained being made easier by machines. The resultant idleness drove women to look for work outside the home in order to preserve their physical vigor and sanity. These factors operated even among those women whose family incomes were not an economic compulsion to female work.

In 1929, therefore, the matter of women wage earners was an unsolved double dilemma: low family income or their own physical and mental health required that women work for wages; if they did work they might at one stage force men out of jobs or reduce their wages; both sexes ought to work but production for profit did not furnish enough jobs to absorb the labor power of the whole adult population nor on the other hand yield the population enough income to afford a leisure devoted to non-economic pursuits. The problem of women wage earners, consequently, was a facet of the kind of society in which the women lived.

Child Labor Laws.—Society, however, in the generation after 1896 did make progress in the solution of the problem of *child* labor. In 1890 there were 1½ million child workers between the ages of 10 and 15 years; or 18% of the total number of children of these ages. In 1930 there were a little more than half a million child workers constituting 4.7% of the children 10-15 years of age.

The improvement was due to the interaction of compulsory school laws with other laws that fixed the age limits and formalities for the grants of work-certificates to young persons. To this generalization there were the qualifications that the laws were most precisely administered in the northern and western states and that the legal formalities applied with slight exceptions only to work in the manufacturing industries.

Enactment of child-labor and school laws did not automatically eliminate children from factories. Inspection and unfailing punishment for violations were never ending responsibilities of the states. In the early years of the generation, Maine, Rhode Island, and Pennsylvania were particularly remiss in the administration of their child labor laws, and even in later years evasions of the laws were not unknown in these states; textile mills were the chief offenders. As some of the northern states advanced the upper age limits of childhood from 12 to 14 and then to 16 years, in the school and work-certificate laws it became almost impossible to hire children under 10 years for factory work because their youth was so obvious.

Where Child Labor Is Worst.—By 1929, very young children seldom were discovered in northern or western factories. Nevertheless, child labor persisted in these states in other occupations. Agriculture was the worst offender and this industry was itself at its own worst in the types of farming that most resembled factory organization. The truck areas, fruit orchards, (northern) tobacco fields, onion acres, and sugar beet ranches were notorious exploiters of very young persons. The street trades also were scarcely regulated at all despite the hard work, long hours, low pay, and hazards to limb or morals of the many children engaged. In the school laws, there were great gaps in the safeguards around children in vacations or after-school hours; thousands of children had these odd time jobs partly in street trades but also in stores, garages and even some factories. Work in tenement homes engaged children far into the night. Complacency among northern people on account of the disappearance of tiny children from factories was dangerously narcotic because it dulled the perception to the continuation of great numbers of children in non-factory jobs.

Southern Child Labor.—In the North and West, there was a consciousness that child labor was an evil; and also considerable appreciation that modern childhood did not end at 12-14 years of age. The South, before 1900, had no conception of either of these two ideas. In the next three decades parts of the South began to awaken to the detriments of child labor; but as late as 1929 only beginnings of restraints upon southern child labor had been made.

Before 1900, a Georgia act (1853) had prohibited night work for children although permitting work from sunrise to sunset.   Alabama (1886-87) had barred mines to child workers less than 15 years old but in 1892-93 reduced the age limit to 10 years, only again four years later to raise it to 12 years.   The same state in 1886-87 limited to 8 hours the work of children under 14 in manufactures but repealed this act in 1894. Georgia in 1889 made 66 hours a week the maximum for children in cotton and woolen mills, while South Carolina in 1892 made an 11-hour day, 60-hour week the legal limits for children in the same two textile industries.   No other southern state before 1900 took any kind of legal notice of child labor.

The tardiness of the South in regard to the safeguarding of children was not due to conscious brutality but to ignorance of the debilitation that accompanied child labor.   Just as the industrial revolution in Britain and New England gave rise to the employment of very young persons without any immediate public protest, so also in the South the first great incursion of mills into rural agricultural counties caused no apprehension when children were enrolled as workers.   All three regions originally regarded the employment of children a blessed means of inculcation of industrious habits; they thought that idleness, not work, was injurious.   In all three places, when the first mutters arose against child labor, there was no general credence in the authority of the state as an agent of control; the care, upbringing, and authority over children was deemed vested in parents.   By the time there was insistent objection to child labor, the hiring of young people had become both customary and profitable; consequently, the demands of reformers for the abolition of child labor were countered by the declaration that "maudlin" interference with child labor would be an economic injury to the state.   Manufacturers who were denied the use of children said the factories would move to places where they were not restrained.   The South passed through this evolution just as had its predecessors, England and Massachusetts.

South Tardy in Regulation of Child Labor.—North and South Carolina, Georgia, and Alabama, as the pioneer southern manufacturing states, were the scenes of the first southern attempts to reduce child labor. From 1900 onward there was scarcely a session of the legislatures in these four states that did not record attempts to erect legal barriers to child labor. It was in 1903, in South Carolina, that the first slight advance was made in the state control of child labor; this inaugural law put a 10-year-old limit to child labor in mills, and provided that the limit gradually be raised to 12 years by 1905. Since the act contained no method of enforcement it was more of a gesture than a restraint. It was 1909 before a law in South Carolina empowered the hiring of two state inspectors to seek for violations of the 12-year age limit. The other three southern states did not advance that far against child labor although all had an ostensible 12-year limitation. In the two decades after 1910 all of the principal southern states enacted laws that forebade the employment in textile mills of children under 14 years of age; but above this age they could work as long as adults. Only in North Carolina was there a provision that for 14-year-old workers a limit of 8 hours was placed if the child had not finished the 4th grade in school.

To set by law a minimum age limit for employment in textile and other factories was, outside the South, a first step toward further restraints upon child labor; among them the extension of the laws to occupations other than factory work, the prohibition of night-work, the fixation of hours of work for young persons, the increase of the age limit for hazardous occupations, the advancement of the compulsory school ages beyond 14 years, and the requirement of certain school standards for the grant of work certificates to minors. Inasmuch as the South was slow to take the first step it did not proceed far with the others. For example, despite the fact that in 1929 the South had the nation's largest numbers and proportionally greatest percentage of its children gainfully employed in agriculture, the southern child labor laws gave specific exemption to farm child labor.

Why Child Labor Exists.—Wherever child labor has existed it has been due to a combination of poverty and ignorance of the harm done to children by too early entrance into employment.   The supply of child workers thus has arisen from families that have not been successful under a system of free competition.   The demand for child workers was created by their cheapness.   Employers persistently agitated and lobbied against child labor laws and against attempts to make the laws more stringent; there was no time from 1896 to 1929 when this was not true.   Hence, there was no possibility of elimination of child labor by shrinkage of the *demand*.

Effects of Regulation of Child Labor.—Adult workers recognized this fact as early as 1828 and thereafter, bent their energies toward restrictions on the *supply* of child labor.   The most plausible means of reduction in the supply was a universal free public school system at which attendance was compulsory. Grown workers never relinquished their pressure for greater school opportunities for children, together with more inclusive regulations concerning attendance.   Reform associations, including in their membership a great many persons other than adult wage earners, made direct legislative attacks upon child labor; the effect of their efforts in legislation was to remove thousands of young people from the labor market.   In so far as this result was obtained it had a double advantage to adult workers; for one thing it reduced the supply, and for another it restricted the competitive menace of the low wages paid to children.   From the viewpoint of the children's welfare, they were saved from too early an entrance into the grind of making a living; and to the extent they were able to utilize their educational advantages, when they became wage earners, they had the equipment to work on a higher economic plane.

Capital

Growth of Capitalism.—Having examined "land" and labor as factors in American production it is fitting to review the story of capital during the years from 1896 to 1929.

Before the Civil War, the dominant group in both the economic and political fields had been the farmers; these except for the compact slavocracy had been so scattered and numerous as to comprise a democracy not an aristocracy. At the end of the Civil War, economic and political power shifted to the merchants, manufacturers, and transporters, without, however, any high degree of concentration. That is, businesses and industries were small-scale and consequently numerous. At the beginning of our era in 1896 the total national wealth was only a little over $65 billion and this was controlled by a large number of persons.

Concentration of Wealth and Income.—The significant changes in the generation were, on the one hand, the five-fold increase in national wealth ($362 billion in 1929) and, on the other, the shrinkage in the number of persons who controlled the wealth. Just as single great corporations blotted out the numerous little businesses, so also a few families attained supremacy over the thousands of little capitalists. As national wealth piled up, the control of it narrowed into a limited number of hands. Without changing the external forms of our society the fact was that a capitalist autocracy functioned as its heart.

Statisticians have supplemented the findings of the Census with special studies that have yielded reliable yardsticks to measure the onrush of capitalism. Whether they have used index numbers, or percentage comparisons, whether they have been satisfied with gross numbers or have refined them by weighting and correction for price changes the same truths emerge in all cases. The capital investment in production and distribution throughout the generation proceeded at an accelerating rate; and so did national output especially that part of it contributed by capitalistic enterprises. The shift from man or beast power to machines was manifested by the mounting figures for mechanical or electrical horsepower used in production and distribution; indeed a gigantic new capitalistic industry for the manufacture and sale of electrical energy was created during the generation. The figures that affirm the constantly tightening grip of capitalism have been made more significant by such comparisons as capital investment per wage earner or per dollar value of output and similar comparisons in respect to horsepower. The results of these investigations clearly confirmed the impression widely held in the generation that nearly every producer and distributor functioned with the aid of more and more capital and that in most cases each decade showed a relatively greater reliance upon capital. The assistance of capital was not only in the forms of buildings, machines, or other investment equipment but in credit instruments that speeded and enlarged business transactions.

Corporate Production.—Another type of statistical confirmation of the growth of capitalism may be found in studies of the corporation. Although the numerical increase of corporations was large it was not so much the number of enterprises conducted under the corporate form that was a revelation of the strides of capitalism, as the more important relative share of the national economic activity done under the corporate form and the vastness to which some corporations swelled. The billion dollar corporation became a reality. The individual proprietorships and partnerships controlled a dwindling proportion of the national output whereas the corporations accounted for the lion's share. For the majority of wage earners the "boss" no longer was a man but an artificial creature of the state. Even some farming was conducted on a corporate basis; and of course a great deal of it was by machine output.

Holding Companies.—In the preceding generation, capitalists had tried to reduce costs and competition by pools and trusts, but these had suffered from human greed and legal reprimand. The generation of "More" got around the law, yet achieved the aims in regard to competition and sometimes as to costs, by the device of the holding company. This was a corporation whose principal function was the ownership of the voting power (usually common stock) in other corporations; thus they gained the results either of combination or of integration. Some holding companies operated in both fields. Of the first type of horizontal combination an example was the United Biscuit Company; while the Kendall Company illustrated integration from raw cotton, through plants for spinning, weaving, and finishing, to the Bauer and Black Company which acted as the selling corporation for the integration. Toward the end of the generation, holding companies were incorporated to own several other holding companies, a practice so much indulged by electrical power magnates that even the creators could not understand the final web they had spun. Samuel Insull was a case in point as a utility magnate; the Van Sweringen brothers as railway barons; and Krueger in the industrial field.

Capitalistic Oligarchy.—So far as society was concerned, there might be a vital distinction between a magnified capitalism whose evidences of ownership were widely distributed among the whole people, or one whose ownership was concentrated within a few hands. The former might be very close to the ideals of socialists while the latter would be at least oligarchic and was likely to become despotic. The proponents of capitalism in the generation of "More" claimed that in the United States inasmuch as the stocks of the greatest corporations (American Telephone and Telegraph Company, General Motors Company, U. S. Steel Corporation) were owned literally by hundreds of thousands of different individuals we reaped all the advantages of capitalism without incurring the dangers of octopi capitalists. To clinch the matter, these proponents pointed to the thousands of employes on the one hand and thousands of consumers on the other who owned stock in the corporations for which the first worked and by which the second were served.

On the contrary, persons who feared capitalists showed that ownership and control of corporations were not synonymous. They claimed that the very fact that stock was held by hundreds of thousands of individuals made it easier for a few with a relatively small investment to control great corporations; this was so because most stockholders were indifferent about the corporation so long as dividends regularly were received, while others felt they owned too few shares to exert much influence, or lived too far from the place of stockholders' meetings. As for employe stockholders, these rarely were wage earners but usually salaried key men; consumer stockholders were invited into the purchase of small blocks of shares in order to reduce complaints about service and to alienate public opinion from too rigorous regulation of public utilities by government commissions.

That a few persons did acquire control, if not ownership, of the mammoth capitalism erected in the generation was proven when the generation's years were finished; witnesses from Morgan and Company, Kuhn, Loeb, and Company, and others who appeared before a Senate Investigation Committee gave testimony which revealed a small group of bankers and industrialists as the real controllers of the national structure of capitalism. The testimony was corroborated in several contemporary court cases and later by the United States Treasury. According to the latter authority a reckoning by families instead of by individuals revealed that a mere score of families controlled the majority of our greatest industries.

Use of Surplus Income.—One result of these changes was the use made of surplus income from our wealth. Before 1896, all of our own surplus plus considerable amounts from foreign countries was re-invested in the United States thus providing homes, goods, and jobs for Americans. During the generation after 1896 ever larger blocks of our surplus income were invested abroad; first in Cuba, Canada, or Mexico and after the World War in Europe or South America. If trade had been unrestricted, this procedure would have benefited American workers both by creating a broader market and by bringing into the country a wider variety of goods. Since trade was hampered by tariffs, bounties, or quotas and because many of the foreign investments were unsound the net result was that American workers' living costs did not decline nor his housing, clothing, or employment improve anywhere near to the extent they should if the income had been more wisely utilized. Our capitalists dissipated the golden eggs and well nigh strangled the goose.

The counters used for wealth and income, namely money and credit instruments, often have aroused the passions of American workers more than the real values which these tokens represented. In previous generations, working people frequently were aroused over questions concerning our monetary systems.

After the defeat of William Jennings Bryan and his "Free Silver" program in the campaign of 1896, the currency for a generation was not an important issue in American life.

Rise of Credit Instruments.—A factor in the quiescence of this formerly burning issue was the rapid and widespread substitution of credit instruments in the place of coins. National bank notes, personal checks, drafts, bills of exchange, warehouse receipts (a dollar silver certificate—our "dollar bill"—was in reality one of these warehouse receipts), and other varieties of commercial "paper" all tended to supersede gold and silver money. Moreover, in these years (1896-1929), every improvement in transportation such as the automobile and airplane speeded the circulation of the credit instruments and thus in effect increased our currency. So universal was the shift in the media of exchange that even many wage earners were paid in checks and in turn paid their own debts by checks—a kind of personal money with a limited circulation.

National Bank System.—To control this new system of exchange we had relied since the Civil War on the United States Treasury and the National Bank system. The chief defects were the inadequacy of governmental power over credit machinery and the inelasticity of it. There were recurrent regional and seasonal jams and the rules tended to tighten circulation when conditions made it tight and loosen it when conditions already created "easy money." In the "bankers' panic of 1907," the worst of all the generation's periodic financial crises occurred; the dislocation was so severe that bankers and others resorted to script money. Unemployment for several months was acute.

This lesson in inadequacy produced a National Monetary Commission headed by Senator Nelson Aldrich of Rhode Island. After four years of study, this commission (1912) recommended to Congress a system comprising a Central Bank with 15 branches scattered strategically over the country; measures for control also were advocated by the commission. Congress and the nation refused to accept the commission's findings. The old Jacksonian fear of a Central Bank together with sus-

picion of the disinterestedness of Senator Aldrich—he had by
his own avowal no sympathy with common people—and the
unpopularity of the Taft administration all concurred to defeat
the proposals.

The Federal Reserve System.—However, early (December
23, 1913) in the Wilson administration, the really valuable
work of the Monetary Commission bore fruit in the Federal
Reserve System. This removed many of the defects of the
previous National Bank system; and the 12 Regional Federal
Reserve Banks were supposed to safeguard against the presumed monopoly power of a Central Bank.

In practice, between 1913 and 1929, the Federal Reserve
Bank of New York dominated the other 11 banks.   By means
of "friends" on the directorate of the New York Federal Reserve Bank, a small group of New York bankers generally influenced the policies and acts of this all important bank.   Thus,
the nation in fact had two centers of financial power, the Congress with its control of coinage, and the clique of New York
bankers who indirectly controlled credit.   Since the nation
rapidly was becoming a credit rather than a money economy,
the banker clique of New York City became the unofficial and
irresponsible—that is not responsible to the people—oligarchy
of finance.   As such, they were the keystone of American capitalism.   The lives of millions of American workers in effect
were dependent upon the wills and intelligence of a few individuals, and not upon their own elected Congress.

Capital vs. Labor.—In a history of labor it is a vital matter
to notice the growth of capitalism together with the identity of
those who controlled capitalism.   Absentee capitalists as a rule,
were not interested in working conditions or hours of work or
wages except as these were factors in costs.   Massed, centrally
controlled capital was more than master of labor organizations
short of a revolution by labor.   Moreover, the American unions
in the generation of "More" persisted in the craft structure of
unionism and therefore rendered it extremely difficult to oppose
massed labor against massed capital.   These facts were behind

much of the story of labor in the more than three decades between 1896 and 1929.

Business Management

Besides the changes in land, labor (population), and capital between 1896 and 1929, there were some significant innovations in business management. In preceding generations, the heads of enterprises generally were the men who originated them. Although many of these themselves in their earlier years were workmen, as a rule they lost sympathy with the problems and feelings of the persons in their employ; indeed on account of the rapid changes in methods these bosses could know little by personal experience of the effects of later working conditions. The lowlier his start, the more "hard boiled" the boss was apt to be. Because he had attained prominence and power he believed all men could who really tried; and conversely he asserted that men who remained common workers had nothing to blame but their own indecision, laziness, or low mentality.

Salaried Experts.—After 1896, such business managers were less frequently encountered. Instead, either the second generation took charge of the enterprise or else salaried experts directed affairs. The sons of successful fathers usually had a more broadening youth than the first generation, and so could bring more tolerance into industrial relations. To the sons, the business was not a beloved creation of their own hands and minds, but an inherited responsibility; therefore, where the fathers had fiercely resented every criticism of their business the sons often themselves were its severest critics and so felt no deep insult when others, even the workers, made objections to policies, practices and equipment. On the other hand, *some* sons knew far less about labor's viewpoint than their lowly born fathers and consequently were more intolerant than the parents.

The cases in which one generation followed another and both in personal contact with their employes were much more rare than the cases of enterprises so swollen in size and intricate in organization as to require the services of salaried experts.

These, in their turn, less and less frequently as the years after 1896 passed were men who had risen from the ranks. Instead they were men who had a special training either in technological schools or in schools that taught the arts of management—the latter were new in this generation after 1896. These graduates started above all the labor ranks although their first jobs were at the bottom of the managerial hierarchy. Competition among the managerial recruits was keen and where "office politics" entered, the competition often was bitter. Yet, promotion either by merit or by knowing the right higher executive was relatively rapid. Hence, even the highest executives frequently were men under 50 years of age. The larger the corporation the younger its active managers were likely to be. In these companies the elder men were not always retired, but were put into advisory positions where the wisdom of their years was useful but where the weight of the daily burdens of management did not have to be borne—the younger more vigorous men took this onus.

Cooperation of Wage Earners Sought.—Many of the younger managers, especially after 1910, brought into personnel relations a new spirit; they sought to WIN THE COOPERATION of wage earners, not to BLUDGEON them. A new kind of Welfare guided by a new managerial profession of Personnel Management furnished workers on the negative side with the means of rectifying their grievances; and on the positive gave workers new incentives to produce by plans of promotion, connection of wages to output, mitigations of industrial insecurities, such as fears of unemployment, old age, accident or death, and attachment to the company either by stock ownership or by participation in the profits. In addition, there was an enlargement of the older forms of Welfare such as the provision of rest, bath, and lunch rooms, building, loan, and savings funds, and the organization and facilities for recreation. Moreover, many of the new managers took a broad view of wages and hours of work; they were willing to pay high wages in order to stimulate both production and consumption; and they believed in short hours as a means of rest and recreation whereby the hours of work could be devoted to more intensive production thus lowering unit costs. In short, the new managers thought that contented workers were efficient workers; the managers out of cold selfishness as much as warm humanity searched for ways and means to make wage earners contented. They succeeded to a surprising extent; and by just so much turned wage earners away from unionism, since unions have found their greatest stimulant to organization to be discontent.

Technology of Production.—Another preoccupation of the new managers was the technology of production. Not just new machines nor new adjustments to old machines but also new methods were eagerly applied in output. So great was the interest in "progress" that many corporations added as staff assistants to management more or less elaborate research laboratories. There was an avalanche of technological changes after 1920. The technological changes increased production, reduced unit costs, and thereby permitted shorter hours of work at higher wages. At the same time, they weakened or destroyed old crafts and eliminated or reduced the number of job holders. Thus, unemployment mounted all through the years of Coolidge Prosperity. Unions were hit two blows in the process; one was that the workers retained were so much better off that union membership seemed futile; the other was that the rising number of unemployed made the supply of labor so much greater than the demand that unions were weakened in their economic power. Men at work did not need union aid; men out of work were too numerous for unions to risk making demands.

In some industries, the acceleration of general managerial interest in technology brought about in their industries the long delayed advent of the industrial revolution. Traditional hand trades not only were confronted with mechanical substitutes but in many instances were suddenly and completely abolished by the introduction of automatic power devices. The trades that suffered the most were those in the glass industry, cigar industry, pottery industry, and textile industry (weavers). Some of the glass workers' unions were destroyed; the cigar workers' union was reduced to impotence; and the weavers by a "stretch out system" (more looms per person) lost even their craft name, becoming known as "section hands." Thus, several once powerful craft unions were either annihilated, or were greatly reduced in numbers with most of their former members permanently removed from the industry.

The Capitalist and the Hired Manager.—The rise of this new type of manager was the unique feature of this generation's (1896-1929) contribution to the arts of management. The former capitalist-manager who in one person performed two economic functions was replaced by two specialists, one the stockholder (capitalist) the other the hired manager. If the specialization had been complete, managers and wage earners might have combined against the capitalists since both were employes. But the segregation was not complete. The managers were so well paid (from $25,000 to 1 million or more per year) that they themselves became capitalist-minded through their own investments. Often, part of their earnings were shares of stock in the enterprises for which they worked. Moreover the managers held their jobs by the dividends they earned for stockholders, and the pressure to do this often was terrific. Sometimes they had a still more direct personal incentive to produce huge dividends because their own compensation in the form of cash or stock bonus was proportional to dividends. Under these circumstances, any labor demands, even those which in the long run would yield higher dividends, were suppressed by the managers if the immediate results were cuts in dividends for that year. A capitalist-manager-owner might once in a while yield to benevolent impulses but a hired manager might find that his humanitarian acts brought about his own discharge. Hence, the new managers rarely made any advances to labor that the managers could not justify as productive of lower unit-labor costs. The new managers, like the old owners, yielded nothing to labor unless labor exerted some kind of force.

Why Labor Sought "More"

The essential question is: "Did the cooperative efforts of land, labor, capital, and business management in the generation after 1896 result in any improvement in output; and if so did labor or the other factors of production get the benefit?" The first part of the answer is simple; production increased at about the rate of 4% per year with special spurts from 1898 to 1907 and again from 1919 to 1925. Therefore, even if labor's share in output remained static there was more to share; that is, in 1896 labor got a part of a robin's egg while in 1929 it had an ostrich egg to divide. As a matter of fact, labor's share fluctuated, the tendency being downward until 1909, then rising until 1921 when another recession set in. Nevertheless, the product was enough enlarged to give labor a net gain in real income if the entire period 1896 to 1929 be smoothed of its minor deviations.

Why then was there labor discontent in the generation? The answer has two parts, one concerning the adequacy of wages, the other the inequality in the distribution of national income. While the generation did witness a net increase in real wages, the wages at the start in 1896 were close to a subsistence level and by 1929 had not risen to a genuine comfort level; the increase left very much to be desired. In the same years, the national income tended to bulge more favorably for the upper middle class composed of managers, landlords, and stockholders. Men could endure a misery that was a universal lot but they resented unevenly distributed favors especially if they felt that the unevenness was unjustified. Besides, men did not live by wages alone; they wanted also security, and opportunity for their children.

Therefore, the workers of the generation after 1896 despite the improvement in their condition, diligently and sometimes belligerently sought "More."

CHAPTER 2

MORE UNIONS

Beginning with about 450,000 unionists in 1896, there was a generally consistent addition to their ranks until the generation's highest record of about 5 million was reached in 1920. In the remaining nine years of the generation, membership in unions—except for "company unions"—fell off about two million. In the period before 1920 there were three groups of years when growth was most intense. The first of these—1897 to 1904—was by far the most important, for unions then added members at a rate slightly in excess of 50% per year. In the second period, from 1909 to 1913, the rate of growth was about 8% per year. The third period from 1915 to 1920 showed a rate of about 20% per year. While the rate of expansion in the second and third periods was much less than the first, the actual increase in individual unionists was not so discrepant because the rate base was so much larger. As we will see, each of the periods of most rapid growth in union membership was followed by one in which employers were most bellicose in their endeavors to stem the tide of unionism.

Where Unions Are Strong.—Until 1915 the types of employment in which unionism spread the most were the building industry, transportation, coal and metal mining, glass manufacture, printing, and stone work. Indeed about half of all unionists were in these branches. Nevertheless, in these strongholds it was principally the skilled men who were organized; the unskilled and women employes as a rule were not included in the union fold. Between 1915 and 1920 unionism advanced most rapidly among the semi-skilled and unskilled in industries that hitherto had been mostly without organized labor. Examples could be taken from the textile industry, packing and slaughter house industries, and within the transportation industry such groups as longshoremen, seamen, railway shopmen, and railway maintenance-of-way men.

After 1920 it was this most recently organized set of employments that lost most heavily in union membership, but the loss also spread through all the fields of unionism. About the only unions that held or increased membership after 1920 were some of the building trades, the makers of men's clothing, and the organized theatre workers, including the actors but not the musicians.

The Position of the A. F. of L.—Up to the peak year of 1920, the American Federation of Labor increased its dominance among organized workers; in 1896 its national unions enrolled about 60% of all unionists and in 1920 a little over 80%. At the beginning of the generation the important unions of bricklayers, miners other than coal miners, and four railway brotherhoods all stood outside the American Federation of Labor. In addition there were numerous scattered, completely independent local unions. By 1920, the most important national unions that were still independent were the railway brotherhoods; but a new union organized in 1914 among the workers in the men's clothing industry had no connection with the Federation.[1] After 1920 and before 1929 none of the independents joined the American Federation of Labor, although the common loss in membership caused considerable cooperation in the last four or five years of the generation. The railway brotherhoods, especially the Trainmen came into close relations with the Federation, and all four in order to gain support for the Plumb Plan in 1918-1919 petitioned for American Federation of Labor charters. The American Federation of Labor two years earlier (1917) had urged the Brotherhoods to unite with it, but then the Brotherhoods were wary. In 1919 the situation was reversed; for the American Federation of Labor feared the Brotherhood's Plumb Plan (one to nationalize the railroads and then turn the operation over to a corporation con-

---

[1] The Amalgamated Clothing Workers Union joined the American Federation of Labor in 1934. The United Garment Workers Union which long had held an American Federation of Labor charter continued in that body but its membership was limited to the workers who made overalls.

trolled by the unions and management) would plunge it into a labor political party. The passage of the Transportation Act of 1920 cooled the Brotherhood ardor for both the Plumb Plan and affiliation with the American Federation of Labor. The radical unions such as the I. W. W. before 1920 and the Communists after that date, of course, had nothing but enmity for the Federation.

Where Unions Failed.—To confine attention to unions is not sufficient in evaluating them, for notice should be taken of how thoroughly they filled the area in which they tried to operate. Of all persons over 10 years of age about half were wage earners. Before 1910, the proportion was slightly higher than this and later was slightly lower. Throughout the generation agriculture lost members to manufacturing, mining and trade. Since most of our northern and western farm population before 1896 had lived on their own farms the change during the generation was in the direction of building a wage-earning class. After 1910, however, the occupations that grew the fastest in numbers were those in trade, clerical, professional, domestic and personal services; that is, the white collar jobs advanced faster than the overall jobs. Because in the United States farmers and their helpers as well as white collar people before 1929 seldom regarded themselves as members of the working class but rather the middle class, it will be apparent that our national tendencies favored unionism before 1910 more than they did after that date. American unions before and after 1929 always attracted the most members from manual workers.

Within the occupations most amenable to unionism, the workers who were actually members of unions were about one in five. This relatively poor showing was due partly to the geographic limitations of unions; they were strongest in the large cities of the Northeast and Middle West and in mining areas. The magnificent distances in the United States together with the fact that more than half the population lived in small towns, little villages, or on farms made the task of unionization extraordinarily difficult. Likewise, native Americans at that time were too imbued with individualism to be highly cooperative or altruistic.   Hence, unionism progressed best in the area east of Chicago and north of the Potomac or Ohio where most of our large cities, manufacturing and coal-mining enterprises, and foreign-born were congregated.

Finally, some of the unions themselves limited membership in one or more ways such as age limits, skill tests, tenure in industry, high initiation fees, race, or sex.

Variations in Degree of Unionization.—Some industries were unionized to a far greater extent than the one in five ratio.   The most highly unionized were the railway trainmen and other transportation employes, miners, and building tradesmen.   Within the manufacturing industries, which taken as a whole made a poor showing in degree of unionization, some branches were well organized.   For example, the men's clothing industry after 1914 enrolled much more than half of all the workers in the Amalgamated Clothing Workers' Union, and the printing and publishing industry was equally well organized, particularly in the newspaper section where workers were about as thoroughly unionized as the locomotive engineers were among trainmen.   On the other hand the chemical, automobile, paper, steel, rubber, and cement industries had scarcely any unionists among their employes; and the textile industry was only weakly organized in New England and almost wholly lacking in unionization in the South.

Compared with other industrial nations the degree of unionization in the United States was small.   Countries such as the United Kingdom, France, Germany, and Belgium were compact, largely homogeneous, and their workers not only were class conscious but more or less tied their economic unions to a working-class political party.   England, moreover, was highly urban and greatly specialized in industrial occupations.   None of these things was true of the United States.

Internationalism.—Because of this diversity together with the extreme individualism that has characterized American unionists, the worker organizations in this country, except for the Communists after 1920, had scarcely any contact with the labor movements in other countries. Fraternal delegates did cross the Atlantic in both directions and with increasing regularity as the years passed; but these delegates were convention guests. The courtesy of delivering an address to a convention was extended to them but they had no vote, nor did they represent any official international alliance. For eleven years after 1910, the American Federation of Labor was a member of the International Secretariat of Trade Union Centres (name changed in 1913 to International Federation of Trade Unions), but the decided drift of this organization toward labor political action and espousal of socialist doctrine so alienated the sympathy of the individualistic American Federation of Labor that in 1921 the latter withdrew its affiliation. Many American national unions had numerous locals in Canada and the American Federation of Labor was sympathetic to and almost responsible for the union organization in Mexico. In 1924 this fact was affirmed by simultaneous and partly joint conventions (November 17-26, 1924) at El Paso, Texas, and just across the national boundary in Juarez, Mexico. This event marked the last official appearance of Samuel Gompers, for he died, December 14th, at El Paso after his labors at the two conventions.

Explanation of the Tardy Growth of Unionism

No single explanation of the foregoing record of American Unionism of the three decades before 1929 would be adequate. Of the many reasons that have been advanced we can present only a few. First place should be given to the fact that we had no self-conscious, suppressed wage-earning class. Birth in a wage-earning family put no economic or social bar in the path of persons of ability; and politically, wage earners had enjoyed the right of suffrage for at least two generations before 1896. Wage earners themselves were divided into a small group of skilled persons, usually of American birth; and a larger group of unskilled, mostly aliens, women, children or Negroes. The skilled were segmented by the nature of their jobs into mutually exclusive social gradations; and the unskilled were divided into national units often hostile to each other by inherited prejudices. For a union to weld into one unit these unsympathetic blocs, was a well nigh insuperable task.

American Psychology.—Secondly, the psychology of Americans at that time was against subordination of the individual to the will and best interests of the group. Environment so long had placed a survival value on self-reliance that Americans generally practiced a philosophy of each man for himself and the devil take the hindmost. In carrying out this belief, the American-born grabbed for themselves the "soft" and well-paid jobs, thus putting themselves in situations about which they had little to complain. The relationships of Americans to the foreign-born were nearly always those of superiors to inferiors, so that when Americans saw unions led by persons of obviously alien origin and listened to union jargon full of words, phrases, and ideas of plainly foreign significance, the American thoughtlessly dismissed unionism as something itself inferior and of use mainly to inferiors. When employers charged unionism and unionists with being "un-American" they selected a weapon most certain to deaden any appeal of unionism to Americans.

As an illustration, in detail of this psychological environmental influence, take the case of the union rule, which dictated that a job must be done by the man within whose craft it fell. The rule harked back to European craft distinctions minutely drawn and rigidly enforced by long custom. Americans, on the contrary, were by *their* custom, "jacks of all trades"; so in any town or village there were men who could and did perform adequately the arts of several crafts. When informed of the union limitation to one craft, and the union insistence that as many men as there were craft skills needed for a job be actually called to a job—which the American knew that one man with his combined skills could do—American wage earners were apt to regard unions and their rules as silly.

Weaknesses of Craft Unionism.—Thirdly, inasmuch as the selfish creed of American individualism confined our unions mostly to the skilled, they were also mostly limited to manual craftsmen. The unprecedented advance of capitalism in the generation was one which substituted power machinery for manual operation. As the generation clicked off the years, it used its capital abundance to scrap capital equipment long before the machines really were worn out, substituting for partly worn machines new ones that were more nearly automatic. In short, capital increasingly pushed skill out of machine-using industries. In this process capital led a twofold attack on unions; the first was the elimination of the very skill on which unions were based, and the second, the power of massed capital to outwait and defeat any union that objected to anything done by the controllers of capital.

Jurisdictional Disputes.—Another phase of the use of capital to outrun unions was the possibility that capital might hire researchers, or finance the inventiveness of individual geniuses, in the discovery of new products or new processes. These latter tended to wipe out the distinctions between crafts. For instance, a blacksmith and a carriage builder once were distinct; but to what craft did a worker on automobiles belong? A carpenter, a metal worker, and a mason once performed each his own unique work; but to what craft should be assigned a man who erected a concrete wall within wooden or metal forms? As craft lines thus were smudged, unions struggled with each other because each union wanted all the work on new materials or processes it could get for its members. America, more than any other place, witnessed the spectacle of union men on strike against other union men. Bitterness over jurisdictional awards at times caused unions to withdraw from the American Federation of Labor, with the result that two unions, one "official," the other "outlaw," competed for the same membership in one trade. Employers took tactical advantage of this situation to play one union against the other in order to destroy both.

Unions vs. Fraternities.—Lastly, the unions had an unrecognized competitor for membership interest in the numerous fraternal orders in the United States. At first, this assertion may seem incredible, but a little investigation will give it weight. The appeals of both were to the same social and economic motives.

The two greatest attractions of unions were the social features and insurance benefits; to lonely city craftsmen the union hall with its fellowship, parties, outings, and close relationships with "ladies' auxiliaries" might well be the chief outlet for a social urge, while to others the opportunity to insure, at low rates paid in small regular instalments, against unemployment, sickness, or death, was the principle incentive to seek and retain membership in a union. Union insurance was an unusually powerful lure in trades so dangerous that ordinary insurance companies either refused to write it, or else charged exorbitant rates. It was the insurance features that most strengthened the railway brotherhoods, and until 1910 insurance accounted for the appeal of the cigar workers' union.

It was precisely in the social and cheap insurance advantages that the fraternal orders made their most conspicuously successful drives for membership. Unlike the unions, the fraternities were not confined to large cities or to any one geographic area; they flourished in small towns and villages and had numerous lodges in every state. Their membership rosters, even with all due allowance for duplications due to inveterate "joiners," very far overtopped union memberships; the Free Masons alone had as large a membership as the American Federation of Labor. As for insurance, the fraternities wrote in new business each year a billion dollars worth; the B. P. O. Elks disbursed annually in *charities* as much as the American unions paid in benefits.

Fraternities each had their own publicly recognized but seldom-mentioned social status, and they were so numerous that every social gradation had a fraternity very much to itself. The unskilled foreign-born had their own fraternities as did those persons with the self assurance to snub a banker. Unlike unions, the fraternities did not appeal to a man's cooperative spirit but to his individualistic egotism; when he obtained a badge it was a recognition that a desirable group has approved of *him,* whereas a man who joined a union was expected to sink his individuality in order to advance a *group* out of which he could not lift himself.

The oldest fraternity, the Free Masons, originally was a union of men who used the trowel as an implement of livelihood, not as a symbol. As the order matured, it admitted gentry and men of other trades to honorary membership, and called them, "speculatives." The increasing proportion of "speculatives" to the practicing craftsmen eventually converted the craft organization into a fraternity. Lodges of it appeared in America as early as 1710, a whole generation earlier than any known craft union.

On the other hand, the Noble and Holy Order of the Knights of Labor was inaugurated with most of the ritualism of a fraternity; but it was so flooded with workers seeking to use the "order" to further their economic desires that the organization was stripped of most of its fraternal features, and put before the nation as a labor union; the change being marked by the removal of the words Noble and Holy Order from the rest of the name, Knights of Labor. Several modern unions—for example, the Weavers' Union within the United Textile Workers' Union—have retained the use of fraternal passwords, opening and closing ceremonies, and "stations" where officers sit during meetings. The Patrons of Husbandry—Grange—also has been a mixture of union and fraternity.

Hence, it is not too far-fetched to consider fraternities as competitors of unions. The unions tended to win in the largest cities, and the fraternities in the towns and villages. In the cities, the unions' economic bonds strengthened them there; whereas the fraternities, more dependent upon personal knowledge of those invited to membership, were at a disadvantage in cities where this was difficult. In the towns and villages the individual contacts possible between employers and workers hampered union organizers; this is to say nothing of the expense of union membership campaigns conducted in widely scattered towns, where if all the town's craftsmen enrolled, the local would be tiny and weak. For the fraternities, the small-town intimacy in the whole life and living of its inhabitants was advantageous. Already strong in the smaller places, the fraternities captured whatever interest a union might have had if it had entered the town as a novelty offering scope for the social or economic motives of men.

Why Unionism Declined after 1920.—We have reserved for separate consideration an explanation of the causes of weakness among unions that was evidenced by the general decline in memberships after the peak year of 1920. The most hostile critics would mention first, the extreme conservatism of the American Federation of Labor, and of the leaders in the national unions that composed it. Until his death in 1924, Samuel Gompers was President of the American Federation of Labor; thus, save for one year, the same man for 43 years headed this important organization. It is a rare person who, with increasing age, retains mental flexibility; so it is no matter for astonishment, that Gompers continued into old age the policies and shibboleths that in the youth of the generation, confronting simpler industry, had served to make the Federation powerful. Gompers' own adherence to established principles of leadership was not offset by youthful advisers on his Executive Council; for the members of this body also had changed less frequently than the membership of the United States Supreme Court. Likewise, the heads of most of the greatest National Unions were men sustained long decades in office by their own political "machines." Like Calvin Coolidge's, the social and economic philosophy of many union leaders "dated" to their boyhood, and was not attuned to the conditions of the time when they were gray, or bald.

Length of service was not so true of employers or managers, especially those who guided the destinies of large corporations. As we have shown in Chapter 1, the new type of young business managers after 1910 used a new tactic against unions. They did not try to beat unions by force, but cut the grounds from under them by removal of causes for worker grievances. Such innovations as Personnel Management, and company unions in connection with, or separate from Welfare Work, or the startling reversal of attitude toward favoring high wages and short hours were indications of flexible young minds. No such mental dexterity was prominent among the members of

the Executive Council of the American Federation of Labor;
although there were examples of it among some affiliated national unions and unaffiliated unions.   The officers of the Amalgamated Clothing Workers' Union, notably, were as sophisticated in methods as the most adroit young manager.

Unions and the Law—Injunctions.—Within the eight years
after 1920, unions were held in check by legal disabilities.
Probably the most prominent legal restraint was that imposed
by the injunctive process.   Of course, restraint of unions by
injunctions was not something new; nevertheless, the use of
injunctions by employers in this period was unusually extensive.
Moreover, the injunctions at this time were abnormally severe,
both in the minuteness of the acts forbidden and the extraordinary number of things covered by the orders.   The example
was set by the Government itself, when, in September 1922,
Attorney General Daugherty obtained from Judge Wilkerson
against striking railway-shopmen one of the most sweeping and
yet detailed injunctions ever issued up to that time.   Private
employers emulated the thoroughness of the federal department.
    The relief from injunctions—and other suits—organized
labor thought it had obtained in October 1914 by the Clayton
Act, was swept away; for, when the provisions of this act were
presented to courts by labor defense-attorneys, the courts declared that the Clayton Act set up no new rules of law, but
merely interpreted existing law.   The Act in practice granted
to unions no immunities nor privileges.

Yellow Dog Contract.—As a by-product of one famous injunction case, the *Hitchman Coal & Coke Co. vs. Mitchell,* 245
U. S. 229, the Supreme Court in December 1917 declared that
a "yellow dog" contract was legal.   Thereafter, until March
1932 when the Norris-LaGuardia Act outlawed it, an employer
could stipulate in granting employment that an employe must
sign a declaration that he was not, and would not become a member of any union, such a signed statement being construed a
legal contract.

Suability.—Again as the by-product of an injunction, the Coronado Coal Company case 1925, the Supreme Court delivered a severe blow to unions. The Court stated that although a union was a voluntary association and not an incorporated body it nevertheless could be sued, a statement that opened the way for employers to launch attacks on union treasuries. The Sherman Act was used by employers to hamper unions in the Bedford Cut Stone Co. case April 11, 1927; contrariwise, the protection of the Sherman Act did not help unions in San Francisco who asked court relief from a practice of the Employers' Industrial Association of San Francisco; this practice was a "permit" to secure construction materials granted only to those who enforced an "open shop" policy.

The unions were forced to divert part of their energies in contesting the multitude of court cases brought against them by employers. Likewise, in 1920-21, the unions were put upon the defensive by the employers' nation-wide drive for the open shop (See Chapter 6); to the extent that unions were forced to fight to live, they were turned aside from more progressive actions. On the other hand, unions always have been most stimulated when most attacked. To have an openly avowed enemy was a force toward unity and demonstrated the need for organization.

Workers Relatively Well Off.—Beneath all the other causes for apathy, was the relative well being of employed workers. They had more leisure and their real wages were unusually high. With leisure and a bit of money there were many more attractive ways of using time than in attendance upon union meetings or in doing union work. Even fraternities lost members after 1920.

Neglect of Unskilled.—The greatest dereliction of American unions was their inattention to the organization of the unskilled. To be sure, the building trade unions and some others did unionize "helpers"; the miners unions enrolled the unskilled, and the clothing and textile unions embraced all the classes and nationalities found in their industries. For the most part the unskilled were ignored.

Since large numbers of the unskilled were aliens, Negroes, "poor whites," or women, the failure or outright opposition of unions to consider these groups as union material split the working class into factions and exposed the organized workers to retaliatory strike-breaking by these neglected numerous elements. A brief survey of the unskilled groups, therefore, is a necessary part of any American labor history.

Aliens.—Wholly foreign-born groups such as the clothing workers formed their own organizations, and by their extraordinary success put to shame the American unionists that had despised them. In mining and the textile industries, there were so many aliens, that a union to amount to anything was forced to include them. In other trades and industries the foreign-born got no consideration unless or until the weight of their numbers threatened disastrous competition; if the threat did not materialize, because the aliens stayed in the lowest jobs, they were let alone without help to stew in their own miseries. As a result, the unskilled, non-unionized constituted a majority of wage earners.

Negroes.—Negroes were barred from the railway unions and some building trade unions; and indirectly excluded from the blacksmiths, letter-carriers, and many others. Several unions such as the bookbinders, hotel and restaurant workers, painters, teachers, and textile workers admitted Negroes only to separate locals. The longshoremen and miners, both with many foreign-born members, were the least influenced by color considerations. On their side, the Negroes in many callings tried to get into the unions of those trades or sometimes organized separate Negro unions; in either case they were rebuffed by white unionists. Under this treatment, it is not surprising that Negroes frequently were strike-breakers and allied themselves with employers rather than white workers; what is surprising is that some Negroes never ceased the effort to batter down the barriers against their entrance into white labor organizations. The attempts to form working class solidarity were far more by Negroes than by whites.

In southern towns and cities, "poor whites" who attained trade skills readily were admitted to, and just as eagerly desired membership in unions—despite their origin they ceased to be classified as "poor whites." In mill villages and mining camps they formed a separate class of citizenry derided by all others. The segregation did not at first weld them into an economic group of their own, partly because they were highly individualistic and partly because they kept on the move from village to village. Their kind that migrated North to industries that manufactured steel or automobiles and other employments retained their independent attitude. It was not until toward the end of the generation that "poor whites" in the South banded together to rectify grievances and not until then did union organizers pay much attention to them.

Women.—In regard to women workers, the male unionists barred them from the unions and trades if the women were few in number. If the female competition became dangerous, as in the printing industry, the unions reluctantly took in women members. For the most part the women workers, like the aliens, were ignored.

The most prolonged and energetic efforts to enroll women into unions came from the National Women's Trade Union League instituted in 1906. The leadership of the League was unique among American labor organizations in that it came not from wage workers but largely from women of means. The League was not an affiliate of the American Federation of Labor although that organization approved of the work done by the League. With headquarters in Chicago, the League operated through subsidiary leagues in nearly a score of cities.[2] The League furnished the leadership which the youth, temporary service, and unskilled work of most women wage earners made little likely to spring from the ranks. Quite tactfully, the League avoided those occupations where women wage earners were in a minority and where a male union existed; instead it

---

[2] Birmingham, Boston, Chicago, Cleveland, Cumberland, Kansas City, Madison, Milwaukee, Minneapolis, New York, Philadelphia, Seattle, St. Louis, Tri-Cities, Washington, and Worcester.

went after those occupations where women were in the majority and which male unionists had most overlooked. Hence, in so far as women were unionized, it was mostly in spite of, not because of, the incentive and help of male unionists.

As a matter of fact most male unionists neglected to interest their own feminine relatives in unionism. There was a Women's International Union Label League organized in 1905 and intended to promote the purchase of union label goods by unionists' wives or daughters. A few unions had Ladies' Auxiliaries, and miners' wives fought valiantly on the picket line in strikes. For the most part, male unionists failed to realize that unionism was a family matter and that wives and daughters were as valuable allies to win to the union cause as potential male scabs. A strike could be scabbed in the home just as effectively as in the shop; "domestic pressure was slow but sure."

Wages and Hours

To summarize what has been said about the growth of unionism in the Generation of "More," let it be repeated that while the number of unions and unionists increased to a considerable extent they were most powerful in the skilled trades where manual operations still were important, and that the power was most manifest in large cities or in mining camps. However, compared to the total number of wage earners, or even of skilled workers, the unions did not progress as much in getting control in the field of labor as capitalism did in its field. In making these statements, we are apt to minimize too much the power and achievements of organized labor in the generation we have under consideration. To correct this tendency let us examine two of the things, wages and hours of labor, in which the well-being of labor was most closely wrapped.

Prices and Wages.—At the outset, it should be understood that the year 1896 was one which marked the end of a 15-year period in which wholesale and retail prices had been slipping downward from the peak reached in the Civil War—Greenback years, 1861-1879. On the other hand, the year 1929 was the end of 33 years in which the price trend was upward. Wages generally have corresponded in trend with the price curves, although as a rule, they have lagged behind prices both on downward and upward slopes. Consequently, it should be expected that a study of money-wages in the generation after 1896 would show a considerable increase as the years passed; and as a matter of fact this was the case. But at a point a little more than halfway through the generation, the World War upset normal trends so that from 1915 to 1921 prices leaped to heights never before attained. Likewise, money wages, beginning in 1916, set out to climb the heights toward prices. Both prices and wages fell back in 1921-22 but not near to the 1914 levels, and during the last seven years of the generation, the two more slowly began to recover some of the lost altitude.

Real Wages.—To be of real service in understanding the worker's relation to wages, it is necessary to refine the broad generalizations just made. It is real wages, not money wages, that cause workers misery or happiness. The story of real wages through the generation is found by relating the prices that compose workers' costs of living to the money wages. The cost of living for a workingman's family for the years 1896 to 1914 probably rose as fast or faster than his wages. Herein lay a cause for continual unrest and discontent on the part of wage earners.

In the next six "war years," the prices of articles in a worker's budget did not rise quite as fast as his earnings, so he enjoyed a modest increase in real wages. In the further years of the generation the slump in food prices, an item that accounted for more than forty per cent of the workers expenditures, enabled him with his increasing money wages to enjoy the most substantial improvement in real wages his generation had known. The status of real wages may be the secret of the worker's attitude toward unions after 1896.

Variations in Well-Being.—Truths, applicable in general to all workers, have to be modified when applied to particular groups. Before 1914, when most workers were barely holding

their own, two groups, farmers and teachers, were improving
their economic condition.   Farming at that time was relatively
undercapitalized and undermanned, so farmers and farm products had a scarcity value.   This meant that wage earners in
cities or mining camps had to pay relatively high prices for
food.   On the contrary, the things farmers bought were being
cheapened in price by the progress in other industries, especially
that of manufacturing.   For teachers, the explanation of their
better fortune was the increased demand for special training of
children to fit them for better jobs.   Thousands of the children
of manual workers went to school, or were sent there by their
ambitious parents, in order to get on and up in the world.   The
public school year was lengthened, the high schools were getting crowded, and the one-room local school was beginning to
give way to consolidated schools in towns.   Teachers of higher
quality were in demand, and since this necessitated longer and
more expensive training, the teachers demanded and received
more pay.

After 1914, workers in manufacturing enterprises led in increases in *money* wages; those engaged in production of food
products gained somewhat more than others, while those in
textile manufacture and the leather groups did not advance as
much as most of the others.   Iron and steel, clothing, paper and
printing, and automobile workers all advanced at about the
same pace, and at the pace that was average for all manufactures.   Transportation workers reached the levels of manufacturing employes, but did not get there quite so quickly.
Clerical workers and government workers, while they got advances, were far below the leaders in pay increases.

When these *money* wage increases are translated into terms
of *real* wages, we find that employes in manufacturing and
transportation secured a genuine increase, as did also the teachers; but those in clerical positions probably lost, for prices outran their wage advances.   Within the manufacturing group,
the highest real wages were obtained by the workers in the
lumber and wood, and food industries, followed by paper and
printing, clothing, automobile, iron and steel, and textiles.
Tobacco workers were worse off in purchasing power than they

had been before 1896, due to the attrition of hand cigar rollers by machinery, and the low-wage policy of the leading corporations that produced cigarettes, pipe tobacco, chewing tobacco, and snuff.

Did Unionism Raise Wages?—Some statistical experts who studied real wages came to a conclusion like that of Paul H. Douglas, who asserted that it was difficult to ascribe any large share in the real wage gains which labor made to the union movement inasmuch as the increases were about as rapid and as great in unorganized industries as in the organized trades. To this conclusion, other statisticians objected on the grounds that the available wage data was by industries, whereas unions with few exceptions were organized on a craft basis that cut across industrial lines and varied in strength in different cities or localities. The Bureau of Labor Statistics in a report on the *History of Wages* (October 1929) showed that in the generation after 1896 in wage rates per hour the advances made in the union scale failed only in the one year (1922) to hold the gains already made; whereas the hourly rates of all labor fell off in three different years; and that after 1922 the rate of increase was higher among unionists than among all labor taken together.

In individual industries, such as mining, we know that after 1902 the organized anthracite workers fared better than the partially organized bituminous miners, and that of the latter the unionized obtained higher rates (but not always higher earnings) than the non-unionized. Again, in the railroad industry, we have evidence that the organized trainmen got preferential treatment over partly organized employes in other railroad service, and that as between railroads the non-train employes who were organized in free unions had fatter pay envelopes than those unorganized or in company unions. Compare the unionized *Baltimore and Ohio* employes with those of the "open-shop" *Delaware and Hudson*. In the textile industry there was a wage advantage to Northern workers over those in the South, and within the North a unionized plant such as the Naumkeag at Salem, Massachusetts, had better wage rates and hours of

work than the non-unionized Amoskeag at Manchester, New
Hampshire.   Similar favors in pay or hours were noticeable
among unionized building craftsmen over those in the same
trades who were unorganized; and the same situation could be
observed in the clothing industry.

High Union Wages Raised the Wages of Unskilled.—
There was a negative argument put forth by friends of unions;
that is, the pay of non-unionists was influenced either by the
presence or absence of unions in the industry in which the unorganized were employed, or by the threat that unions would enter
the industry if low pay gave them a rallying cry.   In all industries, there are well-established differentials in wages that distinguish one set of workers from another so that a change in
any one is likely to create corresponding shifts in all others in
order to maintain the differentials.

Thus, if a small, skilled, unionized group was able to force
higher wages for itself, the action sooner or later pulled up the
wages of the unorganized below or pushed to higher levels
those differentially above the union.   Statistical tables would
not credit the union with this effect on the non-unionized and
neither does the concept in economic theory called "non-com-
peting groups" give sufficient recognition to this matter.

Also, if a trade highly unionized, say in Boston or Detroit,
set a pay standard, the employers with non-union men in the
small towns or villages of New England in the one case or
Michigan in the other had to approach the union city-wage-
scale.   In instances such as these, the unions got no statistical
credit for their effect on the unorganized.

Fear of unionization in many an enterprise as well as in
some whole industries, undoubtedly was a compulsion upon
employers to keep pay close to levels that would be exacted by
unions if they did penetrate the concerns involved.   We have
had the employers' own statements to verify this truism.   Potential unionization, therefore, was a factor in wage increases
among the unorganized which neither they nor wage statisticians always recognized.

Wages in Relation to Size of Family

After all, statistical tables of money wages or real wages did not cover all the changes in working family finances after 1896. One important matter, that bore upon family fiscal affairs, was the progressively smaller size of working class families. The wage of the breadwinner had to be shared by fewer claimants, with the result that families could save more of the income or could raise the standard of living. Both occurred; increased savings were evidenced by the published reports of savings banks, postal savings accounts, insurance companies, and building and loan societies; while improved standards were shown by the homes or home-furnishings of workers as well as the number of children of manual workers in high schools or technical schools, including business colleges. The decline of child wage labor in the generation was a product not solely of more stringent laws but also of fewer children per family and rising standards of family living.

There was considerable difference in the size of families between the skilled and unskilled workers. With all due allowance for exceptions, the unskilled had more children per family. Since the wages of unskilled were below those of skilled, the difference in number of income-sharers heightened the differences in standards of living of the two groups. Among the skilled, there was a reciprocal relationship between size of family and standards of living; small families permitted an improvement of standards, while the latter in turn compelled limitations upon births.

More Breadwinners Per Family.—The head of the family was relieved of part of his financial burden also by his wage earning daughters over the school age. The increase in the employment of women throughout the generation was even more remarkable than the decrease in the size of the family. The daughters of skilled workers became school teachers, librarians, secretaries, stenographers and clerks while the daughters of the unskilled became clerks, waitresses, servants and factory hands. Inasmuch as most women workers were under 24 years of age and generally lived at home, their earnings either positively by their contributions aided the family treasury, or negatively, to the extent that they were self supporting, had a similar result. However, the movement of women into industry partly defeated itself because the bulk of the women flooded into a few occupations which, by the oversupply of workers, remained relatively low waged. The poor statistical showing of clerical wages in the generation may be accounted for on this basis. At any rate, in 1896, most working class families had only one wage earner but by 1929 there were few that did not have more than one.

Now if we put together the two movements, one a smaller number of children, the other a larger number of breadwinners, it is apparent that worker family standards had considerable opportunity for improvement; if we add the third element, an era of rising money wages and higher real wages, we can understand the unusual well-being of American workers in the generation.

City vs. Village Workers.—Offsetting, somewhat, the advantages stated was the partial disadvantage of greater urbanization of wage earners. City workers usually could not supplement money incomes with kitchen-gardens, chicken-yards, pig-pens, and cow-barns. Generally, city workers had to buy vegetables, eggs, or poultry, bacon, lard or pork, and milk. Nevertheless, there continued to be an astonishing amount of village practice even in the largest cities. Wherever, as in Philadelphia, workers could command a back yard there was more often than not at least a chicken-coop, and frequently little vegetable plots. The sanitary codes of most cities barred back yard pig-pens or cow-sheds, but among some of the foreign-born, goats were urbanized in place of cows. In all cases, city rents were high in proportion to the number of rooms, air space, and sunlight they commanded. Moreover, some goods, such as water which often were free in villages had a money price in cities; and the city worker usually had to pay for transportation to and from the work place, whereas in villages he had walked the short distance between home and shop.

On the other hand, the city furnished wage earners with many low priced or free services. Visiting nurses or clinics, organized charities, inexpensive playgrounds, public free concerts, public libraries, and accident compensation all were virtually community additions to worker incomes. It might be said also that one measure of real wages is leisure; and that city workers as a rule gained shorter work hours before this boon extended to smaller communities.

Finally, any wage could be made to go further if consumption were efficiently directed. The greater competition of city sellers gave workers' wives an education in buying; but sometimes this advantage over village wives was offset by the greater number of false "bargains" offered in the city.

Shorter Work Day

Although there may be some doubt as to the part played by unions in getting real wages advanced in the generation of "More," there can be little question that they were leaders in obtaining for workers a shorter work-day, particularly prior to 1917. There had been a mass effort to bring about an 8-hour day in 1886, and a plan for a similar general strike in 1890; the latter in spreading to Europe, giving rise to the celebration thereafter of May 1 as Europe's Labor Day. In the United States, it was the carpenters who led the 1890 struggle and this craft was the chief beneficiary of the fight. Although the onset of a depression in 1893 halted for a time the campaign for shorter hours, by 1896 organized labor had adopted the principle as one of its leading tenets.

Unions discovered that the 8-hour agitation, more than any other labor demand, had the effect of unifying all labor; and in addition that reduction of hours more easily could be secured from employers than increases in wages. However, after hours were reduced, employers sooner or later could be forced to raise hourly rates; so that the shorter work-day eventually led to greater pay.

In 1900, the American Federation of Labor resolved to secure a shorter work-day for at least one trade each year. In carrying out this policy, the greatest of the contemporary strikes was one in 1905, conducted by the International Typographical Union. At the time the strike succeeded, there were 26 trades that in whole or in part had won the 8-hour day.

By Law.—Soon thereafter, a minority in the American Federation of Labor questioned the slower policy of trade-by-trade fights for the 8-hour work period, and sought instead to swing the American Federation of Labor behind a movement to get to the goal quickly by blanket state legislation.

The issue, after hot debate, was settled by a careful statement of policy. It was declared that the questions regulating wages and hours of labor should be through trade union activity, and not made subject to laws through legislative enactment, excepting in so far as such regulations affected or governed the employment of women and minors, health and morals, and employes of federal, state or municipal governments. Occasionally, in later years, the policy was challenged by those who favored work-hour legislation for all labor; but the American Federation of Labor steadfastly, throughout the generation, maintained that the best way for wage earners to decrease their work periods was by trade union pressure upon employers.

The experience of the generation justified the policy: for the legislative regulation of the hours of work of women and minors was in the first place difficult to secure and limited to a few states; while secondly, the legislation as passed was often poorly administered and frequently held in abeyance by suits brought by employers to test the constitutionality of the laws. For government employes it was relatively easy to obtain limitation of hours by legislation or ordinance; but it was a task imposing constant vigilance to compel government administrators to observe the intent of the rules laid upon them.

Varied Success in Attainment of 8-Hour Day.—The pressure of individual trade unions for shorter hours resulted in varied success so that the same union had different hours of work in different places; and between groups of workers there was wide divergence in the hours of employment. A universal 8-hour day was very slowly approached before 1917.

As illustrations of these discrepancies, we can cite the case of the stationary engineers who, in 1900 had a 48-hour week in Massachusetts, and an 84-hour week in Pennsylvania. In the group of building trades, the plasterers and plumbers in some places had had the 48-hour week for 5 years in 1896; and the painters for 2 years; but it was 1900 before any electricians got 48 hours; 1903 before stone masons did; and 1907 before building trade laborers fell in line. In the leather industry, some shoemakers obtained a 48-hour week in 1896; but it was 1910 before any tannery workers had such a short week. Machinists, outside of railway shopmen, equalled their fellow craftsmen. Newspaper compositors in 1907, after about two years of strikes, skipped the 48-hour week and put their hours down from 54 or more to 45; but press feeders had to be satisfied with 48 hours in 1908. Blacksmiths, boilermakers, iron molders, pattern makers, and many other trades had to wait for the World War to reduce the work week hours to 48; and only in Massachusetts did any textile workers have 48 hours regularly at any time up to the end of the generation except during the World War.

Steel workers, many railway workers, and some miners trailed way to the rear for most of the generation; these unfortunate groups labored 12 hours or more per day. New industries, such as automobile manufacture, resisted the 8-hour movement; and likewise new industrial areas, such as the South, fought against the adoption of so short a day.

World War and 8-Hour Day.—Considerable sporadic progress had been made by the time of the World War but it was our entrance into that conflict that brought hasty and general adoption of the 8-hour day. At the very beginning of our participation, pressure was brought upon the trades in munition works to suspend any rules of working time they may have had. The result was a compromise; the trades permitted hours longer than 8, but all time over 8 hours counted in pay as time and a half. Since the compromise recognized the principle of 8 hours but allowed more output and increased earnings, the workers were satisfied. Railway unions in 1916 forced from Congress the Adamson Act by which the "basic 8-hour" day was legally imposed upon the railroads; this law was intended more to increase the earnings of railway workers by the exaction of increased pay rates for the time over 8 hours than it was to reduce actual working hours. Indeed, a prior law which was not modified, permitted a maximum day of 16 hours for railway workers.

In 1917-18, so much of the productive capacity of the country was devoted to war work that nearly every industrial employer had government contracts. For that matter, in order to get raw materials, fuel, or freight space for *any* product, employers virtually were compelled to have some work being done on government contracts. Under President Wilson's advice the contracts were drawn with a clause that forced those producers, accepting government contracts, to conduct their operations on an 8-hour basis. The War Labor Board set up to hear and decide industrial disputes during the war adopted as standard an 8-hour day.

Consequently, when the war was finished, most workers and nearly all unionized workers were, and continued to be, in enjoyment of at least an 8-hour day. Some employers, such as those in the textile industry, increased the hours over 8 as soon as the government contracts were filled or cancelled. But three-fourths of all wage earners in manufacturing enterprises enjoyed 54 hours or less and only 3% still had to toil 60 hours or more.

The 44-Hour Week.—Further reduction of the work week to 44 hours began in 1921-22. When manufacturers of men's clothing planned to take advantage of the depression of that period to revert to "open-shop" operation, the Amalgamated Clothing Workers' Union seized a strategic advantage by declaring a strike. Among the demands made by the strikers—a demand put forward merely as a bargaining point—was one for a 44-hour week. The strike so routed the employers that when a settlement was signed it contained a provision for a 44-hour week. Painters (40 hours, 1920), press feeders (1921), bookbinders (1925), furriers (40 hours, 1926), plasterers (40 hours after 1915), were other trades that pressed the hours below 48 per week. The agitation for a work week of 40 to 44 hours spread much faster and further than had the earlier 48-hour campaign.

The 6-Hour Day.—The proposals that soon eclipsed all others were ones that set either 5 days of work, or 6 hours per day, as the standards—some declarations were for a 30-hour week. The 6-hour day had been proposed in an American Federation of Labor convention as early as 1913; but the convention, while expressing its sympathy for such a short work day, thought it appropriate at that time to strive for a more general application of the 8-hour day. The action was reaffirmed in 1914, with an added phrase to the effect that the convention believed in progressive decreases in working hours in keeping with the developments of machinery and productive forces. The 6-hour program was advocated by Lord Leverhulme in a special article in the *New York Times* (May 25, 1919); and by the coal miners,—in their case however not as a means of decreasing, but of increasing the average weekly work period.

The 5-Day Week.—Until after 1928, the 6-hour day was not as much discussed as the 5-day week. Henry Ford gave the talk a considerable impetus in 1922 when he professed his belief in the 5-day week. He brought the topic startlingly to every one's attention in the fall of 1926 when he announced his orders to give the 5-day week a trial in his plants; and again September 25, 1927, when he told the world that this work period was confirmed as the standard for his companies. A few days before Ford's statement in 1926, the American Federation of Labor officially endorsed the 5-day week, and began its first nationwide campaign since 1886 for a reduction of working time. The organized effort was especially directed at the automobile, mining and construction industries; the first, to enable unions to penetrate it; the second, to take up the slack of part-time work and unemployment; and the third, because in that field there seemed a good chance of securing it. In the

spring of 1928, the New York City building trades won a demand for a 5-day week; and by that time department stores in
some cities had adopted it, at first as a summer schedule, and
then as an all-year practice.   Consequently by 1929 there probably were 500,000 wage earners who had obtained the 5-day
week.

Steel's Long Hours.—Aloof from all these changes, the
anachronistic 12-hour day in the steel industry continued without any modification.   During the World War, unions had appeared once again in this industry; so almost as soon as the war
was over the capitalistic corporations grappled with the labor
organizations to which they were relentlessly opposed.   Although the Steel Strike of 1919 was epic, it was lost by labor.
Nevertheless, public sympathy rested with the strikers, especially in their demand that the 8-hour day be substituted for the
12-hour day.   An investigation made by an Inter-church body
scathingly condemned the 12-hour day, and other investigations
bore out the main points of the Inter-church report.

The spokesmen for the steel companies showed that the
12-hour day was not universal, and that it was least in vogue
in the open-hearth department (50%), more general around
blast furnaces (63%), and most common in the Bessemer
plants (75%).   They also pointed out that the work where
12 hours prevailed was intermittent in intensity; and that the
men loafed or slept with the unofficial sanction of foremen on
time for which they were paid.   It was assumed by these pro-
tagonists that the nature of the processes in the steel industry
was unique and demanded 12-hour shifts.   They asserted that
a three shift, 8-hour program, was too costly to consider.

The antagonists of the 12-hour day found, that in the forty
continuous process industries of the United States, the 8-hour
day prevailed; they claimed that a 48-hour week (or even less)
was generally accepted in non-continuous process industries.
They argued that an 8-hour day in steel would produce more
alert men, better morale, and win public approval.   As for the
intermittency of the tasks, these champions of labor asserted
that was of less consequence than the time a worker had at

home with his family. The cost of the change would be—so
it was said—only from 3% to 15%; and this was actually less
than the differences in costs that already existed between different steel plants. Moreover, the cost could be reduced by the
installation of more labor saving devices.

Steel Reduces Hours.—The debate in the public press ran
so hot that President Harding called the steel magnates to a
conference at the White House in May, 1922. As a result, a
committee of steel makers was formed to seek information as
to the feasibility of an 8-hour day. This committee's report
was adverse. A year later the American Steel Institute, composed of steel manufacturers, made a tentative gesture toward
a shorter day. President Harding published a letter urging the
Institute to weigh carefully all the evidence and to hasten, so
far as possible, the abolition of the long work-period. On
August 16, 1923, the Carnegie Company of Pittsburgh announced its adoption of the 8-hour day. The other principal
steel producers immediately fell in line; and the 8-hour day became the avowed standard for the steel industry. In reality,
this was a victory for public opinion, an elusive thing, but more
powerful than the steel corporations. The latter, however,
cheated on their standard wherever they could go unobserved.

Arguments for Shorter Work Day

Health.—Before 1896, the principal reasons put forward
by labor in support of a demand for a shorter work period had
been "the citizenship" argument—workers needed leisure in
order to gain information upon which intelligent voting depended—and the health argument—the physical strain of long
hours.

In the generation of "More," the reasoning was changed in
order to attract public approval. In the face of constantly increased labor saving devices, the health argument had to be
shifted from the *physical* strain of long hours to the *nervous* and
mental strain of closer attention to monotonous repetitive
motions through long hours. This argument came very much

to the fore after 1908 when the successful use of it by Louis
Brandeis and Josephine Goldmark in the *Muller vs. Oregon*
case in which the Supreme Court's decision validated the state's
10-hour law for women. It was strengthened after 1910 by
various studies in fatigue made by researchers in *Scientific
Management* (e.g., Gilbreth).

· **Share in Production.**—After the World War, the principal
talking point for shortening hours was the startling advance in
output per worker. If wages depended upon production, an
average increase in output per worker of 43% between 1919
and 1923—as shown by the employers' National Industrial Conference Board—"then," the workers said, "an increase in earnings as well as a decrease in work time was justified." Moreover, the unions claimed that the improved efficiency of workers
was having the effect of adding to unemployment; so work
time should be reduced in order to give all workers an opportunity to gain a livelihood. As each passing year witnessed
still more remarkable records of output, a further supplementary
argument was urged. It ran thus: Low unit costs are obtainable by mass output; mass output requires mass consumption;
mass consumption requires more leisure. Not only wage earners but several prominent employers zealously promulgated this
connection of relationships; so it got a "good press."

Against Shorter Hours.—Those employers, who fought the
successive decreases in work-time, used the same points of objection that their kind had made in 1830 against the 10-hour
day.

John E. Edgerton, president of the National Association of
Manufacturers, quoted the Biblical command to labor six days
(thus utterly misinterpreting the statement "six days shalt thou
labor," which was a limitation to six days so as to keep free the
seventh day) and also distinguished between the leisure which
is conducive to culture and that which grants time for criminal
pursuits. It was the latter use that labor made of leisure, he
believed. This was the old 1830 "Puritan argument" that
leisure was sin.

Mr. E. H. Gary, head of the U. S. Steel Corporation, used the same points, but added that a shorter work week would lower wages and lessen production because industry could not supply human wants in less time than was then the rule.

A large number of employers threatened to close their works because, said they, "they could not compete with other employers who resisted or escaped coercion for shorter hours." The Edgerton and Gary comments were made in 1926 against the 5-day week, but others had said similar things between 1896 and 1917 against an 8-hour day or 48-hour week.

As a matter of fact, diligent search has failed to reveal any really new arguments against shorter work time; the employers of each decade and generation repeated the same points as made by the first employers who were faced with a demand for lessening the work period. Consequently, advocates of shorter hours had a strategic advantage, for they had answers prepared for the employers' standard objections; whereas the advocates kept changing the arguments or emphasis so as to present the most plausible appeal to the public. Furthermore, before the 1908 Brandeis-Goldmark Oregon brief, both labor and employers had depended upon oratory to win their cases before the public; but throughout the remainder of the generation, and increasingly so with the passage of time, reliance to gain victories was placed on data revealed by statistical, medical, and other research. A battle of tongues was replaced by a battery of tomes.

Unionism in Relation to Shorter Hours

In recapitulation of the unions' attainment of shorter work periods, it is noticeable that the unions were much less successful in this endeavor than in their pressure for higher wages. The results after 1896 were few and scattered for two decades. Then the power of organized labor in a war period plus a favorable national government administration, and later a technological advance accompanied by managerial acceptance of the economy of short hours, did at last cause most workers to gain an 8-hour day. When this goal was reached, it suddenly was passed by many workers who went on to the 44- and 40-hour week. Thereupon a new goal was set up: a 5-day week of

6 hours per day.   The principal credit to unions in this reduction of work hours was their leadership in bringing it about, together with an unremitting pressure that served to make the public conscious of the program.

Since in this chapter we have confined our attention to the growth of unions and their success in the raising of wages or reduction of hours, we have left for a later chapter (Chapter 7) the legislative actions in regard to wages and hours of work.

CHAPTER 3

STRIKES IN GENERAL

To compel employers to bend to labor's desires, the most powerful weapon in labor's arsenal was the strike.

Notwithstanding that most persons assumed that strikes and unions were inseparable, this idea was short of the truth. There have been many strikes that were spontaneous revolts of unorganized workers. Whenever these happened, it is true that union officers, if possible, hastened to the scene; and in return for experienced counsel, endeavored to persuade the strikers to enroll as unionists. With this qualification, along with the further one, that strikes among established unions were not weapons of first, but of last resort, then the popular conception that unions and strikes went together was reasonably accurate.

The Number of Strikes

In writing about the number of strikes and strikers, the success, or cost of strikes, it is necessary to deal in generalities; for there has been no complete official record made of them in this country. From time to time, Congress has appointed committees to report on the subject; and beginning in 1916, the United States Bureau of Labor Statistics began to collect and publish monthly figures. The committees were not continuous and usually were confined to some especially sore spot in employment; while the Bureau of Labor Statistics had no mandatory power to force the reporting of strikes, and so depended upon its own ingenuity in ferreting the facts.

Some of the difficulties that blocked accuracy were the definition of a strike, the determination of when strikes started and ended, and the number of persons involved. Nearly every one thought he knew what a strike was, but when the attempt was made to put into words a definition that covered all varieties of

strikes the task was formidable.   Accurate counting depended
on accurate definition.   The hour and day when a strike began
or ended could not always be ascertained; some strikes just
grew, and some were confused with lockouts; some strikes never
had an official termination, and some really were ended long
before the official declaration.   The number of persons on
strike almost always was differently reported by employers and
by the strike-leaders; for the one sought minimization as much
as the other tried exaggeration.

With these qualifications in mind, it seems as if strikes
tended to increase until 1919 and then to diminish considerably
until the close of the generation in 1929.   Soon after unions
are formed they are apt to engage in a strike, partly as a test of
strength, partly because unseasoned members insist on getting
some immediate results.   While unions were growing after
1896, numerous strikes were a mark of youthfulness; the decline after 1919 was correspondingly somewhat of a sign of
maturity.

In the first years after 1896, when union interests to a considerable extent still were local, the number of strikes was large
but the number of strikers relatively small.   The nearer a union
came to truly national organization the more it hesitated to precipitate a strike, thus keeping down the numbers of strikes;
when such a strike did occur the numbers involved were large.
Again, when national unions were a new creation of locals, the
latter engaged in strikes with little attention to the sanction of
the national; but with the passage of time many national unions
became so ascendant over locals that the latter could be expelled
or disciplined if they called a strike without authorization by
the national.

Relation to Corporate Business.—Still another explanation
of the history of strikes is that in the earlier part of the generation many unionists worked for individual employers rather
than for great corporations.   From this circumstance several
results arose.   One was that many of the individual employers
used every art to get the public to condemn strikes.   In answer
to this attack, unions glorified the strike and used it as often as

they dared.   Secondly, as soon as unions perceived the drift of business toward large-scale corporate organization, the unions mistakenly thought the shift gave them more power.   "Whereas an employer with a small capital investment could outwait a strike, a corporation," thought the unions, "could not afford to let its capital equipment lie idle; especially could it not permit a large plant to wait for a dispute to be settled with one small craft unit of workers."   "Corporations," said unionists, "would find concession less costly than conflict."

By 1920, unionists had learned the bitter lesson that corporations, endowed with immortality, could take the long range viewpoint; and so, in order to avert future costly conflicts, the corporations were willing in test cases to let the strike drag to lengths the union itself could not afford.   Capital could outwait labor.   Moreover, when holding companies appeared in the business field, a strike against one plant was worthless; if the union lost, it was because the company diverted the work to other plants; if the union won, it was a pyrrhic victory, for the company soon picked another quarrel, or permanently closed the unionized plant in favor of some other non-unionized plant. Corporations with abundant capital sowed all varieties of anti-union propaganda against striking unions, thus successfully alienating public support from the unions.   Large funds also were useful in erecting legal entanglements around a union on strike.   Unionists were hauled into jails on personal charges of misdemeanor or crimes, while the union as a body was halted by injunctions, or hampered by suits for damages, under the Sherman Act.

In 1896 a strike could be a blithe hand-to-hand scrap with an employer; but by 1920 a strike against a corporation or a whole industry was an impersonal contest of rival strategies and resources.   In short, in 1896 strikes could be impulsive, but by 1920 they had to be warily planned.

Industries Most Often Affected By Strikes

Because in the generation after 1896 the chief burden of strikes was carried by the building trades, the clothing workers, the miners, and textile operatives, the economic factors affecting the industries in which these wage earners were engaged merit attention.

Building Trades.—The building trades were the least disturbed by the generation's increasing dominance by capital. Throughout the generation, building, only to slight degree, was subjected to mass methods; nearly all public and private construction was both unique for each job, and local in its relationships. Seldom were there duplicate structures. Rarely were exactly the same men employed on two successive buildings; and except for a few key men, it was seldom the case that craftsmen continually had the same employer. Some machinery entered the industry, but for the most part, manual skill remained its chief characteristic. All the local craftsmen of each building craft could unite each in the union of his craft, and thus set up a monopoly that was not much more subjected to competition than medieval city craft gilds. The inter-community craft competition that did exist could be minimized by the fact that the local crafts each had their own national. Wandering craftsmen from small towns or other non-unionized places generally were not sufficiently numerous to scab a whole job, and so were made to secure employment through the union and to abide by union regulations. The unions, therefore, fairly well controlled the supply of labor, and this labor was skilled; hence, building trade unions had the bases for power. When allied with politics, the union power often was tyrannical.

Weakness of Contractors.—Set against the local monopoly of labor power was an unusually powerless set of employers. Responsibility for the erection of a building was taken by a general contractor, who, in turn, sublet much or all of the actual work to other contractors. Thus, no one subcontractor had much stake in the entire enterprise; but if his share of the work was interrupted, his dereliction could halt the whole structure. The subcontractor, moreover, was a kind of broker who brought together materials and labor without much capital investment in or for either. All subcontractors were under pressure to complete their own job within contracted time limits; besides which, the weather sometimes imposed a time limit.   Although general contractors and subcontractors often formed local associations in order to deal with labor, the construction business was so viciously cut-throat that members of these associations found it difficult to act in harmony with each other.   They not infrequently hated each other more than they did unions.

Under these circumstances, building trade unions utilized their power to boost wage rates, lower working hours, and impose rules relative to use of materials, tools, appliances and the number or kind of men employed.   Strikes were frequent in order to enforce these demands; and since the strikes were by trades against subcontractors, there often were several in the course of the erection of one building.   No one strike as a rule was very serious, but any one in which perhaps only a small minority of all the men were engaged, could interrupt progress on the structure, and render idle most or all the men.   Frequently it was cheaper to grant even exhorbitant demands of the few rather than delay the many.   In some places, such strikes— or threats of them—were associated with racketeering.

→ **Jurisdictional Strikes.**—The building trades, also, were grievously afflicted with jurisdictional strikes to determine which of several crafts was to do a particular job.   New materials and methods gave rise to strikes of this kind because the materials or methods created a border zone between crafts without exactly conforming to previous practices in any one of them. For example, were carpenters or tilers to lay synthetic shingles, who was to construct forms for concrete walls—the masons, carpenters, metal workers, or laborers?   Since the decision meant more jobs for the craft selected, and fewer to the crafts rejected, the jurisdictional disputes and strikes of union against union often were more bitter and violent than strikes of a union against a contractor.

In the small towns, except those that were satellites of cities, the building crafts for the most part were non-union; if any were organized they were generally the masons and plasterers, the latter sometimes not as a separate trade but included among masons.   Nevertheless, the small town craftsman had an interest in the strikes of his city fellows partly because he had been, or expected to be, a city artisan himself; and partly—a growth from the first alternative—his wages and hours followed a rough differential adjusted to the city standards.

Clothing Trades.—In contrast with the building trades, the frequent strikes in the clothing trades had quite a different set of causes; the former were engagements in which a powerful group wrested special privileges for itself, while the latter were struggles of an overly exploited group to rise to American standards.   Until 1910, the stories of workers in the men's and women's branches of the clothing industry were much alike; after that date they diverged.

Characteristics.—The clothing industry, by 1896, had developed two characteristics; it was one in which there was slight advantage in large-scale centralized control of operations; and it was one that was notorious as an exploiter of the needs of poverty-stricken workers who being largest numerically in cities, fixed the cities as the location for clothing manufacture. In the making of clothes, the first operation of cutting the cloth was one of the most important; if this were carefully supervised the rest of the sewing or pressing could be passed out to individuals who ran sweatshops, or to others who worked at home.   About the only advantages of the factory system in this industry were closer timing of the finish of all parts of the completed garments, better inspection at lower costs, and greater security against thefts, and possibly improved sanitary conditions of the premises where clothes were made.   Against these, was the undoubted advantage to the manufacturer of the low labor-costs if actual sewing was submitted to keenly competitive bidding by contractors who ran sweatshops, or the equally competitive prices obtainable from those who had to work in their homes or die.

Jewish Dominance.—With the tide of immigration in 1896, which swept into our country from central and southern Europe, was a horde of Jews from eastern Germany, Poland, and Russia.

The German Jews first invaded the clothing industry, and quickly pushed out the Scotch and Americans who had been the manufacturers. The German Jews, as bosses, put work in the hands of Polish and Russian Jews to such an extent that most of the widows and indigent females who had been the wage earners were ousted. A male Russian Jew could work more intensely for longer hours at lower rates than most of the city's poor women. Soon, some of the Russian Jews became contractors; and in hiring their own kind in their sweatshops, drove them without mercy. The sweatshops' operators, in turn, were inhumanly pitted against each other by German-Jewish manufacturers, the latter term meaning the men who bought materials, received orders from wholesalers and retailers, and made deliveries to these outlets. As quickly as the Russian-Jewish wage workers became socially acclimated to America, they began to hold meetings, publish papers, and otherwise seek solace for their grievances.

To these particular immigrants, the American freedom of assembly, freedom of speech, freedom of press, and freedom of movement were unprecedented boons. Liberated from so many accustomed pressures, they all the more resented the economic pressure exerted in the clothing industry. American workers and union leaders gave them scant heed, and besides they were long used to following their own leaders; so the clothing industry, first in New York, and then in other cities, soon was peppered with craft unions. Thereupon began two decades of continual strife. Directed against the employer, the struggle was to abolish sweatshops, raise wages from the subsistence to the American comfort level, and reduce hours from those set by human endurance to those that conformed to the best in other industries. Directed against each other, rival unions sought the allegiance of the same workers; and within unions, rival factions fought for control.

Men's Clothing.—After 1910, unionism in the men's branch of the clothing industry began to forge ahead of the women's branch. Since men's clothes were less subjected to the vagaries of style, it was more feasible to manufacture them under the

factory system than women's clothing; hence by unionizing the
factories the unions used factory employers to club into subjection the sweatshop manufacturers.   The influence of style in
women's clothing militated against large investments in plant
or manufacture in advance of orders; so the sweatshop remained
dominant in this branch.   In the second place, workers in the
men's industry after 1914 abandoned craft organization in
favor of industrial unionism.   By the time this new union—the
Amalgamated Clothing Workers—was stabilized, the industry
was swamped with war orders; and the union without hesitation or scruples seized its chance to consolidate its position.
After the World War, in Chicago and Rochester, the union was
powerful enough to bring about city-wide trade-agreements;
in New York City, the agreement covered nearly all the market
except a few recalcitrant sweatshop groups.   In Baltimore and
Philadelphia, headway was slower, but certain.

Secure, prosperous, and an immigrant example to Americans
for a few years, the men's clothing union after 1925 began again
to encounter difficulties.   One was the slow seepage of sweatshops back into the industry brought about in part by the high
price of men's clothing.   Accompanying the revived sweatshops, were still newer immigrant groups, of which the one leading in the men's clothing industry was the Italian.   Jewish
union leaders had to learn how to induce a dozen or more nationalities to work together; and moreover, along the Atlantic seaboard, Negroes were filtering into the industry.   By strikes,
or threats of them, the union held its grip quite well in the cities;
thereupon, manufacturers unfriendly to unions and quite cordial
to excess profits began to set up small shops in rural villages and
towns.   In these places, Americans were employed at wages
and for hours that the city immigrants had learned to despise
and from which they had liberated themselves.

Technological changes after 1920 brought problems to this
industry as to many others; on the one hand, union control was
sufficient to enforce sharing between capital and labor of the
proceeds of improved mechanical aids, but on the other hand,
the devices added to union unemployment.   One of the solutions
tried by the union was a joint union-employer unemployment

fund; but the insistence upon this proposal was one of the causes of disputes with employers.

Women's Clothing.—Meanwhile, in the women's clothing industry, a peak of progress was reached, at least in New York, in 1910 when the Joint Board of Sanitary Control was established to set health standards in work places; this was a direct attack on the sweatshops and was maintained through and after 1929. Nevertheless, the workers in the women's clothing industry did not escape from the contract (sweatshop) system.

The trades included in this industry—waist, suit, coat, dress, and raincoat producers—were involved in an uproar over Communism for a half dozen years after 1922. Communists bored into most of the clothing unions and in the women's branch succeeded for a while in capturing control. Employers were constantly held up by demands and strikes by one faction or the other, the worst set of strikes taking place in 1926 over a period of 26 weeks. In the internal union struggle by one faction over another, no interest of the employer, as well as no sanctity of the person or property of the unionists themselves, was allowed to stand in the way of factional supremacy. The strife within the unions and between the unions and employers almost destroyed some of the unions and weakened them all.[1] The gains in wages, hours, and working conditions, and the control over sweatshops attained by 1910 were slipping away in the years after 1917. The industry also was scattering to new localities; it had been highly concentrated in New York City with a dispersal of the remnant to small towns in New Jersey and a new center in Hollywood, California. After 1920, employers fled from the strife in New York City.

Dispersal.—Some went into the coal and steel towns of Pennsylvania, some settled for a time in small villages in New Jersey, and many went into Connecticut and Massachusetts, particularly where abandoned textile factories could be con-

---

[1] The International Ladies' Garment Workers is in effect a federation of separate unions in the branches of the industry—e.g. waist, suit, cloak, dress, and raincoat makers. Moreover each of these branches has locals in New York, Cleveland, and other places.

verted into clothing lofts. From these new locations, the finished garments were taken by motor trucks to the wholesale or retail outlets in New York City. An additional complication was the entrance of department and chain stores into the industry; these usually designed and sometimes cut the garments which then were turned over to manufacturers or jobbers and in turn to sweatshops for finishing. The latter might be located anywhere along the Atlantic seaboard. Outside of New York City, the new workers in the industry generally were Americans by birth.

Exploitation.—In these new locations labor generally was exploited, and deliberately cheated to an unbelievable degree— unbelievable that Americans would accept such low standards of pay, hours, and working conditions, and that human beings could be so much without conscience in respect to other human beings. The competition of the substandard country shops increased and embittered the employer-employe revolts in the cities. Hence, strikes or lockouts were frequent in this branch of the industry during the whole of the generation. After 1920, the I. L. G. W. was one of the unions that lost most heavily in membership, although much of the loss was recovered by, and after, 1929.

Miners' Strikes.—After organization in 1890 in the industrial form, the United Mine Workers' Union set out to capture the workers in the soft coal fields. To gauge the task confronting the union it should be realized that soft coal was found in 32 of our states and employed more than a half-million workers, a third of whom did not speak English. On the other hand, in the soft coal division there were few large-scale operators; for of the approximately 5,000 engaged in the business, the average operator employed less than 20 miners. This fact was a source of both strength and weakness to the union; strength, because it was easy for a powerful union to overawe little employers, weakness, because the ease of entrance into the business constantly produced new employers to be brought under union contracts. In addition, the large number of small-scale operators led to a condition of cut-throat competition.

Since the largest cost of coal-mining was the labor charge, the easiest way to cut prices was to slash wages and prolong hours of work. Against this tendency it always was the policy of the union to stabilize competition by bringing all employers under union contract.

National Agreements.—At first the union made individual contracts; but early in the generation after 1896 it was able to establish joint agreements throughout the Central Competitive Field; that is, the operators of mines in western Pennsylvania, Ohio, West Virginia, Michigan, Indiana, and Illinois, through representatives, met the collective bargaining agents of the union and by agreement set standard wage scales for the entire area. Separate meetings provided for subregional and local rate adjustments. The final step was the making of biennial national trade-agreements.

Local Strikes.—In such a sprawling industry, considerable autonomy had to be granted to the district federation but no local union could strike until sanction was granted by the executive board of the district. Local strikes were numerous, usually brought about by dispute as to the interpretation of the trade agreement, or by the acts of operators who tried to sneak out of the terms of an agreement.

National Strikes.—General strikes were by a referendum vote of the entire membership. This kind of strike generally was a pressure tactic used against operators at the time of biennial wage-scale meetings. The chief causes of them—besides delay by operators in signing agreements—were first the efforts of operators to return to state or regional negotiations, secondly to abolish the "check off" and thirdly a resistance to "check weighmen."

The "check off" was the system whereby the operators deducted union dues from pay envelopes thus acting as union collection agents. The scheme first had been proposed by the operators in order to keep local union treasurers on pay days off the mine premises, where their presence created confusion and (sometimes) fights. After the first two years of the "check-off," the operators realized it was one of the union's surest devices in holding its members, as well as in building a strong union treasury.   Thereafter the operators struggled, not always in vain, to be relieved from carrying their own cross.

The "check weighman" was an employe of the union who stood with the operator's man at the coal scales each recording the weight of each miner's car.   Miners were paid by the weight of coal mined.   Since the weighing was done at the surface out of sight of the miners deep underground, the miner had no way of telling if he really was honestly paid for the coal he sent above ground.   In truth, some operators cheated outrageously on the weight records.   Hence, the union demanded a weigher of their own.   State laws in some mining states provided for check weighmen; but the laws were evaded where the vigilance of the union relaxed or where the union had no locals. Wherever pay was by the carload, there was constant dispute as to what constituted a car load—the standard car or an oversized one, a level full car or one heaped up, run of mine load or screened load.

Sweep of Industrial Unionism.—Although the United Mine Workers' Union, from its inception in 1890, was an industrial union it did not for 11 years attempt to include every worker in or around a mine.   But in 1901 it did begin this policy.   Always when an industrial union does this it runs afoul of craft unions whose members work for the same companies.   Two reasons made the policy, as carried out by the United Workers, give rise to the minimum of jurisdictional disputes and strikes: one was the wilderness environment of many soft coal mining camps making one labor spokesman preferable to several bickering voices; the other was the fact that the miners' union had the largest number of votes in the American Federation of Labor conventions, (after 1902; before that the carpenters contested first place with the miners). The Brotherhood of Coal Hoisting Engineers were expelled from the American Federation of Labor in 1903 because they then, as they had for some time previously, refused the jurisdiction of the U. M. W. over that craft.   In the end, the U. M. W.

acquired jurisdiction over some 50 different occupations about mine properties; but the core of the union always was the miners and their helpers.

The invasion by the miners union of the hard coal fields in eastern Pennsylvania was one of the most spectacular achievements in all American union history. The strike of the anthracite workers in 1902 is an epic in itself; this story is told in a later section (Chapter 4).

War Prosperity.—During the World War, the American coal miners enjoyed the greatest prosperity they had ever known. The industrial boom, at that time, was reflected in extraordinary demands for coal; so both the wage rates and the number of days worked rose to new heights. In regard to days of work, the anthracite miners, as always, fared better than the bituminous; for the soft coal could not easily be stored. Car shortage on account of war demands for railway service, therefore, prevented the bituminous miners from getting full years of work. Even so, they had more work than usual. In the absence of immigration and the actual departures of numerous combatant aliens, the chronic oversupply of miners was relieved; in fact in some areas the shortage of mine labor pulled many mountain farmers into the mines. These were the days when coal miners, even if they lived in shaky shacks, wore silk shirts, drove their own cars, and danced to the music of their own Victrolas. After the World War, few trades were faced with such difficult problems as the coal miners.

Post War.—The anthracite miners were able to hold their gains. Their product was unique, mostly used in domestic heating plants, found only in one small area of 148 square miles, and the employers were small in number and united in interests. Moreover, a Pennsylvania law required an anthracite miner to get a certificate of proficiency from a state commission. Scabbing was thereby made difficult, and the commission was friendly to the wishes of the miners' union in granting certificates.

The principal problem in this branch of the coal industry was the increasing use of fuel oil and gas in domestic heating, a competition hard to meet on a price basis, because the anthracite deposits cheapest to mine were well nigh exhausted. At first the operators ignored the competing fuels, until decided drops in anthracite sales, after 1925, compelled the anthracite operators to be less haughty and far more helpful to consumers. Coal was more carefully prepared for market, its price was somewhat shaded, and consumers were given personal instruction in the most efficient use of the fuel. One company went so far as to immerse its coal in a blue dye so consumers could distinguish it! Nevertheless, the operators and miners were shut inside an industry that steadily was confronted with a relative shrinkage in consumer demand.

Excess Capacity.—However, it was in the bituminous industry where the real knotty problems lay. The war had further over-expanded an industry that chronically was over-expanded. Mining machinery reduced the demand for miners at the same time that it increased output per man. Among consumers, startling innovations increased the efficiency of the use of soft coal so that a pound did far more work than formerly; this is to say, that improved combustion reduced demand for volume of coal output. Furthermore oil, natural gas, and hydro-electricity swept into the industrial market and narrowed the possibilities of sales of soft coal.

There were so many excess mines, miners, and operators that the miners' union decided the wisest policy was to force the retention of the high war wages and low hours. By doing so, the union hoped to force out of the industry the high cost (marginal) mines. It believed that concessions in regard to wages and hours would simply lower retail prices, and by competition from the over-capacity, force continuously more concessions without advantage to anyone except consumers.

Southern Coal.—The union's policy had the effect of driving the industry toward greater production in the non-union areas of West Virginia and the South. The effort of the union to close this loophole led to virtual civil war particularly in West Virginia and Kentucky. Since the union was not successful in fastening unionism upon the mines in West Virginia and the

South, the union had to abandon nation-wide trade agreements, and revert to agreements by districts.   At this point the situation was complicated by factional strife within the union, and by the appearance of a rival Communist miner's organization. Membership in the union dwindled rapidly, and open-shop employers gloated in public that they had the union "licked."

The union's strategy had been correct, but it overlooked the fact that the union was not in complete control of all the coal mining areas, therefore the *union* mines became the high cost marginal mines in danger of elimination.   The bulk of soft coal sold shifted in production from the older mining centers around Pittsburgh, and westward in Ohio, Indiana, and Illinois to the newer centers in West Virginia, Kentucky, and Alabama.

From the time of the World War to the end of the generation, the soft coal industry was the scene of turmoil.   As a whole, the industry was one of the least well managed of all of our major national enterprises, and it was divided and subdivided into warring factions both on the side of employers and on the side of labor.   It knew little of either progress or peace.

Textile Industry.—Textile manufacture, the oldest manufacturing industry in the United States, never before 1929 had a powerful union extending its sway throughout the industry, although after its organization in 1901 the United Textile Workers Union provided a central body to which any textile craft could affiliate.   The record of its membership enrollment is indicative of its position in the industry; the record shows certain years such as 1902-1904, 1907-1908 in which considerable increase was registered, but in the whole decade following 1902 there was scarcely any perceptible gain.   For 5 years after 1915, the union gained more than a fourfold increase in membership.   Since this was mostly a war exotic the figures after 1920 showed an almost equally great decline.   Special textile trades joined and withdrew from the central body whenever advantage or pique dictated action.   Rival organizations appeared at various times and places and for a while foliated astonishingly, but generally just as quickly withered and either perished or were absorbed in some other body.

Cheap Labor.—The explanation of the situation is that the textile industry battened on cheap labor; and just as soon as an employed group grew restive and assertive the industry drew upon a new uninformed source of labor, even if to do so required new location of plants. Of the general truth, the specific applications were the succession of various nationalities drawn from the stream of immigrants into the textile mills; and the withdrawal of companies from old established places of production such as New England and Philadelphia to new areas in the South.

Explanation of .Cheap Labor.—At the beginning of textile manufacture (1790 and 1814), due to a fluctuating labor supply, the machinery had to be both so accurate and so simple in operation that "green hands" soon could learn to manipulate it.   The premium, thus, was on machines and not upon labor; as a result there were few jobs in a textile mill that called for any great degree of skill.   Workers who troubled managers could easily be replaced.   As soon as managers detected signs of unionization among employes, intimidation and a few warning discharges checked the movement.   If intimidation and discharges failed or only partly succeeded in halting unionization, the managers secured fresh human stock never before used in the mills.

At times and in places there was no local supply of labor ignorant of mill practices and standards; so employers or their agents defied the letter and spirit of the federal contract labor law by search for some hithereto untouched southeastern European region where by promises of jobs with rich rewards they induced immigrants to leave home for American mills. Conditions which to persons of some residence in the United States had become intolerable, might be to newly arriving immigrants, a step upward in income and living standards.   As the mills dipped into human reserves of lower original standards, they found many men willing to undertake jobs whose wage had been the minimum for female employment.   An industry, historically one for feminine occupation, was in the process of being converted to masculine preponderance.

Hard to Organize.—Unionists who sought to organize textile workers were faced with one of the hardest of tasks. Semi-skilled workers always have been difficult to unite, yet this was the prevalent type in textile manufacture. The youth of both sexes, and especially young women, are little likely to see advantages in unionism; yet the majority of textile workers were young women. Newly arrived immigrants are not aware of grievances, and when they first suspect them are too timid to voice complaints. In groups of mixed nationalities inherited animosities tend to keep the people apart as much as common grievances bring them together. Yet it was a constantly more heterogeneous mass of aliens that fitted textile mills.

When all the difficulties were surmounted and a union began aggressively to assert its rights to improved wages, hours, and working conditions, employers ruthlessly discharged leaders and harried them out of town; and then proceeded to break up the union by infiltration of still greener "green hands." If the measures taken by the employers left a stubborn nucleus of unionism, the employers set up branch plants in new places. By the transferal of work to the branch—or the threat to do so—the employers strove to keep subjected the workers in the old mill town. Mill strikes consequently ran in cycles in the order: strike, greater or less defeat, substitution of laborers, slow reorganization of union, increasing truculence, strike.

Migration of Industry.—The practice of employers in setting up branch mills to escape unions took different directions in different sections. The smallest movement was from large cities to towns or villages in the same state. Larger migrations were from the three southern New England states to the two northern states of Maine and New Hampshire. Vermont was too truly rural to get many migrant mills. From the three middle Atlantic states, textile mills sought out interior locations where heavy work was being done by men. Thus the cement mills, coal mines, iron fabricators, and steel mills were foci for textile plants. Of course the principal mecca for new mills from all regions was the South. To the employers, change of location brought only temporary relief. Sooner or later the mill labor began to complain of low wages and long hours; thereafter union organizers began to haunt the scene.

Employers' Case.—In defense of the apparently senseless greed of employers, it should be understood that the textile industry since the Civil War was fiercely competitive. In no branch of it was much capital necessary to start in business; machinery was nearly standard, for with few exceptions, no one had any patent protections on his own mechanical equipment; no one location had any superlative advantages over any other and in this we include the South; the rewards for good management were not sufficient to induce many outstandingly keen intellects into the business, so managers were much alike in ability.

Since the business was old, the control in many of the companies lay in hands that had no other interest in the mills save the dividends; so that any policy that for even one year reduced dividends was negatived. It was easy for old companies to build new branches and thus add to an already bad competitive situation, but it was hard for managers with new ideas to get opportunity to try them. When dividends shrank, the only alternative that occurred to most executives was some method of reducing labor costs. The easiest was to secure a new, cheaper labor force. The effort at reduction of labor costs usually brought a covert or overt labor revolt.

Change in Style.—The industry was subjected to several trials during the generation. While Queen Victoria still lived, women and furniture were swathed in layers of textile materials; but after her death in 1901 both began to unveil. With furniture the process did not take long, although the loss in textile demand was considerable; but for women to reduce their layers of clothing required twenty years of shifts in fashion. The trend, however, was all in the same direction; that is of reduction in volume. By the time of the World War, women's clothing was reduced to a maximum of three pieces, brassiere, pants, and dress; so for 10 years after 1917 the continuing process of reduction was in making these articles scantier. At the same time decorative textile trimmings on all feminine wear were banned by fashion. Undoubtedly the changes were beneficial to female health, but by 1926 they brought despair to textile manufacturers, for they reduced the textile yardage per woman from 30 or more to 5 or less. The point to be realized here is that an expanding textile productive capacity was confronted with a shrinking demand.

Case of Hosiery Manufacture.—The only textile producers who profited by the style trend were the manufacturers of hosiery. The more the leg was exposed the greater the demand for attractive stockings. Cotton and wool—except for sportswear—were routed by silk, at first only in part, and then wholly, as dresses drew away from the ground. The fragility of silk stockings made replacements a constant necessity. Established stocking mills expanded and new ones were built with the result that the skilled labor supply was depleted. The Full Fashioned Hosiery Workers' Union, an autonomous affiliate of the United Textile Workers' Union, seized its opportunity; so that for the latter two-thirds of the generation this craft was the most successful of all textile crafts in getting its conditions of work improved, especially its wage rates. Indeed it went so far, that in the last decade of the generation, employers tried to escape by placing hosiery mills in the South, in the mining and steel areas, and in Middle West agricultural centers. The hosiery workers were responsible for many of the strikes registered in the textile industry. While the trend of styles favored stocking makers, the trend was a source of discontent and unemployment among many other textile workers.

Effects of Introduction of Rayon.—The second disruption to which the textile industry was subjected was the introduction of a new textile fiber, rayon. Before 1910, this product was in an experimental stage and not satisfactory, because then it was not resistant to water. It suffered the handicap of being named "artificial silk." When these faults were corrected, rayon production started a meteoric career; with a million pounds output in 1912, and more than 100 times that by the end of the gen-

eration.   Made of wood fiber in the North, and of cotton lint
in the South, its manufacture was a chemical process, and required relatively few—but trained—workers whose wages ran
50% or more above those of textile operatives.   When the same
labor force was drawn upon, the rayon mill got the pick.

The important effects of rayon upon the textile industry
began after rayon was in the form of yarn.   The first assault
was felt mostly by silk mills; soon every branch of the textile
industry was made aware of the presence of the lusty infant.
In weaving and knitting it was mixed with yarns of other fibers,
so these branches of the textiles benefited by the novelties possible with rayon; but the spinning branches suffered from competition with the new yarn.   Of course in this country most
plants did both spinning and weaving; nevertheless, the entrance of rayon hurt the spinning department.   Even the weaving department had to buy rayon yarn since it was not made
on the premises, and so perhaps added a new cost to production.   The least disturbance made by rayon was to add a new
uncertainty to nearly every part of the textile industry; its most
violent disruption was the forced closing of some silk mills, and
specialized yarn mills based on other fibers.   In its own production, rayon yarn did not absorb as much labor as it displaced, or disturbed in other textile branches.

Raw Material as Cost Factor.—The third general change to
which all parts of the textile industry was subjected was the
price of raw material after the start of the World War in 1914.
Until then the industry was accustomed to low priced raw materials with any change tending toward lower rather than higher
prices.   The War itself created a huge demand for cotton, wool
and silk and pushed their prices higher than they had been for
half a century.   Manufacturers were accustomed to a normal
spread between material and goods prices; but for nearly all the
period after 1914 this spread tended to narrow and disappear.
Styles caused a relative decline in demand for goods at the
same time that raw materials were advancing in price, so the
greater raw material cost could not all be passed on to consumers.

Finally the South was a great bugaboo to almost all northern textile manufacturers. The speed and ease with which, in the generation, the South wrested leadership in the cotton branch from New England caused producers in other branches to fear their turn was next. Knitting manufacturers did start a movement toward the South. The magnet was cheap, mostly unorganized, labor worked for long hours.

With declining demand, the intrusion of rayon, rising raw material costs, and the threat of southern competition to say nothing of increasing local taxation (for that was not a special thorn pricking textiles alone) the employers in the textile industry were short tempered with labor grievances, especially when voiced by unions. The uncompromising hostility of employers toward correction of labor complaints provoked labor to strike for their demands. Because the textile industry was a sore spot, to it flocked the I. W. W. before 1917 and the Communists after 1920.

Summary.—In each of the four great industries—construction, clothing manufacture, coal mining, and textiles—there were special conditions that led to grievances. Analysis of any other occupations would have revealed that these too had individual backgrounds for the strikes that occurred. While it was true that grievances were the seeds of unionism, and that unions conducted strikes to bring about reforms, the real causes of strikes lay in the backgrounds and seldom got publicity or tabulation.

CHAPTER 4

THE GREATEST STRIKES 1896 TO 1919

While it would be pointless, even if it were possible, to give the detailed story of the 100,000 strikes that occurred in the 33 years after 1896, it is profitable to select a half dozen or so of the most significant for description.

Anthracite Strike of 1902

Background.—The first notable strike in the generation was that of the anthracite miners in 1902. To get a proper perspective on this strike it is well to recall the high points in the previous history of anthracite miners. Before the Civil War, anthracite mining had been desultory; and because it dealt mainly with surface outcrops, resembled quarrying more than mining. Aside from the four British nationalities who furnished most of the miners, there were some Germans in the work. Although an English miner, John Bates, had formed a union in 1849 in Schuylkill County it had been short-lived; so the miners expressed their grievances in brawling and lawlessness, features for which these early miners were notorious.

The Civil War brought a great stimulus to the anthracite industry, partly for the war demands, but more importantly for the general substitution of steam for water power in industrial plants. Anthracite, not bituminous coal, at that time was the principal fuel for eastern factories. The anthracite miners joined with The American Miners' Association, a union that had been started in 1861 among soft coal miners in Illinois. Strikes among the anthracite miners during the war period were frequent, but were confined to one colliery at a time, or to one field, or the coal shipped by one railway line. After the war the industry suffered from glut; the consequent slicing of war wages and slackening of work produced a number of local unions and hotly contested local strikes in 1867 and 1868. The loss of these strikes almost entirely destroyed the unions.

Soon afterwards, in 1869, under the courageous leadership of John Siney, a new union, the Workingmen's Benevolent Association, spread throughout the anthracite area. At the same time the 6 railroads [1] that specialized in the carriage of coal tightened their hold upon coal mining operative companies and began acquisition of coal bearing lands as reserves for the future. Railroad intrusion into the mining industry brought some benefits to miners in the technical improvements of mines (e.g., better ventilation), somewhat better dwellings, and more accessible and more fully furnished retail stores; but no change for the better was made in regard to wages or the hours of work. Siney's union, therefore, in the early part of 1875 went on a five months' strike, the largest and most general known up to that time in the anthracite area. The coal railroads and their captive operating companies used every endeavor to crush the union and by June 1875 had it annihilated. The miners' reaction to this defeat was the bloody reign of the secret "Molly Maguires."

Grievances.—After the hanging of the leaders of the "Molly Maguires," the railroad-coal companies imported miners from Austria, Hungary, Lithuania, Poland, Russia, Italy, and other places so that before 1900 there were 20 nationalities among the anthracite workers. The mixed and supposedly docile group was exploited by the rail-coal companies. In defiance of the Pennsylvania law—secured March 30, 1875, by Siney's union—which had set a standard ton for coal mine cars, the operators introduced a car holding 3,190 pounds and insisted that this oversize car be further overloaded by a heaped ("topping") rather than a level filling. The miner's pay was "docked" by deductions for various penalties or services such as $1 a month for medical care. Powder, which miners themselves had to buy, was sold to them for $2.75 per keg although elsewhere it

---

[1] (1) Philadelphia and Reading R. R.; (2) Lehigh Valley R. R.; (3) Delaware, Lackawanna and Western; (4) Pennsylvania R. R.; (5) Delaware and Hudson; (6) Erie R. R.

was purchasable for $1.10. Evictions from company houses for complaints about mine conditions were frequent occurrences, as were overcharging (despite state law) in company stores. The company doctor's fees, too, the miners thought bore little relation to services rendered. Along with this exploitation the work was very irregular (190 days a year average) and on the long 10-hour day basis at low wages. For a decade or more after 1875 bituminous miners had better pay and working conditions than the anthracite miners.

First Preliminary Strike.—For 10 years after 1875, except for the "Mollies" and for sporadic local unions which employers killed off by setting one against another, the only organization among the anthracite workers was a feeble Assembly of the Knights of Labor. In 1885 the bituminous miners organized a miners National Progressive Union, locals of which eventually began to spread in the anthracite fields. In 1890 this union was merged with the K. of L. Assembly No. 135 and the two together became the United Mine Workers' Union. Membership in the new union tended to decline rather than grow but in 1897 when the whole union had only 9,000 members, few of whom were anthracite miners, a strike was called which developed so much support from miners that the union gained appreciably in the next three years.

Quasi-Monopoly of Coal Operators.—This tendency toward organization for the sale of labor power by one union was overmatched by the monopoly of producers. Since it was so highly localized in eastern Pennsylvania and had a large demand (100 million tons), anthracite offered the natural basis for monopoly control. Nevertheless before 1892, competition was just as keen—and disastrous—among the railway-coal companies as among soft coal operators. In that year, efforts were started to bring the anthracite producers together, initiated by the Reading Railroad, the largest owner of coal lands. The first attempts at agreement were not permanently successful; but they demonstrated the value of "cooperation" because while the agreements lasted, profits were high, and when they were broken demoralization set in.

Beginning in 1898, a new method of control was established. The interested railroads in control of three-fourths of the coal property, purchased each other's stock and thus gained a community of interest. Each railroad had its own separate mining companies whose stock it controlled. But after the railroads were interlocked, the stocks of the different operating companies were also interchanged. These practices in fact constituted an anthracite monopoly, behind which were New York City bankers, "gods of the machine."

By 1900, therefore, the United Mine Workers confronted in the anthracite area, not a crowd of warring operators but a monopoly rooted in Wall Street.

Second Preliminary Strike.—Yet in 1900 the anthracite workers were ready to test their new union, and called a strike which lasted two months. With an actual membership of 8000 the union took more than 80,000 anthracite miners out on strike with them. Since the strike fell in an election year at a time embarrassing to the plans of Mark Hanna, he is said to have influenced the capitalists behind the railroad-coal companies to settle the strike. Wages were increased, the company-store charges for powder were reduced to $1.50 a keg but the union was not granted recognition.

The Strike of 1902.—Both sides realized that this 1900 strike was a preliminary skirmish; so both prepared for the real battle to come. Unready in 1901, both sides continued the agreement of 1900; but by 1902 the railroad-coal companies deemed themselves fortified to force a conclusive test of strength. The employers refused every negotiation, every compromise, except an offer of arbitration from Mark Hanna acting as chairman of the National Civic Federation; and this one produced no results. The miners temporarily suspended work May 12 to 15th, and on the latter date a workers' vote having favored resistance, a strike was declared. In June, after a 10 days' warning, the strike was joined by the mine engineers, pumpmen, and firemen, whose principal grievance was a 12-hour day with double shifts on alternate Sundays.

The strike of 150,000 men and boys dragged on all summer, the miners being supported by a fund of $2,645,324 raised by assessment upon bituminous miners (who had remained at work under a trade agreement which was not to expire until April 1903) and from gifts from many American trade unions and individuals, as well as from union miners in England and Wales. In August there was a riot in Shenandoah against a sheriff, and in other clashes some 20 miners were killed and 40 wounded. The deaths or injuries due to the strike were far less than the 262 who would have been killed if the miners had been at work.

The railroad-coal companies were losing business and accruing expenses at the rate of approximately $4 million a week. Incidentally they lost almost all of their industrial consumers because these, by changing grates and drafts were able to use soft coal; after the strike they did not return to anthracite fuel. It has been estimated that the strike had an immediate cost of $100 million in lost sales, lost freight, and lost wages. But since neither side budged, September found the situation deadlocked and anthracite coal quoted at $20-$30 a ton.

President Theodore Roosevelt Intervenes.—Then, with winter approaching, President Theodore Roosevelt intervened. Earlier in June he had ordered U. S. Labor Commissioner, Carroll D. Wright, to confer with both sides, an action which had brought no results. Now Roosevelt invited the railroad presidents and the union officers to a meeting in Washington, October 3, 1902. Roosevelt appealed to both sides on the grounds of patriotism and public needs. The union offered to arbitrate, but the railroad presidents dealt in invectives and urged military occupation of the coal fields. The refusal of the railroad presidents to arbitrate caused a national wave of resentment against them which was all the more bitter because the railroad executives were identified with the unpopular "trust magnates." Their stiff-necked attitude really was the turning point that led to the workers' victory.

Roosevelt next (October 6) tried to get John Mitchell, union president, to order his men back to work on a promise by Roosevelt to appoint a commission of investigation. When Mitchell refused on the ground that to comply would constitute a surrender to the railroads, the Governor of Pennsylvania ordered the entire National Guard into the anthracite areas. On the same day the miners' convention voted with Mitchell to continue the strike. Roosevelt at this point planned to seize and operate the mines with the help of the United States Army, at the same time appointing a commission to get the facts of the situation whether or not the two sides were willing for him to take these actions.

Morgan Steps In.—On October 13th, J. Pierpont Morgan perhaps sensing that the public had swung to the miners' side, communicated with Roosevelt through Secretary of War, Elihu Root, that the employers offered to submit matters in dispute to a commission of five men to be appointed by Roosevelt and selected in the manner prescribed in a letter of submission tendered by Morgan.[2] Upon news of this proposal the strikers at a meeting in Wilkes-Barre October 20-21 decided to resume work on October 23rd.

Strike Commission.—The Commission was organized in October and held hearings from November to February, and then listened to 5 days of argument from February 9 to February 13 inclusive. Upon the basis of this evidence and statistical exhibits that had been presented contained in 10,000 legal cap pages, the Commission made its award in a document of 120,-000 words on March 18, 1903. The award was to run from April 1, 1903 to April 1, 1906.[3]

---

[2] (1) Engineer officer from U. S. military or naval service; (2) A mining engineer; (3) A judge of a Federal Court of eastern Pennsylvania; (4) An eminent sociologist; (5) A man acquainted with the business of mining and transporting coal. To above was added Bishop Spaulding and Labor Commr. Carroll D. Wright.

[3] The features of the award were: first, a permanent Board of Conciliation comprising 3 representatives of a majority of the workers in each of three divisions of the anthracite area together with 3 similarly appointed representatives of operators. If this Board failed to agree an umpire was to be selected by one of the local Circuit Court judges. Secondly a wage increase of 10% above the rates of April 1902 for contract miners and all other employes together with a 9-hour day after April 1, 1903. Thirdly, an increase of 1% in wages for each increase of 5 cents per ton in the price of coal.

The award provided increases in wages totaling $7 million to $8 million a year; it reduced the hours of engineers from 12 to 8, and of men on day wages from 10 hours to 9; it validated checkweighmen whenever a majority at a colliery demanded them; and provided for a Board of Conciliation to interpret the award. Most important to the union was that the award indirectly recognized the United Mine Workers as one of the contracting parties, thus fixing the status of the union.

Gains by the Strike.—It should be noted here that these were the provisions on *paper,* for at the collieries less than full compliance with the award was the rule. The clause relative to checkweighmen was ignored for a dozen years; and the recognition of the union was not frank and open but so indirect as to be furtive. Frank recognition of the union would have been public admission of the employers' defeat; and, still more important, would have aroused workers in many industries to attempt the snaring of their own employers into trade agreements. A short anthracite strike in 1912 succeeded, in addition to increasing wages, in getting a more complete acceptance of the spirit of the award of 1903. But it was not until 1916 when the imminence of our entrance into the World War, together with the lack of immigrants already felt after two years of war, that the railroad-coal companies at last not only gave full recognition to the union but granted the 8-hour day; not until then were the fruits of the 1902 strike gathered.

For the remainder of the generation the miner's union had an established place in the anthracite areas, and although there were later strikes, (1920 for 19 days; 1922 for 138 days; 1923 for 14 days; 1925-26 for 146 days), the anthracite coal miners were better off in every way than soft coal miners. Indeed in the period of decline after 1920, the anthracite miners held their ranks and nearly all their gains whereas other miners left the

On May 7, 1906 and again on April 29, 1909 the agreement was renewed. The term was lengthened to 4 years on May 20, 1912 at which time the sliding scale was dropped but an increase of 10% in wages granted. On May 5, 1916 another 4-year agreement was made with a further wage increase of 7% and the 8-hour day accepted.

union and lost ground. The anthracite *industry,* however, lost most of its western customers due originally to war restrictions and then began losing to fuel oil in its eastern market.

Immediate Effects.—The immediate effect of the strike of 1902 was a revival of confidence among all union men; for in this struggle against organized capital it was organized labor that had triumphed. Naturally at the moment of victory, unionists overlooked that the anthracite coal industry was unique. It was confined to a small area, employed relatively few persons, produced a luxury fuel sold principally to house-holders (for as we have said the 1902 strike itself lost to the industry most of the industrial customers). Householders would stand considerable price gouging but strikes that cut off supplies brought public pressure immediately to bear including the power of government to compel capital to submit.

These considerations came later; at the moment union enthu-siasm ran high and was exemplified in 1903 by a series of strikes in many trades and in many places. Of these, the ones that attracted the most attention were in Chicago. There, using the teamsters' union as a coercive weapon over any and all em-ployers, the unions forced the city employers to operate on the closed shop basis. This tactic had been successful in 1901 in making San Francisco a closed shop town and in putting labor in control of the city government.

Samuel Gompers, writing his autobiography in 1923, stated that in his opinion the coal strike of 1902 was the most impor-tant strike ever staged by American unions. It *was* the genera-tion's most successful assault by organized labor upon organized capital.

On the other hand, another immediate effect was the unifica-tion of employers to resist the onrush of unions which they feared and detested. Anti-union, "open shop," anti-boycott, belligerent employers' associations were formed. Also, to aid themselves, employers turned to the law seeking every legal weapon they could wield over unions. Hence the coal strike of 1902 intensified for more than a decade the struggle between unions and employers.

Colorado Fuel and Iron Co. Strike 1913-14

The United Mine Workers Union was involved in another of the notable strikes of the generation, that one of 1913-14 against the Colorado Fuel and Iron Company. While outstanding in itself, this strike is given here also as typical of others arising from similar grievances in West Virginia, Kentucky, and other non-union areas.

Background.—Unionization of soft coal miners came earlier than the organization of anthracite workers. A fairly strong union movement in 1886 had swept the Central Competitive Field. Tom Tippett's novel, "Horse Shoe Bottoms," was based on his family's personal experiences in this movement. In the eighties there was a relative scarcity of miners in that area, where a large number of small mines operated upon a narrow capital margin. This situation was favorable to workers, so that after their unionization the bituminous miners got better pay and treatment than the contemporary anthracite miners. Except for West Virginia, the union operated under a trade agreement with operators in the Central Competitive Field between 1886 and 1890.

Hard times and increased numbers of immigrant miners caused the abrogation of the general trade agreement for 7 years after 1890 and a reversion in some cases to individual local bargains or in others to non-union operation. Only in Ohio did the union hold its former position. In 1897, there was a three months' strike which accomplished for the union among bituminous miners what the 1902 strike did for the anthracite workers. Operators in the Central Competitive Field were forced by the strike to recognize the union, adopt a general interstate trade agreement, institute the "check off" (1898), accept the 8-hour day, and mitigate the extortions of company stores.

Every two years, after 1896, the trade agreement came up for revision; so always there was tension at these times and often there were strikes. The most frequent causes of trouble were the blanket agreement—the operators preferred individual district or state agreements to one that covered the whole field—and the basis for setting wages, the miners insisting upon payment for the full weight of all the material sent out of the mine whereas the operators as strongly urged the payment only for the net weight of salable fuel contained in a mine-car's load.

Both the union and the operators who signed with the union realized the competitive disadvantage of partial union control of a district, and the limitation of union dominance to any one district. The soft coal industry was so fiercely competitive that no one mining area was certain of its most natural market; for operators in their stress to make sales raided markets a long way from their own mines and near to their rivals'. Hence, small differences in labor costs per ton could make or break sales. Since labor was the chief cost of production, union labor cost per ton tended to run higher than non-union; therefore, the union to preserve its hold and to protect its associated operators was forced to campaign in non-union fields so as to have one union dominate the coal miners of the whole nation.

After 1897, the United Mine Workers spent millions of dollars and sacrificed hundreds of lives to carry union power into non-union areas. The fiercest resistance from employers and consequently the bloodiest contests were in West Virginia, Colorado, and Kentucky. As typical of the continuous warfare in these places, it is pertinent to give some detail of the 1913 strike in Colorado.

Grievances.—The coal camps of Colorado in 1913 were in canyons remote from any large community. The site of a coal mine was wholly owned by the Colorado Fuel and Iron Co. (or lesser operators of the same kind). Houses, stores, schools, churches, the site of the Post Office, and even the streets and roads were the private property of the mining company. Armed guards patrolled this property, and on the legal claim of trespass ejected or denied ingress to all persons objectionable to the mining company. Naturally no known union organizers got by the guards, no peddlers were permitted on the property to compete with company stores and even state officials were denied access to the mining communities.

Politically, the mining company was the chief and generally the sole taxpayer so mine officers were themselves village, town, and county officials or else put their own creatures into these positions.   A mine worker who troubled his foreman was in difficulties at the same moment with his landlord, his store-keeper, the village police, and the village magistrate or mayor. He could not even collect his mail without running the risk of arrest for trespass.   If he left one village for another he was in no safety; for the mining company controlled both the opportunities for work and the forces of government through-out southern Colorado.

The attitude of the company toward labor was feudalistic. No free meetings were permitted, no free purchases were allowed, not even medical care was open to choice, for the miners were made to pay for the services of the company doc-tor whether or not they employed him.   Despite the fact of engagement in one of the most hazardous occupations (more so than soldiers in time of war), there were areas as large as Connecticut without a single hospital and the whole burden of accident or sickness fell upon the worker.   The Colorado legis-lature had enacted laws which granted an 8 hour day to miners and permitted them the services of a check-weighman; but the mining company ignored these laws and resisted state officials who endeavored to investigate their non-compliance.   The directors of the company lived and met mostly in New York so the local officials of the company in Colorado did about as they pleased in respect to labor relations.

The miners' union secretly crept into the mine camps. Meetings were held late at night, each person slipping furtively to a designated place in the hills or on a plateau beyond the eyes and ears of mine guards.   Of course sometimes the unionists were exposed by mine spies.   But by 1913 enough were organized to make a show of resistance to the company.

Strike Begins.—On September 23, 1913 the miners em-ployed by the Colorado Fuel and Iron Company went out on strike. Their demands were that the company obey the state laws, abolish the guard system, allow freedom of choice as to lodging, purchases, and medical care, increase wages, and recognize the union. The company's answer was immediate eviction of all the strikers and their families from houses and villages, the swearing in of an army of marshals and sheriffs, and the employment through "detective" agencies of a host of strike-breakers many of whom had come directly from similar service in West Virginia.

Battle of Forbes.—The strikers set up tent colonies on the outskirts of mine property. Strikers' wives and daughters mocked and harassed arriving scabs and both the guards and male strikers took snipers' shots at each other. There were daylight murders on the streets and roads. These disorders culminated in what the miners have called the "Battle of Forbes" (Oct. 16, 1913) in which an armored car with machine guns fought all day against strikers' riflemen hidden behind their tent colony.

Militia Used.—Within 2 weeks Governor Ammons had sent the state militia into the disturbed area. At first the militia fraternized with the strikers; however, as the weeks of irksome duty wore on, many of the school boys, professional men, and others in the militia resigned and went home. Their places were filled by the idle from Denver and Boulder, by imported gunmen and by enrollment of the camp guards. With the change of personnel there was a change in conduct; the new militiamen were brutal, immoral, and roisterous. Strikers were arrested without warrant and left in jail without charges or trial. Strikers retaliated in kind whenever they got a chance at a guard. This period of strife ended with the "Battle of Ludlow," May 1914.

Ludlow.—The tent colony at Ludlow was subjected to an all-day machine gun fire because it stood between an attacking group of militia and a defending corps of miners entrenched behind it. To escape the rain of bullets, the women and children retired to cavities under the tents. At the day's end, the militia were victorious and first looted the tents and then set them on fire. In consequence, two women and eleven children were smothered to death in the pits. Five other members of the strikers' group had perished from shots during the day and evening. Some of the "captured" strikers including one of the strike leaders, Tikas, were victims of the Latin-American "law of flight." Prisoners were tricked into an attempt at escape and then shot down as they fled. This was an innovation in Colorado brought there by militia Lieutenant Linderfelt as a result of his services below the Rio Grande.

The day following the Ludlow "massacre," the strikers issued a "call to arms" which was a defiant resort to violence to meet violence. For a week, in all of the mining properties of the C. F. & I. Company, buildings were looted, wrecked and burned, and company servants were shot in their tracks. Riot and murder raged.

U. S. Army Used.—With virtual civil war sweeping the southern portion of the state, the Governor called upon the federal authorities for aid. In response, detachments of the U. S. Army occupied the mining area. From the moment of their arrival in May, and for the remaining seven months of the strike, peace ruled.

Peace Offers.—In November 1913, the first effort external to the combatants was made to bring about a settlement. This was an offer to mediate made by Governor Ammons, but the strikers did not believe in his disinterestedness and refused his offer. Subsequent offers of aid for adjustment—all refused by the company—were made by the U. S. Department of Labor; a U. S. congressional committee proposing federal judges as arbitrators; President Woodrow Wilson, offering a commission and a three-year truce; and the New York directors of the company offering a plan of peace negated by Colorado company officials. Finally J. D. Rockefeller, Jr., representing his father as the largest stockholder in the C. F. & I. Co., intervened; and the exhausted strikers capitulated December 10, 1914.

Aftermath of Strike.—Mr. Rockefeller visited the mining region with W. L. McKenzie King, former Secretary of Labor for Canada (later Prime Minister), and with his advice and assistance brought forth a plan for employe representation, the first nationally known "company union." This "Rockefeller Plan" began to function in January 1915.

In Colorado, despite whatever ameliorating influence there was in the "company union," the strike left bitterness. On the side of the state some 400 strikers were indicted by a Grand Jury which contained six men with business affiliations with the C. F. & I. Co. In the trials that followed, 6 weeks were consumed in a futile effort to impanel juries and then in desperation juries were picked off the streets. Two of the cases were heard before Judge Hillyer, who formerly had been an attorney for a coal company. The judge caused the arrest of the defense attorney for perjury and contempt of court. John Lawson, a Board Member of the U. M. W., was found guilty of the murder of John Nemmo, a mine guard and condemned to life imprisonment, a sentence later (June 1917) overruled by the Colorado Supreme Court. The evidence against Lawson had come from two mine guards, one an ex-forger and one a blackmailer. Judge Hillyer, who tried the case, had committed gross errors in his conduct of the trial.

The state legislature was influenced by the strike to enact in 1915, at King's suggestion, a law almost identical with the Canadian Investigation of Industrial Disputes Act. This law forbade strikes during a time when a state-appointed committee heard the issues and published its findings.

On the side of the United Mine Workers, a monument was built by them at Ludlow over the cemented pit that was the grave of so many children smothered in the "massacre"; and yearly at that spot commemorative services were conducted by the union. The union continued to organize miners and although the company refused to "recognize" the union it was tolerated and its officers indirectly, unofficially for a while given a voice in labor affairs. Finally, after quiet was restored to Colorado a committee appointed by the U. S. Congress investigated the whole affray.

Importance of this Strike.—Although this strike had slight national significance from the viewpoint of interruption of the supply of consumers' coal, it was important in other ways. To all organized workers, the C. F. and I. Co. had epitomized all that was merciless, domineering, and lawless in large-scale capitalistic enterprise; to have brought it to terms would have heartened every union votary. The failure of the strike, together with the Rockefeller innovations, checked in Colorado for some years any true balance between labor and capital; for the scales were weighted on the side of capital.

The Rockefeller "company union," first instituted as a result of the strike, was installed in other industries and localities where the Rockefeller fortune had weight. Moreover, the early rise of "company unionism" in nearly all other large-scale capitalistic industries was traceable to the publicity which was given to the "Rockefeller Plan." Company unionism most effectively blocked ordinary unions in our greatest industries throughout the rest of the generation.

The Colorado law, that as a result of the strike, provided for a state investigation before any strike (or lockout) could be declared was not imitated in other states despite proposals to that end. In Colorado the law undoubtedly reduced strikes although it did not eliminate them. The C. F. and I. Co. itself, in 1927-28, had another strike on its hands when the I. W. W. led the company's miners in combat.

Lawrence, Massachusetts, Textile Strike 1912

Grievances.—Massachusetts, in 1911, enacted a law that reduced the legal work week for women from 56 to 54 hours. At the time the law was to take effect (January 10, 1912), the Lawrence mill managers announced an immediate pay cut to correspond with the reduction in hours. Since the average weekly wage in the mills at that time was $6—or if skilled are included was $8.75—the workers, two days after the notice, walked out rather than accept less than these amounts.

I. W. W. Takes Charge.—When the strike occurred, the I. W. W. had 400 members among the mill help. One of these, an Italian, wired Joseph Ettor who—with several leading I. W. W.'s, including William Haywood—was in New York City for a meeting. Haywood sent Ettor at once to Lawrence in order to start a strike organization. In the days that followed most of the I. W. W. field organizers went to Lawrence on strike duty.

With Ettor's help, and that of Arturo Giovanitti, a strike committee of 56 persons representing 27 languages and all of the divisions of all the mills, was organized. This committee demanded the 54-hour week, a 15 per cent pay increase, double rates for overtime, the abolition of the bonus and premium systems of wages, and a return to work with no discriminations against strikers. An I. W. W. strength of 400 thus managed a strike of 23,000 persons.

Strike Tactics.—Besides usual strike tactics this strike gained unusual publicity by means of two methods new to New England. One was to place women, especially pregnant mothers, on the picket line; when one of these was so beaten by the police as to give premature birth to her child almost losing her own life in the process, the news won many sympathizers for the strike. The other was to ship children of strikers out of town to places of safety; the interference of police with this exodus again emotionally reacted in favor of the strikers and it was the chief cause for raising the strike to national attention. Then wide publication of existent earnings did much to gain support for resistance to further wage reduction. Through Victor Berger, Socialist Congressman, a Congressional hearing was obtained and to this Margaret Sanger piloted a committee of 16 boys and girls all under 16 years of age to Washington to appear before the Rules Committee. This strategy too was effective in publicizing the strike grievances. Mass picketing of course was adopted.

On the other hand the employers made use of prejudices against the radicalism of the I. W. W. To increase this they plotted dynamite explosions; but the plot was discovered and its tool, the county coroner, was arrested, convicted and fined $500. However, the owners got ample support from police, militia, and press and all three of these aids capitalized one of the incidents of the strike. One day as the police jostled the mass picket line, and as pickets counter-attacked the police with snowballs and wads of ice, a shot was fired killing little Anna LaPiza. Two days later Joseph Ettor and Arturo Giovanitti were arrested as accessories to the murder of the child. A non-strike leader named Caruso also was jailed. This removed Ettor and Giovanitti as strike leaders for they were not tried until the conflict was finished. Then, with 19 witnesses swearing that the fatal shot was fired by a police officer named Benoit, the three Italians were acquitted. Ettor's statement, "I am not being tried for my acts, but for my views" carried considerable weight with the jury and the public. Haywood, James Thomson, and Elizabeth Gurley Flynn continued as leaders in the absence of Ettor and Giovanitti.

Strike Wins.—Finally, after nine weeks (March 17, 1912), the mill owners capitulated. The 54-hour week was instituted, with pay raises of 5% for skilled, and 25% for unskilled, and a provision for a rate of 1¼ for overtime. Moreover, the owners promised to modify the system of bonus and premium, and to take back the strikers without discrimination. The outcome at Lawrence spread to all the textile workers in the state, and to many in other New England states; so that a quarter million textile operatives gained pay increases by the Lawrence strike.

This strike was important because it introduced new technique, because it marked the invasion of the East by the I. W. W. and made its name nauseous to all conservatives, because it proved that the immigrant worms would turn, and because it was a spontaneous mass rebellion. Yet, as was true of nearly all I. W. W. conflicts, the strike did not leave behind it a strongly organized work-force ready again to do battle. The I. W. W. always hit hard, and ran, not always to return some other day.

The Record Year of 1919

The year 1919 was notable not for one great strike alone, but for a series of them, averaging 292 a month. More than

4 million American workers went on strike in that year, a number never before in any generation reached and never again in this generation. The outstanding strikes of the year were a general strike in Seattle that temporarily paralyzed that community, a strike of Boston policemen that eventually put Calvin Coolidge in the White House and brought laws that forbade police and firemen to join any union that sanctioned the strike weapon, a strike of all the bituminous coal miners and one of all steel workers. To get clearly what a disturbed year 1919 was, glance at the list of outbreaks that made headlines in the *New York Times*:

January 21	Strike of 35,000 New York City dress and waist makers.
February 6	General Strike in Seattle.
February 8	I. W. W. Strike at Butte.
April 15	Strike tied up New York telephone system.
May 2	A North Carolina judge declared congressional child labor law was unconstitutional.
May 16	Winnipeg seized by striking metal workers, firemen and postal employes.
June 2	Homes of 10 prominent Americans bombed including that of Attorney General Palmer.
June 2	Winnipeg strikers seized control of Manitoba legislature.
June 11	Order for nationwide strike of telegraphers.
June 16	Ocean liners and coastwise shipping tied up by strike of firemen.
July 17	Boston traction strike.
July 19	Rhode Island street railway operatives strike.
July 20-22	Race riots in Washington, D. C.
July 27	Race riots in Chicago, 31 killed, 500 injured.
Aug. 1	Nationwide railway shopmen's strike.
Aug. 8	New York theatres closed by strike of Equity Association.
Aug. 12	U. S. War Labor Board goes out of existence for lack of funds after adjusting 1,200 disputes in 15 months.
Aug. 17-18	New York strike of subway workers.

Aug. 24   Strike on railways in southern California.

Aug. 30-31   Race riots in Knoxville, Tenn., 2 deaths.

Sept. 9 to   Boston Police Strike. Threat of sympathetic
Oct. 5   strike of workers in electric light plants,
                       power houses, and telephone industry.

Sept. 22   Steel workers' strike.

Sept. 22   Railway workers adopt Plumb Plan—worker
                       participation in management of railroads to
                       be government owned.

Sept. 23   Coal strike threatened.

Sept. 28   Lynchers in Omaha burned new court house.

Oct. 1   All New York weekly and monthly periodicals
                       suspended by employe's "vacation."

Oct. 6-24   Wilson's National Industrial Conference.
                       Broken by withdrawal of labor on Oct.
                       22nd over inability to define "collective
                       bargaining."

Oct. 7   New York longshoremen on strike.

Oct. 31   Bituminous miners strike, 400,000. Judge
                       Anderson's injunction orders union head to
                       stop strike before 6 P. M., November 11.

Nov. 24   National Labor Party formed at Chicago.

Dec. 5   Lusk Committee New York organized to in-
                       vestigate communism in that state.

Dec. 8   Attorney General Palmer asks for more
                       stringent laws against "Reds" of whom he
                       said 365,000 in the United States.

Dec. 10-15   Hundreds of "Reds" assembled at New York
                       for deportation.

Dec. 13   Labor's "Bill of Rights" issued by American
                       Federation of Labor and 4 Railway Brother-
                       hoods.

Dec. 18   Federal jury Kansas City sends 27 I. W. W.
                       to jail for 3½ to 9 years.

Dec. 22   The old U. S. Army transport "Buford" takes
                       300 "Reds" from New York under sealed
                       orders. Among the "Reds" were Emma
                       Goldman and Alexander Berkman.

Causes.—For this roisterous year there were many explanations although it might be said that several of them stemmed from a psychological condition, a reaction from the self sacrificing emotionalism of the war months. One concrete cause was the attempt of radicals, while the nation was undergoing readjustments—made harder because the Armistice in November 1918 came with the seasonal natural peak of unemployment—to seize the opportunity to agitate reforms of an extreme nature. The fount of this radicalism was the example of successful revolution in Russia. The Seattle general strike enthused American adherents of revolutionary doctrine. The steel strike leader, William Z. Foster, was an extremist who later became one of the principal American Communists.

On the other hand, some employers used the hysteria over radicalism as an excuse for repressive measures which in their turn brought revolt. Unions also brandished the "Red Scare" as a club both to clean out "undesirables" within the unions and to frighten employers into signing agreements with the "conservative" labor forces.

The radicalism of railway workers, shown during the war by the manner in which they forced Congress to pass the Adamson Act, again came to public attention in their syndicalistic plan for railroad ownership by the government and joint operation by management and labor. This "Plumb Plan", named for the railroad unions' attorney, Glenn E. Plumb, was the most radical native-born proposal of the whole year of 1919.

Not Revolutionary in Purpose.—It has been said by some writers and speakers that American labor in 1919 was on the verge of revolution; but such an assertion probably is inaccurate because the causes of the disorders of that year were not intimately connected with each other, nor did they exemplify different facets of one underlying impatience with social and economic institutions.

Many workers struck in order to preserve gains acquired in the war. This was the primary motive behind the coal strike. Defensive action was forced upon many wage earners by the outspoken attitude of some employers who declared that "labor must be deflated." Actual attempts at deflation at a time when prices still were rising, brought conflict.

Again some of the strikes, and more of the threatened walk-outs, were by workers who had not shared in increased wages or shortened hours to the extent of other workers, or to the extent of preserving real wages. Policemen, firemen, railway shopmen, reporters, desk men employed by periodicals, subway and street railway workers, were some of the wage earners in this category.

Strikes, in some instances, were as much against union leaders as against employers. The heads of unions had been notably conciliatory during the war and had refrained from taking advantage of the power inherent in labor's position. Large numbers of the rank and file in the unions had been keenly disappointed in the leaders' tactics. In 1919, when the same officers advised against strikes, and even when they explicitly ordered men not to strike, the membership disregarded their own officials and walked out. The railway shopmen's strike was unwanted by union leaders; and so, too, in the steel strike most of the chief officers of the national unions involved were forced against their will to endorse it. As for the coal strike, although miners' President John L. Lewis obeyed Judge Anderson's injunction to call off the strike by November 11, the miners remained away from the pits for months after Lewis's order. In this instance probably Lewis was not incensed.

Anti-Negro Demonstrations.—The scarcity of unskilled labor in 1917 and 1918 had produced a large Negro migration to northern plants bursting with war orders. The influx was greater than accommodations in existing Negro quarters, and some cities had no special Negro residence district. When the Negroes overflowed into former white living areas, friction between the races started. As soon as the cessation of hostilities in Europe removed the need for restraint upon home passions these broke loose; and once again the Negro was made the victim of his own ambition to better his economic status. A race riot in this country primarily is a strike of lowly whites against the competition of blacks.

Strike Wave Continues.—The year 1919 by no means witnessed a settlement of all the variety of causes for unrest, so for two years more there were startling strikes. Mingo County, West Virginia, in 1921, was the scene of such serious rioting over the issue of unionization in the United Mine Workers that the county was put under martial law.[4] In 1922, a general strike of all coal miners both bituminous and anthracite was marked by a reign of terror in Herrin, Illinois. The same year there was an outlaw (unauthorized) strike of 300,-000 railroad shopmen in which was issued the notorious Wilkerson injunction. These strikes and riots were not revolutionary; that is, they were not intended to change society. Their chief motives were retention of war wages, raising wages to meet prices, and recognition of a union's right to speak authoritatively for labor in work bargains.

Noteworthy Strikes of 1919

Three of the strikes in 1919 merit special mention; these are the General Strike in Seattle, the Boston Police Strike and the Steel Strike.

Seattle Strike.—The germ of the Seattle General Strike was in the discontent of workers in the shipyards. During the war, shipbuilding was greatly extended in Seattle, for in pre-war days this activity was mostly confined to the government Bremmerton plant, but the war witnessed the building in Seattle of more than a quarter of the ships for the United States Shipping Board. The Seattle war-yards were unusual in that they operated on a closed shop basis, the union agreements not being made with the 21 individual shipyard crafts but with the Seattle Metal Trades Council, their representative negotiating body. The local agreements caused no unrest. When in December 1917, the Macy Board was created—by agreement between the

---

[4] The union spent $2½ million in this effort.

national officers of shipyard unions, the Navy Department and the U. S. Emergency Fleet Corporation—to provide a national tribunal for the settlement of shipyard labor disputes, its decrees were binding upon all local shipyard contractors, and the wage decrees as applied to Seattle upset accepted wage differentials.   For example, some trades were granted 60 cents per day above their going rate while others were reduced 22 cents below their prevailing wage.   Few things irritate labor more than upsets in established pay differentials; for by the differentials the status of crafts is made manifest.   Although the Seattle crafts protested the Macy Board rulings, they did not strike while the nation was at war.

With the arrival of the Armistice, the crafts tried to pluck this thorn; but all efforts at relief from the Macy Board pay rates were unavailing.   So a strike vote was taken by the 35,-000 shipyard workers; this vote being favorable, the Metal Trades Council declared a strike for January 21, 1919.   On that date the workers quit the yards in Seattle, Tacoma and Aberdeen.   Their demand was for $8 a day for skilled men with a scale graded down to common labor whose minimum wage should be $5.50 a day.   These rates were not out of line with war-shipyard wages.   Demands for an 8-hour day and a 44-hour week were coupled with the wage demands.   When the shipyard contractors used the time-honored tactic of an offer to comply with the skilled rate but a refusal to grant the unskilled rate, the skilled men refused to be lured from their unskilled associates.

The General Strike at Seattle.—At this point, January 22nd, the Metal Trades Council requested the Central Labor Council—representing *all* the trade unions of Seattle and Tacoma—that the shipyard strike be joined by a sympathetic strike of all the trades in both cities.   This proposal was submitted to the locals concerned, which by the end of the week voted acceptance. ˙ A General Strike Committee was formed and the date of 10 :00 A. M. Thursday, February 6, 1919, was set for the strike of 30,000 workers to aid the 35,000 shipyard men already out.

This was the first General Strike in American labor history, notwithstanding that a nationwide strike for an 8 hour day had taken place in May 1886; this earlier strike was not truly *general* because it involved only a minority of highly skilled craft workers.

By February 2nd, it was obvious what was impending in Seattle. The prudent laid in stores of food, and took out riot insurance; the imprudent set up shrill cries "You can't do this, it is revolution." The Minute Men, an unscrupulous adjunct of the American Protective League of Washington, scurried into positions where they might both thwart the strike and lay the train which would blow organized labor out of the state of Washington.

Meanwhile, the General Strike Committee in continuous session organized the campaign. So thoroughly did they do their work that they held Seattle in their grip for 6 days after the zero hour on Thursday morning, February 6th.

No Disorder.—Utterly unarmed patrols, 300 in number, maintained public order. There was no violence, whatsoever, connected with the strike in the 6 days. A detachment of the U. S. Army in camp near Seattle did not leave their tents. Milk stations were provided for children and invalids; 21 eating places served 30,000 meals a day at 25 cents to unionists and 35 cents to others; one laundry did all the wash-work for hospitals; one print shop served the Strike Committee; light and water services were unimpaired; garbage regularly was collected but not waste-newspapers and ashes. On the other hand there was no shipping, no street car services, no newspaper (each of two papers got out one issue toward the end of the strike), no theatre entertainments, no hotel engineers, maids or laundry service, cooks or waiters (but guests had plenty of food stored in advance); in short, no usual city activities except those granted permission by the strike leaders.

For two days the Strike Committee ran the city as it pleased; but for the other four there were slips in its power. Several of the presidents of International Unions, in person or by communication, ordered their Seattle locals to go back to work, or else forfeit their union charters—several did lose them—; and the American Federation of Labor severely censured the Central Labor Council.

Mayor Hanson's Acts.—Mayor Ole Hanson, of Norwegian ancestry, hired $50,000 worth of special police and called for and got the protection of 1,000 federal soldiers at nearby Camp Lewis; although the regular police did not receive a single trouble call as a result of the strike, nor as we have said did the soldiers leave their camp. Hanson, also by interviews with correspondents of outside newspapers, broadcast that Seattle was in the throes of a revolution, which, if successful there, would be spread to the rest of the country. So after the strike was over the Mayor took an extended speaking tour reiterating this statement concerning "revolution," and then claiming it was his valiance which broke it. (He was right to the extent that a general strike *was* a revolution no matter how peaceably it was conducted.)

The "revolution" cry did alienate outside support of the Seattle strike. However, it was the seepage back to work of hundreds of unionists that caused the Strike Committee to set noon Thursday, February 11th, 1919, as the termination of the strike.

Original Strike Loses.—The General Strike did not win the shipyard workers' issue. Their strike dragged for another month, when, on March 17th they returned to work on the same terms as had existed. In Seattle, as well as along the Pacific Coast, employers were more reactionary after the General Strike than before it; from this the I. W. W. and the Socialists were the most immediate sufferers although neither had any responsibility in connection with the strike. Labor political candidates lost in all Seattle elections for a year after the strike. The only result of the Seattle General Strike was a heightening of the sense of labor solidarity both in that city and across the nation, and a resolve by conservatives to prevent at all costs another general strike anywhere in the United States.

In evaluation of the shock of the Seattle General Strike, it should be recalled that a much more serious one immediately followed in Winnipeg, Canada, starting on May 15, 1919, and running through the 26th of June. This was one of the longest, most bitter general strikes in world labor history although conducted without violence. The government of Manitoba, and to a less extent that of Ottawa, were subject to intense but peaceful mass pressure. This strike, therefore, made the "revolutionism" of the Seattle strike seem pale indeed, despite the fact that one of its leaders later became Mayor of Winnipeg and two others entered the Dominion Parliament.

CHAPTER 5

THE GREATEST STRIKES 1919-1929

The Boston Police Strike 1919

The strike of the Boston Police on September 9th, 1919, in brevity was disparate to its national importance; it lasted only four days.

The original complaint of the Boston police, shared by many other police forces and public servants, was the extreme tardiness of wages behind run-away prices, together with the long hours of police duty. Getting no satisfaction from hints to headquarters, the Boston police observing the readier ear given to unionized firemen, municipal clerks, and treasury workers decided to organize a police union and affiliate it with the A. F. of L. The contemporary unionization of policemen and firemen in London also contributed to the Boston patrolmen's decision.

On August 10, 1919, acting through the policemen's "Boston Social Club," 1,290 of the men formed a union and got an A. F. of L. charter. Three days later, Commissioner Edwin U. Curtis announced as a new police rule, that no Boston police could become members of any outside organization except the Grand Army of the Republic, Spanish War Veterans, or American Legion. Nevertheless, the police went on with their unionization, getting 1,400 men signed of a force totaling 1,544 men and 96 officers. The Boston Central Labor Union commended the police upon the new union, and a local A. F. of L. officer assured the police they had the backing of 80,000 locally organized workers.

On August 22, Commissioner Curtis brought charges against 19 policemen for the violation of his new rule of the 13th; among these "culprits" was John P. McGinnes, the president of the police union, and the rest had been active in the

formation of the union.   On the 27th, these 19 were tried
before Commissioner Curtis who in this case was sole judge
of the infraction of his own "law."   The union had decided
that if the Commissioner found against the 19 men the rest
would strike; since the issue involved the existence of their
union.

The Commissioner, on September 9, declared against the 19
men.   On the same day at 5:45 P.M., the time of evening roll
call, the police left their posts.

City Unprepared.—The only preparation made by the city
for a possible strike had been the recruiting of volunteers by
former Commissioner Pierce, and the swearing in of Harvard
students, and some employes of banks and other large business
houses.   The responsibility for this situation ever afterwards
was disputed; for in Massachusetts the Commissioner of the
Boston police was appointed by the state governor, not the city
mayor.   Mayor Peters afterwards claimed he had pressed Commissioner Curtis to make ready for an emergency, but the
Commissioner had said "all necessary steps are taken."   Governor Calvin Coolidge claimed he had been ready to call state
troops upon Mayor Peters' request but no petition came; Peters,
in turn, stated that he could not ask for militia until overt acts
had occurred.   In this wrangle Commissioner Curtis in the long
run was made to take the blame while Governor Calvin Coolidge
got the accolades.[1]

Riots.—At any rate, at the zero hour of 5:45 P. M. September 9, 1919, Boston was without guardians.   All that night and
the next day crowds jeered police sergeants, lieutenants and
captains—who did not strike—and mobs of boys smashed windows and looted stores.   The next day—the 10th—the rioting
became more serious so Peters-Coolidge called out local units

---

[1] Among Boston newspapermen there were rumors that the police strike
easily could have been settled but that Boston and New York financial interests insisted that it be fought.

The reporters thought that the purpose was to distract attention from the
impending steel strike.   Another explanation was that the bankers wanted to
precipitate a general strike in Boston and then to crush it so overwhelmingly
that all unionism would be discredited.   All of this was newspapermen's
gossip but some claimed to have facts to support their off-the-record opinions.

of the militia.   The presence of these few soldiers made the rioting so much more vicious that two persons were killed and an unknown number wounded.   The militia used machine guns on the mobs, acts which were supposed to account for the two deaths.   The newspapers said that crooks were arriving at the Boston stations on every train.

On the 11th, Governor Coolidge took command; he called out the entire state militia and wired Secretaries Baker (War Department) and Daniels (Navy Department) to be in readiness to furnish federal assistance if the situation got further out of control.   With business houses barricaded, lit from cellar to roof and guarded by armed employes, with several hundred volunteer patrolmen, and trained policemen drawn from more than 200 on retired lists, together with steel helmeted mounted militia charging the streets and sidewalks—in Pennsylvania "cossack" fashion—there was no need for the federal army and navy.   President Wilson, in the course of a speech at Helena, Montana, denounced strikes by police, and in the United States Senate the riots in Boston were deplored by a conservative Senator from Colorado—of all places, one noted for its lawless unions and employers.   Sentiment throughout the country unmistakably was against the Boston strikers.

While the state was moving to restore tranquillity to Boston, the Central Labor Union of that city was discussing a general strike in sympathy with the police strike.   During the several days that it took the unions to vote on this proposal, the greatest uneasiness was felt by Bostonians.

Elsewhere events were moving.   The police of Washington, D. C., actuated by the same motives as their Boston brethren had unionized.   For this they were about to be discharged when President Wilson, in the week of the Boston strike, persuaded the Police Chief to let the case rest until his Industrial Conference, called for October 6.   In Macon, Georgia, unionized police forced the removal of an unpopular Chief and the latter's principal henchman, a lieutenant.   There were 37 American cities with police unions, and all these cities and their policemen watched Boston with anxious eyes.

Efforts at Adjustment.—On September 12, Samuel Gompers asked Governor Coolidge and Commissioner Curtis to take the strikers back into the force, and let the grievances as to wages and hours go over to the President's National Industrial Conference set for the next month. This move, together with all the known national hostility to the strike, caused the Boston police to vote on September 13 to return to duty. Four men anticipated the vote and appeared at headquarters where Commissioner Curtis instantly suspended them.

The next day Coolidge replied to Gompers that in his (Coolidge's) opinion and that of the State's Attorney General the term "striker" was a misnomer; they considered the men deserters and as such unworthy of any favors. The same note was struck by Commissioner Curtis. It was apparent they meant what they said, for the Civil Service Bureau opened a special office for the examination of recruits for a new police force. Five hundred ex-service men applied for the jobs but most of them were refused on account of flat feet. At this time, September 13, Montpelier, Vermont, sent a quantity of guns and ammunition to assist the Vermonter in the Governor's chair in Massachusetts.

Strike is Lost.—On September 14, with the city quiet under the militia, there was a definite decision to refuse to treat in any way with the men who had gone on strike. The Park police, too, who had refused to quell the first day's riots were all discharged. Instead, an entire new police force was to be enrolled and trained; for this work the city still had all its old police Captains, Lieutenants, and Sergeants. This day marked, then, the real defeat of the strike.

Clemency Denied Strikers.—However, the ex-police were not through trying to get back their jobs. Special pleas were made to reinstate the older men—if some were old enough to belong to the G. A. R. they must have been well along in years. This petition was denied. The Central Labor Union, never much in favor of a general strike, now on September 22 refused to strike for a lost cause; some constituent unions though did so vote, e. g., the bartenders and United Hebrew Trades; and the Amalgamated Clothing Workers' Union refused to make uniforms for the new policemen. The police strikers, therefore, as a last resort turned to the courts.

On October 31, they applied for a writ to compel Commissioner Curtis to re-instate the 19 patrolmen on the ground that they were really members of a union before Curtis made his rule, the violation of which caused their discharge. On November 8, the Massachusetts Supreme Judicial Court denied this petition. The decision crushed any further action. Even 16 years later when one of the strikers tried to get re-instatement on the force he was rejected.

Coolidge Wins.—Through October, November and December, the national guardsmen on duty in Boston gradually were relieved as the new police took over the job. In November, organized labor of Massachusetts campaigned against the re-election of Coolidge as Governor; but he won. The national Democratic platform also condemned Coolidge "for failure to protect lives and property." As early as the first week of the strike Coolidge was the recipient of Republican praise; it began with Massachusetts' Senator Lodge, Sr., was carried on by Elihu Root, and ex-President Taft. The result of this adulation made Coolidge Vice-President, and then President upon the death of Harding.

In the labor field, the strike's principal lesson was that public opinion would not tolerate ordinary labor tactics with such public servants as policemen. Several times it was proposed to make it a matter of law—as England did—that policemen cannot strike. Whether the public realized that this decision put a responsibility on the public to secure decent pay, hours of work, and working conditions for these public servants only policemen could tell.

The Steel Strike of 1919

On September 22, 1919, some 300,000 steel workers "walked out" of their work places. Three and a half months later (January 8, 1920), a remnant of 100,000 still sticking by a lost strike were ordered "to walk in" again, on whatever terms they could secure.   Although these official dates are convenient pegs, they do not bound the steel strike of 1919; for its roots struck back to 1892, and its fruits extended to the end of the generation (1929).

Background.—For 9 years after the defeat administered by the Carnegie Company at Homestead, Pa. (1892), the Amalgamated Association of Iron, Steel, and Tin Workers, held itself together only by meekness.   Confined as it always had been to the "tonnage men"—heaters, rollers, blast furnace men and others paid on the basis of tonnage output—it made no effort to enlarge its scope of membership, and retained what it had, mainly in the smaller companies, independent of the Carnegie giant.

In 1901, the Amalgamated feared (rightly) that the new United States Steel Corporation would practice the Carnegie hostility to unions, and so tried to make binding agreements with various parts of the new corporation before it had a chance to exercise its strength.   The Amalgamated did not know that the U. S. Steel Corporation had formulated at its inception, a labor policy from which it never deviated.   This was a double one; the part given publicity was that the corporation had no objections to unions, but that it would deal only with its own men; the secret part was a resolution to eliminate all existing union contracts as soon as possible without arousing resentment, and, thereafter, for the corporation to dictate its own terms of employment.   The Corporation decided that in its early days if it met great union resistance it was to "sign up" with the union in the mills involved; and then shut those mills. Since this policy was adopted before the early action of the Amalgamated, the union made no headway in getting contracts with the subsidiaries.

A strike, in 1901, to force the signing of union contracts, lasted only a few weeks.   It was such an utter defeat that the union barely maintained existence in a few independent plants. The Steel Corporation promptly closed those few mills in its own group that had unexpired union trade agreements.

The Strike of 1909.—In 1909, the U. S. Steel Corporation led the independents in crushing the remnant of the Amalgamated. First, the union was notified that its members must take a cut in pay, and then that the union must dissolve. With little to lose, the union met this challenge by a 14 months' strike; a gallant gesture, for the union was destroyed as an active force. Only a skeleton organization survived, and this had no power even in the very few independent small companies where its name was still used.

Corporation Tactics.—Meanwhile, the U. S. Steel Corporation adopted tactics to segregate its hundreds of thousands of employes into disunited groups. About a third of its men were very highly skilled. These were won to the Corporation by high wages, bonuses, stock ownership, and home ownership. Almost entirely, too, their ranks were closed to every one except native Americans, Irish and a tiny sprinkling of English, Scots, and Welsh. At the other extreme, another third of the total workforce was composed of recently arrived aliens, representing at the maximum 54 nationalities. Some American and West Indian Negroes were mixed with this workforce. These unskilled were poorly paid, and given none of the "extras" enjoyed by the top rank Americans; all were lumped under the term "hunkies" and treated like plantation mules. In between the Americans and hunkies was another third that held jobs that required training rather than skill. Some of these men were Americans but most were naturalized foreigners or second generation aliens. Their pay never was above the market rate for semi-skilled workers. All three groups were held apart by the status of their jobs; the Americans and skilled were made conscious of a superiority over the alien unskilled; and the foreigners were subdivided into nationalities that hated each other.

The U. S. Steel Corporation, to insure control of labor, had a large force of spies throughout the works. At critical times these "undercover men" were re-inforced by spies hired from "detective" agencies. Every spotted union sympathizer or grumbler was fired without notice, no matter how long or how

faithfully he had worked. Living in an atmosphere of distrust, steel workers did not dare voice opinions either in the
shop, at social gatherings, or even in their own homes.

The Corporation, in distinction to most of the independents,
spent thousands of dollars upon all kinds of "welfare."   Also
as a distinction, it applied and enforced after 1910 many safety
methods.

But until August 16, 1923, about half of the steel workers
had a 12-hour day, the worst departments in this respect being
the blast-furnaces, (pig iron) and open hearth furnaces (steel).
About half of those on 12-hour shifts worked 7 days a week,
alternating between day and night shifts usually twice a month.
When the turn came, the men put in 24 hours at one stretch.
Some men spent 106 hours out of 168 under the plant roof every
week.   Nearly all the work was hot, noisy, heavy and dangerous.

With no union to enforce better working conditions, the
chief relief was by the individual strike; that is, a high labor-
turnover.   Among the immigrant unskilled, turnover was especially high.

The Strike Planned.—The World War emphasized the
working conditions in the steel industry, and led directly to the
strike in 1919.   Nevertheless, the strike was not a spontaneous
revolt; for John Fitzpatrick, President of the Chicago Federation of Labor, and William Z. Foster, then a member of the
Carmen's Union and organizer for the A. F. of L., laid and lit
the fuse that brought the explosion.

In 1918, Fitzpatrick and Foster planned and managed a
successful strike in the packing industry whose labor history
had been much like that in steel manufacture.   At that time we
were in the World War and the steel industry was the hub of
our war manufactures.   The leaders thought the times most
propitious for forcing unionism into steel manufacture.

On April 7, 1918, Foster presented a resolution to the Chicago Federation of Labor requesting the executive officers of
the A. F. of L. to call a general labor conference and to inaugurate thereat a national campaign to organize the steel work-

ers.   In June, the resolution was presented and unanimously approved by the A. F. of L. convention in St. Paul.   On August 1-2, 1918, representatives of 15 national unions met in Chicago to plan the organizing campaign and later 9 other unions joined the movement.[2]   These unions at that time had about 2 million members which was about half the entire membership of the A. F. of L.   To conduct the campaign, the unions set up a "National Committee for Organizing Iron and Steel Workers." Of this, W. Z. Foster was made Secretary-Treasurer.   Samuel Gompers served as the committee's Chairman until June 1919, when this office was taken over by John Fitzpatrick who had been Acting-Chairman.

Plan Altered.—Foster's original plan had been a whirlwind national organizing effort in every steel center capped by a strike threat.   Under war conditions, he thought the steel industry would capitulate rather than risk a strike.   The delay from April to August 1918, brought the start of the campaign just before the Armistice.   Still more crippling was the faintheartedness of the 24 national unions, illustrated by their contribution of only $100 apiece for a campaign fund and their niggardly response in furnishing organizers.   With this scant war chest and tiny force of officers, the simultaneous national attack was abandoned for an encircling movement of steel's citadel in the Pittsburgh area.   The new plan called for capture of the outlying steel districts and then a concerted drive on Pittsburgh.

---

[2] These were (1) Int. Bro. of Blacksmiths, Drop-Forgers and Helpers; (2) Bro. of Boilermakers, and Ship Builders and Helpers of America; (3) United Brick and Clay Workers; (4) Bricklayers', Masons and Plasterers' Int. U. of A.; (5) Int. Assoc. of Bridge, Structural and Ornamental Iron Workers; (6) Coopers' Internat. U. of N. A.; (7) Int. Bro. of Electrical Workers; (8) Int. Bro. of Foundry Employes; (9) Int. Hod Carriers' Building and Common Laborers' U. of A.; (10) Amalgamated Assoc. of Iron, Steel and Tin Workers; (11) Int. Assoc. of Machinists; (12) Int. Union of Mine, Mill and Smelter Workers; (13) United Mine Workers; (14) Int. Molders' Union of N. A.; (15) Patternmakers' League of N. A.; (16) United Assoc. of Plumbers and Steamfitters; (17) Quarry Workers' Int. U. of N. A.; (18) Bro. Railway Carmen of America; (19) International Seamen's Union of America; (20) Amalgamated Sheet Metal Workers' International Alliance; (21) International Bro. of Stationary Firemen and Oilers; (22) Int. Union of Steam and Operating Engineers; (23) Int. Bro. of Steamshovel and Dredge-men; (24) Switchmen's Union of North America.

In September 1918, the first outpost was easily taken, namely the Chicago steel district. Through the rest of 1918, the strategy was carried out so that the final drive in the Pittsburgh district came in the summer of 1919.

Grievances.—The steel workers were ripe for organization on account of an accumulation of grievances. The long hours had been applied to a greater proportion of the men during the war. Although wages were raised several times, they had begun at low levels for two-thirds of the workers, and did not catch up with catapulted prices. It was common knowledge that the steel industry had made enormous profits during the war. Indeed, during our two years' participation in the war, the dividends of the U. S. Steel Corp. exceeded by a comfortable margin the entire par value of the Common Stock—*all* of which originally was "water." The steel industry was believed to be capable of paying higher wages. During the war, the alien unskilled were treated with unprecedented consideration because their kind of labor was extraordinarily scarce; but beginning on November 12, 1919—the day after the Armistice—the usual "Hunky-skinning" methods by foremen and skilled workers returned. This was especially resented because for many of the nationalities the war had brought a heightened national pride. The example of British labor, in 1919, reaching for control of the Parliament, and of Russian labor already rulers of their country, made the contrast of the powerlessness of steel labor all the more bitter. As a consequence of all these factors, the lower two-thirds of steel labor did not need much persuasion from organizers to join unions.

Counter-moves by Employers.—The employers moved energetically to block the organizing campaign. The "under-cover men," much augmented by agency spies, reported every man they could catch showing interest in the unions. Thousands of workers were fired for this cause. In the Pittsburgh district, the U. S. Steel Corporation so thoroughly controlled the public officials that union organizers were denied access to halls and were arrested if they conducted meetings in the open,

even on land owned by proponents of the meetings.   Thereupon the unionists raised the cry of "suppression of free speech,
and free assemblage"; they held meetings in defiance of ordinances and jails, and boycotted the merchants of towns that
denied assemblage.   Since the unionists generally won on this
issue, the tactic turned out to be favorable to the union cause;
for it dramatically forced home to steel workers that the steel
autocracy could be defied.   However, the full power of the steel
manufacturers was not applied until after the strike began.

Preliminary Negotiations.—During the summer of 1919,
those steel districts that earliest had been organized, pressed
upon the union leaders for a strike.   Piece-meal strikes of this
kind would have upset the union plans for a simultaneous national demand upon steel manufacturers; so the leaders had to
oppose the local restlessness.   Toward the end of summer, when
it was evident that a strike was imminent, several steps were
taken to negotiate with the companies' spokesman, Elbert H.
Gary.

The first of these was a letter, written June 20, 1919, by
Gompers asking for a conference with Judge Gary; to this Gary
made no reply.   During July and August, while a strike vote
was being taken in the mills, the National Committee tried, on
August 26, to interview Mr. Gary at his office; he refused to
meet them, instead asking that the Committee's proposals be
submitted in writing.   This was done on the same day.   Gary
replied on the 27th that the Committee did not represent the
majority of the employes of the U. S. Steel Corporation, and
anyway the Corporation's policy was that of "the open shop."
For the purpose of record, the Committee sent a challenging
reply to this letter on the same day; Gary paid no notice.

On September 4, 1919, the Committee wired to President
Wilson—then on his fateful tour speaking for support of the
League of Nations—asking him to arrange for a conference
between the Committee and representatives of the steel industry.
On September 9, a reply stated that no progress had been made
toward a conference and another interchange of telegrams
brought the same lack of results.   The strike vote meanwhile

had been about 98% favorable. So on Sept. 10 the orders were issued for strike action on September 22. On the 11th, Wilson wired Gompers, who in turn communicated with the Committee, requesting a postponement of the strike until after October 6 when Wilson would endeavor to place the issues of the steel workers before the President's Industrial Conference.

Strike Begins.—These requests of Wilson and Gompers came too late. The men no longer were willing to delay. The strike began on September 22, 1919.

Approximately 300,000 steel workers obeyed the strike order during the week after September 22. The task then was to keep up the enthusiasm by means of mass-meetings and a strike news bulletin; and to furnish the necessaries of life to destitute strikers and their families.

The first was impossible in the Pittsburgh district, for the public officials banned all meetings except in the Labor Temple in Pittsburgh itself. Elsewhere in the 10 states, 25 districts and 50 cities or towns in which steel was made, the meetings for a while were permitted.

The strike bulletin was required because the newspapers everywhere, but mostly in western Pennsylvania, printed scarcely anything save what was unfavorable to the strikers. The care of the destitute was difficult because except in two or three unions none of the unions paid strike-relief. The maximum treasury of the organizing committee was half a million dollars, most of it from $1.00 per capita membership fees—the fee was a flat $3.00 but $2.00 of this went to the national unions —and from voluntary gifts from non-steel unions; one gift of $100,000 came from the Amalgamated Clothing Workers' Union then not a member of the A. F. of L. The A. F. of L. unions separately from the committee raised another half million dollars during the entire campaign, half of it during the strike itself. On the commissary there was spent a little less than $350,000, which figured out to 9⅓ cents per striker per week. (The total cost of the entire campaign from start to finish was $4.02 per man.)

Opposition to Strike.—Against the strikers, enormous forces were raised.   First there was the press.   Never, at any time during the strike, did the newspapers tell the real grievances of the strikers in regard to wages, the 12-hour day, and the atmosphere of repressed fear in which steel workers lived. Instead the papers printed pages of material fed to them by agencies of the steel companies.   Two misrepresentations were most frequently printed.   One which began on September 23 was that the strike was broken by the men flocking back to the mills.   William Hard kept a file of these accounts and counted the men said to be going into the mills; the total was 4,800,000 whereas the maximum on strike, according to the unions, was 365,600.   Secondly, the newspapers called the strike revolutionary in intent; basing the charge on a book then out of print (the steel companies reprinted and distributed it in uncounted numbers) entitled "Syndicalism" written 8 years before by Earl C. Ford and W. Z. Foster in the latter's I. W. W. days.   In fact, the strike was an orthodox trade union affair—too much so to succeed.   The "Red" charge however was a vital blow against the strike.

Especially in the district near Pittsburgh all the powers of the community were invoked against the strike.   The officials suppressed free speech and free assemblage.   The ministers, who spoke at all, preached against the strike, except for a few Roman and Greek Catholic priests and Lutheran clergymen whose pulpits were not amenable to local pressures.   The small business men and professional men by hundreds were sworn as deputy sheriffs, and the regular police increased.   Besides, the state constabulary in Pennsylvania and New York (Buffalo) rode their horses through the strike towns, into stores and even homes.   In fact the Constabularies were so terroristic in their methods, that they were dubbed "Cossacks."   The steel plants themselves were infested with hired armed guards.   The courts imposed jail terms and fines upon strikers, whose offense in some instances, was being wounded by the "Cossacks."

The United States Senate, on September 23, was brought into action by an investigation committee composed of Senators Kenyon, McKellar, Walsh (Mass.), Sterling, and Phipps; their report on November 8, while silent on the workers' real grievances, embellished the "revolutionary" aspects of the strike. The United States Army was used in the Chicago area. The steel companies of course hired thousands of "scabs." They made especial use of Negroes who were shipped in sealed carloads from the South. Their own striking workers were terrorized by every possible method in order to induce them to "scab" the strike.

Internal Weakness of Strike Organization.—Despite the great forces operating in favor of the steel companies, the greatest handicap was in the unions themselves. In a struggle, in which the natural and most effective form of organization would have been an industrial union—all the workers in the industry enrolled in one union—the battle was fought by an alliance of 24 *trade* unions. At the start of the campaign in 1918, these unions were both timid and defeatist in attitude and so hesitated to plunge money and organizers into the struggle.

In 1919, just before the strike order was imminent, the Amalgamated Association of Iron, Steel, and Tin Workers tried to make an independent exclusive agreement with Chairman Gary. After the strike had been in full swing for a couple of months, this same union ordered its men back to work in some of the "independent" mills on the plea that the union had inviolable trade agreements with these mills. The return of these skilled workers at a crucial time made the alien unskilled strikers feel that they had been betrayed by the skilled Americans; so they too started to pour back into the mills. In general, the skilled had justified Mr. Gary's policy of favoritism, for they gave the strike the least support of any of the three groups of workers—of course they had more to lose than the footloose unskilled immigrants.

Another union—the International Union of Steam and Operating Engineers—boycotted the strike in its first week because they had lost a jurisdictional decision to the International Brotherhood of Electrical Workers over the membership of steel mill electrical crane operators. The officers of the engineers were forced to support the strike when the rank and file went on strike in disobedience to the officers' orders.

Still another example of union exclusiveness was the attitude of the railroad workers. Steel plants in any one district are connected by a network of private rail lines. Halt these and steel production stops. The 24 unions that fought the strike pleaded with the railroad men to join the strike where they could do so in mill yards without violation of agreements. But the railroad men kept on working.

Finally, some strikers themselves acted as scabs outside their home districts; for instance, a Gary mill man might scab in Pittsburgh, explaining his absence to his home mill associates by any story that sounded reasonable. The fact that so many southern Negroes scabbed, can be attributed in part to the long standing hostility of unions toward the admission of Negro members.

Strike Fails.—The strike lines held fairly well for two months but thereafter they crumbled. The effort in October, to get the steel strike before the President's National Industrial Conference failed on the technical definition of collective bargaining—this caused the Conference to fail too, for the labor members walked out. An attempt at mediation by the Commission of Inquiry of the Interchurch World Movement likewise was a failure. By January 1920, although 100,000 strikers still were out, the mills were running at between 50% to 75% capacity. To avoid longer sacrifice of the most staunch 100,000, the strike committee, on January 8, ordered them to return to work on the best terms they could get. The strike was a failure.

Shortly after the strike was broken, the U. S. Steel Corporation announced a wage increase for the unskilled with a corresponding "adjustment" for the other two groups of workers.

Interchurch Report.—The grievance, in respect to hours, was influenced by the "Report of the Steel Strike of 1919" issued by the Commission of Inquiry, Interchurch World Movement. The Interchurch body had authorized an investigation

in the second month of the strike (October 1919) and its agents
were busy collecting facts throughout the strike.   Between November 28-December 5, the Commission of Inquiry was drawn
into the strike as mediators, but Mr. Gary, although he talked
with them (on December 5) for two hours, refused to recognize
their status as mediators.   The Report of the Commission, one
copy of which had been forwarded to President Wilson on July
27, was given to the press on July 28, 1920.   In essence, the
Report was an indictment of the steel industry with dates, figures, and names duly cited.   It was given, for two days, large
space in every important American newspaper and later was
commented upon by many European papers.   The *Christian
Science Monitor* conducted a symposium upon the report for
8 weeks in 17 "stories" and editorials.   Nineteen national
unions bought the Report in large quantities.

As a result, the contents of the Report were common knowledge, and for many persons overturned their former conception
of the strike.   Yet the thing that gripped the public the most
was the Report's exposure of the 84-106 hour week in the steel
industry.   The Commission's second report "Public Opinion
and the Steel Strike" issued in 1921, although it did not deal
with hours of labor but spies, newspapers, civil rights, the
Pittsburgh pulpits and the Corporation's Welfare work, nevertheless, served to remind the public of the hours issue in the
strike.

Even in advance of the first "Report," William Z. Foster
had published, "The Great Steel Strike And Its Lessons."   This
book was peppered with derogatory adjectives but on the whole
was a remarkably temperate account, to have been written
within a few weeks after the strike by its most maligned leader.

Counter-Report.—Therefore, despite the ending of the
strike on January 8, 1920, publications concerning it went on
through that and the following year.   To Foster's book, the
steel companies gave no heed, but to the two "Reports" they
felt they had to reply.   In 1922-23 they sponsored "Analysis
of the Interchurch World Movement Report On The Steel
Strike" compiled by Marshall Olds.   This book alone was

nearly as voluminous as the two "Reports" put together.   It was a masterly piece of sophistry, covering on the one hand a diatribe against unions and on the other a criticism of "radicals" who published calumnies against an industry about which they had no real knowledge.   Mr. Gary made personal gifts of this book to college and other libraries and to many individuals; but the volume never got out of the shadow of the "Reports."

White House Conference.—So great was the public's continual debate over the steel workers' long hours that in May 1922, President Harding called the steel manufacturers to the White House to discuss a shorter work period.   From the conference emerged a committee of steel makers for study of work hours, but their report, months later, was that 8-hour shifts in steel making were infeasible.   This whetted, not blunted, the public clamor; so at last on August 16, 1923, the Carnegie Company announced it was going to adopt the 8-hour shift.   To the strike in 1919, much of this result must be attributed.

It may be permitted to mention two more historical facts. The American iron and steel industry rarely has originated a new principle in the manufacture of its products, except the mechanical handling of masses; nearly every other innovation came from Scotland, England, or Germany.   Secondly, the United States Steel Corporation never, until the late 1920's, had research laboratories comparable to those of the Bell Telephone, General Electric or General Motors; in steel works the laboratories merely tested materials to insure compliance with specification.   Except for size, therefore, our largest steel companies contributed scarcely anything to steel technology; whatever of this has been done in the United States has been by relatively small independent companies such as the American Rolling Mills Company.

Soft Coal Strike of 1919

The bituminous coal strike of 1919, (Nov. 1-Dec. 10) we will not treat in detail, but we must describe its unusual feature, an injunction issued under the Lever Act.

The Lever Act of August 10, 1917, provided for federal wartime control of food and fuel. Section 4 of the Act made it unlawful "to conspire, combine, agree, or arrange with any other person (a) to limit the facilities for transporting, producing, harvesting, manufacturing, supplying, storing, or dealing in any necessaries, (b) to restrict the supply of any necessaries, (c) to restrict the distribution of any necessaries, (d) to prevent, limit, or lessen the manufacture or production of any necessaries in order to enhance the price thereof."

The Act was aimed at war profiteers and it was administered so far as fuel was concerned by Harry Garfield—president of Williams College and son of President Garfield—to control the prices of fuel during the war. While still as a bill before Congress, friends of labor feared its application to unions, and Senator Hollis of New Hampshire introduced an amendment providing that nothing in the Act should be construed to prohibit labor unions from conducting their ordinary functions. The amendment was not voted because Senator Husting of Wisconsin stated that he was authorized by Secretary of Labor Wilson and Attorney General Palmer to say that the administration did not and would not construe the bill as prohibiting strikes and peaceful picketing. Gompers, in a speech at Washington on November 22, 1919, reiterated that this had been the understanding and that U. S. District Attorneys had been so instructed.

Injunction Issued.—Neverthless, after the action of the United Mine Workers' Convention on September 22, 1919 foreshadowed a soft coal strike on November 1, 1919, unless the operators increased wages 60% and introduced a 5-day, 6-hour work period—the latter to insure regular work not to get out of work—the Attorney General, on October 21, petitioned the United States District Court in Indianapolis for an injunction restraining the officers and members of the United Mine Workers from carrying on the proposed strike. The Fuel Administration, having lapsed a year earlier after the Armistice, Garfield was now hurriedly brought back to Washington to reinstate it. On October 23, Judge A. B. Anderson gave Attorney General

Palmer what he wanted, a restraining order commanding the 84 national and district officers of the United Mine Workers and all persons whomsoever to refrain from doing anything whatsoever to bring about the strike.   The *officers* obeyed. Inasmuch as the strike orders already had been issued, on November 1, the *miners* 425,000 strong stayed out of the mines thus tying up about 75% of the bituminous industry.

Therefore, on November 8, which Judge Anderson had set for a hearing on the restraining order, he not only made the injunction permanent but added to it an order compelling the officers in the same manner that they had issued the strike mandate to cancel it.   This too was obeyed.

Since men cannot be forced to work—13th Amendment to the Constitution—the miners remained on strike until December 10, 1919.   Then the operators granted a 14% wage increase and agreed that a Presidential commission of three persons should decide the still unsettled questions of wages, working conditions, profits, and proper coal prices.   This action quashed all but one of the 84 contempt of court charges that had arisen from the injunction; the one exception was Alexander Howatt, leader of the Kansas miners, and an exceedingly ardent laborite who also ran afoul of the Kansas Industrial Court law.

In summation: this injunction was based on a war measure nearly a year after the Armistice; the application for it by Attorney General Palmer violated his, and Secretary of Labor Wilson's promise that the Lever Act would not be used against unions; the Lever Act provided that violations should be subject to criminal penalties, and it is a rule of law that crimes as such are not the basis for petitions in equity.   Finally, the injunction was useless, for it did not stop the strike.

This injunction case became one of the favorite "horrible examples" used by unions to show the lengths to which even the government would go to thwart what unionists thought were their own legitimate actions.

Shopmen's Strike of 1922

Background.—The Shopmen's Strike of 1922 had its prologue in 1919.   In this earlier year, the Shopmen had been aggrieved because their wages during the war had advanced the least of any such large body of men (500,000), and were inadequate to meet the still mounting costs of living. They had gotten one increase, July 2, 1918, which brought their rate to 68 cents an hour; this was not only lower than the rate paid to machinists in private employ but was 12 cents under the rate for shipyard machinists. On January 1, 1919, the Shopmen asked that their rate be raised 17 cents; that is, to 85 cents an hour. After laborious conferences and an abortive "outlaw" (unauthorized by national officers) strike on August 1, they finally got a raise of 4 cents an hour. Nearly a year later (July 20, 1920), the newly created Railway Labor Board granted them 13 cents an hour more; thus giving the men the full 85 cents an hour they had asked for in January of the preceding year.

Strike Begins.—On June 6, 1922, the Railway Labor Board cut off 7 cents an hour from the Shopmen's rate and thus precipitated the Shopmen's troubles in the year of 1922. Another grievance was that several railroads—the Pennsylvania was one that was named—had ignored the Railway Labor Board's order that prohibited the sending of repair work to non-railroad shops. When the Railway Labor Board (June 7) informed the Shopmen that the Board had no way to force the stoppage of "contracting out," the union leaders were authorized to reply (June 27) that the shopcrafts would strike unless the railway executives granted an immediate conference and promised both to ignore the Board's wage reduction and to stop giving repair work to outside shops. On June 29, the executives refused to comply, and added that a strike would not be against the railroads but against the government inasmuch as the railroads still were under the federal war control.

Hopeless of gains by negotiations, the shopcrafts on July 1, 1922, walked out in ranks 400,000 strong. This strike immediately was hit two hard blows: the Railway Labor Board announced (July 3) that it considered the shop jobs to be not struck but vacated, and therefore invited recruits to fill the jobs without stigma of scabs or strikebreakers; at the same time, the

railway executives declared that all strikers' names were dropped
from payrolls and their seniority cancelled.   These moves at
once placed the demand for retention of seniority above those
for a wage increase and abolition of contracting out; that is,
the strikers were put on the defensive.

Before the month of July was finished, complaints came from
southern U. S. Marshals that the strike was interfering with
the transport of mail.   This claim was countered by complaints
from the railroad Brotherhoods that the bad condition of rolling stock together with the presence on trains of armed guards
was subjecting them to intolerable hazards.   In fact, the trainmen struck at Joliet, and on the Sante Fe R. R. train movement
in Arizona and California was crippled.

President Harding Intervenes.—Meanwhile, after a futile
conference on July 14, the Railway Labor Board stopped trying
to find a solution for the strike, with the result that President
Harding on July 29 and August 7 took over the task.   In his
first effort he was rebuffed by the railway managers and on his
second, by the Shopmen.   The President then (August 18)
used a message to Congress to inform the nation that the government would enforce the statutes forbidding conspiracies to
hinder interstate commerce, and other laws that assured the
highest possible safety in railway service.

Daugherty Injunction.—After a flurry of Cabinet meetings in late August, Attorney General Daugherty on September 1 took the step that put the Shopmen's strike in a special
niche in American labor history.   Daugherty went to Chicago
and from the U. S. District Court, for the Northern District
of Illinois Judge Wilkerson in the chair, secured a restraining
order against the Shopmen that was the most sweeping preliminary injunction ever issued in a labor dispute.

The grounds stated for the order were a "conspiracy" as
defined by the Sherman Act, a contempt of Decision 1036 (the
wage cut) of the Railway Labor Board, and a contempt of the
Board itself.   Only the first ground had any standing in law.
The order forbade every normal activity of a union in the con-

duct of a strike, and in addition denied to the strikers and their unions the rights of speech, press, and assembly.

This restraining order produced such a storm of protest not only from the strikers but from a great many noted citizens that Daugherty, and President Harding himself (September 5), stated that the government had no intention of violating the constitutional guarantees concerning personal liberty, free press, speech and assembly; nevertheless on September 23, Judge Wilkerson converted the order into a temporary injunction against the Railway Employes' Department of the A. F. of L. et al. A second preliminary injunction was obtained on October 5, 1922. Motions for dismissal, filed on October 6, were denied on January 5, 1923. The injunction was made permanent on July 12, 1923, a final hearing having convinced the judge that the government's plea was justified.

Meanwhile in Congress on September 11, 1922, Representative Keller of Minnesota entered impeachment charges against Daugherty, but the House Judiciary Committee postponed action and the matter never again was considered.

Baltimore Agreement.—In the midst of the furor over the Daugherty-Wilkerson restraining order, the union leaders and certain railway executives held conferences from which emerged what became known as the "Baltimore Agreement." Its terms included an immediate return to jobs at existing pay rates and without loss of seniority, a system for adjusting disputes over the return to work that avoided jurisdiction to the Railway Labor Board, and a mutual promise against discrimination. The Baltimore and Ohio R. R., the Chicago-Northwestern, and the Chicago-Milwaukee and St. Paul signed the agreement on September 15, followed within 4 days by the New York Central R. R. Within the same month, 78 railroads had settled and by October 30 some 100 railroads and their shopmen again were working in harmony.

Partial Failure of Strike.—This limited success was the total result of the strike. Many railroads, including the Pennsylvania and its quasi-subsidiaries, the New England railroads, never did permit the strikers to return to work except as "new" employes.   As late as March 6, 1923, over 120,000 shopmen were still out on "strike"—by that time and later they really were not strikers but the unemployed.   The shopmen's unions did not recover from this ill-starred strike during the remaining 7 years of the generation.

Southern Textile Strikes 1929-30

Of the notable strikes in the generation of "More," the last ones were in the South, and were connected with the places named Elizabethton (Tenn.), Gastonia (N. C.), Marion (N. C.), and Danville (Va.).   All were in the textile industry and although differing in detail all arose from similar causes and exhibited common characteristics.   The first three took place in 1929; while the Danville strike was from September 29, 1930, to January 29, 1931.

Causes.—An imponderable but important reason for disturbances in the South was in some cases the disappearance of the traditional semi-feudalism that had prevailed among mill owners and workers in the generation before 1896.   Formerly, the "best people" in any southern community had felt responsible for the welfare of common white or black folk; the latter in turn had depended upon the advice and assistance so freely rendered.   Before 1929, a new generation of mill owners or managers, and a second generation of mill workers, generally had replaced the earlier easy give and take with a tight fisted profit and wage relationship.   Absentee ownership had appeared.   For example, a Miss Sarah Baldwin of Baltimore was the principal owner of the Marion (N. C.) mills; while German capitalists were the chief stockholders in the Elizabethton (Tenn.) enterprise.   Absentee owners primarily were intent on the maintenance of high dividends, and workers no longer got gratuitous additions in money or services to their meager wages.

In other cases, such as the mammoth Cone enterprise, "the Proximity Mills" at Greensboro (N. C.) and the "Riverside and Dan River Mills" at Danville (Va.), it was the retention of feudalistic attitudes by the owners carried over into an industrial sphere that underlay much of the trouble. Both of these companies were large, and in both the paternalistic statements of the heads of the concerns that their workers were "happy and contented" had been accepted as true. The South had regarded these as her model cotton-mill enterprises.

In 1928, the southern workers were not ignorant of the lot of workers elsewhere. Some individuals had been "outside" on railroads, or other jobs, and some had been in the World War; upon return these travellers brought tales of living or working conditions superior to those in southern mill villages. Some few workers by their reading became cognizant of their own exploitation, while others were made aware of it by school teachers, preachers, and visiting kin. With many workers aware of their own relatively degraded situation, the stage was set for clashes.

The "Stretch Out."—The explosive agency that brought outbreaks was the installation of the "stretch out" system, a name given by workers to the increase of machines per worker and also to advanced speeds of machines.

The "stretch out" originated under Scientific Management, and when properly introduced, it did not necessarily impose greater burdens upon workers. For example, a weaver was paid for completed yardage of goods; therefore, if yarn was poor, the weaving loom in poor repair, or the pattern or style of cloth frequently changed, the weaver's attention was so constantly required and the looms so frequently stopped by broken yarn or changes in set up, that the weaver could not manage many looms (four to twenty say), the loom speed was retarded, and weaver's earnings low. If standardized, strong yarn was steadily supplied to the loom, the pattern and style of the cloth to be woven also standardized, and the looms maintained in first class condition, then the weaver could attend more looms without strain. If the number of looms was gradually increased so that the weaver accustomed himself to the changes, and the weaver given interest in the process by upward adjustment of earnings, then the number of looms (on certain grades of cloth) not only could be stepped up to 148 or more per man but each loom could be run at greater speed.   In the best managed plants this was the manner of the installation of the "stretch out," and the results were accomplished without serious worker opposition.

In the poorly managed mills, little effort was given to standardizing conditions before abruptly speeding the looms and increasing their number per weaver and at the same time cutting wage rates.   Inasmuch as the consequences were more work at less earnings as well as augmented technological unemployment, the weavers revolted.   Hence, it was not so much the "stretch out" itself that constituted a grievance, as the improper method of its application.

Supplementary Causes.—With a common soreness against the unscientific sudden thrust of the "stretch out" system, other causes for bitterness cropped up, and thus added to the worker's desire to fight the employers.   Chief among these supplementary issues were the perennial ones of wages and hours of work. In the mills, where strikes occurred, the wages averaged from $10 to $14 for a 60-hour (or more) week; and for about half the workers the long week was on night work.   At that time, the average wage for the entire industry was $15.65 per week for an average 53-hour week.   In Georgia and Alabama wages were slightly less than $12.50, while in New England they were about $20.   In Georgia the hours of work averaged 56, while in Massachusetts they were 48, with night work for women prohibited.   These data are cited to indicate that the strikers had slightly better wages and hours than in many other southern cotton mills but were distinctly inferior to the work conditions in New England mills.

As to the southern strikers' superiority in wages or hours to the majority of southern textile workers, it may be noticed that strikes often have been absent among the most exploited labor because it had neither the energy nor the resources to conduct them; but have been common among workers in whom a margin of energy, or resources led to hopeful efforts still further to improve their lot.

As to the contrast with New England textile operatives, the customary southern rejoinder had been that southern living costs were less, so a lower wage secured as much satisfaction as in New England. A survey conducted by the National Industrial Conference Board in 1919 showed that the costs of living differed only slightly as between Greenville and Pelzer, S. C., or Charlotte, N. C., and Fall River, or Lawrence, in Massachusetts.

This statement is somewhat obscure, because the investigation covered the prices of the same or similar things in the different places. These were things in a budget considered reasonable for workers. Actually the southern mill people did not buy those things. There was a real difference in the *standards* of living between North and South with the latter at the lower level. We may conclude that it was not a fair argument to say that southern wages were low because living *costs* were low, when the fact was that *standards* of living were low because wages were low.

From other studies made in 1926, the conclusion was reached that a differential of 12 cents in hourly rate would cover the variation in living standards between the two cotton manufacturing sections. The actual average hourly rates in 1928 ranged from 24 cents in Alabama, 26 cents in Georgia, 29½ cents in North Carolina, to 32 cents in Maine, 39 cents in Massachusetts, and 41 9/10 cents in New Hampshire. Bearing in mind that these are *average* rates, it follows that many southern operatives received rates less than the 12-cent differential.

Another southern defense for low mill wages was that the worker there received benefits in the mill village system that more than offset the differential in wages. The amount of services in villages varied greatly, as for instance between the Proximity Mills (Cones') in Greensboro (N. C.) and the Riverside Mills in Danville (Va.); in the former the village services covered every aspect of life while in the latter there was no "village," for the help lived in private houses in Danville and mingled indiscriminately in the life of the town. In Danville itself, there was a contrast between the employes of the Riverside mill and those of the Dan River; the latter lived in the mills' Schoolfield village. The Riverside and Dan River Cotton Mills Company owned both sets of mills, those by the river in the heart of the city and those in the village on the outskirts. Disregarding such differences competent persons [3] have estimated that the average money worth of mill services did not exceed $1.62 per week. The pay differential North and South was greater than this.

Company Houses and Stores.—Still another cause for soreness among southern mill operatives was the compulsion of living in company houses and trading at company stores. Originally, southern mills were located outside, and sometimes remote from ordinary communities; hence, when mills were built it was necessary to construct houses and furnish stores for workers. Whether or not company houses and stores were means of exploiting workers depended upon the spirit with which the mill managers conducted these subsidiary enterprises. To combine in one group of persons the functions of boss, landlord, and merchant was at best an irritation to workers, and at worst—there were many such—led to virtual slavery. Whenever wage earners can be heard they always have voiced opposition to company houses and stores, and this was true of the strikers in 1929. In fairness it should be stated that, in these strikes the mill managers did not indulge in wholesale evictions from company houses, although some strikers in each strike were compelled to get out of company houses.

Managers Stubborn.—In all of the strikes the managers were obdurate. They refused to deal with strike committees or to heed offers of mediation from outside persons including state and federal officials. The managers claimed that their employes were not exploited, and were not discontented, and so attributed the strikes to the plottings of outside "agitators." In the Danville case, the manager was so certain that his mill and village were models for the South, that the shock of the strike

---

[3] Main and Gunby of the Society of Mechanical Engineers; and Broadus Mitchell, Professor of Economics, Johns Hopkins.

together with the extra burdens it put upon him, resulted in his death.

Yet impartial investigators were convinced that the strikes originated among the mill helps, and that "outsiders" had no part in the strikes until after the walk outs; even then, in most instances, the outsiders were invited by the strikers to come to the towns in order to furnish experienced skilled leadership, the management of the distribution of food, clothing, money, or other assistance. In three of the strikes, the outsiders to whom appeals were made were officers of the State Federation of Labor, officers of the United Textile Workers' Union (A. F. of L.) and agents of the Federal Council of Churches, and Society of Friends (Quakers). The Red Cross would not aid strikers. In the Gastonia strikes, the Communists were the principal "outsiders" so the A. F. of L. affiliates shunned this affair; the church agents, however, participated in relief measures in this strike. Funds and relief supplies were solicited from workers and others throughout the nation for all of the strikes.

Violence.—All four strikes were marked by violence. Firearms and dynamite were used, sometimes to terrorize, sometimes to inflict mortal injury. Social pressure within the villages to keep strikers in rank, and to expel scabs did not always fall short of terroristic coercion. The police, deputies and militia called upon to preserve order were themselves guilty of bloodshed and—allegedly—outright murder, e.g., Gastonia and Marion.

The strikes, therefore, had an aftermath in the courts of which the trials connected with the Gastonia strike were most vindictive. Two sets of murder trials arose from the Gastonia violence, one against the public officers for alleged wanton killing of strikers—resulting in acquittals—the other against the Communist leaders for the shooting of peace officers and these resulted in convictions from which the condemned escaped by disappearance while freed under bail. The Marion sheriff, with his deputies, accused of unprovoked murder of 6 strikers not only was acquitted but re-elected. During the strikes, the employers besides resorted to armed protection of property, appealed to the courts and secured injunctions against the strikers.

A. F. of L. Assistance.—After the Elizabethton, Tenn., double strikes, a wave of strikes swept the Piedmont cotton mills. In the following weeks about 18,000 textile workers in 15 places walked out of the mills. The inability of the United Textile Workers by itself to cope with the organizational demands raised by these strikes caused the A. F. of L. in convention at Toronto, in the fall of 1929, to vote in favor of a general organization drive throughout the South. President Green, beginning at Charlotte, N. C., in January 1930, conducted a speaking tour of the South in which he emphasized three things; the objects of unionism, the virtues of management—union cooperation—he was trailed by an A. F. of L. efficiency engineer—and the assumption that if southern managers did not accept the conservative A. F. of L. they would be overwhelmed by the Communists. The strategy of the A. F. of L. campaign favored quiet, peaceful, business-like penetration and frowned upon both noisy dramatic demonstrations and strikes.

In October 1930, the A. F. of L. reported the formation of 112 locals organized as a result of their campaign; but 81 of these were in occupations other than those in cotton mills. The textile workers were inclined toward noise, drama, and strikes; and when the A. F. of L. did not supply these the cotton mill workers set out to produce their own. These came not in the areas affected by the strikes of 1929, but in the northern parts of North Carolina and in Virginia. The Danville strike was the epitome of this second series.

Results of Strikes.—The strikes in both years were prolonged into many costly weeks: expensive because the mill managers in business lost to rivals in an extraordinarily competitive industry, as well as in the extra charges for legal fees, property protection, rent losses, and hire of strike breakers; and equally onerous to workers in lost wages, savings, short rations, clothes, and sometimes in evictions.

Yet the results of the strikes were inconclusive. The managers wore out the strikers but did not break their morale; while the strikers did not gain recognition for collective bargaining nor secure much reform in the stretch-out, wages, hours, company houses, and stores. To the workers the principal gain was proof of their ability to endure a strike, and maintain co-operation with each other in organized effort. In getting the support of national public opinion, the strikers also counted a gain; for the publicity given the strikes spread before the whole country the anachronistic attitudes, and practices, of some southern mill managers and owners. To all the latter, whether or not their works were involved, the strikes were a warning that the advertised "docility" of southern white wage earners was on the wane, partly because the great surplus of labor had been whittled down, partly on account of the increased proportion of second or third generation workers among mill hands, and partly for the reason that wage earners were getting better informed as to the extent they were being exploited.

Thus, despite the lack of direct, concrete results, the strikes probably were not vain efforts: perhaps the temporary improvements under the Cotton Textile Code (N. R. A.) in 1933 were traceable in some degree to these strikes in 1929 and certainly they were the fore-runners of the Great Textile Strike of 1934.

CHAPTER 6

EMPLOYERS' ACTIVITIES

Associations.—Business and industry (1896-1929), in all their aspects, were regimented. Associations of business men and industrialists were based upon geography, product, materials, business, industry, customers, pet hates, and true loves. Rare was the employer who belonged to only one "union"; employers were as inveterate "joiners" as any small-town lodge enthusiast. The business man and industrialist had a choice of 1,500 national organizations, 200 state and 7,000 local ones; if they wished, they could sink a goodly proportion of profits in dues.

It was true that most of these organizations did not touch labor matters or did so only incidentally; but there were several whose primary function was the employer-employe relationship. Some of these bargained collectively with unions while others fought unions with tooth and claw.

Employers' "Unions."—The employers' associations for collective bargaining were found in industries in which a boycott or strike were peculiarly damaging. Some were seasonal industries such as coal mining, or clothing manufacture. Others were activities in which time was a factor in value; newspapers, the theatre, and railroads were cases in point. All were industries or businesses that depended upon skilled labor; for this reason not only miners, garment cutters, the workers in the mechanical division of newspapers, all the employes of a theatre, including the actors, but also the railway train crews, the men in potteries, glass factories, stove works, and in construction were able to force employers to sign trade agreements. To do so effectively, the employers associated themselves into organized labor-trading units.

The employers were not unwilling to enter union agreements because in their businesses the payroll usually was one of the greatest costs of production, and if this cost could be standardized for all employers, the danger of cut-throat competition was reduced.   It was not eliminated; for a few employers outside the organization might still attempt to capture trade by undercutting labor.   These were factors in the garment, coal, and construction industries.   Newspapers, and the theatres found it cheaper to deal with labor than suffer the complete temporary loss of business occasioned by strikes.   Until quite late in the generation, sanitary pottery and glass were produced almost entirely by the skill of labor; so in these instances employers had no power of massed capital with which to fight labor. Sensibly, they sought peace by agreement.   Some employers, as for instance building contractors, saw a chance for a double monopoly in trade agreements; the two—employers and unions —acting in harmony, could beat off competition and charge the consumers all they were able to pay.

Trade Agreements.—The first national trade agreement was written in 1891 between the Molders' Union and the Stove Founders' Association.   Between 1898 and 1902, the Newspaper Publishers' Association, the National Metal Trades' Association, and the National Founders' Association—foundrymen, other than stove makers—all signed trade agreements.   After 1897, the soft coal industry was wholly or partially operated under trade agreements; likewise, the anthracite coal industry, after 1902, used long-term agreements but without official recognition of the union until 1916.   In the garment industry, trade agreements became customary after 1910.   The railway train crews had trade agreements throughout the generation, but other railway workers either had intermittent agreements or none.   Pottery and glass workers were consistent negotiators of agreements until automatic machinery abolished their jobs and their unions.

Anti-Union.—For reasons set forth in later sections of this chapter, the Founders' Association, the Metal Trades' Association, and that part of the United Typothetae that operated book and job printing, abandoned trade agreements after 1902; they joined the bitterest enemies of unions and fought them for the rest of the generation.　Country newspapers and the *Los Angeles Times,* the *Buffalo Commercial,* the *Phoenix Gazette,* and *Hamilton* (Ohio) *Daily News* were among the principal newspaper publishers that refused to deal with unions.

In manufacturing, those varieties that were most typical of the generation's large-scale capitalistic industries excluded unions, and of course had no agreements of any kind with them.　The most active combatants against unions were the automotive, rubber, iron and steel, cement, electrical equipment, oil and textile industries.　Their substitutes for unions in the earlier years after 1896 were labor spies called "undercover men," and later the setting up of personnel departments in charge of many kinds of "Welfare," and after 1917 the organization of plans of employe representation ("company unions").

Industrial Spies

Espionage of their own work-forces was conducted by individual corporations, employers' associations and by detective agencies that specialized in this work.　Details concerning corporation undercover men cannot be given because their activities were necessarily secret.　Despite public denials by many corporations that they maintained spy systems, the corporations' own private admissions, adventitious disclosures, and the confessions of spies substantiated the fact.　To uncover spy systems, a good guide was to look for the most bellicose employers; when these rocks against unionism were upset, generally there was revealed under them a nest of borers.　That the steel companies were riddled with spies was proved at the time of the strike of 1919.

Undercover Men.—Usually, it was the largest corporations that had permanent espionage corps; the little fellows nevertheless thought they needed spies at times of threatened strike or ebullient grievances.　Their associations then came to their rescue. Association undercover men were inserted among the aroused employes, discovered the causes of unrest, and spotted the leaders of incipient revolt. The latter were discharged upon some pretext and the soreness of the others was either salved or ignored.

An identical procedure was followed when one or more employers in a community wanted to rid themselves of recognized unions so as to operate "open shops." Among the associations that rendered these services were the National Metal Trades, Manufacturers (N. A. M.), Erectors, Founders, Employing Printers, and United Typothetae. Also engaged in kindred services were the Local Builders' Exchanges, Citizens' Alliances (Denver, Minneapolis, St. Paul, and Duluth), the Associated Employers of Indianapolis, American Plan Association of Cleveland, Industrial Association of San Francisco, and numerous other Associations, Alliances, Councils, and some with such other terms in their titles as American (Plan), Constitutional, or Citizens'.

Spy Agencies.—The first well-known commercial spy organization was Pinkerton's, earliest attracting notice in the Molly Maguire Case (1876). Incidentally, the career of this organization and the acknowledged methods of its successors cast doubt on the justice rendered the Molly Maguires. The Pinkerton Agency, without going out of business, yielded primacy to other competitors just before the World War, its last conspicuous notoriety being in the Governor Steunenberg murder trial involving the Western Federation of Miners. It appeared indirectly in the Sacco-Vanzetti case. At about the time of the *Los Angeles Times* case, the William J. Burns Agency came to the fore, followed by the Sherman Detective Agency (later, successively, the Sherman Service, Inc., and Sherman Corporation), the Baldwin-Felts Detective Agency, Mooney and Boland, Corporations Auxiliary Company, the Railway Audit and Inspection Company, and the most appropriately nicknamed "Black Jack" Jerome. A later conspicuous strike-breaking agency was that of Pearl L. Bergoff.

Their Services.—These agencies not only furnished spies upon demand, but served as strike-breakers, armed guards, and—when sworn—deputy sheriffs. Previously, these same men had broken nearly every criminal law and engaged in every underworld activity. The companies' own prospectuses boasted their ability to bore into any union situation and get themselves elected to union offices. From the inside, they sent reports to their clients and, at times of tension, influenced the union in ways to weaken it or bring discredit upon it. When industrial relations were too peaceful for the profits of the agencies, they were known to organize a union, or stir discontent so as to frighten clients into signing contracts. They never called this racketeering, but considered it sales promotion. While the spy chiefs shook down their clients, the strong-arm men on duty mulcted the scabs.

The heyday of these spy corporations was in the troubled years that came right after the World War, 1919-22. They reaped a harvest in the employers' Open-Shop Campaign of 1920-22 which was the employers' counter attack of the strikes of 1919-22. The Bergoff agency alone, by 1924, had made a profit of $10 million.

During the remaining years, until 1929, both employers and many spy outfits became more sophisticated. Employe representation (company unions) and Welfare Work were most popular in those years; therefore, the espionage emphasis was dropped. Faced with dwindling income from their straight stuff, the spy corporations shifted to advice on personnel matters, in some cases pointing this shift in function by a change in title. Upon need, though, they could revert to strong arm methods, e.g., against "Reds." Moreover, there were secret methods of supply to employers of arms, ammunition, and war-gases.

In the wake of the big espionage companies there swam a number of little ones. As a rule, these were more unprincipled than their prototypes.

Agency Patrons.—Among the known patrons of professional spies were about a dozen Class 1 railroads, several city transit systems, individual corporations in the paper, packing, textile, steel, arms and ammunition, flour, electrical equipment, oil, rubber, and wire communication industries. Banks and hotels also had been clients.

What did they get for the millions paid to spies? On the one hand they were freed from the restraints of unionism while on the other they were preyed upon by their own spies—every parasite feeds on its host—and the presence of spies among the work-force made the latter suspicious, sullen, and venomous. To the unions, the public knowledge of the employers' "stool pigeons" and hired espionage agents furnished an excellent alibi; any violence could be charged to spies and disowned as a union tactic.

Anti-Union Employers' Associations

Employers, of the kinds we have described, acted as individuals or if perchance there was agreement between them it was secret. There were, however, many employers' associations that openly defied unions. One of these was the National Erectors' Association composed of companies manufacturing iron and steel, together with fabricators of this material, such as the American Bridge Company and Marshall-McClintock. The latter was a Mellon concern until sold sometime after the World War to the Bethlehem Steel Company.

National Erectors.—The National Erectors' Association's belligerency was aimed at the Bridge and Structural Iron Workers' International Association with whom the Erectors had signed trade agreements, between 1902 and 1905. A strike that year, against the American Bridge Company, marked the end of a two year closed-shop agreement and converted the Erectors into an implacable foe of unions. The fights between these two organizations were little short of war; for on both sides the men were selected groups of physically strong, mentally daring individuals. Dynamite, one of the "tools" of the industry, was freely used against each side. When in 1910 the *McNamara-Los Angeles Times* case "broke," and when in the next year suits against more than 30 of the union officers and members resulted in sojourns in Leavenworth Penitentiary, the Erectors might be termed the "war's" victor.[1]

The Erectors then turned their power against construction contractors in large cities who hired any kind of union men. Contractors who would not operate on an "open-shop" basis got no steel from manufacturers closely allied with the Erectors' Association. This was a secret tactic so the Erectors never were cited for restriction of interstate commerce; after the World War (December 15, 1920), Mr. Eugene Grace, President of the Bethlehem Steel Company, admitted while on the witness stand in New York that his company had used this means of extending the "open-shop."

The Bridge and Structural Iron Workers' International Association which, before its "war," had a membership of about 12,000 lost steadily until after 1914. From that year to 1920, the union rose to its peak membership of 24,000 members. Thereafter, it sank back to 12,000. The Erectors never abandoned their hostility; so these membership figures indicated work beyond the Erectors control; that is federal, state, and municipal construction, and building in "closed-shop" cities.

National Metal Trades' Association

An equally irreconcilable enemy of unionism was the National Metal Trades' Association. In 1900, this organization had a national one-year agreement with the Machinists' Union, providing for a 54-hour week and for conciliation of disputes. In 1901, the union asked for an increase in the hourly rate of pay so that the shorter hours would yield the same income as in 1900. When the employers refused, the union, in May 1901, called a national strike; this was so effective, yet at the same time produced so much hard feeling among employers, that the latter through their National Metal Trades' Association agreed to fight unions.

Its Methods.—The methods used against unions by the National Metal Trades' Association were principally three. The

---

[1] These cases are described in Chapter 13.

members helped each other in strikes.   Assistance was rendered not only in money but in doing the work of struck shops, a supplement (more frequently a substitute) for furnishing strikebreakers in the struck shops.   Secondly, the Association became an employment agency.   In each area where it had members, the Association maintained an office from which the members hired their labor.   Each office kept a file of names—furnished by all the members—of workmen who were "trouble makers" or inefficient; that is, a "blacklist."   Hence, a wage earner in bad grace with any member became graceless to every member. Change of name or disguise might get a blacklisted man a job at a distance; but generally the undercover men discovered him or perhaps he himself made a slip leading to unmasking and discharge.   This terrible weapon—terrible because it meant banishment from a skilled trade—was used without mercy.   The third tactic was affiliation with the National Association of Manufacturers.   What this meant is described a few pages beyond. The Metal Trades' Association, if not the backbone of the N. A. M., was one of its strongest ribs.

National Founders' Association

Another rib was the National Founders' Association.   The foundry industry was most complex; for it contained little, one-floor shops doing a few gray-iron castings and also great multiple plants with floor and bench molders able to make any shape that was cast in iron.   Besides, there were little and great foundries attached to machine shops, some as tiny as manufacturers of fireplace shovels, some builders of locomotives.   The whole industry was nearly as competitive as clothing manufacture.   Hence, the attempt between 1900 and 1904 to write national trade agreements was quite unsatisfactory to both sides. Minimum wage rates, the proportion of apprentices to journeymen—the union also insisted on a 7-year apprenticeship—and the hours of work for such disparate plants and such geographically separated places as Atlanta, Moline, Detroit, and Worcester were certain to cause heart-burnings.

Rather than struggle with the Molders' Union, the Founders' Association, in 1904, decided on maintenance of "open-shops."

This policy made them the enemy of unionism, and their Presidents were among the most vociferous opponents of unions. The Association eagerly formed alliances with other anti-union organizations.

It will be noticed that the dates, upon which employers became belligerent against unions, all fell shortly after 1900. There were two reasons for this coincidence. One was the rapid growth and success of unions between 1896 and 1904; the American Federation of Labor had 265,000 members on the first and 1,700,000 on the second date, an average percent increase (5-56.9%) per year never again equalled. The other was the drubbing given to massed capital in the Anthracite Strike of 1902.

These two reasons given here were particularly pertinent in the creation of the two strongest antagonists of unions, the Anti-Boycott Association and the National Association of Manufacturers.

Anti-Boycott Association

The Anti-Boycott Association was conceived in 1901 by Charles H. Merritt, Dietrich Loewe (both hat manufacturers), and Walter Gordon Merritt, then a fledgling lawyer. These men thought that "individual character, incentive, and responsibility are still believed to be the cornerstone of our social structure." They assumed that the United States was unique in the cultivation of these characteristics, and that therefore "it surpassed all other nations." Yet they saw the United Hatters of North America, a union, striding so roughly over the whole hat industry, enforcing the closed shop by strikes implemented with boycotts, that in 1901 there were only 10 "open-shop" hat factories in existence.

In February 1902, letters were sent by the above-named persons to all the manufacturers who had been listed in the A. F. of L. *Federationist* as "unfair," asking opinion as to the feasibility of an organization to fight boycotts. Although the majority of replies were negative, Charles Merritt and his Bridgeport, Conn., legal adviser, Daniel Davenport, decided to go ahead as soon as 100 employers signified approval of the plan.

The 100th charter member was secured in April 1903; some of the 100, however, were afraid to make open avowal of allegiance, and others still more wary of their names appearing in the Association's books, joined through their legal counsel.

The Association's purpose was to invoke the power of the courts against unions.

The First Case.—Their first case was a strike, May 7, 1903, of four unions enrolling 800 employes against the Kellogg Switchboard and Supply Company of Chicago. The Association secured an injunction May 25, 1903, against the strikers and some of these violating it were cited for contempt of court. The injunction was upheld by the Illinois Supreme Court on June 22, 1905, in a decision that became a precedent for a long line of labor cases in Illinois and other states. This success was added to by 12 successful damage suits against Chicago labor.

Danbury Hatters' Case.—The case which really established the Anti-Boycott Association was the Danbury Hatters, against whom Loewe and Company, in 1903, brought a damage suit under the Sherman Act.[2] The Association furnished the funds and the legal talent for the 14 years this case was in litigation. In that time, the case was heard before two juries, was four times before the United States Circuit Court of Appeals, and three times before the United States Supreme Court. A final judgment of $252,300 was obtained against the 240 members of the Hatters' Union, 60 of whom, meanwhile, had disappeared or died.

Other Cases.—Long before the Danbury Hatters' Case was closed, the Association had appeared in others. The first was the Buck's Stove and Range Company injunction and contempt cases which the Association entered upon plea of its member, James W. VanCleave, president of the company involved. For like reasons, the Association supplied the money and lawyers for the Duplex Printing Company Case and Bedford Stone case. It cooperated in the Coronado Coal Case and was sym-

[2] This and the next mentioned case are described at length in Chapter 9.

pathetic with American Steel Foundries in their case against the Tri-City Trades' Council. After the Herrin Illinois "massacre" in 1922, the Association used the suability ruling of the Coronado case to assist the Southern Illinois Coal Company; but the United Mine Workers flanked the Association by buying this company at an excess value—so said the Association—of $500,000.

Lobbying.—The Association was active in state cases and as lobbyist before state legislatures. It was opposed to state anti-injunction laws, so when the Massachusetts law of 1914 was declared unconstitutional by the Massachusetts Supreme Judicial Court, the Association rejoiced; but when the Arizona law, in the *Truax v. Corrigan* case, was declared unconstitutional by the United States Supreme Court, the joy was much greater. Said Walter Gordon Merritt, counsel, "A political commandment [is] thus thundered forth from the greatest tribunal in the world to the legislatures of forty-eight states, 'Thou shalt not deny protection to business.' "

The Association was so active in New York in getting injunctions against building trades and other unions for interference with interstate commerce, that the unions, in 1916, brought the Association into court. The ground was in New York laws of 1909 and 1911 that forbade a corporation to practice or appear as an attorney or to hold itself out as entitled to practice law or furnish legal advice. The unions claimed that the Association was an incorporated "trust" of lawyers. The Association, however, convinced two of the three judges who heard the case that the acts of the Association and its agents were lawful.

The Association, represented by Daniel Davenport and James Beck, lobbied before the federal Congress. The bills that aroused their most strenuous efforts were those that would remove or lessen the legal restraints of labor. For other matters, it supported the lobbies which in states and in Washington acted for the National Association of Manufacturers.

Change of Name.—In 1919, because the name Anti-Boycott Association represented a largely obsolete cause, and because the Association's work had greatly broadened from the original principles, the name was altered to the "League for Industrial Rights." At the same time, a periodical, *Law and Labor,* began publication under League auspices. The journal digested the most important legal cases in which organized labor was a party.

There can be no doubt that the Association and League shaped labor history. It influenced unions to drop the boycott as a weapon, and it circumscribed the effectiveness of strikes as well as of picketing. It hampered unionization by broadcasting the Hitchman case decision that "yellow dog contracts" were legal; and it opened the unions to new attack by utilization of the suability dictum in the Coronado case, to say nothing of the mass of injunctions that arose from the precedent of the Hatters' case which made unions amenable to the Sherman Act.

On the other hand, it stimulated unions to political effort after 1906; and it made organized labor contemptuous of courts, a fact that may drastically change American history. By associating in the popular mind a connection between capitalism, the courts, and the Republican Party, the League may have damaged all three. The Association-League cast its pebble in the stream of history, and the ripples widened far beyond the Leagues' ken.

National Association of Manufacturers

The historians of the National Association of Manufacturers credit the first suggestion for such an organization to Thomas H. Martin, editor of the *Dixie Manufacturer.* But the man who was the leader at the Cincinnati convention in January 1895 when the N. A. M. was formed was Colonel Thomas P. Egan. Among the other organizers were William McKinley and Senator Foraker of Ohio.

For seven years after its inception, the N. A. M. was a small voluntary association whose chief interests were tariff reform (upwards) and the promotion of foreign trade. The Spanish-American and Boer Wars enlarged markets for American producers and turned their attention to further gains of business in foreign trade. At home, profits were satisfactory from the domestic pick-up from the "lows" of the 1893-96 depression as well as from the increase in overseas traffic. Labor was almost fully employed and with the rising strength of new unionism was working under trade agreements.

Becomes Anti-Union.—Around 1900, many employers began to fear the new-found strength of unions and so as trade agreements expired, began to contest their renewal. With this spirit of resistance to union encroachments, the rabid anti-unionism of four leading manufacturers swung the N. A. M. over to an hostility to unions that dominated its later career. These rudders were John Kirby, Jr., C. W. Post, David M. Parry, and J. W. VanCleave.

John Kirby, Jr., organized in 1900 a local association of manufacturers in Dayton, Ohio, whose primary purpose was to make Dayton an "open-shop" city. Succeeding in Dayton, Mr. Kirby assisted in the organization of similar associations with the same purpose in Elmira, Akron, Columbus, Detroit, St. Louis, Indianapolis, and Chicago. Kirby was president of the N. A. M. from 1909-13, and was a dominant figure in that body both before and after his term as administrative head.

C. W. Post, who quickly made a fortune from the manufacture of cereal foods, banned all unionism from his plants in Battle Creek, Michigan, and on account of his prominence there as a citizen together with his investments in other local activities, did all he could to make that city "safe" from unions. He then turned his virulence and money into any association, including the N. A. M., that endeavored to make the nation "safe" from the same "demogogues." In these activities, he was in direct contrast to his fellow townsman, Dr. J. H. Kellogg, and the manufacturing company that developed the Doctor's ideas at Battle Creek.

David M. Parry became president of the N. A. M. at a convention in New Orleans in 1903. It was in his inaugural address that he assailed unions and all their works, a condemnation that was supported by convention resolutions, and so marked the date of the change of the N. A. M. to militancy against unions. J. W. VanCleave was president of his own St. Louis anti-union

Citizens' Industrial Association and first vice-president of the national body of that organization, and president of the N. A. M., following Parry.

Growth.—With these militant men to steer it, the N. A. M. at once after 1903 became the greatest organized combatant of organized labor. In the year after Parry's first attack, the N. A. M. increased in membership more than 100% (990 to 3,000), which indicates that anti-union employers needed only a quartet of bellwethers.

Shortly, several hundred local manufacturers' associations were joined on the one hand into state associations and on the other into special-interest national associations. Then, sired by the N. A. M., all these bodies were united into a National Industrial Council.[3] Throughout its career, the N. A. M. became the parent of individual organizations formed for some specific purpose. The Citizens' Industrial Association was a short-lived body whose purpose was to fight against unionism until the N. A. M. took over the job in its Open-Shop Department (later known as Industrial Relations Department). The National Council had the specialized function of lobbying. The Committee for the Rejection of the 20th Amendment fought against changing the federal constitution so that Congress could legislate on child labor. The National Industrial Conference Board (nominally independent, but nevertheless a creature of the N. A. M.), was a fact-finding body.

Organization.—To conduct all its activities, the N. A. M. set up four internal departments, viz: Trade, Law, Publicity, and Open-Shop (changed to Ind. Relations). The Trade Department carried on the original purposes of the N. A. M., that is, the increase of domestic and foreign trade. In connection with this department, the N. A. M. furnished its members with many services such as trade contacts, translation service, and the like. The Law Department analyzed, digested, and furnished arguments concerning legislative bills, besides giving

---

[3] This was organized in 1907 as the National Council for Industrial Defense but changed its name, in 1919, to National Industrial Council.

other legal services.   The Publicity Department prepared material for newspapers, magazines, and learned journals; and supplied speakers upon demand.   A separate National Manufacturers' Company published the periodicals *American Industries*
and *American Trade Index*.   Other publicity was obtained in
the *Open-Shop Bulletin,* and over 100 special bulletins, pamphlets, and books.   All of this publicity was directly aimed at
the press, magazines, preachers, professors, students (particularly debate teams), and public officials, on the theory that if the
N. A. M. convinced leaders it could swing public opinion in
favor of N. A. M. ideas.

The Open-Shop (Industrial Relations) Department, itself,
was divided into five subsidiaries: (1) Open-Shop, 1920; (2)
Fuel Supply, 1924; (3) Employment Relations (it had several
names besides this one); (4) Junior Education and Employment, 1925 (in connection with child labor proposals); and (5)
Women's Bureau, 1926.   The Fuel Supply division cooperated
with the National Erectors' Association in trying to stop the
spread of the United Mine Workers' Union after the Jacksonville Agreement, a national trade agreement that retained war-
won hours and wages for coal miners.

The N. A. M. was a congeries of units managed through
three offices, one in New York City, another in Washington,
D. C., and the third, in the home town of whoever was president of the N. A. M.   The New York City office was run in
conjunction with the National Industrial Council.

Purposes.—The N. A. M., in its own or paraphrased words,
stood for: "A person's right in a contract is as much property
as any tangible asset."   Personal liberty, free contract, and
property rights are the key stones of America; and the Constitution is their safeguard.   "The real and ideal union is the one
between employer and employe."   "Employers' interests are
those of society, including its working-class members."   "The
interests of wage earners and those of employers are identical,"
"the employers are labor's best friends," and all that labor
leaders can offer labor is "half-baked theories."   It preferred
government control of wages, hours, and working conditions to

union recognition and collective bargaining for "the opinion of the state, at least in its legislative expression, will largely reproduce the opinion of those who hold the keys of economic power." Yet, "state insurance is one of the vicious German ideas yet existent in this country."

The N. A. M. stood for the "open-shop" and pointed to Detroit, Indianapolis, and Los Angeles for illustrations of open-shop beneficence; and to San Francisco, England, and Australia for examples of union-ridden places. It "was not against unions as such" but was against militancy in unions and against collective bargaining "with outsiders." It "was not against the right of labor to organize, but was against vicious misuse of organization."

It was for group insurance—to reduce labor turnover; for piece work; for Americanization; and for employe stock ownership. After 1920, it was for employe representation plans "if properly instituted and operated." It was for the Federal Board of Vocational Education. It was for, among others, Congressmen Littlefield of Maine, Joseph Cannon, and Nicholas Longworth; Senators Foraker, Frye, Aldrich, Smoot, Penrose, and Watson; Presidents McKinley, Taft, and Harding. It favored Carroll D. Wright, his successor Charles Nagel, and James J. Davis as heads of the national Department of Labor. It endorsed the League for Industrial Rights, the Founders', National Metal Trades' Associations, and the Chamber of Commerce of the United States for their "righteous crusades."

What It Opposed.—Some of the things opposed by the N. A. M., together with some of the comments it made about them follow.

The National Association of Manufacturers was against:

1. Any shortening of the work period. For the proposals were merely part of union plans to reduce output. Would increase costs and give our markets to avaricious Europeans. Would increase the cost of living. Would, by the leisure afforded, increase labor's craving for luxuries. Would be against the best interests of the ambitious. Was impractical. Would trend towards the

Arena as it did in Rome; and remember what happened to that empire.

2. Any imposition by governments of hour provisions for labor done under government contract. "For these were serious and unwarrantable interferences with the businesses of many manufacturers." Would increase the costs of government and raise taxes.

3. Any government regulation of wages. So opposed any interference with Taylor scientific management methods in arsenals, opposed the War Labor Board, the Railway Labor Board's power over wages, the Seamen's Act of 1915—"it ignored the right of free contract"—the Adamson Act, and any affiliation of government employes with the American Federation of Labor.

4. Any restriction of immigration save the elimination of the obviously unfit. It opposed the Chinese Exclusion Act of 1906, the Literacy Test bills and law, the Quota System of 1921 and 1924, and the National Origins Act of 1927.

5. Any restriction of child labor by law. For this was a local problem. Would extend control to every feature of a minor's life. Would build an intolerable federal (or state) bureaucracy.

6. Any legislation sponsored by union labor; especially shorter hours, minimum wages, or relief from court and other legal restraints; called it, "class legislation." The N. A. M. in these matters commended both the activities of the League for Industrial Rights and the American judiciary.

7. Against the 16th, 17th and 19th amendments to the federal constitution. The 16th (income tax) "was socialistic and unfair in its exemptions." The 17th (direct election of senators). "Reduces the inherent purposes, powers, and functions of our national charter." "The Senate never was intended to be a direct popular body." Later—"a noticeably marked decadence in the Senate has taken place since the passage of the 17th amend-

ment." The 19th (woman suffrage). "The day may come when men will have to beg the women for the right to vote and govern."

8. Any restriction of property rights, or restrictions on freedom of contract.

9. Against Socialists, Bolshevists, "Vicious Reformers," "Dilettantes," "Sentimentalists," "Agitators," and "Demagogues."

Methods.—In order to realize a society that included its own "fors" and excluded those things the N. A. M. was against, the Association relied upon propaganda, lobbying, and the work of its Industrial Relations Department. In respect to its propaganda, it should be noticed in addition to what already has been said that the N. A. M. by no means relied upon its own publicists, but was able to secure the services—or endorse and distribute the work—of some of our "best citizens." C. W. Eliot, President of Harvard, was a frequent contributor by pen and tongue to the causes of the N. A. M. So, also, were Chancellor Day of Syracuse, President G. B. Cutter of Colgate, and Dean Robertson of New York University. Men in the public eye like John Hays Hammond and Henry Cabot Lodge were on the N. A. M. publishers' lists. From the churches, S. Parkes Cadman and the Rev. John L. Belford were representative contributors of N. A. M. material. The N. A. M. firmly believed in the persuasive power of big names, and used that kind as often as possible.

Lobbying.—The N. A. M. had two main programs; one was propaganda by which indirectly to hamper unions, the other was lobbying. Lobbying was a legitimate activity no matter if the word has gained a connotation of deviousness. There were "good" lobbyists and "bad" ones, the segregation depending on whether lobbyists worked for what a person wanted or against one's pet desires. Lobbying has existed as long as representative government—not that its age alone makes it respectable. In our First Congress, lobbyists worked for or against the funding of our national debt and the assumption of state debts. The site of Washington, D. C., was itself the result of a lobbying and logrolling dinner party at which Jefferson and Hamilton were guests. Lobbying at Washington grew apace after 1880, and after 1911 it became an avowed profession. This kind of pressure-politics increased because the House rules were changed in 1911, shearing much of the Speaker's power over legislation. Other factors were open committee hearings, the direct election of Senators—a breach in the citadel of privilege—and the decline of Party power.

So the N. A. M. and its National Industrial Council, in setting up a lobbying agency in Washington, merely joined 520 national bodies that had listed addresses in the Capitol city. There were twice as many persons in this "Third House" as in the other two,—the House of Representatives and Senate; and if all the employes of the "Third House" were included the total was ten times the size of the bodies the lobbyists hoped to influence.

The N. A. M. was not lost in the crowd of its fellows; for it belonged to the small group of most powerful lobbyists. Exact delineation of this group is impossible; but most persons would agree that there was eligible for it the lobbies for Farmers, Laborers (American Federation of Labor and Railway Brotherhood groups), G. A. R.; V. F. W. and Legion, the Drys, and Big Business. The latter were represented not only by the N. A. M. but by the League for Industrial Rights, the Erectors' Association, the National Electric Light Association, the American Railway Association, Railroad Owners' Association, the Chamber of Commerce of the United States of America, and others, the trade associations alone totalling 100 organizations. Sixty of these lobbying organizations met at the Monday Lunch Club where, under the cloak of sociability, many an item of business was transacted. Daniel Davenport and W. G. Merritt of the L. I. R., Walter Drew of the Erectors consulted with J. A. Emery of the N. A. M. All of these met with spokesmen for the Chamber of Commerce of the U. S. A.

Activities at Capitol.—The N. A. M.'s Washington office kept a file of every bill presented in Congress, analyzed and digested every one that seemed to fit their interests, noted the time and place of committee hearings, and kept all this available for instant reference. Its findings were transmitted to members in a fortnightly *Washington Service Bulletin.* The chief contact-man was James Augustin Emery, a suave, personable, astute lawyer; he was assisted by whoever was Secretary of the N. A. M. and others upon occasion. Emery did not need much help; he had a longer, more intimate contact with Congress than most Congressmen or Senators; he often had the ear of Presidents and Cabinet officers; he was aware of the ways of Washington press correspondents; and in short, he knew his way around. If he needed extra pressure, his word brought bushels of telegrams or letters from the 75,000 concerns affiliated with the N. A. M. and National Industrial Council. These messages came from men who employed 6-7 million workers and controlled the output of about 80% of the manufactured goods of the United States. In the days before 1911, when the Speaker of the House selected committeemen and controlled legislation, and before 1913, when Senators were elected by state legislatures, Mr. Emery's job was not burdensome.

His office in 1913 made a serious slip; it discharged its field agent, Martin Mulhall, without first getting from him his files on matters concerning the N. A. M.

Mulhall had attempted in Maine politics to play off certain liquor interests against the state Republican Party, and so enraged the "dry" Congressman Littlefield, that he used his strong connection with the N. A. M. to cause the dismissal of Mulhall. Mulhall tried to give, without remuneration, his documents to the American Federation of Labor; to W. B. Wilson, then Chairman of the House Committee on Labor; and to W. R. Hearst—but none of these would touch Mulhall's evidence. For a consideration of $10,000, Mulhall sold his material to the *New York World* and this newspaper published the story, in conjunction with the *Chicago Tribune,* on June 29, 1913.

The instantaneous uproar over the article reverberated in Congress, so that both House and Senate started investigations into lobbying. The hearings continued throughout the rest of

1913 and into the next year. The printed hearings of the House committee covered 2,936 pages in four volumes, and those of the Senate 4,013 pages with as many more in an appendix, four volumes for each.[4]

Despite this mass of material, neither house discovered anything upon which to base criminal charges; but it did unearth many inexplicable situations, and cast considerable doubt upon the ethics of the N. A. M. and its representatives, James A. Emery and Marshall Cushing. A Congressman, James T. McDermott, a unionist himself, and supported by unions as Representative from a Chicago stockyard district, had apparently played Judas for the silver of the N. A. M. He was said, also, to have permitted the N. A. M. to use his franking privilege. His page, I. H. McMichalls, appeared to have accepted pay for eavesdropping in the service of the N. A. M. On the other hand, Emery and his associates had hurled "tu quoque" at the American Federation of Labor lobby trying to show that it also had not been free from sin.

The upshot of the whole affair damaged somewhat the reputations of the N. A. M. and Emery, but soon the scandal was forgotten by every one except the unions; they taunted Emery with the memory on favorable occasions.

State Lobbying.—Lobbying at Washington the N. A. M. did for itself; but in the states it relied upon state associations of manufacturers. In both propaganda and lobbying, it cooperated with the League for Industrial Rights, the National Founders' Association, the National Erectors' Association, and the Chamber of Commerce of the United States. These bodies reciprocated. There was a rough division of labor amongst the group; the Founders and Erectors fought unions in the field; the L. I. R. charged them in the courts; and the other two blocked them when they could in legislative halls, and exposed their sins and sophistries in the press or on the rostrum.

---

[4] References: (1) Hearings Before a Sub-Committee of the Committee on Judiciary, U. S. Senate 63rd Congress 1st S. Res. 92. (2) Hearings Before the Select Committee of the House of Representatives, Appointed Under House Resolution 198, 63rd Cong. 1st Session.

Accomplishments.—Was the N. A. M. a success? The answer cannot be given in as positive terms as it was in respect to the achievements of the L. I. R., because the work of the N. A. M. was almost entirely negative. It was *against,* seldom *for.* This creates difficulties in the measurement of things that did not happen. Nevertheless, it can be said that the N. A. M. delayed union programs and other reform projects such as a Child Labor Amendment. It alienated opinion from these measures among people whose opinions influenced a great many more. It may have been, in part, responsible for the fact that the American labor movement had in it scarcely perceptible motion, but instead became a "job trust" fighting capital "trusts" for existence.

Chamber of Commerce of the United States

The N. A. M. was one of the founders of the Chamber of Commerce of the United States. Compared in age with the organizations already discussed, the Chamber of Commerce of the United States was an infant; but if rated according to power, it ranked ahead of all of them.

In 1910-11, a number of commercial organizations felt the need of a national body to speak authoritatively in the name of united business. At the same time, both President Taft and his Secretary of Commerce and Labor, Charles Nagel, made public statements as to the need of the federal government for some organization that could be relied upon to tell administrative officers what business thought about national issues. There were plenty of business lobbies, but since none could speak for a majority the result was conflicting pressures. On their side, business men were restive under the attacks of muckrakers and the drift of governments toward regulation of industry. The Boston and Chicago Chambers of Commerce each tried to start a national organization, but failed. The successful incentive finally came from President Taft and Secretary Nagel who invited representatives of well-known commercial bodies to attend a conference on February 12, 1912, under the auspices of the Department of Commerce and Labor.

This conference succeeded in creating the framework and temporary top-flight officers for a national commercial organization; and called a convention for April 22, 1912, sending invitations to all known Chambers of Commerce, Trade Associations, and business corporations that might be interested. At the convention, with 700 delegates in attendance, the Chamber of Commerce of the United States was launched, with Harry A. Wheeler as President. He had held the same office during the previous year in the Chicago Chamber of Commerce, and also (then) was Vice-President of the Union Trust Company.

Membership.—The Chamber of Commerce of the United States had at first two and later (after 1917) three classes of members. First, there were members representing already organized groups such as city and state chambers of commerce, national trade associations and associations for special purposes. Only those in places larger than 5,000 in population were sought; of this narrowed field, the maximum enrolled in the Chamber of Commerce of the United States was about 17%, or in figures 1,500 out of about 8,000. They paid dues ranging from $10 to $700, but averaging about $\frac{1}{2}$ of 1% of their own collected dues. Secondly, individual corporations or firms doing a business in excess of $50,000 a year were accepted as members. There were about 8,000 of these, paying minimum dues of $25. Finally, about the same class of individuals were installed as associate members, the distinction being in dues; this class, about 5,000 in number, paid up to $10,000 a year, although less than 100 paid more than $1,000 apiece. The financial strength of the Chamber was derived mostly from the second and third classes. In total membership, the Chamber grew steadily until the 1921 depression, and then after 1924 began again to climb, but largely in the second and third membership classes.

Functions.—In functions, the Chamber at first merely mobilized national business opinion by means of referenda. Because this might have seemed a small return for members' dues, the Chamber began expanding the services rendered— such as translation, research, and information—until it had seven service departments, each acting as a research body for a special branch of business. As to the referenda, these, with passing years, became less a compilation of what members thought, than questions, either that the administrators wanted the members to consider or to give statistical confirmation to what the Washington office was asserting to be true. At first a funnel, the referenda became a hammer.

A corresponding change occurred in the Chamber's relations with the federal government. When very young, the Chamber transmitted the data the government requested; and in return asked for defense against invasions of the province of business. Within a year, the Chamber was invading the Bureau of Foreign and Domestic Commerce, and reaching for more influence over Congress. In short order, the Chamber became one of the most influential lobbies in Washington and was rated by some as the most powerful business lobby. The Washington headquarters, at first housing a staff of 11 in two small rented rooms, soon had its own magnificent structure directly across from the White House and operated on a budget of $3 million. The members "back home" were manipulated so as to put weight into the pressure exerted by the lobby.

Lobbying.—As a lobbyist, the Chamber used the technique of the best—files, interviews, prepared speeches, committee hearings, and letters, telegrams, or personal appearances from the constituency. To keep its own members informed, the Chamber published a weekly *Legislative Bulletin,* and the *Week's Work.* For public consumption, the Chamber issued a monthly, the *Nation's Business.* The motto of the Chamber was, "If it is not for the public good, it is not for the good of business." How the Chamber really interpreted this slogan probably was correctly stated in 1927 by its president, Pierson, when he said, "The people cannot prosper unless business can prosper."

In lobbying, the Chamber at first did not unduly run head-on into the American Federation of Labor lobby, for the Chamber's early interests were in taxation, a national budget, trade promotion, a merchant marine, and increased services to business by the Bureau of Foreign and Domestic Commerce. As Wilson's Administration became a plum tree for labor, the Chamber began to whet its axes. With Harding, Coolidge, and Hoover in office and all friendly to the Chamber, its lobby was used not only to advance its own interests but to resist the pressure of the labor lobby. While the Chamber was still very young, one of its originators, the National Association of Manufacturers, censured the Chamber's liberality in inviting labor and other "leftist" speakers to address its formal meetings. The N. A. M. resigned from the Chamber in 1922. In the later 1920's, the most conservative officer of the N. A. M. would have felt quite congenial in the atmosphere of many meetings of the Chamber. As a matter of fact, both organizations cooperated on many a lobbying foray, and both agreed on these principles; "More business in government and less government in business," and "Increase the services but decrease the regulation by government." Because labor believed in more government in business—nationalization of coal mines, railways, power, and credit—and in more regulation by government—minimum wages, maximum hours, the right to bargain collectively, redistribution of income by high taxes—labor clashed with both the N. A. M. and the Chamber of Commerce of the United States.

Post-War Open-Shop Campaign

"War time wages must be liquidated." With this cry, William H. Barr, president of the National Founders' Association rallied the most militant offensive taken by organized employers against organized labor in the generation after 1896. The open-shop drive of 1920-22 was backed by Mr. Barr's membership in 247 cities of 44 states; by J. P. Bird's National Association of Manufacturers and its satellites in the National Industrial Council in 250 cities; the National Erectors' Association; numerous city and state associations; and 470 purely open-shop associations. Among other leaders were the National Metal Trades' Association, the Employing Painters of America, the Associated General Contractors of America, the United

Typothetae of America, the Employing Photo-Engravers' Association, the National Association of Pattern Manufacturers, and the Railroad Executives' Advisory Committee. The members of the United States Chamber of Commerce voted on Referendum 31, June 9 to July 24, 1919, by a ballot of 1,676 to 4 in support of the declaration, "The Right of Open-Shop Operation is an essential part of the individual right of contract."

American Plan.—Andrew J. Allen, of the Associated Employers of Indianapolis, was credited with the suggestion of calling the open-shop the "American plan" and to organize the mass of open-shop opinion among employers into the "American Plan League." As a guide in the campaign 1920-22, the League never got far from its source in Indianapolis but the title "American Plan" was used everywhere, many local open-shop associations even putting it in their own name. The title was a shrewd choice; in 1920 the United States was unusually chauvinistic so any union that by inference was anti-American already was struck the first blow. Conversely, a movement labeled "American" disarmed and captured those of the public who might have rebelled if they had understood the selfishness of the promoters of the open-shop. Samuel Gompers, in a special article in the *New York Times* for September 17, 1922, declared he was ready to substantiate, with documentary proof, an assertion that the "American Plan" was a plot to crush unions. In retort, the open-shoppers charged unions with being monopolies unfair to the non-union workers.

Eugene Grace, president of the Bethlehem Steel Company, testified before the Lockwood Committee in New York City, December 15, 1920, that his company refused to sell steel to builders or contractors in the New York and Philadelphia districts if it was to be erected on a union labor basis. The National Grange, always ultra-conservative on social or non-farm economic questions, at its annual convention in Boston, November 1922, endorsed the open-shop policy. In the same month and place, Calvin Coolidge said that the Republican victory at the polls was a rebuke to organized labor. These various statements had a bearing upon Gompers' declaration of a plot.

Samuel Hayden Church, president of Carnegie Institute of Pittsburgh, Pa., printed a categorical denial of Gompers' plot story.   Church said, "What appeared to be a plot was in reality a country-wide public opinion condemnatory of the oppressive, dictatorial, criminal attitude of labor."

Methods.—Whether or not there was a plot led by the steel interests as Gompers believed, it was a fact that in the earlier part of the 1920's, open-shop agitation was hotly pressed in most parts of the country; it was particularly aggressive in the Middle West, South, Rocky Mountains, and Pacific Coast. The open methods of the campaign were great advertisements in newspapers, literally tons of booklets, folders, hand-bills, and pay-envelope inserts, platform speeches and debates, and open-shop labels.   Injunctions and other legal weapons were openly used against unions.   The secret activities included boycotts by banks, wholesalers, and manufacturers against employers with union agreements or against businesses in towns where a strike was in progress.   The Baldwin-Felts Detective Agency helped operators to keep West Virginia free from unionism; the other undercover agencies were not inactive elsewhere in the same cause.   The employment departments of national and local associations made rigorous use of the blacklist to cleanse towns of unionists.   The "yellow dog" individual contract was another device to preserve the non-unionists' right to free contract.

In contrast with these negative tactics, some of the more astute employers weaned their workers from unions by the introduction of employe representation (company unions) and Welfare Work.   Their own and hired undercover men sometimes helped in the stimulation of an appetite for these predigested substitutes, or, as was more often true, the employers poured propaganda for these things into their work-people. For this work and also for winning public approval, the politic employers hired public-relations counsel.   Formerly, worn-out newspapermen sometimes earned a precarious subsistence as publicity agents; but the example, after 1913, of Ivy E. Lee in changing the public's reaction to the name Rockefeller spurred other ambitious persons to make a profession of what had been hack-work. The demand for these services by large corporations after 1920 put the professional public-relations counsel on the highroad to wealth, a haven of fortune to aspiring newspapermen.

By the brutal force of capital power, or by the persuasive artifice of enticement employers put over the open-shop campaign. Unions reached their peak of power in 1920; never again, before 1929, did they stand in a position of command. The big industries were safely open-shop in 1922. Thereafter, there was no onslaught against unions; but open-shop attrition against unions among soft coal miners, building craftsmen, and printers as well as less conspicuous unionized trades continued, with the result that many local unions were the victims of the open-shop campaign.[5]

---

[5] The employers' use of Scientific Management and "company unions" is discussed in Chapters 1 and 7.

CHAPTER 7

METHODS FOR INDUSTRIAL PEACE

Much of the story of unions versus employers was tinctured with the terms of warfare. Yet, the generation after 1896 was conspicuous for a swelling sentiment against all kinds of war, and this desire for peaceful methods carried over into industrial relations. Since the strike was a variety of warfare, there was, as Stuart Chase has said, a feeling that "knocking a fellow's block off was a suitable method of settling disputes only among blockheads." Although proposals to outlaw strikes got slight sympathy from workers, they were not always hostile to suggestions that would reduce strikes. Their own favorite solution of the strike danger was the trade agreement.

Trade Agreement.—By a trade agreement was meant, an orderly negotiation by collective bargaining of the terms of work for a definite period of time. The terms included standard minimum rates of pay, and maximum hours of work, with overtime safeguarded by extra rates and limited in amount in a given period. Sometimes, further provisions were set down in respect to working conditions. The duration of trade agreements might be as short as six months in businesses subjected to extreme fluctuation, or three or more years in more stable industries. A trade agreement might be narrowed to one trade in one shop—although strictly that was a shop agreement—or broadened to include all the shops hiring a type of craftsman, or all types of craftsmen in a locality. Some trade agreements were national in scope.

When trade agreements were carefully drawn, they contained a method for interpretation of the agreement itself, and also a means for settling disputes during the life of the agreement. Finally, an agreement generally set forth a way of termination,

or negotiation of a replacement agreement when the existing
one expired.

The generation after 1896 did not invent the device of the
trade agreement; for the previous generation had tried them—
e.g., iron and steel workers and stove molders—yet the generation after 1896 perfected the technique and for a while increased the number of trade agreements.   These were described
at the beginning of the previous chapter, and as we showed the
choice between strikes and peace by means of trade agreements
probably was one for which employers were as much responsible
as workers.

Strikes for workers were so much a risk to jobs, savings,
income, health, and even life that workers did not readily resort
to them until all other measures failed, and this was especially
true if the workers were in an experienced union.   If the trade
agreement was available to workers, they generally preferred
it to the uncertainties of strikes.   Employers, who were hostile
to unions and who thought they were in a stronger economic
position than their own workers, made a deliberate choice in
favor of strikes, because they deemed these less costly than the
continuous increase in costs that would follow the recognition of
a union in a trade agreement.   Hence, the paucity of trade
agreements doubtless should be attributed to employers, and
was a result of the relative superiority of massed capital to
massed labor—a superiority that increased as the years advanced
through the generation.

Not a Contract.—Aside from all that was implied in the
recognition of a union in a trade agreement, some employers
objected to them because they were not legal contracts.   If a
union violated a trade agreement, an employer had no recourse
at law.   Inasmuch as scarcely any union was incorporated but
was merely a voluntary association, a union in the eyes of the
law was not a responsible legal "person," and hence, could not
write a work contract enforceable by the courts.   The liability
of unions for suits or injunctions, under the Sherman Act, had
no bearing on the legal compulsion to fulfill a work agreement
arrived at by collective bargaining.   To enforce labor as in-

dividuals or in unions, to comply with work agreements, ran afoul of the 13th Amendment prohibiting involuntary servitude. The only power that forced obedience to a trade agreement was the ability of each side to damage the other.

Of course, employers also were relieved from legal compulsion to carry out any trade agreement they signed; they broke agreements when circumstances favored them just as often as unions did when circumstances were reversed. To the credit of both employers and unions, it should be known that many of them refused to take advantage of conditions to break agreements. Nevertheless, the lack of legal enforcement was a factor in preventing wide popularity of trade agreements as a means of avoidance of strikes. Despite employer opposition and non-enforceability, the device of the trade agreement was effective in the reduction of strife in the cases where it was used.

Beyond its usefulness in the preservation of order, the trade agreement also was notable as a step toward worker control of production. It was a start toward industrial democracy; for it gave workers a chance to legislate the rules under which they worked. By this much it reduced the employers' autocratic control of industry. Doubtless employers sensed this result, and it made them unwilling to relinquish any more power than the nature of their industry made requisite.

Incorporation of Unions.—Digressing for a moment, let us seek the answer to the question, "If trade agreements were unenforceable why did not unions incorporate?" In commenting upon certain San Francisco labor troubles, the National Association of Manufacturers once said, "Organized labor must accept legal and social responsibility for its acts to an extent equal to its power." This meant employers wanted unions to be incorporated instead of being voluntary associations. As early as 1885-86, Congressional acts permitted national unions with headquarters in Washington to incorporate under federal charters. Ten or more states soon afterwards made specific provisions for incorporating unions, while others granted charters to unions under their general incorporation acts. Yet scarcely any unions in the last forty years have incorporated.

They felt that the status of a voluntary association was in the nature of a shield.

Unions feared that if incorporated, suits against them would be brought by hostile employers. Even as associations, unions suffered from suits arising out of either the Sherman Act or injunctions; these so hampered unions that they did not wish to take a status that would facilitate legal assaults, and magnify union vulnerability. Besides their own history, unions read a lesson from the records of several giant corporations that removed opponents by strangling them in litigation.

Moreover, if unions were incorporated, every member who was disciplined, suspended, fined, or expelled might appeal to the courts for redress. An intrigue among a minority might occasion a court intervention in the internal affairs of the union. It would not be unique if employers maliciously promoted one or the other of these sources of union dissension; for, by division, conquest might be made easier.

To file corporation reports with the government would reveal the union's vital statistics; thus perhaps inviting attack from employers if the union figures showed weaknesses, or furnishing arguments for reduction of dues to short-sighted members if the treasury was well filled. All taxation on account of incorporation would add a burden to unions they so far had escaped. Some union philosophers felt that incorporation inevitably would bring centralized authority; this would emasculate the democracy that always has been their ideal.

From incorporation, unions would gain the power to hold employers to trade agreements, for these would become legal contracts; but to most unionists this seemed too small a reward for too large a risk. In short, incorporation to them seemed not a road to peace but an invitation to war.

Welfare Work.—In their turn, employers tried to avert strikes by removal of the grievances that caused them. In the earlier part of the generation, this effort took the form of Welfare schemes. Company eating-places, ranging from crude devices for heating lunches to elaborate restaurants where food was served at cost, company bathrooms, rest rooms, and athletic

facilities were among the Welfare plans.   In addition there
were savings, building and loan, pension, and profit sharing
schemes inaugurated by employers both with and without employe cooperation in their operation.   Housing and gardening
plans, some simple, some extensive, and various social functions
were indulged in by some employers.   Company "house organs," for publicity, and the encouragement of loyalty were
used in connection with some or all of the above activities.
Rewards, prizes, distinguished service medals, and bonuses for
"suggestions" were part of the Welfare plans.

Results were not satisfactory to employers; grievances arose
and strikes followed, even where many costly Welfare schemes
had been in vogue.   Indeed, sometimes the Welfare work was
itself a cause of grievance; "hellfare work" was what Gompers
called it.   Workers were affronted by the charitable aspect of
much of the Welfare, and whenever they suspected Welfare
was granted in lieu of wages, or shorter hours, they revolted.
Said they, "Give us decent wages and hours and let us furnish
our own Welfare."

Scientific Management.—After 1910, Scientific Management pointed to employers the way to bring contentment to
wage earners.   The first step was to analyze jobs in all their
particulars and then select workers to fit the jobs.   This practice removed much of the distress that came from misfits and
had led to strikes.

Workers were given an incentive by the orderly and regular
scanning of records, in order to select workers for promotion
and transfer.   Discontent was lessened; for advancement tended
more to be the reward of merit than the result of sycophancy.
Training and education for promotion, furnished at the employers' expense, was another employer device to promote
loyalty and remove sourness.   Specialists, who were experts in
all that related to personnel, were hired and put at the service
of employes.   To them, any worker with a complaint could go
for a hearing and possibly for redress.   The specialists also
were to search for and remove any possible causes for workers'
grievances.

Finally, in some cases, a works-body representative of the employes was set up in order to give workers and management opportunity to know each other's problems, and to seek solutions of them.   These bodies were the germs of "company unions" and they varied greatly in the amount of real control over conditions of work granted to wage earners.   Always, however, management was the final authority in these "works councils."   Along with all these new managerial devices, sometimes some or all of the old Welfare was re-introduced; if so, the managers turned them over to workers to manage.

If, to this personnel management, the employers also added good wages, reasonable hours, and an even flow of work—all possible under scientific management—the results often were what the employers desired.   Workers did grow contented. Therefore, strikes were not frequent and outside unions got slight attention from the work force.   If the *forms* and not the *spirit* of scientific management or personnel management were introduced, then revolts followed.

Effectiveness.—In general, after 1920 the new "enlightened" managers so often pursued a wise labor policy that strikes became less frequent and less widespread.   In that decade, workers who had jobs in the best managed plants and were not thrown out by the rapid technological improvements, had less cause for those grievances that formerly led to strikes.

On the other hand, those workers who were under employers who seized all the advantages of the new methods of management and production without passing along to labor some of its share, were given more than ordinary grounds for grievances; the speed and nerve-strain of work were augmented with no offsetting compensations.   Finally, workers in plants whose managers were remiss in adopting new methods had all the grievances of persons engaged in marginal or extra-marginal enterprises.   Those unemployed because of the march of scientific management had a 100% grievance; but in the absence of social insurance they had no means of satisfaction for their complaint.

Examples.—Hart, Schaffner, and Marx Clothing manufacturers of Chicago, after a strike in 1910, introduced all the best features of the new type of management. Since they did it with the full cooperation of the Amalgamated Clothing Workers' Union, this company, in an industry notorious for its strife, went through the next 25 years without a single strike.

The Dennison Manufacturing Company of Framingham, Mass., makers of tags and novelties of paper, pasteboard, or wax were perhaps the most famous for the utilization of all the features—including profit sharing—that modern management could devise. This company erected no barriers to unionization of its employes but never suffered from strikes; for, when occasionally one of its crafts was pulled out in a general regional strike, the union leaders, generally after a day or two for the sake of demonstrating solidarity, let the Dennison employes quietly go back to work.

A company that was noted for Welfare and employe representation, and among other things, a guarantee to certain categories of workers of 40 weeks' work per year, was the Procter and Gamble Company, soap manufacturers at Ivorydale, Ohio.

The Columbia Conserve Company, Baltimore and Ohio Railroad, Endicott-Johnson Shoe Company, Kendall Manufacturing Company (cotton textile), Goodyear Rubber Tire Company, Naumkeag Manufacturing Company (cotton sheets), Filene's Department Store (Boston, Mass.), were a few among the better known concerns to apply the arts of the new management with discretion for the labor viewpoint.

On the other hand, the founder of Scientific Management, Frederick W. Taylor, scarcely considered humanitarian factors in developing his new methods. Neither did the steel companies for which he worked, or rarely any other steel companies that later applied his principles. The automotive, rubber, cement, food, railway, and most oil companies made considerable use of the mechanics of Scientific Management without much heed to what labor felt about it. Some southern textile manufacturers applied some of the practices without apparent knowledge or understanding of the fundamental groundwork of Scientific Management. All of these classes of industry suffered from

strikes in spite of, and often because of, their one-sided introduction of the new principles of management.   The same was
true of many retail or wholesale establishments and public utilities.   Scientific Management was like fire, an excellent service
to man only if under proper safeguards.

Company Unions.—In respect to company unions, it can
be said that [1] "since such a union was organized among the
workers engaged by one employer, the scope of the union fitted
the area of the most numerous industrial grievances.   The
company union was a shop affair with outsiders excluded.
The conferences that were features of such organizations informed employers concerning labor problems and educated
labor in management problems so the unions were, or could be,
mutually beneficial.   These unions extended responsibilities to
labor over Welfare as well as over hours and wages.   Thus,
workers were trained to enlarge their functions.   By bridging
the gap between the front office and the shop, company unions
promoted loyalty and discouraged resignations, friction, and
strikes.   Where the unions were best these things were true.

"On the other hand no workers, ever, of their own initiative
have organized a company union—it was a boss-inspired union.
The power that created company unions could destroy them.
Worker-representatives not only must not antagonize the management—for that meant discharge—but were ignorant of labor
conditions in other plants and other sections even in the same
industry, and moreover, were untrained in the tactics of bargaining; thus the representatives usually were timid, ignorant,
and unskilled negotiators.   No truly equal-sided collective bargaining was possible in company unions.   A company union
could not strike because it had neither a treasury nor could it
get help from other workers in the same industry.   Consequently, a company union had no power of compulsion over an
employer."

For these reasons, regular unions fought the company variety
from the moment they became important; that is after 1914.

---

[1] This quotation is from an editorial by the author in the *Christian Science
Monitor*, February 19, 1934.

Since most of them existed where ordinary unions had no footing, the American Federation of Labor and Brotherhoods tried to get the company unions banned by law.   When it was realized that the company unions, after 1920, gained as many hundreds of thousands of members as the regular unions lost—not the same persons—the agitation against them became acute. By 1929, therefore, the company union was not a means toward industrial peace but a bone of contention.

Peace by Legislation

Not only unions and managers sought means for industrial peace but the public—a third party injured by strikes—looked for legislation that would bring order in place of war.   Both federal and state legislation was directed at this problem.

Federal Laws.—Because Congress had no power under the Constitution to enact labor legislation except for government employes and workers engaged in interstate commerce, the principal acts aimed at industrial peace passed by Congress concerned railroad employes.   For these during the generation there was a series of laws, the Erdman Act (1898) passed as a result of the Pullman Strike of 1896; the Newlands Act (1913), Section 8 of the act creating the Department of Labor (1913); Title III of the Transportation Act of 1920; and the Watson-Parker Act of 1926.

Erdman Act.—The Erdman Act, after repealing a law passed in 1888 which had called for voluntary arbitration but which never once had been used, set up a scheme of mediation and arbitration for disputes involving engineers, firemen, conductors, trainmen, switchmen, and telegraphers.   Until just before 1906 there were scarcely any applications of this Act; but during the next seven years either the workers or railroad managers appealed to the government every time they got into a serious dispute.

Neither side really liked the provision of the Act that made an award of arbitrators binding upon both parties.   A compulsory award was nearly as irksome as compulsory arbitration;

for it was not hard to present an issue to the public in such manner that arbitration was practically forced on the reluctant party, therefore, if the award was compulsory, the industry actually had compulsory arbitration.   American workers and employers have been alike in frowning upon compulsory arbitration.

Newlands Act.—In 1913, the Newlands Act repealed the law of 1898 and set up a Commissioner of Mediation and Conciliation with a 7-year term.   He, with two other government officers appointed by the President, constituted a Board of Mediation and Conciliation.   The unusual conditions ushered in by the World War after 1914, the direct appeal and coercion exercised by the four railroad Brotherhoods upon Congress in 1916 when the Adamson eight-hour law was enacted, and the period of government operation of the entire railway system of the nation, rendered the Newlands Act useless.

Act of 1920.—The Transportation Act of 1920 not only provided the method for the return of the railroads to their own stockholders' direction but contained a plan for the adjustment of disputes between railway managers and workmen.   The law directed that disputes, arising from the formulation of trade agreements or from interpretations of these instruments, first be referred to boards on which were representatives of both sides.   If these could not settle the matter, the issue was to be taken to a Railroad Labor Board, which the Act designated was to consist of nine members appointed for terms of five years and representative of managements, men, and the public in equal proportions.

The efforts of railway managements in the early 1920's to reduce labor costs from their war peaks gave rise to numerous disputes.   Labor wanted these referred to adjustment boards of national scope, as had been the decisions of the Railway Administration during the war.   Since managements objected to this standardization which overturned local differentials, and instead insisted on local adjustment boards, the matter of what kind of board to set up, itself became an issue in dispute.   The result was stalemate; the workers refused to participate in proceedings before local systems' boards and the managements balked against appearances before national boards.   Hence, neither kind of adjustment board functioned and disputes, both important and petty, were dumped on the table of the Railroad Labor Board.

This body soon abandoned any judicial decorum it might have had; for each representative group, in its championship of its own partisan affiliations, forgot to search for the merits of cases.   Moreover, because the awards of the Board were not mandatory, either contestant upon failure to secure all to which it thought itself entitled felt free to flout the Board's decision.   Wrangles that produced cases before the Board were carried into the Board's own membership, and continued after the Board had rendered a decision.   Inasmuch as the mechanism which had been intended to preserve peace and deal justice itself became a cause for an increased bitterness of strife, and lost the respect not only of the disputants but the public, a change had to be made.

Act of 1926.—Managers and men sat together with Congressional committees to devise a new method for the settlement of differences.   Out of these deliberations came the Watson-Parker Act of 1926.   This law set as a first step, direct negotiations between railway managers and the representative of the employes.   If these failed to agree, the issue was to be referred to boards of adjustment.   If in turn, no finality was attained by the boards of adjustment, then reference was had to a Presidentially appointed Federal Board of Mediation which need not wait for an actual appeal for its services but could take the initiative as mediator.   In case mediation failed the Board could assist arbitration.   If both parties agreed to arbitration the award of the arbitrators was final; but if arbitration was rejected the President was empowered to appoint a commission of investigation to ascertain the facts and publish its findings.   Thirty days were allowed for investigation during which time neither party to the issue could change the conditions out of which the dispute arose.

Under the 1926 law, all issues had a slow tortuous path to follow. In the first two years after enactment, the provisions of the law were called upon in over 300 cases; these, however, were not of paramount importance. After 1929, when the depression created major problems in respect to wages and dismissals, the two parties preferred direct collective bargaining to the delays inherent in the roundabout methods of the law. Management committees met committees representative of 21 standard railway unions and came to relatively speedy agreements upon the issues. Doubtless, the nature of the law was an indirect compulsion toward direct negotiations; if so, the law was not useless.

Department of Labor.—The Federal Government has furnished one other method of bringing about industrial peace. In the Act of 1913, creating the Department of Labor, its Secretary was given power to act as mediator and to appoint conciliation commissioners. These powers at once became a regular part of the functions of the Department, and not a year passed that did not find the federal conciliators busied with several hundred cases. In about three-fourths of the cases, the intervention of the federal officials produced results satisfactory to the contestants; so they and the federal department claimed.

Industrial Conferences.—Mention should be made also, of President Wilson's Industrial Conferences, called in 1919, as a result of the wave of strikes that swept the country that year. There were two of these Conferences. The first, agitation for which began in August by Secretary Lane, was called for October 6, 1919, and contained representatives of employers, labor, and the public. The function of the gathering was to produce a plan for industrial peace. However, the employers bloc could not agree with the labor bloc upon a definition of collective bargaining, and also, both were so estranged by the injection of the passions engendered by the then current steel strike, that the conference was destroyed. The labor bloc withdrew, whereupon the other two also returned home. The American Federation of Labor and Railway Brotherhoods tried to get a conference with farmer organizations but the plan failed when the National Grange and National Board of Farm Organizations declined to meet with labor.

President Wilson invited 15 prominent men for a second conference in December, avoiding in this instance direct partisan representation or bloc voting.   After due deliberation, the conference presented an elaborate plan for the creation of boards to settle disputes.   Except for contemporary editorial comment and leading articles in periodicals, the plan sank into oblivion. One reason for the complete obliteration of the work of the second conference was the fact that its report came after the crest of the wave of strikes.   There had been 3,571 strikes in 1919, and 3,291 in 1920.   But in 1921 there were only 2,381 and in 1922 the number sank to 1,088.   There were about 1,000 outbreaks per year from 1922-25.   Thereafter, throughout the decade of the 1920's, the number was less than 1,000 per year and the virulence rapidly declined.   Hence, interest in a national plan for the promotion of industrial peace ebbed with slackening in its cause.

State Legislation.—Just as the federal Department of Labor made provision for mediators and conciliators, so too, many states had legislated in similar manner.   Naturally the state provisions were not uniform; some provided for conciliators as part of the functions of the state labor bureau, others set up permanent boards independent of the state bureau, and still others created the mechanism for calling temporary boards to attempt the settlement of special cases.

The results of these varied attempts toward peace were as diverse as the means used.   The personnel of the mediation, conciliation, or arbitration staffs was a greater determinant of success or failure than the structure and legal powers set up by the states.   Men in whom employers and labor had confidence secured gratifying results; appointees, who were merely political "lame ducks," generally were ignored whether or not they attempted to intervene in industrial disputes.

Colorado Act.—Of the state laws relating to industrial peace two had special interest for the generation after 1896.   One was the Colorado Act of 1915 which created an Industrial Commission, the other was a Kansas law of 1920 by which her Industrial Court was started on its brief career.

The Colorado law, as we have shown in Chapter 4, was a direct outcome of the great strike of 1913-14 conducted by the miners against the Colorado Fuel and Iron Company. It will be recalled that J. D. Rockefeller, representing the largest stock holding in this company, invited W. L. McKenzie King to visit Colorado in order to suggest methods to prevent any other such violent outbreak. One result was the famous Rockefeller Employe Representation Plan. Another was the proposal to enact in Colorado, a law similar to the Industrial Disputes Investigation Act, which King and the Liberal Party had secured for Canada in 1907. The Colorado legislature, in 1915, prepared and passed the bill that brought into existence the Colorado Industrial Commission.

The essence of this law was a requirement of 30 days' notice for any change in employment relations. If the proposed change involved a dispute, there could be neither strike nor lockout during the 30 days; in that period the Commission was to investigate the proposal, and get the facts concerning the dispute. Upon the basis of its findings, the Commission was to publish the requisite facts and its opinion thereon; but this opinion was not binding upon either or any parties to the dispute. In short, the law brought about a "breathing spell" in a heated situation, and relied upon public opinion to sway the reluctant party to act in fairness according to the findings of the Commission.

Because time often was the key to success in a strike, the workers of Colorado did not like the enforced delay provided by the law, but they learned to allow for this interval in planning their struggles. For a similar reason, some employers did not approve the law. Both sides, at length, more or less accepted the Act, for each found it at times to operate in his favor. The law by no means stopped strikes or lockouts within the state, although it undoubtedly did restrict their numbers; very few disputes broke into open conflict without statutory notice, a fact that of itself did much to warrant the law.

Kansas Act.—The Kansas experiment did not have so fortunate an outcome.   After the nation-wide bituminous coal strike in 1919, Governor Henry J. Allen in January 1920 called the Kansas legislature into special session, the sole purpose of which was legislation to prevent a recurrence of the strife and distress occasioned by the coal strike.   In a brief session and against the vehement objections of organized labor the Legislature created an Industrial Court.   To this Court composed of three judges was given jurisdiction over disputes arising in any industry affected by a public interest, a phrase interpreted by the Act much more broadly than the usual public utilities. Strikes, lockouts, or other means of industrial warfare were prohibited.   The court was clothed with all the customary judicial powers—calling witnesses, compelling production of records, hiring of experts, and rendering decisions—and its findings were mandatory, (although appeal could be taken directly to the state Supreme Court) carrying punishment by fine or imprisonment for disobedience.

While Governor Allen after the law was enacted traveled in the east to receive the jubilant plaudits of employers, and—so it was said—to angle for political promotion, the disgruntled labor unions loaded the Court with cases, seeking, thus, to entangle it in a web of trivialities.   For the law prohibited strikes, picketing, and all other acts of industrial warfare.   Kansas employers, too, found the Court not such a blessing as they supposed; not so much because they were denied the use of lockouts, but because its orders to them they found burdensome.   Besides, the cases consumed valuable time in appearances before the Court.   It was a displeased employer, the Wolff Packing Company of Kansas City (Kansas) that tested the Court's powers. The Kansas Supreme Court upheld the law but when the trials came to the United States Supreme Court this body, in two decisions, removed most of the effectiveness of the Industrial Court.

Tests of Kansas Act.—In the earlier case (1923), the legal point that was raised was the power of the Kansas legislature to extend the ordinary legal classification of "public utility" to cover meat packing, a private competitive business; if this type of enterprise was not properly classifiable as a public utility, then did the Kansas Court have the right to fix wages in this business? The United States Supreme Court recited the varieties of definition of public utilities and, while recognizing that the enterprises so classified had changed from time to time, the court was of the opinion that the Kansas legislature had been unwarranted in including ordinary dispensable non-monopolistic manufacturing businesses in that category; hence, the Kansas Industrial Court had no legal sanction for setting wages for a competitive industry, for to do so violated the rights of free contract of both the employer and the employes. The U. S. Supreme Court, furthermore, could see no resemblance between this case and *Wilson v. New* (1917, in which it had upheld the Adamson Act) because in that instance, public utilities (railroads) were threatened with a strike that would have brought a nation-wide commercial paralysis; whereas, no public disaster would result if the Wolff Packing Company either made or lost profits or went out of business.

In the second case, involving the same company, the United States Supreme Court denied the right of the Kansas Industrial Court to set hours of labor for the packing house employes, for to do so infringed their right of free contract.

These two decisions so circumscribed the powers of the Kansas Industrial Court, together with a change in the political control of the state government, that in March 1925, the court as such was abolished, and the remnants of its former powers transferred to the state Public Utilities Commission.

The Chief Justice of the Kansas Industrial Court, William L. Huggins, became a Special Attorney for the League for Industrial Rights, his job chiefly to lecture in colleges and before other audiences upon the objects of the League. Wherever speakers for the League for Industrial Democracy (Socialist) appeared, there if possible Judge Huggins was sent with his message.

Until the U. S. Supreme Court emasculated the Kansas Industrial Court, it became an example set before other state legislatures. In many of them bills were introduced to establish similar courts; in New York State the bill was on the verge of becoming law but finally was overthrown by a massed lobby led by organized labor.   In Kansas, the members of Chambers of Commerce were to members of the American Federation of Labor as 10 is to 9; in New York the ratio was 1 to 7.

During 1921-22, a number of anti-strike bills were introduced in Congress.   None of these became law for the same reason that, after these dates, the search for a formula for industrial peace waned; the nation was enjoying the most industrial peace it had had during the generation.

Public Responsibility.—If the public was a third party in strikes, then the public was responsible for a great many of them.   It had shown slight interest in correctives for the conditions that produced strikes, nevertheless when it was hurt it cried for measures of relief.   When unhurt, it forgot.   There is some significance that this chapter dealing with methods for industrial peace is the shortest one in the book.   Peace, like health, had no clinical record.

CHAPTER 8

SIGNIFICANT LEGISLATION

It is convenient, in the description of the labor legislation after 1896, to adopt the classification inherent in the workers' familiar phrase, "wages, hours, and working conditions." Each of these three gave rise to such a mass of federal and state laws that the digests published at intervals by the U. S. Bureau of Labor Statistics [1] cover several thousand pages printed in small type. Obviously a selection of this material had to be made; our criterion was to pick for recital those laws that gave rise to the most contemporary controversy.

In application of this rule to laws concerning wages, it was necessary to omit discussion of a series of laws that aimed to correct exploitations in the payment of wages. These required employers to pay wages fortnightly or weekly at the place of business during working hours in the lawful mediums of exchange. Special rules surrounded the payments to employes of the government or those working for contractors under the government, the employes of public utilities, and of sea-going ships. Other laws protected wages from reduction by fines (e.g., for tardiness) or by attachment, garnishment, or assignment for debts, or contributions to company doctors or company stores, hospitals, playgrounds, and libraries. Exactly opposite were laws that gave workers chattel liens for unpaid wages, priority of claim in bankruptcies, fixed the method of payments due to heirs or claimants of the wages owing to deceased persons, and provided a public defender to collect for living laborers their delinquent due accounts. Other laws forced employers to publicly post wage rates (e.g., for weavers in Massachusetts) and to give timely notice of wage reductions

---

[1] Labor Laws of the United States Bureau of Labor Statistics. 1892; 1896; 1904; 1907; 1913; 1925.

(30 days in Missouri). All the states except five guaranteed to married women their personal control over their own earnings.

None of these wage laws caused much public clamor although every one was necessary to force some employers to give decent, fair treatment to wage earners. The proposal that aroused the most debate in the generation was that the state should fix minimum wages.

Minimum Wage Legislation

New Zealand in 1894 and Australia (Victoria) 1896 had established legal minimum wages as part of a broader system of control of industrial relations. Nebraska in the United States had discussed the matter and submitted a bill in 1909 bearing minimum rates of 20 cents an hour and $9 per week for both men and women in all stores, factories, and packing houses. It was the passage of the British Trade Boards Act (1909) that aroused widespread interest in this country in the subject of legal minimum wages. The study made (1907-10) by the federal government in respect to women and child wage earners in the United States increased the agitation for wage legislation. The startling revelation of low earnings in the Lawrence textile strike of 1912 stirred not only Massachusetts but the rest of the nation to the condition of some workers. The Progressive Party in 1912 included in its platform a proposal for minimum wage laws for women and children.

For four years after 1909 the debate over legal minimum wages filled the press, and resounded from the platform.

Negative Case.—The opponents said that neither employers nor employes, themselves, proposed legal minimum wages so the whole agitation came from reformers, who had confused ethics and humanity with economics and practicality. Said the opponents, "Bad social conditions are not due primarily to low wages but to poor heredity, weak character, and bad habits. Why should the whole burden of social betterment be borne by the one class, employers?" They continued by declaring that a

compulsory minimum wage would do far more social harm than
good.   Most industries were overcrowded with charity cases—
that is, old persons and handicapped people.   A legal minimum
wage would cause these to be discharged and thus the poorest
in society would have to pay heaviest for social reform.   Rome
G. Brown, attorney, asserted, "Compulsion would stifle all
humanitarian motives of employers.   Their gifts of work now
are moral; but compel them to pay minimum wages and you
banish morality from business."   The lowest wages were
earned in home work.   Since no legal minimum wage, on
account of the difficulty of administration, could reach home
workers, such a law would be ineffective in raising the worst
wages.

Theory as Argument.—Another type of argument used by
opponents of the legal minimum wage related to wage-theory.
Some claimed that wages were fixed by Supply and Demand
and no state law could change this situation.   More knowing
persons declared that wages were in accord with the efficiency
in production shown by workers.   The National Association of
Manufacturers said, "You cannot legislate efficiency"; all you
could do was to legislate an unearned gratuity, in the opinion
of the N. A. M.   What were the effects this organization saw?
Either the discharge of inefficient persons, or an addition to
price that robbed the minimum wage of its value.   Many employers would close or move their businesses rather than submit to such an interference by the state with the natural law of
wages.   Many industries would be lost to the United States
and the products of them would have to be imported.   If the
state fixed wages, it next would have to fix maximum prices—
and this could not be done by fiat.   "Efficiency must and can be
the only basis for wages" was the claim of the N. A. M.   This
idea got substantial support from Professors F. W. Taussig
of Harvard, John Bates Clarke of Columbia, Frank A. Fetter
of Princeton, and J. Laurence Laughlin of Chicago University.
    The opponents feared the inelasticity of the proposed laws.
They looked at the size of the nation with its multitude of differing local wage standards and they gazed back at the history of

violent price and wage fluctuations.   How could laws be flexible enough to cope with a situation essentially dynamic?

Moreover, the laws were not needed.   Of the low-paid women workers, 80% lived at home and so did not require a wage sufficient for complete self-support.   A legal minimum wage would attract even more girls from home to compete with those already at work; or else would induce a flood of immigrants.   Roger Babson of Babson's Statistical Organization, Wellesley Hills, Mass., made a contribution to the subject when he wrote, "Give me a law to send home the girl who works for luxuries or the girl needed at home to lift the burdens of her overworked mother, and so save places for girls who *must* work."   It was he too who wrote "Some of the greatest people the world has produced began earning at an almost incredibly low figure; shall such have no opportunity to find out their own possibilities?"   Again Babson, "The wage question can be settled gradually only through education and religion."

Unions Opposed.—Among the opponents of the legal minimum wage were Samuel Gompers and organized labor in general.   Gompers, like Woodrow Wilson, feared that a minimum wage would become a maximum; as the lower paid workers were leveled up, the higher paid ones would be scaled down; an idea that harked back a hundred years to the "wage fund" doctrine.   The American Federation of Labor, in convention in 1913, published, "If it were proposed in this country to vest authority in any tribunal to fix, by law, wages for men, Labor would protest by every means in its power."   In California, the State Federation and the San Francisco Council both were against the legal minimum wage.   The Council said, "The labor movement is thoroughly familiar with its needs; and a statutory wage law is not among them."   But when organized labor discovered that none of the states sought to do more than fix the minimum wages of the least skilled women, and consequently threatened no prerogatives of unions, opposition changed to mild endorsement.

Unconstitutional.—The final charge brought by opponents to the legal minimum wage was that it would violate the 5th and

14th amendments to the U. S. Constitution; the former "nor be deprived of life, liberty, or property without due process of law," and the latter "No state shall make or enforce any law which shall abridge the privileges or immunities of citizens of the United States, nor shall any state deprive any person of life, liberty, or property without due process of law, nor deny to any person within its jurisdiction the equal protection of the laws."

Affirmative Case.—Those who favored the legislation showed that low wages were basic causes of social misery. The answer to the question, how much income was required to maintain a family or person at the American standard of living, was found in wage earners' family budgets. The social statisticians claimed that it took from $600 to $900 a year (in 1910) just to subsist, so an American standard would necessitate twice these incomes. Against these figures, Scott Nearing, then an instructor at the University of Pennsylvania, set the actual earnings of American workers. He found that half the adult wage earners got less than $500, three-fourths of the males less than $600, and nine-tenths of all the males less than $900. For adult females, one-fifth got less than $200, three-fifths less than $325, and nine-tenths less than $500. These figures were later supported by data gathered officially in Massachusetts, Oregon, New York, and other states. "Here then," said the proponents, "is evidence of poverty from which springs bad housing, insufficient and wrong kinds of food, inadequate clothing, early separation from schools, and child labor, low vitality, and incentive either for revolt or crime—the latter one kind of revolt." The inadequate wages also produced the need for organized charity.

Limited to Females.—Legal minimum wages seemed the only reliable solution. Even the advocates did not dare make their proposal applicable to men—as was the case in the British empire—for not only was there a formidable constitutional barrier in a state invasion of the rights of male free contract, but there was slight chance for making an emotional appeal for men. Hence, the American campaign for a legal minimum wage was confined to getting it for female workers; it was hoped that benefits would carry over to men, and at any rate put a floor under men's wages.

The charge of parasitism was hurled at employers who paid women less than a living wage. If their wage was not enough to support them, the balance had to be made up by their families, by private or public charity, or by "gentlemen friends." It was said that if an industry or enterprise could not support its own labor force without subsidy, that that industry or employer had no right to continue operation; to do so constituted a mal-distribution of national labor force. Incidentally, the connection of low wages with prostitution was one of the most telling arguments used in the entire campaign. Of course chastity was less a matter of income than character, as thousands of poorly paid working girls constantly have proved. It was true, however, that a girl who—no matter what her station in life might have been—would easily have succumbed to seduction, was all the more easily tempted if her earnings did not as much as keep her alive.

Some Employers for Minimum Wage Laws.—It should be recognized that many employers, including those engaged in industries some of whose members were "parasitic," were wholeheartedly in favor of legal minimum wages. Competition on the basis of cut-rate wages set at nought competitors who tried to succeed by efficient management; these latter wanted to curb the unfair and brutish competition of those whose sole cause for success lay in constantly pushing wages to lower levels. Unrestrained laissez faire always resembled "Gresham's law;" "bad" employers like "bad" currency tended to drive out the good.

Wage Theory.—The advocates of legal minimum wages severely censured the wage theories of the opponents. There was not, and never had been, a universally accepted theoretical explanation of wages. In the generation involved, the most popular one was the productivity theory, expressed in employers' language as "efficiency" or "worth"; a person's wages depended on that person's productive efficiency. The experts who held this theory qualified it by presupposing complete free competition, mobility of labor, and equality of bargaining power; and even then never professed to discover a mathematical integer of productivity for an individual laborer. The glib phrase, "Supply and Demand," likewise was greatly qualified when used by careful economists. In short, no reputable economist of the generation asserted there was a natural "law of wages"; all an economist could say was that under certain circumscribed conditions there was a tendency for the price of labor to behave in certain ways. Therefore, to decry a legal minimum wage because it interfered with "natural law" was bombast—"bunk," in the language of the street.

The actual wages paid women upset the idea that wages conformed to any principle. Even when narrowed to one operation in one industry in one set of city blocks, the wages paid to women varied over an astounding range. Candy factories in Boston were cases in point; four factories paid no women less than $5, but two factories paid more than half their female work force less than $5 a week. Six Boston department stores had the following percentages of employes getting less than $6 a week—14, 20, 37, 42, 49, and 67. Boston laundries, for a single job, showed the same diversity. The New York Factory Investigation Commission, in 1915, found an identical situation; Oregon official researchers got similar results. Thus, only one rule applied to women's wages; they were low. The degree, however, was in accord with no observable standard.

"Police" Power of States.—For these reasons, the proponents said that for the state to set legal minimum wages was sound practice. It did no violence to natural forces; from the legal viewpoint it was in the category of state acts that set the hours of work for women, provided for sanitary equipment in work places, and prescribed the time, place, medium, and frequency of wage payments.

Beneficial Results.—Additional support was given the affirmative argument in the claim that a minimum wage, by its increase in income, would allow workers to live in better quarters, eat more nourishing food, and wear more protective clothing. All of these together would make workers so much more efficient that they would earn the minimum wage. The degradation of standards by immigrants would be abated. That the minimum would not become the maximum was proved first by the experiences of New Zealand and Australia, and second, by the experiences of American employers who had known for generations that they had to pay superior wages to superior employes or else lose them. As for the oldest, youngest, or most incapacitated employes, these need not be discharged; deserving cases could be paid less than the minimum under special licenses. The genuinely unemployable persons ought not clog the labor market, but be cared for by special local or state aids; certainly their condition ought not set the wage rate for the majority of normal persons.

That legal minimum wages would raise prices was denied. In the occupations most filled by women, the labor cost was not a principal cost of production. Therefore, a considerable increase in a minority cost would exercise slight influence upon total costs and selling price. If the labor cost did tend toward higher prices, employers—because prices were not set by events in a single state—would become more efficient managers. Employers themselves admitted that they got into ruts, and put forth greater effort only when some compulsion forced them.

Effects of Agitation.—In Massachusetts [2] during 1911, the Consumers' League and Womens' Trade Union League, together with the Federal Report on Working Conditions of Women and Children, stirred enough interest in minimum wages to induce the legislature to appoint a committee (May 11) to study work and wage conditions in retail stores, candy factories, and laundries. The United States Department of Labor supplied reports on the conditions of women in cotton mills. The committee report in 1912 revealed low wages and non-uniformity in rates. The Lawrence strike substantiated and gave publicity to the low earnings of women. So when the committee recommended the enactment of a law creating a Min-

---

[2] Michigan appropriated funds for a similar investigation at about the same time.

imum Wage Commission there was slight opposition, the sole change being the substitution of the minority recommendation that the penalty for non-compliance with Commission rates be publicity. This change was deemed by the few opponents to make the law innocuous; so on June 4, 1912, when the vote was tallied, there were only two votes in the two Houses together in opposition to the law. It went into effect on July 1, 1913.

Massachusetts Law.—The law provided for three Commissioners; one the Commissioner of Labor, one an employer of women, one a woman; and a woman secretary. This Commission could act on its own initiative or upon petition from employers or employes. The Commission appointed advisory Wage Boards comprising six employers, six employes, and one or more representatives of the public. If any employer discriminated against any labor member of a Wage Board, he was subject to a penalty of $200 to $1,000. This penalty was an amendment added in 1914, because in the very first Board two brush workers serving on it were fired by their employer. In later practice the penalty never was invoked. The law applied only to women, and minors under 18 years of age, and the wage standard was "that amount necessary to defray the cost of living, and to maintain the worker in health." (But an employer could appeal to the Superior Court or the Supreme Judicial Court "if the Commission set a wage that would prevent a reasonable profit.") Special rates were permitted for learners or apprentices, and special licenses might be granted to defectives. The only penalty for non-compliance was the publication, in newspapers throughout the state, of the employer's name together with his wage rates. Newspapers were subject to a fine of $100 for refusal to print this notice, paid for at regular advertising rates. If employers could *prove* their inability to pay the rate set, they were exempted from publicity.

Massachusetts Law Unique.—Massachusetts was the only eastern or industrial state to enact a minimum wage law until 1933; her law also was the only non-mandatory one except for that of Nebraska (1913), but the Nebraska legislature made no appropriation in 1913, the governor made no appointments, and the law was repealed in 1919. Hence, as the first and also as a unique experiment, the Massachusetts law was important. In December 1919, the law was modified by the abolition of the three Commissioners; their former duties were transferred to a newly created Department of Labor and Industries. In 1918 the Massachusetts Supreme Judicial Court decided the law was constitutional (*Holcombe v. Creamer, 231 Mass. 99*).

Experience in Massachusetts.—Between 1914 and 1927, the Massachusetts Commission made wage decrees for 18 industries with 5,000 establishments and 85,000 female employes. The state industries employing the most women—textiles and shoe manufacture—were not touched by the Commission (there was some intervention in cotton textiles) because the majority of women employes were paid more than the minimum wages. The publicity penalty was first used in 1921 against an owner of an office building and against 11 paper-box manufacturers. In 1923 there were cited 54 retail stores, 22 laundries, 3 paper box manufacturers, 1 maker of muslin underwear, and 1 manufacturer of women's clothing; a total of 81. In 1925 there was a longer list of 156 violators. The effectiveness of the publicity penalty was proportional to the directness of the producers' relation to the public; it quickly reacted on retail stores, and once on Harvard University (which had underpaid its scrubwomen), but it was ignored by middlemen or manufacturers whose products did not bear advertised names.

Other State Laws.—Following Massachusetts, eight states in 1913 passed minimum wage laws for women and minors. These were California, Colorado, Minnesota, Nebraska, Oregon, Utah, Washington, and Wisconsin. During the World War, people were concerned with other matters, so only Arkansas and Kansas in 1915, and Arizona in 1917, were added to the list. Congress enacted a law for the District of Columbia in 1918, and this law in 1923 was the one tested and discarded by the United States Supreme Court. Three laws—North Dakota, Texas, and Porto Rico—were passed in 1919, and in 1923 South Dakota's act was included in the roll.

Of these laws, those of Colorado and Nebraska were inoperative. The Nebraska act in 1919 and the Texan in 1921 were repealed. The Utah (1913), Arkansas (1915), and Arizona (1917) laws differed from all others in setting flat rates. The Utah rates were 75 cents, 90 cents, and $1.25 a day for various classes of female labor and the administration was handled by the pre-existing Commissioner of Immigration Labor and Statistics. The Arkansas law set $1 and $1.25 a day; but the commission, after hearings, could raise or lower these rates. The Arizona statute set a flat $10 a week minimum. All the other acts closely conformed to a pattern recommended by the Consumer's League; all were mandatory.

Court Tests.—These acts at once were submitted to court tests. In the state courts they generally were upheld. The first appeals taken to the United States Supreme Court were concerned with the Oregon law.

Oregon Cases.—Frank C. Stettler a manufacturer of paper boxes, brought action against the Reverend E. V. O'Hara, Bertha Moores, and Amedee Smith, members of the Oregon Welfare Commission. Simpson, an employe of Stettler, made separate suit against the same defendants. These two cases on writs of error reached the United States Supreme Court in December 1914.[3]

Louis D. Brandeis represented the Oregon Commission and Rome G. Brown was attorney for the plaintiffs. Brown's claim was that the law violated the 5th and 14th amendments, depriving Stettler of property and Simpson of the right of free contract. It also was an unwarranted application of the police power. Brandeis' argument turned on three points, "Were the ends sought by Oregon reasonable and of public benefit? Were the means to accomplish the ends reasonable and unoppressive? Was the law within the limits of Constitutional prohibitions?" After both Brown's and his own arguments had been made, Brandeis (1916) was appointed to the U. S. Supreme Court.

[3] *Stettler v. O'Hara et al.,* 243 U. S. 629; *Simpson v. O'Hara et al.,* 243 U. S. 629.

Reargument was set for January 1917, and of course Justice Brandeis did not sit because the case was one in which he had been attorney.   Felix Frankfurter and Mary W. Dewson prepared the second brief, and the former presented it to the Court. The Justices divided equally 4 to 4 and therefore published no decisions nor the personality of the division of the Court.   The result was that the favorable decision (1914) of the Oregon Supreme Court for the time being was the final word.   In view of the later District of Columbia case, lawyers have indulged in much guessing as to the four who favored and the other four who disfavored the Oregon law.

District of Columbia Case.—The definitive minimum wage case was *Adkins v. Children's Hospital* (261 U. S. 525, 1923), an action to test the constitutionality of the Congressional Act of September 19, 1918, providing for the fixing of mandatory minimum wages for women and children in the District of Columbia.   The decision was 5 to 3 against the statute; in this case likewise Mr. Justice Brandeis took no part, neither in consideration nor decision.

As in the Oregon cases, there were really two tied together in this one.   The appellee in one was a corporation maintaining a hospital for children in the district, which sought an injunction to restrain the District Minimum Wage Board from enforcing its wage awards on the ground that the same was in contravention of the due process clause of the 5th Amendment.   The second appellee was an adult woman elevator operator, employed by the Congress Hotel Company at a salary of $35 a month and two meals a day.   She averred she liked the job, was satisfied with the pay, and because of the Board's wage ruling had been discharged and could secure no other job.   She had asked for an injunction on the grounds that her freedom of contract had been abridged.

The Supreme Court reviewed prior cases bearing upon the states' legislation in the field of employment relations and upheld as valid uses of the police power.   The most important were first, *Holden v. Hardy* (169 U. S. 366), a Utah statute restricting the hours of labor in mines and smelters.   "This," said the Court, "was a valid statute because it applied to a limited and admittedly dangerous range of tasks." *Bunting v. Oregon* (243 U. S. 426), an act prescribing a 10-hour day was upheld because it was a health measure. *Wilson v. New* (243 U. S. 332) did not apply in the instant case because it was a regulation of a business charged with a public interest.

The hardest precedent facing the Court was *Muller v. Oregon* (208 U. S. 412), the statute that fixed a 10-hour day for female workers, upheld by the Court on account of structural differences between women and men, and the relation of their maternal functions to the future of the state. The Court said that the structural differences remained, but that all other inequalities between the sexes were diminishing in intensity: "In view of the great—not to say revolutionary—changes which have taken place . . . in the contractual, political, and civil status of women, culminating in the 19th Amendment [woman suffrage], it is not unreasonable to say that these differences have now come almost, if not quite, to the vanishing point." Therefore, the restriction of contract for mature women now comes close to the same legal standing as similar restrictions for men.

In short, the Court held that the case at the bar did not fall within the exceptions to the rule forbidding interference with contract. Moreover, the Court thought the Act had positive faults. It set wages upon no ascertainable standard, for, "what will be necessary to provide a living for a woman, keep her in health, and preserve her morals" was too vague. Moreover, the statute made employers pay wages that had no relation to the value of the service rendered.

The fact that several states had similar statutes, and that a large number of opinions approved the policy "reflected no legitimate light upon the question of validity . . . the elucidation of that question cannot be aided by counting heads."

Finally, "the power to fix minimum wages connotes by like course of reasoning the power to fix low wages." The Court said a precedent would be set for setting a low wage among building crafts, if in the future their high wages precluded people of ordinary means from building and owning homes.

"The act in question passes the limits prescribed by the Constitution."

Chief Justice Taft and Justices Holmes and Sanford dissented.

Hoodoo.—The *Adkins v. Children's Hospital* case had run into a peculiarly unfortunate set of coincidences. When it arrived in the Supreme Court of the District of Columbia, Justice Robb was sick. In his place Justice Stafford was given a temporary seat. This pro-tem Judge agreed with Chief Justice Smyth against Justice Van Orsdel that the injunctions against the statute could not hold. When Justice Robb recovered, he with Van Orsdel demanded that the case be reheard. When it was, these two Justices outvoted Chief Justice Smyth.

Appeal then was taken to the United States Supreme Court. This Court, too, had been much changed since the Oregon case, *Stettler v. O'Hara.* Former Chief Justice White had died in 1921. Justices Pitney, Day, and Clarke had retired in 1922. In their places there had been appointed Chief Justice Taft, Justices Butler, Sutherland, and Sanford. Of the five Justices, who in *Adkins v. Children's Hospital* "vetoed" the D. C. Minimum Wage Act, two—Butler and Sutherland—were recent appointees, and it was the second of these men who prepared the decision. Competent students of the U. S. Supreme Court have declared, that if the *Adkins v. Children's Hospital* case had come before the Court prior to June 1922, it would have decided 5 to 3 (Justice Brandeis not sitting) to uphold the D. C. statute.[4]

This however is surmise. The decision, in fact, raised a storm of protest from both constitutional lawyers and laymen. The old cry that the Court stood in the path of social reform was supplemented by the old demand that an Amendment, limiting the real and assumed powers of the Court, be submitted to the states. However, in the fantastic years after

---

[4] The hoodoo persisted, for in 1936, both the New York Court and U. S. Supreme Court invalidated a New York minimum wage law. Of all the judges who passed on minimum wage laws, a majority favored such legislation, but never (up to 1937) at critical moments in cases was there a majority that sanctioned the laws.

1923 people forgot their anger, even when two more state minimum wage laws, those of Arkansas and Arizona, were overthrown by the Court.

The Arkansas and Arizona acts not only were mandatory but set flat wage rates. In January 1927, in *Donham et al. v. West Nelson Manufacturing Company* (273 U. S. 657), the U. S. Supreme Court chided the legislature of Arkansas. The decisions in both Arkansas and Arizona cases rested upon the precedence of *Adkins v. Children's Hospital.*

The year 1923 marked a temporary halting place for state minimum wage laws and also brought about modifications of those already enacted. Kansas, Wisconsin, and Arizona high courts were forced to follow the U. S. Supreme Court in invalidation of the mandatory features of their laws. Minnesota and Oregon continued theirs in respect to minors. Wisconsin in 1925 found a new formula which it hoped would satisfy the United States Supreme Court. The law first declared "no wage paid . . . shall be oppressive" and then said "any wage lower than a reasonable and adequate compensation for the services rendered" was oppressive. The Massachusetts law, being non-compulsory, escaped the interdiction of the District of Columbia case. It was not until 4 years after 1929 that six states again enacted minimum wage legislation; and then it was patterned upon a novel New York model. [The New York Law was overthrown by the U. S. Supreme Court in 1936.]

Hours of Work

Not only were legislatures appealed to in matters of wages, but also to set legal limits to the hours of work. These bodies had little hesitation in limiting the work period for minors or public servants; when, however, they were asked to set bounds to the work time of women they were cautious, and as for work limits for men the timidity of legislatures made them stop short after setting maximum hours in trades that were related to public health. Before 1896, legislatures in setting limits to the hours of child workers were concerned chiefly with the education of children or indirectly sought to reduce their competition with their elders. In the generation after 1896, the motives turned toward the interests of the child; its own health and welfare. Notice that here we are not discussing child labor, but merely the hours of such work.

Hours of Work for Minors.—Beginning with Illinois in 1903, when that state set 8 hours as the maximum for the labor of all children under 16 years, 35 of the states legislated similar curtailed hours for children. Some put a limit upon the hours of child labor in all occupations, some only on child labor in factories. Several exempted from limitation specific vocations such as work in canneries, domestic service, agriculture, and retail stores, and in so doing freed the worst exploiters of children. Most state acts were more drastic in the protection thrown around the work of young girls than that of boys of the same ages. Nearly all the laws also applied to daylight hours; night work for young persons generally was recognized as an evil.

Court Tests.—Although employers sometimes challenged the laws as violations of the 5th and 14th Amendments, and urged as well the impracticability of having one set of hours for minors and another for adults, the courts consistently upheld the right of states to safeguard the lives and work of minors. The legal rule that minors really were wards of the state was too thoroughly established for any court to question.

Hours of Work for Women.—The hours of work for women was the subject of many a legislative and court battle in the generation. The object of legislative bills on this subject before 1910 was a limit of 10 hours, and in the later years one of 8 hours.

It was at first difficult to get legislatures to consider bills of these natures. When bills were given a respectful attention, employers' lobbies obstructed them with every possible means; a favorite one being the presentation of a delegation of attractive young women before legislative committees, where the girls pleaded for their right to work for as long as they pleased.   Another was the threat that, if hours were limited, the employers would close the works and move to another state where the laws were less constrictive.   In this connection, the loss of tax values to towns and to the state was emphasized so as to arouse farmers or small-scale merchants to opposition. The farmer representatives often were not hard to excite on account of the feeling among their constituents—all early risers and with late chores—that town workers led a soft life. The farmers also foresaw difficulty in holding farm laborers if town work hours were made a great deal shorter than those necessary on farms.

The employers gave legislative committees quantities of statistics designed to show that employers in other states had advantages in production costs, so that if women's work hours were curtailed, the extra cost would bankrupt the states' most important industries.   Shorter hours would entail smaller output from which other evils flowed; one, the higher cost would require higher selling prices and thus either add to competition or lessen consumers' demands; another would be the necessary cut in female wages and these, the women said, were already too low.

A law fixing maximum hours would have varying effects; some industries in which the worker's efforts determined output might be only slightly inconvenienced, but others in which machinery set the output would lose directly proportional to the cut in hours.   It was impossible to compensate for less work time by greater machine speeds, because these had attained maximum.   Women worked so irregularly that in a month or year their work time averaged what the law would set (10 or 8 hours.)   Managers of hotels, telephone services, and drug stores said they simply could not operate on a short-day basis. Men did not want the shorter hours, unions opposed the legislatures' usurpation of this program of organized labor, women's leaders, the Feminists, did not want special legislation for women.   Finally the working women did not want the curtailment of hours; they did wish to earn as much as possible and this meant long hours.

Case Favoring Laws.—Against this employer attack, the adherents of the bills led a battery of arguments. "Women," they said, "carried the seeds of the future." Therefore, if life was to continue, women must not be subjected to unbearable strains. To be sure, women always had worked and perhaps more than men; but their traditional work was enough varied to allow frequent changes in posture and rest periods. In modern mills, or stores and offices, the women or girls were subjected to monotonous repetitive motions with neither variety nor rest. If the job required a standing position or the use of feet on levers there was a decided danger of internal organic derangement. Long hours of modern work therefore threatened women's health.

Moreover, a woman's work day was not confined to her paid employment. If she were married, she had housework before and after her wage-earning day; if unmarried she either had to help at home or do for herself a number of jobs, such as washing, ironing, and mending. This double duty gave women no recuperative time, and hardly enough time for sleep. Their fatigue consequently was cumulative and finally caused more or less serious sickness. Shorter work hours for women were necessary to preserve women and through them, the race.

"As for the employers' arguments," said the proponents, "they were hoary; employers had been saying the same things for a century of lessening hours of work. How many had bankrupted, moved, or failed to discover—when they were forced—better methods of production?"

Whenever legislatures did vote favorably on a limitation of the work hours of women the act was either laxly enforced or submitted to a court test. To insure enforcement, it was found necessary to provide for inspectors and to institute certain formalities, such as the posting at the work place of notices declarative of the hours of work, or the compilation of an open record of the hours actually worked by women employes.

Challenge in Courts.—In the courts, the laws were challenged as to their constitutionality on the grounds that they invaded the free contractual rights of adult women, were class legislation, deprived women of a property right by limiting their possible earning periods, or were not a valid exercise of the police power. Out of the numerous cases, two that reached the United States Supreme Court were definitive.

The first was one that related to an Oregon Act passed February 19, 1903, setting 10 hours as the limit to women's wage-working time in mechanical establishments, factories, or in laundries. Curt Muller, owner of the Grand Laundry in Portland, worked Mrs. E. Gotcher more than 10 hours on September 4, 1905. Tried and fined $20, Muller appealed to the Oregon Supreme Court. When the conviction was affirmed, Muller brought the case to the U. S. Supreme Court on a writ of error.[5]

The attorneys for the state established a precedent in this case by putting in evidence a mass of data collected by Louis D. Brandeis and his sister-in-law, Josephine Goldmark. The material was extracts from over 90 worldwide sets of statistics and competent opinions relative to the health hazards of long hours of work for women. The brief also cited statutes restricting the hours of labor for women in 19 states and 7 foreign countries.

The U. S. Supreme Court in 1908 upheld the right of Oregon to protect its women residents from the dangers of long work hours and also the right of the state to safeguard its future citizens by putting safeguards around prospective mothers. These rights outweighed the individual rights of contract and property and were not an unreasonable segregation, for the purposes of law, of one class of citizens. The Supreme Court said, "The limitations [of contract] are not imposed solely for her benefit, but also largely for the benefit of all. The two sexes differ . . . [and] this difference justifies a difference in legislation. . . ."

In 1915 when a California statute setting 8 hours as a limit to women's wage work was put before the U. S. Supreme Court, this body reaffirmed its earlier position; but while construing 8 hours as reasonable, stated that it did not, thereby, necessarily

---

[5] *Muller v. Oregon* (208 U. S. 412, 1908).

convey approval to hours less than 8, if the state should so legislate.[6]

New Type Law.—In 1913 a new form of hour legislation for women appeared. The former laws set a single standard for all employments covered, with a result that often was injustice. Not all employments were alike in their danger, physical or mental strain; therefore, a standard which for one employment might be too generous, for another employment might be insufficient protection. In recognition of these facts, California in 1913 enacted a general statute, which stated that the hours of work for women should not be dangerous to their health, safety, or welfare; and then provided a permanent commission to ascertain for each employment what specific hours fulfilled the purposes of the statute. The precedent of this act was followed in similar ones in Oregon, Wisconsin, Kansas, and Washington. In Oregon, however, the commission was permitted to set hours that were only less than 8 per day.

Employers immediately contested these acts, advancing as their chief argument against them that the state legislature, by granting legislative powers to a commission, created a situation which deprived employers of property without due process of law. The United States Supreme Court in 1917, upheld the constitutionality of the commission method of setting maximum work hours for women.

Faults in Laws.—One common omission in the laws regulating the hours of work for women was that a standard time for the start or end of a day's work was not set. Consequently, it was difficult to check evasions of the laws by employers, and the flouting of the intention of the laws by some women who held two jobs. Night work, too, was not restricted by a law which simply stated that a certain number of hours was to constitute a day's work. During the generation, only 18 states took steps to combat these tendencies. Ten states defined the hours of night and then prohibited any employment of women for wages during these hours. Three states (Massachusetts,

---

[6] *Miller v. Wilson* (236 U. S. 373).

after 6 P.M.; Pennsylvania, after 9 or 10 P.M.; Indiana, after
10 P.M.) banned night work for women in manufacturing
establishments; two states (New Hampshire, Maryland)
limited the amount of night work; two eliminated night work
in minor industries; and one (South Carolina) prohibited night
work after 10 P.M. for women in mercantile business. Thirty
states took no action at all.

All but five of the states (West Virginia, Iowa, Indiana,
Alabama, Florida) during the generation passed some legal
measure limiting the amount of time women could be employed
for wages. Usually the laws set a maximum number of hours
per day while some made the maximum for the week. A few
established both daily and weekly maxima. In general, the
laws covered occupations in manufacturing, mechanical, and
mercantile industries but each law varied as to its exact application or in the exceptions granted. Five states, at no time in
the generation, set any limitation on the daily or weekly hours
of work for women. Only five (New York, Utah, Arizona,
Wyoming, California) had both an 8-hour day and 48-hour
week; two more (Massachusetts, Oregon), while putting a 48-
hour weekly limit, allowed a 9-hour day. All the other states—
save Kansas with a 49½-hour week—permitted 50 or more
hours per week.

Non-Uniformity.—The largest concentration was 13 states
with a 54-hour weekly maximum. Georgia set 60 hours a week
and North Carolina put 11 hours a day as its limit. The lack
of uniformity may be indicated by the small section of New
England whose six states divided as follows on the weekly
hours: Maine 54, New Hampshire 54, Vermont 56, Rhode
Island 54, Connecticut 55, Massachusetts 48. For daily hours
in the same small area there was this variation: Maine 9, New
Hampshire 10¼, Vermont 10½, Rhode Island 10, Connecticut
10, Massachusetts 9. Only Massachusetts limited the work
week to 6 days. The only states east of the Rockies with an
8-hour day for women were Kansas and New York, but the
District of Columbia also was in this category. Of the eight
states in or west of the Rockies with an 8-hour day, three also

had a 48-hour week of 6 days, one a work week of 54 hours
of 6 days and one of 56, the other three permitted weekly hours
of 56 to 60 (the latter under exceptional circumstances).

Hours of Work for Men.—It was harder to set bounds to
the daily or weekly work of men than to do so for children and
women.   Men were not "wards" of the state as were minors,
and neither was it so obvious, as with women, that the physical
or mental health of men affected future offspring.   Unions
also opposed legislative restraints upon the hours of work for
men; whereas the same unions lobbied for measures that limited
the hours of minors or women.

Consequently, in setting legal bars to the work of men, the
reason less often was the direct effect of long hours on the
men as the indirect danger to the safety or health of the public.
Of course, states could and did regulate the hours of men who
were the immediate employes of the state; clerical workers for
the state got an 8-hour day after 1902, but city firemen were
on 12-hour shifts as late as 1919.   The precedent case that
established the right of the state to regulate the hours of state
employes was *Atkin v. Kansas* (191 U. S. 207), which in 1903
by a 6-3 decision set the seal of validity on a Kansas act of 1891
in which 8 hours was the lawful maximum for the state servants
or contractors under the state or of county, city, township, or
other municipality of the state.

Transportation.—In the steam railroad and electric street
railway services, before Congress and state legislatures intervened, it was not uncommon for train employes to be on duty
for as much as 16 or more hours per day.   Many accidents
were attributed to the overtired condition of workers.   For
trains operating in interstate commerce Congress in 1907
put a limit of 16 hours to work, and any period as long as this
was to be followed by a rest of 8 to 10 hours.   For employes
not actually on trains but whose jobs immediately concerned
trains such as dispatchers, signal men, and telegraphers, two
standards were set: if the men were on continuous duty the
limit was 8 hours; if their duty was divided between two or
more periods, "on" or "off," then the sum of both periods

could not exceed 12 or 13 hours.   The Supreme Court in 1911 upheld the law in the case *B. & O. R.R. Co. v. I. C. C.* (221 U. S. 612).   About half the states enacted similar legislation to protect men engaged in intra-state transportation.

The Adamson Act of September 2, 1916, provided a "basic" 8-hour day for railroad workers in interstate commerce; the time over 8 hours actually on duty was further penalized in 1919 when the law compelled the computation of this overtime at $1\frac{1}{2}$ times the pay rate for the basic 8 hours.   Between these two dates, the U. S. Supreme Court in 1917 had declared the Adamson Act to be constitutional (*Wilson v. New,* 243 U. S. 332), although the railroad attorneys contended it was a pay measure not an hours law, and that Congress had no power to meddle in wage contracts.

In water transportation, the hours of deck officers set by a law of 1913 were 9 out of 24 in port and 12 out of 24 while at sea.   A law of 1915 limited the hours of seamen while in port to 9 in 24.

Hazardous Trades.—Utah was the leader in the control of the hours of labor of men engaged in the hazardous trades of mining and smelting; the court test, over her law of 1896, settled the question of constitutionality.   In this case *Holden v. Hardy* (169 U. S. 366), the Supreme Court in 1898 said the Utah law was constitutional; in reaching this conclusion, the Court reasoned that the police power of the state changed with changing conditions and this dictum played a part in most later cases in which labor legislation was tied to police power.   In the next quarter of a century 16 states, in which mining and smelting were important, enacted 8-hour measures for some or all classes of employments in these industries.   An example of limited application was the Pennsylvania law, which applied only to hoisting engineers in anthracite mines, whereas the Arizona law (1912) broadly covered all employment in all varieties of mines.

Factory Employment.—There were scarcely any attempts to regulate by law the hours of men engaged in factories or workshops.   Mississippi in 1912 and Oregon in 1913 enacted laws limiting the working hours of men to 10 a day. The Oregon law was carried to and upheld by the U. S. Supreme Court. In this case, *Bunting v. Oregon* (243 U. S. 426), the paramount questions were those of the police power of states and the hazard to health and citizenship of long work hours. A legal brief defending the act, drawn by Felix Frankfurter and Josephine Goldmark, used again the method that had been significant and effective in the Brandeis-Goldmark brief ten years earlier, in defense of the 10-hour act for women in the same state.

A law setting 8 hours as a maximum for all workers passed by the Alaska legislature in 1917, was said to be unconstitutional by the Federal Circuit Court of Appeals. This decision was not carried to the Supreme Court. Before the Oregon case was finished, North Carolina in 1915 enacted an 11-hour law applicable to all men in manufacturing enterprises. In 1923 Oregon enacted an 8-hour day for men in factories, to become effective when adjoining states passed similar laws. In 1924 Mississippi placed a weekly limit of 55 hours on men's work in factories. Special employments, on account of their danger to workers or their vital effects to the public, have been singled out for legislative attention. Electric plants (Arizona), stationary firemen (La.), plaster and cement mills (Arizona, Nevada), sawmills and planing mills (Arkansas), bakeries (New Jersey), and brickyards (New York) are cases in point. In a few states there was some hour limitation for workers in drug and grocery stores.

On the whole, the generation after 1896 left men to shift for themselves in the matter of hours of labor, so that for the most part whatever shortening of the work day was done was inaugurated as a rule by men organized into unions.

Laws in Regard to Working Conditions

The legislation relating to working conditions—the third one of the workers' triad, "wages, hours, and working conditions"—fell within the legal classification "laws for safety and health." Nearly all of the acts passed referred to such matters as ventilation, lighting, time for meals and rest, sanitary measures and equipment, seats and rest rooms for women, and facilities for the prevention of and escape from fire. Certain occupations were licensed (e.g., anthracite miners, aviators, chauffeurs, barbers, electricians, horseshoers, movie operators, plumbers, stationary engineers, and firemen). Certain persons were excluded from particular employments (children from dangerous mendicancy, etc.; women from mines, etc.; messengers from brothels; convicts from mines and other occupations). About a dozen types of work or work places were subject to special codes, because the jobs were either dangerous to those who did them or to the public. Among these were cigar factories, docks, laundries, mines, smelters and quarries, public works, stores, street and steam railways, ships and boats, and tunnels. Places for the manufacture or sale of food or beverage were hedged with laws.

Although all these acts to some degree benefited labor, none touched labor's greatest risks: namely, accident, industrial disease, unemployment, and superannuation. Concerning these only the first—accident—got a great amount of attention between 1896 and 1929.

Workmen's Compensation Laws

Under Common Law.—The law, in respect to responsibility for accidents to workers, traced back to the common law decisions regulating relations between Master and Servant, of which Employer's Liability was a separate category. Under common law, employers were expected to provide reasonably safe work places, reasonably competent workers, and reasonably necessary instructions. The test of reasonableness was "ordinary usage." If an employer were negligent in any of the three reponsibilities and in consequence a worker was injured, the latter or his dependents could sue the employer for money damages comparable to the injuries. The employer was able to secure three common law defenses for such suits. He was relieved from payment of damages if he could prove that the worker knew the danger but assumed it by taking, and continuing in, the job; or if the accident was due to the worker's own negligence; or if a fellow-worker, by negligence, had caused the injury.

Before the Industrial Revolution, the common law of employer-liability provided substantial justice. Work was done with hand tools in small groups of men. Tool users, in acquirement of skill, had learned the risks and safeguards of their craft. If their employer unnecessarily increased the risks or omitted the safeguards, the worker knew what happened; if he stayed on the job it was reasonable to say he had assumed the risks. The smallness of the work group made it possible for each member thoroughly to know the others; so if one was so careless as to endanger the others, they could complain or leave. If the careless one hurt himself, the others knew where to lay the blame.

Why Ineffective.—The Industrial Revolution completely altered work relations. The extremes of the change were noticed first in regard to railroads. To be sure, every one knew that most railroad jobs were dangerous; but employers did not always mitigate the dangers as much as they might—indeed the business was so highly competitive, that most railroads had to be forced by law to adopt known safety devices, such as automatic couplers and air brakes. Railroading, earlier than any other industry, made conspicuous the unfairness of the "fellow servant" defense against liability. To say—as courts did— that the engineer on one locomotive and the firemen on another were fellow servants, or that a train dispatcher in Philadelphia, a one-armed gateman in Paoli, and a switchman in Altoona were fellow servants of a brakeman injured in Harrisburg, were taken as stock examples of the follies of legal fictions.[7] Contributory negligence on the part of an injured railroad man was easy to assert and hard to disprove. Railway managers generally said that their injured employes got hurt by reason of the worker's own "carelessness." This word covered cases of men dulled by the fatigue of 20 hours of work, exhausted by blistering heat, or blinded by fog or snow. If they then failed to heed a signal, they were "careless." If the railroader was killed, the managers nearly always covered their own deficiencies

---

[7] The earliest definitive case was *Farwell v. Boston and Worcester Railroad Corporation* (4 Met. 49, 38 Am. Dec. 339, 1842).

by the accusation that the dead man—who could not answer—was careless.

Risk to Employers.—On the other hand, employers always were confronted by the possibility that juries, sympathetic with the injured or dead, would grant enormous damages. Any case in which a skilled lawyer could present a pathetic story or spectacle to the jury, or one in which the injured person and jury belonged to the same class, could almost certainly cause the jury to spend the money of the soul-less corporation for the benefit of the injured plaintiff.

To protect themselves, employers insured their risk in Employers' Liability Insurance Companies. These, too, dated from the earliest days of railroading; at first the policies covered the accident liability of travelers; but when railroads became safer for passengers, the insurance companies shifted to the writing of policies for managers against the risk of suits from railway workers. The broadening sweep of the Industrial Revolution brought more employer clients to the insurance companies. Their tactics in getting immediate releases from hurt workers or in putting their most wily lawyers before juries in damage suits caused them to be more generally detested than the "trusts."

If, despite the suavity of the most skilled insurance attorney, a jury did award damages, these often did little good to the hurt worker. The long delay in the suit—averaging 3 to 5 years—was enough to pauperize a man. Besides, his own lawyer usually had taken the case on a basis of "contingent fee." With honest lawyers this fee ran as high as 26% of the award and with the other kind of attorney the fee might be 75% or more. The poor worker sometimes got nothing from a case he won except the entertainment.

Movement for Statute.—Long before 1896, therefore, there were many proposals to patch the common law of Employers' Liability so as to bring it more in accord with the facts of capitalistic industry. The predecessor of the American Federation of Labor in 1881 called for "stricter laws to make employers liable for all accidents due to their own incompetency or negligence." The next year the same body asked for laws that would remove the "fellow-servant" defense of employers, a demand repeated by the American Federation of Labor in 1909 and 1910. All but eight states did put into statutes their own interpretations of the common law concerning Employers' Liability; although many of these made new rules concerning the liability of railroads and street railways to their workpeople, none removed the real evils.

Meanwhile, led by Germany in 1884 and Great Britain in 1897, the European countries were abandoning the common law principles of Employers' Liability and instead enacting accident insurance laws eventually known in the United States as Workmen's Compensation acts. As usual, Americans except social reformers, gave these scant heed. When the British act of 1897 was passed our leaders began investigations.

Faulty Early Statutes.—Massachusetts in 1898 appointed an investigatory commission that reported in 1901; and in New York John Ford—later a Justice of the Supreme Court of that state—introduced into the state Senate (February 22) a bill for Workmen's Compensation. The Social Reform Club of New York sponsored the Ford bill vainly, as it turned out, because the bill was smothered in the Judiciary Committee. Maryland in 1902 passed a law applicable to workers in coal and clay mines, quarries, street railways, and steam railroads. Nine employers agreed to accept the law's provisions, and five fatalities were settled under it, before the Baltimore Court of Common Pleas in 1904 declared it unconstitutional.

Massachusetts again in 1903 appointed an investigation commission which among other things looked into the operation of the law on liability. Its report January 13, 1904, advised against amendments to the Employers' Liability Act; it did strongly recommend the enactment of a Workmen's Compensation Act. The advice went without action. The same things happened in Illinois in 1905.

Massachusetts in 1908 and New York in 1910 passed Workmen's Compensation Acts and so also did Montana (1909) and

Maryland (1910). The Massachusetts law, as amended in 1909, offered Workmen's Compensation as a substitute for Employer's Liability if both or either employers and workers elected the choice; since none did, the law was a dead letter. The New York act made compensation compulsory; it was declared unconstitutional on March 24, 1911 (*Ives v. South Buffalo Ry. Co.,* 201 N. Y. 271) because it denied jury trial and by its compulsion took property without due process of law. A Washington law of 1911 similar to the New York statute was upheld in the state of Washington, September 27, 1911. The Montana law applied to coal mines and washers and by an assessment of .01 cent per ton created an "Employers and Employees Cooperative Insurance and Permanent Disability Fund" from which the injured were paid $1 a day, and the dependents of the killed got $3,000. This was declared unconstitutional (*Cunningham v. Northwestern Improvement Co.,* 44 Montana 180) because a worker could elect *after injury* whether to take the compensation of the law or to sue at common law, and this the Court said, "made the employer pay into the Fund without release from damage liability."

Contribution of President Theodore Roosevelt.—About this time two powerful forces got behind the proposals for Workmen's Compensation. One was Theodore Roosevelt who in messages to Congress urged action in protection of government workers. Congress complied with the act of May 30, 1908, a narrow application to wage earners in arsenals, navy yards, rivers and harbors work, reclamation projects, and Isthmian Canal employes. In 1911 all Canal Zone workers were included; and the next year the employes in the Bureau of Mines, Forestry Bureau, and Light House Service were added. In April 1908 Congress made all interstate, Territories, Canal Zone, and District of Columbia railroads liable for all accidents to employes. Contested by the New York, New Haven, and Hartford Railroad (*Mondou v. N. Y., N. H. and H. R. R.,* 223 U. S. 1), the United States Supreme Court in 1912 upheld the statute. The same year, Congress broadened the Compensation Act for government workers.　All of this activity got the publicity always granted to the major legislation of Congress.

Pittsburgh Survey.—The second force was an investigation of work accidents in the Pittsburgh area during 1907-08, as part of a larger Pittsburgh Survey carried on by the Russell Sage Foundation.　One of the six volumes of the Survey was "Work Accidents and the Law," by Crystal Eastman.　This book first gave the startling results of a thorough investigation of the 526 wage earners killed in Allegheny County, Pennsylvania from July 1, 1906 to June 30, 1907 on railroads, in coal mines and steel mills, and in other local industries.　The results were startling: first, because the majority of men killed were not "hunkies" but Americans; secondly, because Pittsburgh accepted such death tolls with equanimity; and thirdly, because neither the state nor the employing companies gave adequate, if any, relief to the dependents.　From this revelation, as well as from other stimulations, there was organized the American Association for Labor Legislation; the first campaign of this body was for Workmen's Compensation.

The Opposition.—Likewise, the opponents of this kind of law (or of some of its details) organized into several associations.　There was the Insurance Economics Society of America (Chicago), Insurance Federation of America (Detroit), National Workmen's Compensation Service Bureau (New York), and Workmen's Compensation Publicity Bureau (New York).　These counted on the assistance—not in vain—of the National Civic Federation, the National Association of Manufacturers, the United States Chamber of Commerce with its affiliates after 1912, and for a time of organized labor.

The proponents showed how obsolete were the old common law rules in respect to Employers' Liability; how great was the need for Workmen's Compensation; that it had desirable bases in the fields of morals, social good, and economics.　They pointed out that the costs were small and could be carried as insurance.　They prodded national pride by reference to fact all industrial nations had such laws save United States and Turkey; and no nation ever had repealed its compensation law.

The opponents claimed that the workers were not urging the law, but in fact were opposed; so the real agitators were impractical reformers, together with Socialists and Progressive Republicans. These being more skillful with words than facts grossly exaggerated the distress of workers. Relief already was organized by unions, fraternal societies, and employers' Voluntary Relief Associations, e.g., the Pennsylvania R. R. Voluntary Relief Department, the International Harvester Industrial Accident Department (May 1, 1910), and the U. S. Steel Corporation Voluntary Accident Relief Plan (April 15, 1910). Workmen's Compensation would burden industry with an obligation not theirs but that of society. "Good" industries would be taxed for the inefficiencies of "bad" ones. The tax would depress wages for it was really part of the return paid to labor. Workmen's Compensation had been defective in Norway and England. Finally it was unconstitutional, for it denied jury trial, denied equal protection of the laws (if limited to "dangerous" trades or any specific list), took property without due process of law, infringed liberty of contract, and by making employers liable for *all* accidents, constituted a liability without fault.

New Method.—In 1911 the proponents found a way to make a law that on the face was voluntary but really was compulsory. (The opponents called it "legislative trickery.") The law was "elective"; but if employers did not "elect" its provisions, they were denied their common law defences. If workers did not "elect" it, they had to run the gauntlet of the employers' common law defenses. To guarantee payment of compensation, the employers had to secure some kind of insurance. A commission of 1-5 persons was to decide disputed cases of compensation. In that year of 1911 no less than ten states enacted statutes after this pattern, with New Jersey taking the lead.

Immediately the opponents took these laws into court. Only one state court (Kentucky, 1914)[8] disqualified the laws, and the United States Supreme Court, 1917, completely substan-

---

[8] An earlier elective law of New York, enacted in 1910, had been declared unconstitutional almost at once. The state constitution was amended and New York in 1913 passed another law that stood the tests of both state and federal courts.

tiated them (*New York Central R. R. Co. v. White,* 243 U. S. 188).

Before the U. S. Supreme Court spoke, the drift of state decisions was unmistakable. Therefore, the number of states taking action steadily progressed so that by 1918 there were 38 (and 3 territories) that had legislated. By 1929 all but 5 states (Arkansas, Florida, Mississippi, North Carolina, and South Carolina) had joined in the movement for Workmen's Compensation; so had the District of Columbia (1919 and 1928), Hawaii (1915), Philippines (1905 and 1927), and Porto Rico (1916).

Opposition to Details.—Despite this sweep, which virtually abrogated the common law defenses of Employers' Liability, the opponents continued their attacks. These, however, were directed against details of the new Workmen's Compensation legislation, and especially against state insurance in the new laws first adopted by Washington in 1911 and followed by Oregon, Nevada, North Dakota, and Wyoming. The National Workmen's Compensation Service Bureau (P. Tecumseh Sherman, spokesman), a subsidiary of insurance companies that together commanded a billion dollars, and with branch offices throughout the nation—this agency kept an unremitting pressure against state invasion of the field of insurance, for insurance was the companies' private domain. So also, the Association of Casualty and Surety Executives (F. Robertson Jones, general manager), agitated against state invasion of the field of private business, as did likewise the National Council of Insurance Federations (Fred L. Gray, President).

Case Against State Fund.—Their argument ran as follows: Insurance was a highly technical business and the state, a newcomer in operation in a little corner of the whole industry of insurance, could not command the ability possessed by giant companies with generations of experience. Levy of assessments and awards ought not be in the same hands; for when expedient both would be juggled. When the state controls the insurance, the employer loses all feeling of responsibility; he says, "I've paid my assessment, now let the state take care of the workpeople." The state insurance was supervised with an eye to politics, not to business efficiency, and justice. Hence, the political-insurance men, for political patronage, would be too liberal with malingerers and those with political "pull." Anyway, who would trust a politician? The private insurance companies were kept efficient and expert by competition; the state monopoly would become slothful and consequently inefficient and behind the times. The very idea of monopoly was repugnant to Americans. The state system was more costly and slower in action than the private companies. The private companies, also, were more secure; they distributed risks upon a national, not state basis, and if their assets shrank, their stockholders could be assessed; and finally, if they failed, the worker could collect directly from his employer. Not so the state fund; it had to be self-sustaining without legislative appropriations for deficits, and when an employer paid his dues he was finished with his liability.

Case for State Fund.—To these contentions, the first reply was the finger pointed at the record of the old Employers' Liability Insurance Companies. Between 1900 and 1910, some ten of these companies had collected $181 million in premiums and paid $37 million in damages. The New York State Insurance Fund alone, in its first three years, paid $36 million in compensations. The record of the old companies was in such odorous repute, that the mere suggestion that they share the new compensation business raised a fierce growl of protest. Why should any insurance stockholders make profits out of human suffering? The need to earn profits made the insurance of private companies much more costly than state insurance. By the records per dollar of collections, the companies took 40 cents for "expenses" while the state insurance scheme took only 10 cents, a difference in one state and one year of several million dollars. The state was more prompt and equitable in payments to the injured because the companies either threw every slightest doubtful case into the courts or coerced a man to take less than was his due. The reserve funds of the state insurance furnished an excellent market for state securities.   It was the state that created the compensation insurance industry, so the state ought to get the benefits, passing them to employers in lower rates and to workers in higher compensation allowances.

By one means or another, the insurance companies persuaded most legislatures not to establish a state monopolistic state fund. At the other extreme, a few states did not force employers to carry any kind of indemnity insurance.   The majority of states made employers take some kind of insurance, but left the variety at the option of the employer.   His choice lay between a State Fund—this was not true of all states offering options— stock insurance companies operated for profit, mutual non-profit insurance, and self-insurance.   Another form called "reciprocal" or "inter-insurance," by which one employer insured another by means of an attorney-in-fact—to whom power of attorney was granted—was so easily subject to evil practices, that some states (e.g., New York) prohibited it in connection with compensation affairs.

Special Decisions.—To administer the law, a few states depended entirely on the courts, usually with a proviso that the courts must place compensation cases at the top of the docket. Most states created Commissions of from 1-5 persons to do all the tasks necessary to operate the compensation law.   In practice, one of the most frequent duties of the commissions was to decide doubtful cases of liability.   Here are illustrative cases:

> Massachusetts: A hand-bill distributor suffered an injury because he failed to wear gloves on a day when the temperature was 17 degrees below zero.   Held that such failure did not constitute wilful misconduct.
>
> New York: An inmate of an old men's home was injured while doing carpentry work about the premises for a nominal consideration.   Held he was not an "employe" and therefore not entitled to compensation.
>
> Ohio: A workman, while fooling around in a part of a factory where his duties did not call him, suffered burns from a hot can inserted in his overalls, as a joke, by another employe.   The "joker" was fired and the injured

workman was denied compensation on the ground that the injury was not sustained in the course of his employment.

Nebraska: A truck driver employed to deliver gasoline drove to a town some four miles outside his territory for a purpose of his own, and on his return to his territory but before reaching it, was injured in an accident. Held that injury did not arise out of and in the course of the employment.

New York: A man and his wife were janitor and janitress of a building. She threw lye in his face when he reproached her for using too much coal in a heater. Held that the resulting injury arose out of and in the course of employment.

Unions' Stand.—We have said that organized labor at first opposed Workmen's Compensation laws. In Connecticut and Illinois, the officers of the State Federations appeared in the legislative halls and urged the law-makers not to produce these statutes. The unions had two fears: one was that state compensation would reduce the effectiveness of union benefit schemes; the other was that in accepting the state law, workers would waive their rights to suits, and then if the laws were declared unconstitutional by courts, the workers would be left with no legal redress for injury.

The abatement of the latter fear in 1917, together with the number and undoubted popularity of the acts, caused unions to "get on the band-wagon" in order to use their power in cooperation with other agencies to increase the scope of the laws.

Scope of Laws.—Some of the laws were limited to hazardous occupations (12 states); some exempted government (federal states, county, city) employes (5 states); some did not apply to casual labor or work done that was not in the usual course of an employer's trade or business. None of the laws included domestic servants and only New Jersey included farm laborers. There was constant effort to abrogate these exemptions so that all labor would be compensated for injuries.

All except the Washington and Oregon laws, in order to prevent malingering, self-injury, or shams, provided for some kind of waiting period, with two weeks the most frequent time limit. This delay and loss was attacked as unjust. Some of the states compensated for the waiting period if the injury extended beyond specific times. Nearly all the states whittled the waiting period down to a week or less, but most of them refused to abolish it.

The amount and price of hospital, nurse, medical, or surgical service was a constant source of dispute. So, also, were the provisions, where they existed, that workers must patronize specified medical practitioners. Likewise, the financial limits of compensation gave trouble. At first the compensation varied as to the hurt, and did not exceed 50% of the weekly wage. This, too, was limited as to the number of weeks it would be paid, and subject, in most states, to minimum and maximum sums per week and per injury.

Workers Still Carry Burden.—Taken together, all these exceptions, limitations, and special rules, pared the amounts paid and also the numbers of those considered within the scope of the laws. Therefore, the laws did not, as popularly supposed, lift entirely from the wage earners the burdensome cost of accidents. Besides the exclusions already mentioned, the little employer with less than 10, 5, or 2 workers usually was exempted and so were big ones in particular industries in certain states, e.g., distilleries in Kentucky, cotton gins in Texas, and loggers in Maine. The friends of labor drew statistics that showed workers under the most favorable conditions still bearing 50% of the costs of accidents, and under the least favorable the percentage mounted from 65 to 80. Therefore, there was no recession in the pressure for changes in the laws that would bring greater relief.

Industrial Disease.—No one proposal was more insistent nor more rigidly opposed than the inclusion of industrial diseases as compensable industrial accidents. In Iowa, Massachusetts, California, and the Federal Act this was no problem, for the courts interpreted the laws to cover both disabilities, since the wording was "personal injury" not as elsewhere "personal injury by accident." That certain occupations did give rise to specific ailments was accepted fact. Illustrations were lead poisoning; the "bends," due to too hasty decompression of workers who had been under compressed air; "spelter shakes," a disease afflicting some brass-casters; anthrax, a wool sorter's infectious pustular disease; and silicosis, a rock or sand injury to the lungs. Dusty work such as stone-cutting, grinding or buffing operations, and textile crafts all were conducive to eye, ear, nose, throat, and lung ailments. Heavy lifting was likely to produce hernia.

Case Against Inclusion of Diseases.—The opponents of compensation for occupational diseases said they were not against payments to victims of unquestionable industrial diseases; they were afraid, according to F. Robertson Jones, that once these were made compensable, the legislatures next would admit borderline diseases and finally force employers to pay the sickness bill of the entire community. "It already was noticeable," said C. B. Auel of the Westinghouse Electric and Manufacturing Company, "that hernia seldom occurred outside working hours; never on a Sunday or holiday."

If a disease directly resulted from an accident, it was compensable in nearly all the states. For other occupational diseases, actions were taken by the legislatures of 14 states. Some covered certain scheduled diseases, some stated occupational diseases either without definition or in vague terms, some defined the diseases as "peculiar to occupations and due to causes in excess of the ordinary hazards of employment as such." The Wisconsin 1919 and 1931 laws covered "mental or physical harm caused by accident or disease." Minnesota, New Jersey, New York, and Ohio were among the earliest to compensate for diseases; in all of these states the compensable diseases were listed and the laws operated with a minimum of litigation. In Connecticut the original law covered only accidents, but was amended in 1919 to include any kind of disability, whether or not directly connected to occupations. The flood of claims and litigation caused a change in 1927 by modifying clauses that ruled out pre-existing lowered vitality.

The insurance companies at the end of our period, 1929, were most resistant to the inclusion of silicosis as a recognized compensable occupational disease, because it was so widespread, so progressive, and so costly—a loss cost sometimes $24 per $100 of wages. The trend in 1929 toward adding occupational disease to laws that had not already done so, and liberalizing the definition in those that had done so, alarmed the insurance companies. Said P. Tecumseh Sherman, "Before we commit ourselves too far in making compensation into ordinary invalidity and life insurance for workers, we should pause and carefully consider the consequences. The true welfare of the wage workers is not served by ill considered and impracticable perversions of the principle of workmen's compensation. These new rules of compensation would spell widespread ruin for industry unless it weeds out the ailing and the aging from among its workers [bringing to them] more of a curse than a blessing."

At the end of the generation (1929), as at the beginning of the compensation movement in 1911, the insurance leopard had the same spots in the same places.

Results of Laws.—What have been the results of the Workmen's Compensation Acts? One was immeasurable; that was the mental comfort and financial aid rendered to injured wage earners and their dependents by the certain family income during the time when the bread winner was laid low. Only those who know the narrow money margin on which most worker families have to live can fully appreciate this.

Other results were more visible. At once in 1911 and increasingly so afterwards, employers rushed to make their work places safe; exposed gears, belts, fly-wheels, saws, and blades were covered; floor and elevator openings were guarded by rails or doors; dust conveyors were installed; workers who toiled amidst flying chips were forced to wear goggles; handlers of raw materials had to don gloves; molders and others were commanded to buy easily removable fireproof shoes; and so on down a long list. Windows were cleaned, and fitted with panes that gave the proper distribution of light, cluttered aisles cleared, electric switches covered, glaring lamps shaded, danger signs posted, and in general the premises made safe.

Although these precautions produced some startling reductions in accidents—as much as 60%—nevertheless an expensive lot remained. Since most of these were due to men and not material things, employers indulged in endless "safety campaigns." Indeed the states, the insurance companies, and the engineering profession created a new branch called "safety engineering."

Next, the medical profession was called into the mills. Some employers bought merely a first-aid kit and trained an employe (s) in its use; every slightest scratch was treated. The larger enterprises went into medicine on grander scales; the most elaborate were fully equipped and regularly staffed plant hospitals and dispensaries. Then dentists, oculists, and dietitians were employed either full time or on call. Workers were given periodic physical examinations from hair to toenails. The plant also was searched for germs, and their cultures cleansed; likewise, illumination, sanitation, and ventilation were scrutinised from the health viewpoint. In 1929 the average medical expenditure for a group of plants, investigated by the National Industrial Conference Board, was $5.10 per worker. Department stores spent $1.11 per worker; tobacco factories, $2.41; paper mills, $7.10; and metal plant, $7.44. The largest expenditure per plant was $75,000 (10,000 employes).

Rehabilitation.—The most delayed result of Workmen's Compensation was to rehabilitate those drawing partial or permanent disability allowances. The work done by the federal government for soldier and sailor casualties of the World War drew attention to the far larger and continuous casualties of industry. Congress, on June 2, 1920, appropriated sums to be matched by states for rehabilitation and re-training. Some of the states got their funds from the death benefits of workers who left no heirs or dependents. The insurance companies and employers protested this but were overruled by the United States Supreme Court in *Sheehan Co. v. Shuler* (1924, 265 U. S. 371).

Social Insurance.—A final result of the new laws was the direction of attention to other forms of social insurance, such as health insurance, mothers' pensions and maternity aid, unemployment insurance, and old age pensions. Health insurance was studied by nine states before 1919, and in 1920 a bill was introduced in the New York Senate; then and later, these proposals were unitedly opposed by the associations of medical doctors but were given increasing support by the surgeons. The American Association for Labor Legislation prepared a model health insurance bill as early as 1914, and it was this that started the agitation. No state before 1929 enacted legislation on the subject but there were thorough studies made on the "Cost of Medical Care."

Mothers' pension laws were passed by Minnesota (1917) and 41 other states before 1925. This was the only kind of social legislation in which the United States led the world. Congress in 1921 passed a grant-in-aid act for maternity cases and 45 states matched this financial assistance.

Unemployment insurance was talked about, but no state except Wisconsin acted before 1929. Bills were introduced in the Wisconsin legislature in 1921 and 1924 and this state after 1929 was the first to enact an unemployment insurance statute. The law was passed in 1932 but not immediately operative.

Old age pensions however, to replace almshouses and other institutional care of the aged, were toyed with in Massachusetts in 1903 and got a real start in Arizona in 1914, although the law was declared void. [*State Board of Control v. Buckstegge* (1916), 18 Arizona 277, 158 Pac. 837]. Congress as early as 1906, by an act amended in 1913, provided pensions for Alaskans; deriving the funds from liquor, occupation, and trade licenses outside of incorporated Alaskan towns. Alaska itself provided a law in 1915, Montana in 1923; and Nevada and Pennsylvania in the same year set up old age pension schemes, although the last named was voided by the Pennsylvania Supreme Court. Congress set up a compulsory contributory pension scheme for civil service employes in 1920. The movement did not make headway until after 1929; our terminal date. (There were laws by 28 states and 2 territories by 1935.) Nevertheless, old age pension laws were the next great social security measures, aside from mothers' pensions, to get considerable national attention after the rising wave of Workmen's Compensation Acts. (The federal Social Security Act was passed in 1935.)

Syndicalism Laws.—Opposite to all the legislation so far described, all of it favorable to labor, were the laws known as "criminal syndicalism statutes" whose intent was hostile to certain kinds of labor.

Criminal syndicalism was defined as "the doctrine which advocates crime, sabotage, or unlawful methods of terrorism as a means of accomplishing industrial or political reform." Sabotage was defined as "malicious damage or injury to the property of an employer by an employe." By the definitions, it is easy to see that the laws were aimed first at the Industrial Workers of the World and could be used against Communists or any other revolutionary union. Employers used the hysterical World War period to get the criminal syndicalism statutes enacted.

Idaho, March 14, 1917, and Minnesota the next month were the first states to pass these measures. Almost standardized duplicates of the first pair of laws, a fact that emphasized their common origin, were voted by the legislatures of Alabama, Arizona, California, Iowa, Kansas, Michigan, Montana, Nebraska, Nevada, Ohio, Oklahoma, Oregon, South Dakota, Utah, and Washington—17 states in total. In addition, Alaska and Hawaii had similar statutes while Indiana and Wyoming had laws directed in the first case against the general strike and in the second against crime as a means of political or industrial changes. New York revived an old statute that prohibited criminal anarchy.

Upheld by Courts.—These laws where tested in courts were upheld; e.g., Minnesota, California, Michigan, Idaho, and Kansas. Two cases in 1927 reached the U. S. Supreme Court, *Whitney v. California* (274 U. S. 357) and *Burns v. United States* (274 U. S. 328). Miss Whitney was convicted for membership in the Communist Labor Party, although she had tried (vainly) to confine its activities to those that were legal and political. The Supreme Court upheld this conviction. Burns, convicted for membership in the I. W. W. in Yosemite National Park, likewise got no relief from the Supreme Court. These two cases validated the state criminal syndicalism laws. Prior to these two cases, the U. S. Supreme Court in *Gitlow v. New York* (45 Sup. Ct. 332) had upheld the state's criminal anarchy statute, on the ground that Gitlow's rights of free speech and press could be suspended when he exercised them "when there was a clear and present danger" as he did in the war years.

The use of criminal syndicalism laws against the I. W. W. in the war years, and later, almost completely destroyed that organization; in California, mere membership was ground for imprisonment. The laws were turned against the Communists perhaps much to their delight, because the cases attracted attention, martyrised the defendants, and in general furnished pegs for propaganda.

Civil Liberties Union.—The syndicalism laws, together with federal war-time acts, aroused such fears that constitutional guarantees would be weakened or abrogated that a group of lawyers and others formed, in 1917, the National Civil Liberties Bureau. The principle for which this body stood was "the right of free expression is the only sure guarantee of orderly progress." The Bureau arranged for defense counsel for persons indicted under the above laws. In 1920 with a national network of members pledged to aid persons charged with or jailed for offenses that in essence were political, the organization became the Civil Liberties Union.

In the early 1920's, the C. L. U. was busied with obtaining the release of state and federal political prisoners of whom there were more than 100 confined in American penitentiaries. In the later years of the decade, the organization transferred its services almost entirely to the industrial field against legal or armed restraints upon assemblage, speech, press, and picketing.   Most of its work required both courage and knowledge of the law.

The Communists after the middle of the decade had their own "defense" organization.   Since Communists at times broke up meetings of opponents or factions, they themselves were objects of persuasion by the Civil Liberties Union to preserve the rights of assemblage and speech.

Two other pieces of legislation of unusual significance were the Clayton (1914) and Adamson (1916) Acts.   If 1929 were not the limit of our discussion, the Norris-LaGuardia Act of 1932 also would be included.   We will allude to all three of these laws in the next chapter.

CHAPTER 9

IMPORTANT COURT DECISIONS

Although we have cited numerous legal cases involving labor, none was given more than passing glances. Inasmuch as labor history, and perhaps the broader history of the United States, were conditioned by a continuous series of court battles after 1896, it is necessary to intensify our scrutiny of a few of the most important cases. Those that ended in state courts were too numerous to be included in our survey; we therefore will confine attention to cases brought in one way or another to the United States Supreme Court.[1]

1898.—Early in the generation, citizens were made aware of the powers of judges to hasten or halt social reform, and to erect restraints or safeguards upon organized labor and its leaders. The first important case, *Holden v. Hardy* (169 U. S. 366; 1898), arose over an act of the legislature of Utah, March 30, 1896, limiting to 8 hours per day workmen employed in underground mines and in smelters and ore-reduction works. The statute was contested on the grounds that it infringed the 14th Amendment by abridging the privileges or immunities of citizens, that it deprived both labor and employer of property without due process of law, and denied them equal protection of the laws.

The U S. Supreme Court did not deal separately with each of these points, but considered them together because the authorities upon each were more or less pertinent to the others. In opening its opinion the court made an observation, important not only in itself, but because it later was so often quoted. Mr. Justice Henry B. Brown said:

In passing upon the validity of state legislation under that [14th] Amendment, this court has not failed to recognize the fact that the law

---

[1] In its printed opinions, this body does not use capital letters in references to itself or other courts.

is, to a certain extent, a progressive science; that in some of the states methods of procedure which, at the time the Constitution was adopted, were deemed essential to the protection and safety of the people, or to the liberty of the citizen, have been found to be no longer necessary; that restrictions which had formerly been laid upon the conduct of individuals, or of classes of individuals, had proved detrimental to their interests; while, upon the other hand, certain other classes of persons, particularly those engaged in dangerous or unhealthful employments, have been found to be in need of additional protection. . . .

While the cardinal principles of justice are immutable, the methods by which justice is administered are subject to constant fluctuation, and the Constitution of the United States, which is necessarily, and to a large extent, inflexible and exceedingly difficult of amendment, should not be construed as to deprive the states of the power to so amend their laws as to make them conform to the wishes of the citizens as they may deem best for the public welfare, without bringing them into conflict with the supreme law of the land . . . and the law [must] be forced to adapt itself to new conditions of society, and, particularly, to the new relations between employers and employes as they arise.

In digression, may it be remarked that few better statements of the mutability of law have been recorded. If judges, including Justices of the U. S. Supreme Court, always had borne it in mind there would have been much less ill repute and abuse heaped upon the law and its interpreters.

In the instant case, this view of the law was adhered to. The argument that the Utah statute was a deprivation of property, and a violation of free contract, was submerged under the power of states to limit both, in order to preserve health, safety or morals, or abate nuisances. Mining frequently had been brought under this police power; the Supreme Court of Utah had found that poisonous gases, dust, and impalpable substances in the state's mines or smelters had produced morbid, noxious, and often deadly effects upon the human system when too long exposed to the dangers. Both courts agreed that the correction of these things properly came within the police power of the state, and that a short work-period was an effective curb upon the dangerous consequences of the work. Self-interest was no safe guide in such matters because the bargaining powers of employers and workers was not on an equality. In this case the prosecution was against the employer whose defense was not so much the infringment of his own right to contract, but the right of his employes to labor as long as they pleased. "The argument," said Justice Brown, "would come with better grace and greater cogency from the latter class." In this case the facts of employment clearly supported the legislature in exercising the police power to protect the health, safety, and welfare of the workers even if they, themselves, were reckless.

Mr. Justice Brewer and Mr. Justice Peckham dissented.

1903.—The second case, *Atkin v. Kansas* (191 U. S. 207; 1903), also dealt with state regulation of the hours of work, that of a Kansas Act in 1891, setting 8 hours for public work. This case differed from the earlier one in that the work regulated was not especially dangerous to health or life. The point here at issue was whether the state could regulate the hours of a person working for a contractor who in turn was engaged by Kansas City to repair, grade, and pave certain streets. The city contract contained no specification in respect to hours of work.

Atkin, a contractor, had hired George Reese, common laborer, at the rate of 15 cents per hour for a 10-hour day, the then current wage and time for that class of worker engaged by private persons or corporations. Arrested for violation of the state law, Atkin was fined $50 on each count of the complaint. His appeal to the courts of Kansas was not sustained so he turned to the United States Supreme Court.

The claim was made that the statute violated the first section of the 14th Amendment, deprived of liberty without due process of law, and denied equal protection of the laws.

Mr. Justice Harlan said that Atkin's counsel attached "too little consequence to the relation existing between a state and its municipal corporations. . . . They were in every essential sense only auxiliaries of the state for the purpose of local government." The work done by Atkin was one which the state, if it had wished, could have done by its own agents. "Whether done by the state directly or by one of its instrumentalities the work was of a public, not private character." There could be no possible ground to dispute the power of the state to regulate the working standards of any one working for the state or one of its municipal agencies.   If state statutes for state work were mischievous, the remedy was with the legislature, not the courts. "No evils arising from such legislation could be more far-reaching than those that might come to our system of government if the judiciary, abandoning the sphere assigned to it by the fundamental law, should enter the domain of legislation, and upon grounds merely of justice or reason or wisdom annul statutes that had received the sanction of the people's representatives. . . . The public interest imperatively demands that legislative enactments should be recognized and enforced by the courts as embodying the will of the people, unless they are plainly and palpably beyond all question in violation of the fundamental law of the Constitution."

The judgment of the Supreme Court of Kansas, upholding the 8-hour law and its authority to collect fines from Atkin for violations, was affirmed.   The Chief Justice, Melville W. Fuller, and Justices Brewer and Peckham were in dissent.

1908 (3 Cases).—The year 1908 saw three decisions of the United States Supreme Court, each an oft-quoted precedent in later decisions.   In order of time these cases were first: *Adair v. United States* (208 U. S. 161) ; *Loewe v. Lawlor* (208 U. S. 274) ; and *Muller v. Oregon* (208 U. S. 412).   We will not linger on the third case for that was the one that validated Oregon's 10-hour law for women, already treated in our previous chapter.

Adair Case.—The Adair case was based on Section 10 of the Erdman Act of 1898.   That section (a) prohibited "yellow dog" contracts in the railway industry, (b) discrimination on account of union membership, (c) forced contributions to charitable, social, or beneficial funds (devices used at times to evade employer's liability), and (d) "black-listing."   In the Act these terms were couched in legal verbiage, totaling 254 words.   Adair was indicted for the discharge of a railroad employe contrary to the provisions of this section.

Adair's defense was that Section 10 was unconstitutional for it was repugnant to the 5th Amendment which forbade deprivation of liberty or property without due process of law.   He further averred that Congress had no right to write such provisions for they had no direct relation to interstate commerce.

Mr. Justice Harlan, speaking for the court, assented to both these contentions.   He held that Section 10 was an invasion of personal liberty and of property.   He could find in Section 10 no real or substantial relation to or connection with interstate commerce.   If it was a crime to discharge a man because he was a unionist, Congress equally might legislate that it was criminal to hire any but unionists or only those who were not unionists.   Therefore the court set aside the verdict against Adair and, in effect, wiped out Section 10.

Mr. Justice Joseph McKenna entered a vigorous dissent.   He pointed out that the Erdman Act was passed [1898] in consequence of the Pullman strike of 1894.   The Act of 1888 had failed to avert this strike conjecturally because that Act did not contain the matter of Section 10.   Unions, by their unity, could be an aid or obstacle to the arbitration features of the Erdman Act; Section 10 was a bid for aid.   But how could it aid if railway officials could flout it by mere whim or caprice?   "Liberty is an attractive theme, but the liberty which is exercised in sheer antipathy does not plead strongly for recognition."

The Justice said that "a provision of law which will prevent or tend to prevent the stoppage of every wheel in every car of an entire railroad system certainly has as direct influence on interstate commerce as the way in which one car couples with another, or the rule of liability for personal injuries to an employe. . . . We are dealing with rights exercised in a quasi public business, and therefore, subject to control in the interest of the public."

Justice Oliver Wendell Holmes also filed a dissent.

The importance of this decision lay in its denial of special protections to unionists; if these were not valid in a public utility industry, Congressional or state legislative safeguards of unions in private industry were indeed remote.   The decision virtually sanctioned the practices by which employers closed

their shops to unions under the misnomer of the "open-shop."
In parenthesis it may be noted that the *Adair v. United States*
decision was overruled in 1930 by the *Texas and New Orleans
Railway Company v. Brotherhood of Railway and Steamship
Clerks* (281 U. S. 550).

Loewe v. Lawlor and *Lawlor v. Loewe*.—Of even larger

importance to organized labor than the foregoing cases was the
nearly contemporaneous action generally called the Danbury
Hatters Case. This suit, whose origin was in 1901 and in
which the last chapter was written 16 years later, involved the
question as to whether or not unions were subject to the Sherman Anti-Trust Act.

In March 1901 the United Hatters of America, pursuing a
policy begun in 1897 to make all hat shops exclusively union,
approached the D. E. Loewe Company of Danbury, Connecticut, with the object of enrolling in the union all the hat workers
in the plant, and threatened if resistance was offered "to take
the usual measures." The managers were not compliant; and
so on July 25, 1902, the union ordered a strike of the company's
250 employes to force the Loewe Company to employ only
union members. The strike was backed by a boycott on
Loewe hats, shipments of which were traced in order to clamp
on the boycott in whatever town or state the hats were placed
for sale. The strike-boycott was so effective that the Loewe
Company could not operate during 1902, and when the factory
was reopened in January 1903, it had to rely on an unusual
proportion of unskilled workers. Moreover, the boycott created
a stiff sales resistance, so that the strike and boycott together
caused the company, which in 1901 had cleared a profit of
$27,000, to sustain losses that between 1902 and 1904 amounted
to about $75,000.

Aid was offered to the Loewe Company by the Anti-Boycott
Association and with this assistance the company, August 31,
1903, began a series of suits which, in the next 14 years, ap-
peared four times in federal courts, and two times before the
United States Supreme Court. The suits were taken under
Section 7 of the Sherman Act which reads: "Any person who

shall be injured in his business or property by any other person
or corporation, by reason of anything forbidden or declared to
be unlawful by this Act, may sue therefor in any Circuit Court
of the United States in the district in which the defendant re-
sides or is found, without respect to the amount in controversy,
and shall recover threefold the damages by him sustained, and
the costs of suit, including a reasonable attorney fee."

The Loewe Company on August 31, 1903, in the Circuit
Court for the District of Connecticut, brought suit under the
Sherman Act for damages in the amount of $240,000 naming
the individual members of the Danbury local union and the
officers of the United Hatters as the accused parties. These
demurred on the grounds that the Sherman Act was inappli-
cable to unions, and that a strike in Danbury, with boycotts at
the places of sale, did not interrupt or hinder interstate commerce. Judge James P. Platt on December 7, 1906, in uncertainty as to the position of the United States Supreme Court on
the application of the Sherman Act to unions, and hesitant to
cause the expense of a long trial to decide the suit, dismissed
the complaint of the Loewe Company.

The latter then appealed to the United States Supreme Court:
Loewe v. Lawlor (208 U. S. 274). At the hearings before
this court the defendants entered the same demurrer upon the
same grounds as before, adding that the defendants were not
themselves engaged in interstate trade.

On February 3, 1908, Mr. Chief Justice Fuller delivered the
opinion of the court. He said that in two prior cases, the
Sherman Act had been construed to apply to unions; referring
to: *United States v. Workingmen's Amalgamated Council* (54
Fed. Rep. 994, and 57 Fed. Rep. 85 Louisiana) ; and *In re Debs*
(158 U. S. 564). The instant case the court thought to be
within the statute. Quoting the Louisiana case, the court referred to the Congressional debates prior to the passage of
the Sherman Act, and averred that when spokesmen for farmers
and unions had sought specific exemption, Congress had made
no exceptions; instead the Act applied to *any* conspiracy in restraint of interstate commerce. The court pointed out that a
secondary boycott, itself, was illegal at common law. The fact

that interstate commerce was not physically obstructed or that the defendants themselves were not engaged in interstate trade the court deemed untenable objections. The court's reasoning brought unions under the Sherman Act, made secondary boycotts affecting interstate commerce illegal under the Act, and made it possible to bring damage suits against individual union members.

This decision was a terrible blow to unions although it did not, as they at the time thought, make it necessary for them to become secret societies. The precedent of this case kept unions in litigation most of the time until the close of our period in 1929, not so much in damage suits—there were at least 50 of these—but in multitudes of suits arising from injunctions. The decision was one of the most important and far reaching in its after effects upon organized labor ever rendered by this or any lesser court in this country.

It caused a commotion among lawyers who analyzed the Congressional debates to discover whether or not the Supreme Court's assertion as to the intention of Congress was the truth. One group, agreeing with the court, was represented by James A. Emery (N. A. M. Counsel) in 20 Journal of Political Economy 599-612, 1912; W. W. Thornton, "A Treatise on the Sherman Antitrust Act," 1913; and Alpheus T. Mason, "Organized Labor and the Law." On the other hand, Professor Edward Berman in "Labor and the Sherman Act" devoted most of his book to proving that the Supreme Court not only was wrong, but merely took the plaintiff's word as to what Congress had debated.

To return to the further steps in the case: After the 1908 decision the Loewe Company returned to its suit in the lower court. The trial there lasted from October 13, 1909 to February 4, 1910, when Judge Platt gave instructions to the jury to find for Loewe in the sum of $74,000 damages, which tripled and with costs amounted to $232,000. Upon the basis that the judge exceeded his authority in instructing the jury, an appeal was taken to the Federal Court of Appeals for New York and New England. This court (April 10, 1911) reversed the decision of the trial court; "because the jury," so the court said, "should have decided if any damages were warranted, and if so, how much damages." The case was remanded for retrial.

On August 26, 1912, the retrial started and a verdict was reached on October 11, 1912. The jury found for Loewe and granted damages in $80,000 which tripled equaled $240,000, plus $12,000 in costs and counsel fees. Again a petition for a writ of error was presented, and allowed on January 18, 1913. In December of that year the U. S. Court of Appeals 2nd Circuit heard the case and confirmed the lower court. Upon appeal to the U. S. Supreme Court, this body on January 5, 1915, reaffirmed the decision.

This latter case, *Lawlor v. Loewe* (235 U. S. 522), was a plea first, that a combination and conspiracy had not been proved, and secondly, that the defendants—individual unionists —were not responsible for what was done by the sanction of the United Hatters and American Federation of Labor. The U. S. Supreme Court, speaking through Mr. Justice Holmes, agreed with the Circuit Court of Appeals that combination and conspiracy, primary and secondary boycott had been proved. The court deemed it a tax on credulity to say that the Danbury members did not know what the United Hatters and A. F. of L. were doing. The struggle, moreover, got newspaper and other publicity "so it was almost inconceivable that the defendants, all living in the neighborhood of the plaintiff, did not know what was done in the specific case." The members paid dues after the suit was begun, thus affirming approval of their organization's acts. "Neither the argument nor the . . . brief for the plaintiffs in error show that they suffered any injustice, or that there was any error requiring the judgment to be reversed."

When the Supreme Court decision of 1908 had attested the applicability of the Sherman Act to the union's members, Loewe had secured legal attachments on the property and bank accounts of 250 Danbury union hatters. In the following seven years some 64 of these hatters had died or disappeared, and many of the remaining 186 had suffered hardships because their savings and property were tied up pending the court action. No repairs were made on the houses during the long years that they were under attachment. As soon as the final 1915 decision was given in favor of Loewe he commenced actions to obtain the long-impounded savings and property. The judgment with interest—the addition of interest gave rise to another suit— amounted to $310,000. The A. F. of L. came to the aid of the hatters and circularized all unionists to give one day's pay on "hatter's day" in January to help lift the load of damages from the hatters. This collection did not bring in the whole sum required, and it was not until August 1917 that the A. F. of L. sent the final certified check to the treasurer of the United Hatters of America. The workers' homes were restored to them but in a woeful condition; their savings were not restored.

On Loewe's side the next to the last act in the case took place in the late 1920's, when the National Manufacturers' Association granted him an annuity of $5,000 a year to save him from destitution, and as a reward for the benefits conferred by him in lending his name and business troubles to one of the most satisfactory cases ever brought in aid of the organized employers against organized labor. Dietrick E. Loewe died in September 1935, a last act which stirred memories of the bitterness his name connoted among all unionists.

This case was of paramount importance not so much (as unions then feared) because it set a precedent for damage suits under the Act, but because of the declaration that unions could be brought under the anti-trust laws. Employers seized this weapon eagerly as a basis for injunctions, and says Berman, "approximately 18% of all cases which have arisen under the Sherman Act have been brought against trade unions or their members. From 1890 to December 10, 1928, labor was defendant in a total of 83 Sherman Act cases of which a record could be found." As new cases arose the courts extended the applications of the Sherman Act (and of the Clayton Act) so that in one or another case nearly every ordinary activity of a union was prohibited in respect to a specific complaint. The employers' use of the Act so much hampered and restricted organized labor, that it was forced to enter politics in endeavor to secure exemptions from the legal entanglements. The Clayton Act (1914), the chief such piece of federal legislation, upon its passage was hailed as a "Charter of Freedom," and Labor's

"Magna Charta," but its chief final result was to make it possible for private persons to do what only the government could do under the Sherman Act, namely to sue for injunctions. Sixty-four of the 83 cases against labor came after the passage of the Clayton Act and half of the 64 were private injunction suits.

Buck's Stove and Range Co. Case, 1907-1914.—While the Danbury Hatters' Case was in the courts, organized labor and particularly its topmost leaders were caught in the toils of the Buck's Stove and Range Company Case.

This case arose in 1906 out of a strike of metal polishers, buffers, and platers employed by the Buck's Stove and Range Company of St. Louis to resist an increase of working hours from 9 (which they had enjoyed for 18 months) to 10 per day. The strikers got no hearing or satisfaction from James W. Van Cleave, President of the company, a result understandable when it is recalled that he was President of the Citizens' Industrial Association of St. Louis, first Vice-president of that national body and also President of the National Association of Manufacturers. The workers' plight was presented by the International Brotherhood of Foundry Employes to the A. F. of L. convention of 1906 with the request that the name of the Buck's Stove and Range Company be put upon the Federation's "We Don't Patronize List," so as to effect a boycott by union labor of the company's products.

Before granting the plea the Federation sent one of its Vice-presidents, Joseph F. Valentine, who also was an officer in the Iron Molders' Union of North America, members of which were involved in the St. Louis dispute—to confer with Van Cleave in order to secure facts and procure a settlement. Van Cleave had just cancelled all his orders to a local printer because the latter had put his work force on an 8-hour day and Van Cleave, by circular, had urged all other employers to take the same action, so he was not the kind of man to grant an interview or arrange settlements with a union leader. When Valentine reported his failure, the Federation induced two officers of the National Stove Founders' Defence Association, an employers' organization in which Van Cleave was an active member, to approach Van Cleave to get his terms for a termination of the dispute. These men also failed. Thereupon (1907), the A. F. of L. placed the company's name on its "We Don't Patronize List."

Immediately afterwards, December 18, 1907, Van Cleave petitioned Justice Gould of the Supreme Court of the District of Columbia—the A. F. of L. headquarters were in the city of Washington—for an injunction prohibiting the Federation from publication of the boycott. On December 23, Gould issued a temporary injunction, after a preliminary hearing, and on March 26, 1908, made the injunction permanent. The terms of the injunction were minutely detailed; by it the officers and members of the A. F. of L., of all of its affiliated unions, its friends and sympathizers, were prohibited from publication by word of mouth, by print or in any other way the fact of the inclusion of the Buck's Stove and Range Company on the "We Don't Patronize List" or from communication, in any manner, of the fact of a labor dispute between this company and its employes. The A. F. of L. took an appeal from this injunction to the Court of Appeals of the District of Columbia.

Before the appeal had been heard and adjudicated, Van Cleave appealed to Justice Gould to adjudge Samuel Gompers, John Mitchell, and Frank Morrison in contempt of court for violation of the injunction. Gompers was said to have mentioned the boycott case in his editorials in the *Federationist,* on the lecture platform, and on the stump in a political campaign. Frank Morrison, as Secretary of the A. F. of L., had mailed copies of the monthly *Federationist* containing proceedings of the A. F. of L. convention in which the case was discussed, and John Mitchell as head of the United Mine Workers had, in a convention of that body, entertained a resolution of that union to endorse the boycott. For months the three cited men were harassed by the court and by Van Cleave's attorneys, and extraordinarily voluminous union records were read into the official hearings with the result that on December 23, 1908, Justice Daniel Thew Wright, in an unusually biting decree, adjudged the three men guilty of contempt of court and sentenced Morrison to three months in jail, Mitchell to nine months, and Gompers to one year. The A. F. of L. attorneys appealed this case also to the Court of Appeals of the District of Columbia. To separate the two cases we will return to the original injunction, and later pick up the story of the contempt.

The Court of Appeals affirmed the injunction on March 11, 1909, but in doing so gave recognition to the Federation's plea that the original injunction violated the constitutional guarantees of free speech and free press. So the Court of Appeals ordered the injunction to be modified in a manner to forbid the boycott but not to invade the rights of free speech and press. Chief Justice Shepard of the court dissented from the opinions of his colleagues in that he deemed the injunction void because it contravened the constitutional guarantees. The other two judges of the court reached their decision to uphold the injunction, each on different grounds. So there were really three decisions, two being in agreement only that a modified injunction was valid. The *Federationist* published the judicial opinions and decree in its April 1909 issue. The Federation took an appeal to the United States Supreme Court still on the ground that the original and modified injunctions were unconstitutional because of the invasion of free speech.

Before the United States Supreme Court could reach the case on its docket Van Cleave died in May 1910. His successor, Fred W. Gardiner, at the head of the Buck's Stove and Range Company and its largest stockholder was so friendly to union labor that he at once began negotiations for a trade agreement that would satisfy not only the original grievances of the polishers, platers, and molders but include all his employes. An agreement, satisfactory to the unions and the company, was reached on July 19, 1910. This agreement was published in the September 1910 issue of the *Federationist*. But since the Federation and the Anti-Boycott Association—the latter had furnished to Van Cleave upon his application as a member the legal talent to prosecute the cases—both wanted very much to get a Supreme Court decision on the issues involved, the case was not withdrawn. The Supreme Court, however, threw it out; since no longer was there a real legal dispute between the parties the court refused to pass upon a case that was purely moot. *B. S. & R. Co. v. A. F. of L.* (219 U. S. 58). The injunction itself was not disturbed by this action.

It is an interesting side light that C. W. Post, the breakfast food "king," a violent anti-unionist, brought a damage suit as a minority stockholder in the Buck's Stove and Range Company against that organization, *Post v. B. S. & R. Co. et al.* (200 Fed. 918). His grievance was that in Gardiner's agreement with the unions there was a provision that the company waived its right to sue the unions for damages because of past controversies. These damages had been a loss of 40% of the company's business on account of the boycott most advertised by Van Cleave's court actions. Post claimed that the boycott had violated the Sherman Act and caused a loss of $250,000. He said the waiver was without consideration and was illegal and void. Post lost his case in the Circuit Court; his appeal to the Circuit Court of Appeals for the Eighth Circuit brought him no comfort, for on November 22, 1912, that court affirmed the judgment of the court below.

Meanwhile the contempt case was confirmed by the District Court of Appeals, Chief Justice Shepard again dissenting. The three defendants were allowed liberty under bonds— Gompers $5,000, Mitchell $4,000, and Morrison $3,000—in order to appeal the case to the Supreme Court. This court (*Gompers v. B. S. & R. Co.,* 221 U. S. 418) said that since the contempt arose out of a civil case whereas the punishment inflicted was for a criminal proceeding, Justice Wright had been in error and referred the case back to him. The Justice hastily convened an advisory legal committee which recommended that, since the three men had acted upon the supposition that the original injunction was null and void on account of its infringement of free speech and free press, they be allowed to appear before the Justice and render apologies for disobedience to his orders. None of the three came forward with an apology. The Justice then ordered a new trial which the defendants vainly urged be held before another judge. Testimony was taken for 25 days, through December 1911 and January 1912, and included as evidence of contempt the publication in the *Federa-*

tionist of the various court orders and decrees relative to the original injunction.   Judgment was withheld for three months and then on June 24, 1912, Justice Wright again declared the three men guilty of contempt of court and imposed the same sentences as before.

Once more the three took an appeal to the District of Columbia Court of Appeals.   A decision was rendered May 5, 1913, which confirmed the contempt but said the punishment was excessive, and so changed the punishment to 30 days in jail for Gompers and $5,000 fines for the other two.   To this decision Chief Justice Shepard dissented.   The three carried the case on appeal to the U. S. Supreme Court and so also Justice Wright took the unprecedented step of appealing against the reduction of the punishment by the Court of Appeals.   On May 11, 1914, the United States Supreme Court finally by a 7 to 2 decision—Justices Van Devanter and Pitney dissenting—disposed of the case by finding for Gompers, Mitchell, and Morrison, thus reversing and discomfiting Justice Wright.   Eight years of litigation thus closed.

What significance in labor history, as contrasted with legal doctrine, attaches to these cases?   On the side of Van Cleave, the National Association of Manufacturers, and the Anti-Boycott Association the cases were a strategy to hamper, entangle, frighten, and financially embarrass organized labor. This group also had hoped to gain either information or grounds for accusations of fraud by the compulsory presentation of union records in the open court.   Underneath there was a desire to get the courts to clarify the legal status of boycotts. On the side of the Federation the cases gave the leaders a chance to pose as martyrs to the cause of labor, and to arouse such indignation against recalcitrant employers that union membership rolls would grow.   More fundamentally, the cases were invaluable as trumpets to blow through the land the injustices involved in injunctions when applied to industrial disputants. Moreover the Federation also wanted a judicial definition of the status of boycotts.   Justice Daniel Thew Wright was worth to the Federation tons of pamphlets and gales of oratory in fixing public attention on the prejudices of some judges sitting in labor cases.   The financial costs of the cases to the Federation were recompensed by the publicity they aroused, and a year in jail would have been a small misfortune to bear if the serving of the sentences convinced wage earners that leaders were willing to suffer in order that labor's rights be vindicated.

Incidentally, the Federation got revenge upon Justice Wright in 1914.   Early in that year Mr. Wade Cooper, president of a Washington bank, submitted to President Wilson charges of alleged illegal and other improper transactions against Justice Wright, all of which got newspaper publicity.   Next, on April 10, 1914, Hon. Frank Park, Congressman from Georgia, offered a resolution in the House citing alleged unethical, dishonest, and unlawful acts and asking that the Judiciary Committee investigate the charges as a basis for impeachment of Judge Wright.   On October 6, 1914, the Justice sent his resignation to the President, an act which not only closed his career as a judge but prevented his further career in the law except as an occasional adviser.

Clayton Act 1914.—To get relief from damage suits or injunctions taken under the Sherman Act the legislative representatives of organized labor secured two sections in the Clayton Act of October 15, 1914.   Section 6, after declaring "that the labor of a human being is not a commodity or article of commerce," went on to state that unionized labor, agricultural, or horticultural non-profit organizations, "or the members thereof shall not be held or construed to be illegal combinations or conspiracies in restraint of trade, under the anti-trust laws."

Section 20 dealt with the issuance of injunctions forbidding them except where necessary to prevent irreparable damage for which there was no adequate remedy at law.   A second clause was intended to prevent the issuance of injunctions to prohibit strikes, picketing, the use of strike benefits, strike or other meetings, boycotts, or doing anything which could be done if there were no industrial dispute.   None of these acts, furthermore, was to be held to be in violation of any law of the U. S.

Organized labor thought that these two sections of the Clayton Act freed labor from nearly all the court actions of the kinds that for 10 years had been tanglefooting the labor movement. When the federal provisions were incorporated into eight state statutes,[2] union men and their leaders hailed the Clayton Act as a labor Magna Charta.

By the end of another decade, however, labor was sure it had been swindled by the Clayton Act. Judges, led by the U. S. Supreme Court, said that the statute did not blaze new law but simply declared existent law. Some state courts were reluctant to follow this ruling; nevertheless most of them did. In the end, because it allowed private suits, the Clayton Act became another fetter. Among the cases that follow we have some of those in which the judges stripped the flesh from the Clayton Act leaving only the grinning right to private suit.

1915 "Yellow Dog Contract."—In obedience to our chronological order the case, *Coppage v. Kansas* (236 U. S. 1), which was decided on January 25, 1915 comes next, but it does not have any bearing upon the two anti-trust acts. Instead it was a test of the validity of a Kansas statute of March 13, 1903, which prohibited the "yellow dog" contract. T. B. Coppage, on July 1, 1911, as superintendent of the St. Louis and San Francisco Railway Co., discharged at Fort Scott, Kansas, a switchman named A. R. Hedges who had refused to sign an agreement to withdraw from the Switchmen's Union while in the employ of the railway. Coppage was convicted in a Kansas Court, a judgment affirmed by the Kansas Supreme Court. Thereupon Coppage appealed to the U. S. Supreme Court on the ground that the Kansas statute conflicted with the 14th Amendment on the point that it was a deprivation of liberty and property.

Mr. Justice Pitney delivered the opinion of the court. He said that the court could find no evidence that Hedges was coerced or was not, in every way, a free agent; except that in dropping out of the Switchmen's Union he would lose the pecuniary advantage of the union's benefit scheme. Both parties had equal freedom of contract. The court cited the Adair case

---

[2] Arizona, Iowa, Minnesota, North Dakota, Oregon, Utah, Washington, and Wisconsin.

and could see no difference in principle between that and the one under scrutiny although the Adair case involved a federal act and this one a state statute. The court's reasoning was elaborate but began and ended with the assumption that the Railway and its switchman had reasonably equal and constitutional freedom of contract; this being so, the state had no power to interfere with special provisions and penalties nor could the state seek to disguise its purpose by using police power terminology. Any inequality was a corollary of private property and existed in all, not solely employer-employe, contracts. To say that membership in a union was a private and personal affair which bore no relation to the member's duty to his employer was a problem not for the courts but employers to decide. Therefore the court declared the Kansas statute invalid as a violation of the 14th Amendment, Justices Holmes, Day, and Hughes dissenting. Justice Holmes thought the statute actually prepared the way for freedom of contract instead of violating that freedom. Justice Day said, "In view of the relative position of employer and employed, who is to deny that the stipulation here insisted upon and forbidden by the [Kansas] law is essentially coercive? No form of words can strip it of its true character."

1917.—The year 1917 was the occasion for three U. S. Supreme Court decisions in labor affairs. The first case was *Mountain Timber Co. v. Washington* (243 U. S. 219) in which the state's Workmen's Compensation Act was upheld by a 5 to 4 decision, Chief Justice Edward D. White and Justices McKenna, Van Devanter, and McReynolds in the minority. Because we referred to the validation of such acts in the previous chapter we call attention to it here only to place it in its proper sequence.

Adamson Act.—The second decision in the year 1917 was in *Wilson v. New* (243 U. S. 332). The case had arisen from an injunction obtained by railroads to bar the Adamson Act of September 5, 1916, one that established a basic 8-hour day for railway trainmen in interstate commerce. The railroads claimed

Congress had no power to deal with the subjects embraced by the statute; and second, if the power was possessed it was so abused as to render the statute unconstitutional. Said the railroads "this is a wage fixing not a time standard."

The court, in an opinion delivered by Chief Justice White, took cognizance of the conditions prevailing at the time Congress acted—a threatened nation-wide railway strike on the eve of war. The court believed that the extraordinary emergency justified extraordinary measures. Section 2 of the Act provided for a Presidential commission to observe the operation and effects of the law for a period of 6 to 9 months. The court looked upon this section as an indication of fairness and an intention to correct any injustices. The railways were public utilities engaged in interstate commerce. As such, Congress in an emergency, when private rights had not been exercised as a result of dispute between the parties, had authority to fill the want; in substance it compulsorily arbitrated the dispute between the parties by establishing a standard of wages. Congress, in the court's opinion, acted within its powers, and there was no abuse of those powers.

Justices Day, Pitney, Van Devanter, and McReynolds dissented, so the Act was upheld by a 5 to 4 decision.

Hitchman Coal and Coke Co. Case.—The third case, decided in 1917, was *Hitchman Coal and Coke Co. v. Mitchell* (245 U. S. 229). This West Virginia company after a strike in 1906—preceded by two others—resumed operations with miners who signed, as a part of the employment agreement, a statement to the effect that they were not members of a union and would not become such during the course of their employment. The attempt of the United Mine Workers' Union, on October 24, 1907, to organize these men led the company to seek and obtain an equity injunction against the union. In 1909 this was amended on the grounds that the union sought to monopolize labor in violation of the Sherman Act. On December 23, 1912, the District Court declared the union was an unlawful organization under the Sherman Act because it attempted to monopolize mine labor and had joined a conspiracy to restrain the coal trade of West Virginia. Therefore, as an unlawful body, the union had no right to induce the company's employes to join it. The injunction was made perpetual.

Upon appeal to the Circuit Court of Appeals, 4th Circuit, this court May 28, 1914, completely reversed the lower court; it declared the union was lawful, the Sherman Act could not be invoked by a private party, and that the union's attempt to organize contract-bound workers was not unlawful. The Hitchman Coal and Coke Company thereupon appealed to the U. S. Supreme Court whose decision was rendered on December 10, 1917, by Mr. Justice Pitney.

The court ignored the Sherman Act and confined itself to discussion of the legality of "yellow dog contracts." It referred to the Adair and Coppage cases, and pointed out that the case at bar had no action of a legislature as a justification. "That the employment was 'at will' and terminable by either party at any time [was] of no consequence." The union according to the court was not agent for the employe under contract; the company had a legal and constitutional right to exclude union men from its employ; the right of workers to form unions and urge others to join was not absolute, exercisable under any circumstances without qualification. The union, averred the court, in plain defiance of the contracts sought a method of enlarging membership which would inflict the greatest injury upon the company and its loyal employes. The court believed that every contract-bound miner who joined the union was guilty of breach of contract, at which the union connived. The excuse that the union induced the employes of the company only to *agree* to join the union not *actually to join* was a quibble that a court of equity "which looked to the substance and essence of things and disregarded matters of form and technical nicety" was able to ignore. Therefore the court declared that an injunction against the union was a lawful remedy.

Justices Brandeis, Holmes, and Clarke dissented.

Employers' journals published the ruling in this case in order to call it to the attention of executives who might otherwise have missed it. The result was a large number of employment agreements ("yellow dog contracts") containing wording similar to that used by the Hitchman Company. Such contracts were strongly recommended by the League for Industrial Rights and the American [Open-Shop] Plan Association. Against the United Mine Workers' Union it became a most effective weapon. Many employers on railroads and other public utilities used the contracts and so did a large number in the industries making clothing, metal, shoes, textiles, and upholstery; it was even thrust on public school teachers. In fact the "yellow dog contract" became anathema to unions, second only to injunctions; and many injunctions arose from violations of the contracts.

1918 Child Labor Case.—The year 1918 was noted for only one important decision with a special labor interest; however, the paucity of numbers was offset by ponderance of effects. In *Hammer v. Dagenhart* (247 U. S. 251), the United States Supreme Court, by a 5 to 4 decision, destroyed the federal child-labor law of September 1, 1916.

Legislation upon child labor under our federated constitutional government had been left to the states. Experience had shown that states, although every one had some limits to child labor, were laggard in prohibitions of child labor because employers and parents regarded them as violations of free contract, and the employers claimed the prohibitions set up intolerable competitive burdens. In the recently industrialized South where legislators were either rural or "master-minded" restrictions on child labor were inadequate. For example, Georgia had a law forbidding "bosses or other superiors from inflicting corporeal punishment upon minors." If they did, the child had ground for collection of damages which, the law stipulated, belonged to the child not its parents. On the other hand, in North Carolina where the case arose, the law allowed children to work at 12 years of age for 60 hours a week.

Congress was petitioned to correct the disparity in state child labor laws and to impose a national rule applicable to all states, especially those that had inadequate ones. It was a long-deferred (10 years) response to such pleas that led Congress in 1916 to enact the statute that forbade producers, manufacturers, or dealers to ship in interstate commerce the products which within 30 days of shipment had been made where children under 16 for work in mines and quarries or under 14 in any manufacturing establishment had been employed. The products manufactured by children employed for more than 8 hours per day, more than 6 days per week, or between 7:00 P. M. and 6:00 A. M. likewise were barred from interstate commerce.

Roland H. Dagenhart, father of Reuben, aged between 14 and 16 years, and of John, younger than 14, asked Judge Boyd of the U. S. court for the western district of North Carolina for an injunction in behalf of himself (Roland) and his two boys to prevent the enforcement of the federal act against the employment of the sons. Judge Boyd held the statute unconstitutional and issued the desired injunction. Thereupon an appeal carried the case to the U. S. Supreme Court. *Hammer v. Dagenhart* (247 U. S. 251, 1918).

Roland H. Dagenhart, although a "poor white" of Charlotte, North Carolina, was able to secure as counsel a prominent New York attorney as well as two attorneys from his own state. Moreover, the southern textile manufacturers rallied almost to a man in assisting Dagenhart to secure the rights of his boys to go to work under 16 and 14 years of age.

Mr. Justice Day delivered the opinion of the court.

First the court distinguished this case from many others that had invoked the commerce clause to prohibit in interstate commerce, lottery tickets, impure food, prostitutes, and intoxicating liquors. In these—acts all upheld—the court said there was no other remedy. In the present case the court declared that the goods themselves were harmless, and the regulation of their manufacture was within local powers. The labor of production was finished before the goods entered the province of congressional regulative power. This power, according to the court, began only when goods actually were delivered to a common carrier or the actual commencement of its transfer to another state. "If it were otherwise all manufacture intended for interstate shipment would be brought under Federal control to the practical exclusion of the authority of the states—a result certainly not contemplated by the framers of the Constitution when they vested in Congress the authority to regulate commerce among the states."

The argument that the 1916 Act was necessary to prevent unfair competition between manufacturers in states without child labor regulation and those so regulated was—in the court's opinion—untenable; because Congress had no power to require states to exercise their police power to prevent unfair competition. The grants to Congress were not intended to destroy local powers reserved to the states. The 10th Amendment reads "The powers not delegated to the United States by the Constitution nor prohibited by it to the States are reserved to the States respectively, or to the people."

"It may be desirable that [child labor] laws be uniform, but our Federal government is one of enumerated powers." This 1916 Congressional Act was doubly repugnant to the court; it not only transcended Congressional authority but exerted a power in a purely local matter which, if allowed, would destroy our system of government.

Mr. Justice Holmes dissented and his dissent was concurred in by Justices McKenna, Brandeis, and Clarke. These four Justices believed Congress had the power both to regulate and prohibit any part of commerce that it saw fit even if this utterly stopped certain kinds of transportation. Congressional power over commerce, in their opinion, could not be cut down or qualified by the fact that it might interfere with some domestic policy of a state, e.g., tax on state bank notes, and oleomargarine, and breaking up of monopolies. "Is it permissible to regulate and prohibit strong drink and not the product of ruined lives?" "Congress may carry out its views of public policy in respect to interstate commerce regardless of effects on state activities. The national welfare, as understood by Congress, may require a different attitude within its sphere from that of some self seeking state."

Justice Holmes' strong hint as to the use of the taxing power supplemented the advice of others. Congress the next year on February 24, 1919, enacted a new child labor measure based on the taxing power, only to be upset in 1922 in the case *Bailey v. Drexel Furniture Company* (259 U. S. 20), which we will discuss later in its proper time sequence.

1921.—Three cases important to labor were decided by the U. S. Supreme Court in 1921. The one earliest in the year January 3, 1921, was *Duplex Printing Press Co. v. Deering* (254 U. S. 443).

Duplex Case.—The Duplex Printing Press Company of Battle Creek, Michigan—a town, many of whose plants were made "open-shop" by the avid anti-unionism of C. W. Post— was one of five companies actively in competition with each other. Four of these concerns had trade agreements with the International Association of Machinists. The destructive competition from the Duplex Company caused the other three to inform the union that if it could not write a trade agreement with Duplex the other three would have to abandon their union agreements. Negotiation with the Duplex Company was useless, and a direct strike was of no avail; so the union endeavored to block the market for the printing presses made by the Duplex Company. A secondary boycott was clamped on the company's product through the assistance of organized pressmen, teamsters, installation mechanics, repairmen, and others. An exposition company in New York was threatened with a strike if it displayed Duplex presses—but this menace was composed. Purchasers of Duplex machines were warned that they, too, would be boycotted if they installed or operated the Duplex presses. In short, a thorough secondary boycott was conducted against the sale and use of Duplex products.

The Duplex Printing Press Company availed itself of the powers of the Clayton Act that permitted private suitors to ask for injunctive relief, and petitioned the District Court, southern district of New York, for an injunction. This court on April 23, 1917, denied the petition on the ground that the Clayton Act forbade this particular kind of injunction. Upon appeal to the Second Circuit Court of Appeals the court split 2 to 1 upon the applicability of Sections 6 and 20 of the Clayton Act; the majority held on May 25, 1918, that under these two sections there could be no injunction in this case.

Consequently, the Duplex Printing Press Company carried the case to the U. S. Supreme Court. *Duplex Printing Press Co. v. Deering* (254 U. S. 349, 1921).

Mr. Justice Pitney on January 3, 1921, delivered the opinion of the court. As to the facts, the court thought this case was four square with the Danbury Hatters' boycott, but the defense offer of the Clayton Act introduced a new feature. Most of the court's opinion, therefore, was an analysis of Section 20 of the Clayton Act. The court thought the defendants were clearly guilty under the Sherman Act if the decision in the Hatters' case was to be upheld.

The court dismissed Section 6 of the Clayton Act because this merely asserted what already was true—courts could not hold unions as such to be illegal combinations. Nor could courts forbid union members from *lawfully* carrying out the unions' *legitimate* objects. [It was the Anti-boycott Association's attorney, Daniel Davenport, who had gotten into the law the words italicized and twice emphasized by the Supreme Court.]

Section 20 gave the court considerable difficulty and was treated by single paragraphs. Some paragraphs were said to be only declaratory of the law as it stood before. The words "between employers and employes" were ones on whose interpretation the Circuit and Supreme Courts differed; the former gave them the meaning "class to which litigants belonged" while the latter said they meant a single employer and his own immediate servants. This interpretation disemboweled the case of the defendants because the chief boycotters stood in no such proximate relationship. To accept the lower court definition seemed, to the Supreme Court, to repeal by implication the Sherman Act [just what the A. F. of L. and Congress intended] and to confer on voluntary associations, formed within the states, a control over interstate commerce that was denied to state governments. The Supreme Court said the legislative history of the Clayton Act indicated a decided denial of intention of legalization of secondary boycotts. Therefore, since the defendants had conducted an exceedingly harmful and unlawful secondary boycott and inasmuch as the Clayton Act did not authorize such conduct, an injunction should be issued and the defendants should pay the costs of this and the two suits in the lower courts.   Justices Brandeis, Holmes, and Clarke dissented, saying that the secondary boycott had been legalized by the Clayton Act.

This decision went far to knock out the supposed benefits of the Clayton Act, and by becoming a precedent for this court and many state courts—states which had passed laws akin to the Clayton Act—did shortly put the unions back where they were after the decision in the Danbury Hatters' case.

American Steel Foundries vs. Tri-city Trades Council.— The picketing sections of the Clayton Act were disposed of by the U. S. Supreme Court in the same year (1921) and shortly after the Duplex case.   Indeed the *American Steel Foundries Company v. Tri-city Trades Council* (251 U. S. 184) was almost a definitive case upon picketing, because it influenced nearly all later decisions on this subject, especially in the state courts.

There had been a strike of three weeks' duration against the low wages of the plaintiff, and in accord with union technique the plant had been picketed by four groups composed of 4 to 12 persons.   The plaintiff secured from a federal district court an injunction restraining the City-central Union and 14 individual defendants from using persuasion, threats, intimidation, force, or violence in picketing the strike breakers.   Carried to the Circuit Court of Appeals, this court struck out the word "persuasion" and inserted after the clause restraining picketing the words "in a threatening or intimidating manner."   The case then went to the United States Supreme Court where Chief Justice Taft delivered the opinion of the court.

The first question in the case was whether Section 20 of the Clayton Act applied.   Only two of the defendants in the court's opinion, Cook and Churchill, who left at the time of the strike —that is, were directly employed by the plaintiff—could invoke in their behalf Section 20.   As to these men, attention was called by the court to the Duplex case in which was emphasized the words in the act "peaceable" and "lawful."   The intent of

Congress was to safeguard peaceable persuasion. "But," said the court, "what is peaceable persuasion?" Answering its own question the court said that peaceful persuasion must not be persistent, importunate, dogging of an uninterested person. It must not be massed near the place of business. It must not be of a nature to attract crowds so as to obstruct highways. Numerous pickets, in the court's mind, constituted intimidation; the very word "picket" was militant and sinister, and was entirely avoided in the framing of the Clayton Act. "What can be done?" asked the court. "Each case must turn upon its own circumstances. It is a case for the flexible remedial power of a court of equity, which may try one mode of restraint, and if it fails, or proves to be too drastic, may change it. We think that the strikers and their sympathizers, engaged in the economic struggle, should be limited to one representative for each point of ingress or egress in the plant or place of business, and all others be enjoined from congregating or loitering at the plant or in the neighboring streets by which access is had to the plant. . . ." These pickets, according to the court, were to have a right to persuade but not to coerce or intimidate. Then the court added these words, too often later overlooked. "This is not laid down as a rigid rule, but only as one which should apply to this case under the circumstances disclosed by the evidence, and which may be varied in other cases."

Churchill and Cook therefore could, under the Clayton Act, be enjoined from all picketing except peaceful persuasion.

What about the Tri-City Council and the other defendants not direct employes of the plaintiff. "Was interference of a labor organization by persuasion and appeal to induce a strike against low wages under the circumstances without lawful excuse and malicious? We think not. Labor unions are recognized by the Clayton Act as legal when instituted for mutual help and lawfully carrying out their legitimate objects. They have long been thus recognized by the courts. . . . To render this combination at all effective, employes must make their combination extend beyond one shop. It is helpful to have as many as may be in the same trade in the same community united, because in the competition between employers they are bound to be affected by the standard of wages in their neighborhood. Therefore, they may use all lawful propaganda to enlarge their membership, and especially among those whose labor at lower wages will injure their whole guild. It is impossible to hold such persuasion and propaganda, without more, to be without excuse and malicious. . . ."

So the district court's injunction of "persuasion" had to be modified; but the Circuit Court's restraint of picketing otherwise was sustained.

Mr. Justice Brandeis concurred in substance in the opinion and judgment of the court. Mr. Justice Clarke dissented.

Truax v. Corrigan.—Almost at once the U. S. Supreme Court handed down another opinion about picketing, in *Truax v. Corrigan* (257 U. S. 312). Truax operated a restaurant in Bisbee, Arizona, and must have been a wholehearted believer in individual freedom; six years earlier he had cooperated with one Raich, an alien, by firing him in order to test an Arizona Statute that compelled employment of American citizens in preference to aliens and Raich had fought for his rights all the way to the U. S. Supreme Court *Truax v. Raich* (239 U. S. 33, 1915) where he got them, not at all to the disgust of Truax. In the instant case the cooks and waiters employed by Truax went on strike; in order to exert fullest pressure they picketed peacefully, but in mass, the Truax restaurant, thus interfering with patronage. Truax sought and got an injunction to stop the picketing. The workers contested the order because their acts were peaceful, and because an Arizona statute, in paragraph 1,464 (an almost literal transcription of Section 20, Clayton Act), protected this kind of picketing from injunctions. When these contentions were upheld by the Arizona Supreme Court, Truax carried his complaint that the statute violated the 14th amendment to the U. S. Supreme Court.

Chief Justice Taft again delivered the court's opinion, one that was a 5-4 decision. "Truax's business was a property right; with free access for employe's owner and customers incident to such right. Intentional injury to either right by conspiracy was a tort. Concerted action was a conspiracy if its object was unlawful or if unlawful means were used. Here the real question was; were the methods of picketing unlawful means? Of this the answer could not be in doubt. The defendant had patrolled with banners within five feet of the restaurant and filled the air with insistent and loud appeals to customers not to enter; and likewise hurled epithets and libelous statements at Truax. The result was a reduction of business from $50,000 to $12,000. Violence could not have been more effective. It was moral coercion by illegal annoyance and obstruction, and thus was plainly a conspiracy."

"A law which operates to make lawful such wrongs deprives the owner of the business and the premises of his property without due process, and cannot be held valid under the 14th Amendment." By denial of all remedies at law to the plaintiff or if only his right to injunction was denied, he was deprived of equal protection of the laws. *"The equal protection of the laws is a pledge of the protection of equal laws,"* (italics by the court). . . .

"It is urged that in holding paragraph 1,464 invalid we are in effect holding invalid Section 20 of the Clayton Act. Of course, we are not doing so. In the first place, the equality clause of the 14th Amendment does not apply to Congressional but only to state action. In the second place, Section 20 of the Clayton Act never has been construed or applied as the Supreme court of Arizona has construed and applied paragraph 1,464 in this case . . . a construction as far from [the words] of Section 20 of the Clayton Act as if they were in a wholly different language."

Justices Holmes, Pitney, Clarke, and Brandeis dissented.

This decision despite the court's denial, took the heart out of both the Clayton Act and state acts similar to the one of Arizona. None was repealed although as protections to the technique of unions they might as well have been.

1922.—The next court entanglement of labor came in 1922 when Attorney General Daugherty secured, from Judge Wilkerson, the notorious injunction against the railway shopmen then on strike. We discussed this in Chapter 5.

Second Child Labor Case.—A Congressional act of February 24, 1919, had tried to regulate child labor by imposing an excise tax on all products so made.   The tax was 10% on the entire net profits received for the year in which persons under 16 were employed in mines or quarries, or under 14 in any manufacturing plant.

The same groups that had opposed the 1916 child labor law were up in arms against this one.   The legal contest over it began in the same western district of North Carolina and before the same judge as had the case *Hammer v. Dagenhart*.   This time, however, a different industry, furniture manufacturing, was picked to carry the shield.

Bailey v. Drexel Furniture Company (259 U. S. 20) was the arena in which the children of the nation were sacrificed; if their parents were so poor as to require this victimization.

On September 20, 1921, the Drexel Furniture Company received notice from one Bailey, U. S. Collector of Internal Revenue for the district, that it had been assessed $6,312.79 for having, during the taxable year of 1919, employed a boy under 14 years of age and thus incurred the tax of 10% on its net profits for that year.   The tax was paid under protest and a refund was claimed, and denied.   The company then brought suit in the District Court where judgment was entered for the company against the collector for the full amount with interest. The case then went to the U. S. Supreme Court.

Chief Justice Taft delivered the opinion of the court.

The company attacked the law as a federal invasion of state rights since the law was not for revenue but for a kind of regulation reserved to the states under the 10th Amendment.   The defense contended that a mere excise tax was involved.

The court held that the tax was merely a means of regulation and was imposed as a penalty.   The court said that it was true the law did not declare child labor illegal; but the intention was plain.   It did set up a standard and imposed a penalty (tax) on those who transgressed it.   It did not graduate the tax in accord with the number of children employed or the length of service; just one employed for one hour would cause the tax to be levied.   It did relieve employers who unknowingly em-

ployed children under 16 or 14 and this kind of release was
peculiar to penalties and not to taxes.   Inspectors were not only
Treasury officers but those of the Department of Labor.   "Its
prohibitory and regulatory effect and purpose [were] palpable.
How [could] we properly shut our minds to it."

The court recalled that in the many previous cases in which
the court had sustained taxes that in fact were regulatory, the
laws did not on their faces plainly indicate that the tax was a
device; and the machinery of collection had a reasonable relation to the enforcement of the tax.   "The case before us cannot
be distinguished from *Hammer v. Dagenhart.* . . .   We hold
the Child Labor Tax Law invalid, and the judgment of the
District Court is affirmed."

Mr. Justice Clarke dissented.

Child Labor Amendment.—With both the commerce power
and tax power forbidden to Congress as a means to regulate
child labor it passed a resolution by the House April 26, 1924,
and by the Senate June 2, 1924, for amendment to the Constitution, as follows:

Section 1.   The Congress shall have the power to limit, regulate,
and prohibit the labor of persons under the age of eighteen years.
Section 2.   The power of the several States is unimpaired by this
article except that the operation of State laws shall be suspended to the
extent necessary to give effect to legislation enacted by the Congress.

In the states this amendment was fought by newspapers,
national and local employers' associations, the Roman Catholic
Church, farmers' organizations, and prominent citizens, among
them President Nicholas Murray Butler of Columbia and President Charles W. Eliot of Harvard.   Invasion of states rights,
federal interference with the home, and federal bureaucracy
were the principal published arguments of these groups.

As a result only the following five states voted approval of
the amendment before 1929: Arizona (1925), Arkansas
(1924), California (1925), Montana (1927), Wisconsin
(1925).[3]

---

[3] Nineteen others did also between 1931 and June 1936.

Coronado Cases.—The Bache-Denman Coal Company controlled eight other mining companies, among them the Coronado Coal Company of Arkansas. All the members of this combine operated in a contiguous region and all were run on the "open-shop" basis. District 21 of the United Mine Workers' Union in 1914 conducted a strike against the Coronado Co. that was so destructive to the latter's business and property that it was forced into receivership. Dowd, the receiver, in September 1914 brought under the Sherman Act a damage suit in the District Court for the Western District of Arkansas against the officers of District 21 and the members of 27 of its constituent locals, the officers of the United Mine Workers of America, and 65 individuals—not all unionists. These were charged with conspiracy to wreck the "open-shop" mines of the Bache-Denman Coal Company and in doing so restrained interstate commerce. The defendants asserted that they were a voluntary association and therefore not suable, and moreover, they had not violated the Sherman Act.

When the District Court sustained the miners Dowd appealed to the Circuit Court (8th Circuit) which on July 21, 1916, reversed the lower court and ordered the trial to proceed. The trial before Judge Elliott at Fort Smith, Arkansas, was a bitter one. The jury finally got the case and then remained in retirement for 48 hours. Judge Elliott summoned them, told them he would not discharge them and they must bring in a verdict. He then told the jury that in his judgment the case should be decided in favor of Dowd. Federal judges have that power of revealing their minds to juries when the latter cannot reach an agreement; in theory, the juries are not bound by the judge's opinion. The Fort Smith jury was. It awarded $200,000 damages tripled to $600,000 plus $120,000 interest (July 17, 1914 to November 22, 1917) and a further addition of $25,000 for counsel fees.

This 3/4 million dollar blow made the miners appeal first to the Circuit Court (lost) and then the U. S. Supreme Court, *United Mine Workers v. Coronado Coal Co.* (259 U. S. 344).

Before this body the miners' case was: first, that the national union was incorrectly joined in the suit with the District organ-

ization; second, as an unincorporated association neither national nor district unions were suable; third, there was no evidence of conspiracy with either union; and fourth, Judge Elliott
erred in practically making the jury's decision for them.

Chief Justice Taft, June 5, 1922, rendered the court's decision. It held that there was no evidence to show that the
international union was officially responsible for the strike, that
the strike was purely local, and that any restraint of trade by
reason of the strike was relatively unimportant. But the courts
ruling on the suability of unions was such as to make this case
stand high among labor trials.

The court admitted that ordinarily voluntary associations
could be sued only as individuals. Unions, however, had become distinctly different from the associations guided by the
common law of suability. The United Mine Workers itself
had then 400,000 members. "To remand persons injured to a
suit against each of these to recover damages and to levy upon
his share of the strike fund would be to leave them remediless."
In the court's opinion unions in general and the United Mine
Workers in particular had as great unity of action and as highly
centralized control and acted fully as much as a business entity,
as any corporation. The union label had been protected against
pirating and deceptive use just as if it were a trade mark.
The court said that in England, in the Taff-Vale case, unions
were adjudged suable and in the United States the Clayton Act
recognized them as lawful; they were tendered formal incorporation as national unions by an Act of Congress, June 29,
1886.

"In this state of Federal legislation we think that such organizations are suable in the Federal courts for their acts, and that
funds accumulated to be expended in conducting strikes are subject to execution in suits for torts committed by such unions in
strikes."

As an aside let us revert for a moment to the Danbury Hatters' case; there it was not the union as an entity but its individual members who were sued. Now the way was opened to
sue the union just as if it were a corporation; it's long protection
within the status of voluntary associations was cancelled. No-

where in its decision did the court say that unions could sue; but lawyers assumed that the inference was plain that this new power must accompany the new liability.

Returning to the case: the court's decision referred the case back to the District Court. In October 1923 this court found for the unions, a judgment sustained on July 12, 1924, by the Circuit Court of Appeals. Thus, the case on appeal again reached the U. S. Supreme Court, *Coronado Coal Co. v. United Mine Workers of America* (268 U. S. 295). A decision on May 25, 1925, released the national union but (on new evidence) held the District 21 organization guilty of violation of the Sherman Act and thus liable for damages. A new suit was started against the District 21 but was dismissed October 17, 1927, by an adjustment between the parties whereby the union paid the company $27,500, the costs of the trial scheduled for the next month. This outcome was hailed as a union victory. So far as money was concerned it was an ant hill beside the original ¾ million dollar mountainous damages; but there was that 1922 ruling that unions were suable, in which were Sierras of possible damages.

1923.—The *Adkins v. Childrens Hospital* (261 U. S. 525) and *Wolff Packing Co. v. Court of Industrial Relations* (262 U. S. 522) both came to a conclusion in the U. S. Supreme Court in 1923. The first may be regarded as another blow to labor, but the second was deemed a godsend. Each of these cases was referred to elsewhere in this book.

1927.—April 1927 was a black month to unions; within a week of each other the U. S. Supreme Court handed down decisions in the *Bedford Cut Stone Co. v. Journeymen Stone Cutters' Association of North America* (April 11) and the *Red Jacket Consolidated Coal and Coke Co. v. United Mine Workers et al.* (April 18).

Bedford Cut Stone Co. Case.—The Bedford Cut Stone Co. of Bedford, Indiana, was one of a combination of quarries that produced the famous Indiana limestone. In 1921, following several years of agreement with the union, the company broke away and began operations on an "open-shop" basis.   The local members of the same union worked on the placement of the stone in buildings wherever these might be located.   When the quarries in Indiana went over to the "open-shop" these stone-cutters in distant cities refused to place the products of the quarries.   The Bedford Cut Stone Company and 20 other concerns brought suit in the District Court of Indiana for an injunction against the union, asserting that its acts constituted a conspiracy to restrain interstate commerce.   The District Court of Indiana and the Circuit Court of Appeals, 7th Circuit (on October 25, 1925) both denied the plea; but upon appeal to the U. S. Supreme Court that body on April 11, 1927, declared the union was guilty of violation of the Sherman Act.   Justices Stone and Sanford concurred only because they thought the Duplex decision controlled.   Justices Holmes and Brandeis dissented. Virtually this was another 5/4 decision (47 Sup. Ct. Rep. 522, 274 U. S. 37).

The significant facts about this decision were that this union was not engaging in a *secondary* boycott; for the same union was involved at both ends, one the quarry, the other the market.   Neither did it use any violence, threats, or any other intimidation save its own strikes against setting the stone.   Its sole offense was its refusal to handle at the building a stone which had not been quarried by its members.   This was a situation quite different from those in the Hatters and Duplex cases; nevertheless the court considered the stone-cutters equally guilty with the Hatters and machinists in conducting a boycott that restrained interstate commerce.   The decision took away from the union its only effective method of bringing pressure upon the employers at the quarries.   Said Justice Brandeis in dissent, "If on the undisputed facts of this case refusal to work can be enjoined Congress created by the Sherman Act an instrument for imposing restraints upon labor which reminds of involuntary servitude."

Red Jacket Cases.—Between 1920 and 1922, the United Mine Workers put on an intensive drive to organize coal miners in West Virginia.   A series of injunctions, totaling a dozen, were brought against the union in this period by 316 companies. In reaching the U. S. Supreme Court, the series was lumped and became known by the name Red Jacket Cases (18 Fed. (2) 839, 1927), taking the title from the name of one of the companies involved.   The injunctions all were sustained as modified by a lower court.   In modified form the injunctions stopped the unions from receiving dues from West Virginia miners, from paying miners any benefits, from requiring companies to use the "check off" (collection of dues by company for payment to union) from union trespass upon company property, from union interference with the "yellow dog contract," or from assisting unionists in remaining in company houses contrary to company desires.   The severity of these restraints prevented the union from getting a hold in West Virginia and by this failure contributed to the rapid attrition of the union elsewhere for 13 years after 1920.   By 1930 this once-powerful union was close to collapse, having lost two-thirds of its members.   Judge John T. Parker of the 6th Circuit Court, who had a decisive part in these cases in the West Virginia courts, when nominated in 1930 by President Hoover to the U. S. Supreme Court failed of confirmation in the Senate. His humiliation was laid to opposition of both organized labor and organized Negroes.

Labor's Reactions.—This, then, is the record of the principal U. S. Supreme Court decisions 1896-1929, affecting labor. What was labor's reaction to them?   The 1896 convention of the A. F. of L. demanded amendments to the Constitution depriving judges of power to set aside laws enacted by Congress "as we believe the proper function of courts is to expound and administer law but not to make it."   Beginning in 1897, bills were introduced in Congress to restrict judges in the issuance of injunctions in labor disputes with what futile result in the 1914 Clayton Act we have seen.   In 1897 also the A. F. of L. convention recorded the following: "We believe judges should stand in the same position as every other officer of the government, and every power and safeguard be exercised to protect the people against unjust encroachment from judges as from all other officials and that the power of impeachment should be used in all cases where courts have clearly violated the law and the constitutional rights of the people." A third proposal appearing frequently in A. F. of L. debates was that all judges be directly elected by the people and that their terms be limited to three or four years.

After the first Coronado decision Gompers said, "This means that big business has won its objectives in its long campaign for trade unions' incorporation . . . and the Supreme Court of the United States has arranged matters to suit the convenience of big business which can, hereafter, turn its strike-breaking over to the judiciary"—A. F. of L. Weekly News Letter, June 10, 1922. As the years passed labor became more openly contemptuous of the fairness of judges, more outspoken in their declarations that "judges were the principal tools of the employing class for the suppression of labor."

All of these suggestions or criticisms were met by shocked incredulity that labor dared uproot or question "the fundamentals of American institutions under which we had grown and prospered for more than a century." "The Law" was regarded as something impersonally perfect, and its judges so remote from passion, prejudice, and emotion that justice was both automatic and unimpeachable. Americans had no "divine right of kings" but came close to acceptance of "divine wisdom of judges."

CHAPTER 10

LABOR IN POLITICS

The political affiliations of American wage earners were not determined as a rule by class feelings, but rather by geographical environment, or nationalistic and hereditary tendencies. A white carpenter who in Savannah, Ga., was a Democrat might in Burlington, Vt., be a Republican; if he was Irish he probably would be a Democrat wherever he lived. An Iowa grandfather who was a Republican would have a Republican son in North Dakota, and a Republican grandson in Los Angeles County—where grandfather would spend his last days. There was little connection between occupations and political loyalties.

Organized labor had neither a party of its own nor did it pledge allegiance to any one political organization. Labor leaders, in truth, tried to suppress political discussion in union meetings, in order that reliance might be upon labor's economic power. But, to paraphrase Robert Burns, "the best laid plans of mice and men often go astray." This happened to the plan to keep unions out of politics. They so often found economic power frustrated by political power, and judges so frequently curtailed the acts of unions, that organized workers were compelled to equip themselves with a political policy and exert political power. For that matter, a minority always had pressed the A. F. of L. to use its potential political power.

American Federation of Labor Political Policy.—The proposal to combine action as a separate labor political party, with economic efforts as a federation of trade unions, arose in the very first convention in 1881. Resolution 13 of that initial gathering, although it approved of attempts to seat unionists or their proved friends in all law making bodies, also carried a ban on any member of any union legislative committee from publicly advocating, as a partisan, the claims of any political

274

party.   For 14 years thereafter, a minority persistently endeavored to secure an endorsement of partisan political activity;
with equal pertinacity the leaders were backed by a majority in
rejection of such policy.   Four of the conventions in this period
went on record with specific resolutions disavowing any intention of partisan endorsements.

The debates of the 14 years crystallized a general form of
statement on the political issue.   Insistence that the primary
function of trade unionism was betterment of the position of
craftsmen by economic pressure upon employers was put first
in most resolutions.   Following this affirmation of purpose
came clauses whose purport was that, in politics, the unity of
labor was upon *measures* not upon a *party,* and finally that it
was possible and necessary to separate united interests in politics
from espousal of a particular political party.

The convention of 1895 inserted as section 8 in the A. F. of
L. constitution a clause reading, "Party politics, whether they
be Democratic, Republican, Socialistic, Populistic, Prohibition
or any other shall have no place in the Conventions of the
American Federation of Labor."   Partisan politics, along with
religious or social resolutions, thus were to be kept out of convention activities.   The following year a resolution was approved that "no officer of the A. F. of L. be allowed to use his
official position in the interest of a political party."

Non-partisan Political Efforts.—The definite separation
from any one political party did not prevent the Federation from
sharing in politics; discussion of measures of reform desired
by labor was a regular part of union conventions.   After measures were selected, the unions backed candidates for office who
promised to work for the enactment or enforcement of the desired laws and this support was given the candidate irrespective
of his party label.

Why American Federation of Labor Was Non-partisan.—
This non-partisan political policy of the A. F. of L. was a result of several forces.   The leaders were aware of the story of
the National Labor Union; indeed some of the leaders as young-
sters had participated in that organization and had first-hand

knowledge of the manner in which partisanship had wrecked that body, both as an economic union and a political party. Leaders regarded political partisanship as a disruptive force in any union. They blocked all moves to turn the new A. F. of L. down the allegedly dangerous road toward a labor political party. To this reading of the lesson in history, the leaders added a knowledge of the newness and relative weakness of the A. F. of L. and most of its affiliates. The organization was still in a nursing stage; so partisan politics was then too strong a diet for its infancy.

Both the Populist and Socialist parties valiantly strove to secure endorsement from the organized labor bodies. The socialists were especially insistent. The A. F. of L. refused to seat socialists as representatives of socialists' groups; but always there were many bona-fide trade union delegates who were also socialists. It was in fact the constant pressure from socialists that made the A. F. of L. conventions, one after the other, affirm the position on politics and partisanship. When in 1895 the socialists, in despair of "capturing" the A. F. of L., set up socialist trade-unions that soon collapsed, the leaders of the A. F. of L. were more positive that their own policy was expedient.

Finally, in quite a number of cities and states, union leaders were in alliances with a locally dominant party. Imagine the predicament of these officers if the A. F. of L. tied itself to one party: if it endorsed the Republicans, local labor leaders in New York City or South Carolina would get cold comfort; or conversely those in Philadelphia [ante 1936] and Maine would suffer if the Democrats were favored, and all would be distressed if the A. F. of L. had a party of its own.

Results of Early Non-partisanship.—For 10 years after 1895 the A. F. of L. remained steadfast in giving approval to friends—whatever their political connections—who supported the A. F. of L. legislative programs. By the end of the decade, when results were canvassed, they were dismally scant. Moreover, within the decade, organized capital not only greatly had progressed but had so brazenly controlled legislators as to give rise to an outburst of muck-raking exposures in newspaper and magazine articles. The most outrageous affront to labor was the "packing" of the Congressional Committees on Labor with the friends of Big Business, and of course hostile to any reforms proposed by labor. Since the committees originally had been created by the insistence of labor, this almost complete "sell out" to labor's supposed enemies was unbearable.

Along with these factors, the successful attack on labor through the courts was driving labor to action in order to secure an unbiased if not friendly judiciary. Through the court decisions, labor's old weapon, the boycott, was rendered useless as an effective instrument, a loss that put more emphasis on the perfection of a new political instrument. Moreover, employers after 1902 had been especially energetic and successful in drives for what they called the "open shop." Where the employers' open-shop was established, the strike as a union weapon was impotent. Finally, the example of contemporary British unionists in their success in getting unionists into Parliament was an inspiration.

Change in 1906.—As a consequence of all these influences, some 117 representatives of unions met in 1906 with the Executive Council of the A. F. of L. and drew up a Bill of Grievances. A document of considerable length, the core of it was contained in specific legislative proposals. These were a demand that the federal 8-hour law be made effective and extended to workers engaged to build the Panama Canal; that the products of convict labor be denied admittance to interstate commerce; that relief from induced immigration be granted; that seamen be relieved from involuntary servitude; that labor be redressed against injunctions and suits under the Sherman Act; that government employes be granted the right to petition for redress of grievances; and that sea-going tugs be limited to a single barge in tow, to prevent the loss of life incident to cutting adrift in storms, when a number of barges were in tow.

This Bill of Grievances, on March 21, 1906, was delivered to President Theodore Roosevelt, Speaker Joseph Cannon of the House of Representatives, and Charles W. Fairbanks, Vice-

President and presiding officer of the Senate.   The final clause
in the Bill read "but if perchance you may not heed us we shall
appeal to the conscience and support of our fellow citizens."

Still Non-partisan But Active.—Since none of the recipients did "heed" them—except in ridicule—the leaders of labor
on July 22, 1906, proceeded to organize a political campaign
for the fall elections of that year.   From headquarters in Washington, the A. F. of L. committee sent advice and instructions to
state and local labor leaders in order to take the political battle
into Congressional Districts and into counties, the latter not
only for state purposes but to bring pressure on the U. S.
Senate whose members at that time were elected by state legislatures.   No new party was proposed or set up.   Local committees were instructed to scrutinize the records of candidates and
then, first of all, seek the defeat of enemies, next try to elect
friends of labor.   If no local party had a friendly candidate,
then the local labor groups at their discretion might nominate
independent labor candidates.

The unions were warned to keep free from partisanship and
not to let the campaign degenerate into a scramble for offices by
local unionists.   Labor principles were to be kept to the front;
office was to be secondary.   As additional precaution against
distortion of the real purposes of the campaign, city elections
were passed over in favor of state and Congressional, the latter
being most stressed.

The Maine Campaign, 1906.—Because Maine's elections
came earliest, the first intensive drive was made in that state.
There, labor's chief enemy was Congressman Charles E. Littlefield from the 2nd Maine District, chairman of the House Committee on the Judiciary, and sometime counsel for the Anti-
Boycott Association.   Thirteen labor speakers, besides Gompers, invaded the district arousing building craftsmen, paper
makers, lumbermen, lime burners, and fishermen, the first rally
being held in Littlefield's home town of Rockland.   The Republicans in defense sent some of their best-known men into the
state; among them W. H. Taft.   The Congressman in his own
speeches paid little attention to his Democratic opponent, but

fired his greatest salvos at the labor group. When the votes were counted, Littlefield's normal plurality of 5,000 was reduced to 1,000; part of the loss possibly may have been due to the Republican "dry" stand on Prohibition — an issue in Maine long before it got into national politics — but by most people the cut in the vote was attributed to the labor campaign. Two years later, when Littlefield ran for re-election, he was defeated. Incidentally, 29 new local unions were chartered in Littlefield's district during the 1906 campaign.

Results in 1906.—After the fight in Maine, organized labor carried the 1906 battle into 17 other Congressional districts. Not a single enemy was defeated nor a solitary unionist elected; nevertheless, the labor campaign committee expressed gratification that the campaign had made many a politician study labor's position, and had broken the prejudices against labor in the minds of several successful candidates. These results seemed enough to justify further campaigns in 1908 and 1910.

Policy Continued.—When the elections of these two later years were over, labor took stock on accomplishments of the three struggles. By that time it felt certain that non-partisan politics was worth while. It could point to several of its most bitter enemies removed from public office by its efforts, joined to those on the one hand of muck-rakers and on the other of Progressives. It claimed credit for aiding in the widespread popular revolt which curbed the powers of Speaker Cannon and modified the House rules. Its friends again were being appointed to Congressional committees, and Big Business was being apprised that organized labor was not politically supine. Within the states, labor's political power had risen to acknowledged heights in California, Oregon, Kansas, Iowa, Minnesota, Wisconsin, New York, and Maine. Labor also felt that its political strategy had broken the tradition of tight party allegiances so that the number of independent voters had increased; these voters cast their ballots upon the basis of issues and candidates rather than upon blind party loyalty.

However, this kind of independence was far more general than the voters under the influence of the A. F. of L. Because labor believed that its political policy produced these results, it continued to engage in politics upon a non-partisan basis. Notwithstanding these truths, there was a hint of change in 1913 when the A. F. of L. declared, "when our present political activities have fully matured a new political party will be the logical result."

Labor and Democratic Party.—Before 1912, because the Democrats were out of federal control, this party, more often than the Republicans, gave attention to the labor platform planks, and its candidates more often were endorsed as friends of labor. Hence, when the Democrats rode into Washington in 1912 there was for the first time an administration and Congress officially "friendly" to organized labor. Soon many measures were enacted that labor alone, or labor in conjunction with many other groups, long had besought.

In these categories were the creation of a Department of Labor separate from the Department of Commerce, the ratification of the 16th Amendment (income tax), the Underwood Tariff including especially the income tax provisions, the ratification of the 17th Amendment (direct election of Senators), the Federal Reserve Bank Act, the Federal Trade Commission Act, the Child Labor Act(s) (these as we have seen were declared unconstitutional), the Woman Suffrage Resolution, the Seamen's Act, Literacy Test Act for Restriction of Immigration, and Federal Highway Aid, which matched federal dollars with state dollars for the construction of roads.

The special boons most cherished by labor were the appointment of W. B. Wilson as the first Secretary of Labor, the Clayton Act of 1914, the Adamson Act of 1916, and the Seamen's Act. Secretary Wilson had been an officer in the United Mine Workers' Union, the largest union affiliated with the A. F. of L.; by his appointment, labor not only had a direct representative in the Cabinet but the Department of Labor, during his incumbency, became almost an annex of the American Federation of Labor.

Clayton Act.—Labor's peculiar interest in the Clayton Act was that it declared that the labor of a human being was not a commodity of commerce, and other sections ostensibly removed the likelihood of injunctions against normal union activities including strikes, picketing, and the boycott; in short, breaking all the barriers judges had raised out of the Sherman Act.   In 1914 Labor regarded the Clayton Act as the most magnificent piece of legislation gained for labor anywhere or at any time. This exaggerated exaltation later was deflated as judge after judge, including those in the U. S. Supreme Court, interpreted away the liberties of the Clayton Act; eventually, as we have seen, all this Act accomplished was to tighten and add one more strand to the bonds of the Sherman Act.   The extra strand was the Clayton Act provision that private suits for injunction could be instituted.   But labor in 1914 could not foresee these results.

Adamson Act.—Two years later (September 3, 1916), the railroad brotherhoods, coercing Congress with the threat of a nationwide strike upon the eve of war, secured the Adamson Act.   This law set the basic 8-hour day as standard for railways engaged in interstate commerce; the administration of the law did not actually shorten work-hours, but set a standard day's work at 8 hours from which overtime work could be charged at overtime rates.   Thus, the act in effect, was one to raise wages rather than decrease hours.

Labor and the World War.—Besides all these general and special Congressional acts for some of which labor had agitated for years, labor rose to new heights of prestige by the manner in which the Wilson administration took labor into the councils and commissions that administered the economic life of the nation during our participation in the World War.

On March 12, 1917, a little less than a month before the Congressional declaration of war (April 6, 1917), 148 representatives of 79 affiliated and 5 non-affiliated unions met with the Executive Council of the A. F. of L. and drew up an elaborate statement of the stand to be taken by organized labor in the event the nation entered the war.   The essential feature of the document was a pledge of unreserved allegiance to the institutions and ideals of the Republic, and an offer of service in every field of endeavor to defend, safeguard, and preserve the Republic.   In later years this action was looked upon by some as pitiably naïve and by others as a "sell out"; at the time it was praised by conservatives, endorsed by rank and file workers, and censured only by a few ultra pacifist socialists.

When war came, the pledge was accepted by the administration, and labor representatives were placed on almost every body created to conduct the war.   Beginning with a unionist in the Cabinet, and with Gompers as one of the seven members of the Advisory Committee to the Council of National Defense, labor had one or more representatives in practically every administrative body down to a committee of the Surgeon General to prepare a bill for the rehabilitation of soldiers.   Never before in the nation's history was labor so thoroughly recognized in official conduct of a war.

Critical voices at the time, and more bitingly censorious ones in after years, said that the labor appointments gave more the appearance than the fact of recognition to labor's viewpoints. Gompers, especially, was assailed for his lack of impression on the Council of National Defense.   These complaints were mostly "hindsight" not prescience.

Benefits of War Position to Labor.—It would be difficult to say what were the most important benefits derived by labor by whatever intimacy its representatives had at headquarters; among the benefits might be mentioned the clauses in war contracts setting the 8-hour day as standard and providing for overtime rates of pay for overtime work.   Another, considered a benefit at the time, was the creation of the War Labor Board, a body composed of representatives of employers and unions with F. P. Walsh and W. H. Taft as chairmen, which board acted as a court for the settlement of industrial disputes.   Its decisions, generally (especially in the earlier months of the war) were favorable to labor and its aid in recognition of collective bargaining undoubtedly helped to expand unionization during the war.   On the other hand, the Board sponsored many new company unions which, in later years, proved to be formidable substitutes for regular unions.

A system of Federal Employment offices, which labor had desired for many years, was instituted during the war. When peace returned, the opposition of employers who did not want their own local surplus of labor moved through the federal offices caused Congress to cripple the system by failing to appropriate funds for its maintenance. A skeleton organization was kept, however, until the depression of 1929, after which the system was revived.

Defensive accomplishments were the toning down of the restrictions upon free speech and free press, originally included in the Espionage Act (1917), and by some employers and judges interpreted as a prohibition of strikes during the war. However, unionized labor did not interfere when employers and judges used the Espionage Acts to harass and jail socialists, anarchists, and members of the I. W. W. In 1918 labor prevented the enactment of a bill that would have admitted 30,000 Chinese coolies to do unskilled work (principally on farms), and a later proposal to use convicts for the same purpose. The A. F. of L. let pass a waiver of the literacy test to admit Mexican laborers.

Labor also insisted that none of the legal safeguards thrown around the work of women wage earners be lowered during the war, and maintained the principle (not very successfully) that women who did the same work as men receive the same rates of pay. The Women's Bureau in the Department of Labor daily was besieged by employers—always with the excuse that an emergency war order demanded it—that labor laws in respect to women or minors be suspended. The Bureau did not yield even to great political pressures; in its staunch rigidity it was supported by organized labor.

The National Association of Manufacturers pressed Congress continuously to enact a measure that would make arbitration compulsory during the war, but labor's friends in Congress prevented the introduction of any such bill.

President Wilson Recognizes Labor.—President Wilson in 1917 gave significant and public recognition to organized labor when he made a speech at the A. F. of L. convention in

Buffalo, the first President who ever appeared before that body. The Canadian Parliament at Ottawa invited Samuel Gompers, while visiting in Canada upon union business, to address the Parliament on April 26, 1918. The only precedents for this invitation were similar requests made to Arthur Balfour, of the British Mission, sent to Canada and to Rene Viviani, the head of a French commission, on the same errand in Canada. In 1918 President Wilson was unable to attend the A. F. of L. convention, but he sent the body a cordial letter to which, in the official reply, the A. F. of L. pledged "whole-hearted support to the world's chief spokesman for democracy and human justice."

Toward the close of the war, Gompers was sent to Britain, France, and Italy to stop the socialists' campaign for a peoples' peace, and to bolster the spirits of war-worn European labor. For his success in these efforts, Gompers got several flattering notices from the rulers of the Allies and everlasting condemnation from radicals. The final accolade bestowed on labor was the inclusion of Gompers as American labor's representative to the conference that produced the Versailles Treaty of Peace. Gompers took a special part in drawing up the labor provisions of the League of Nations; and afterwards, the International Labor Office of the League was considered one of few solid accomplishments of the Versailles Treaty.

"Work or Fight" Laws.—In only one set of acts during the war did organized labor fail to take a stand; that was on state laws that forced men to "Work or Fight." On May 19, 1917 the West Virginia legislature enacted a law under the guise of a vagrancy act, that forced every able-bodied man either to get a job and labor at least 36 hours per week or be enrolled in the military forces. Immediately, other state legislatures seized the idea and measures, differing in details, were passed in Maryland, New Jersey, Rhode Island, New York, and North Dakota. The solons of Massachusetts debated such an act but did not put it on the statute books.

These laws were effective in rounding up crowds of idlers; but the placement of these men in jobs proved difficult, for so many of those that did not lack skill lacked the will to work. Turnover was extraordinary. Although these laws skirted the thin edge of involuntary servitude, organized labor did not protest them, except mildly to advise that proper safeguards against exploitation be included in the measures.

Draft Act.—Labor also at first was against the proposal for a Selective Service Act by which a universal draft upon males of military age was to be used to fill army and navy ranks. When President Wilson took representatives of labor into the conferences that prepared the bill, organized labor put no further obstacles in the path of the Act. When it was made law, labor gave it support. Only the radicals opposed the war fervor by refusal to accept the draft, a defiance that was met by jail sentences, in the serving of which the radicals, in some instances, were subjected to as many terrors, injuries, and deaths as befell soldiers.

Farm Labor.—One problem that was acute during the war, and which organized labor did nothing to solve, was the distressful shortage of farm labor during a period of marked expansion in farming and demand for farm produce. Although part of the shortage was due to the migration of farm labor to the highly paid jobs in war industries, and the movement of young men from farms into military service, the primary cause was the expansion in demand for agricultural products. Some of the "Work or Fight" laws (e.g., in North Dakota) were aimed at an increase in the supply of farm labor. Mexicans, Porto Ricans, and Hawaiians were admitted in large numbers for this work. School children and college students were urged to spend their vacations in farm labor; some colleges gave academic credit for this kind of application.

Probably the largest and most effective body of recruits came from the women of the nation. One organized group of women agricultural workers was the Woman's Land Army started in 1918 and continued for a while after the war. In 1919 it was associated with the Farm Service Division of the United States Employment Service, and was not disbanded until February 1920. In addition, there were hundreds of unorgan-

ized "farmerettes" scattered across the country.   To the women
must go a considerable credit for enabling the farms to turn out
more than their normal quota of products at a time when male
labor was so scarce.

Post-War Disappointments.—After the war was finished,
organized labor, in imitation of British unionists, prepared a
program of social reforms to be brought about as soon as
democracy was "safe," but was rudely shocked by the drastic
slump in idealistic fervor that set in as soon as peace was
assured.

Instead of getting acceptance for reforms, labor found all
of its energies engaged in holding what it had won since 1912.
After Wilson was stricken September 26, 1919, his enfeebled
condition prevented his control of his own administration.
Labor no longer was so essential as to be placated; with President Wilson hidden in the White House, the subordinates either
ignored labor or snarled at its least bulwarked members.   Attorney General Palmer's rabid harassment of "Reds" was notorious; but even Secretary of Labor Wilson "passed by on
the other side" when certain workers were in need of help.

Employers, many of whom had chafed during the war at
their forced compliance with labor demands, seized their chance
and began a savage campaign to "deflate" labor.   The result on
the one hand was the nationwide series of strikes in 1919 averaging 292 a month and on the other was the "open-shop campaign" already described in Chapter 6.

Labor and Republican Party.—When the Republicans returned to Washington in 1921, the non-partisan political policy
of the A. F. of L. had built up one of the most authoritative
lobbies at the nation's capitol, and had acquired considerable
power in local or state politics in Pennsylvania, Massachusetts,
Michigan, Illinois, and Rhode Island, and only slightly less influence in New York, Ohio, Indiana, Connecticut, and New
Jersey.   Every item in the 1906 Bill of Grievances, except the
ban on convict-made goods in interstate commerce, had been
obtained; besides many new demands had been met, and a number of measures inimical to labor had either been quashed or

modified.　As early as 1917 the A. F. of L. listed 129 major measures obtained by its political policy.

In 1920, however, the "fat years" ended and the "lean years" began.　Through the decade after 1920, the policy of non-partisanship was subjected to many strains.　One was that the party in national office no longer was friendly to organized labor.　Another was that within its own ranks there was a powerful minority urgent for an American labor party.　Both of these were complicated by the authorized support rendered the LaFollette candidacy in 1924, and were further influenced first, by the continuous shrinkage in trade union membership during the decade and secondly, by the left wing political aspirations of communist or farmer-labor groups.

Laws Passed by Republican Administrations.—From the Republican administrations of the 1920's, the principal benefits derived by labor were the successive laws that imposed drastic limitations upon immigration.　After 1926 the Republican "Progressives" held the whiphand in Congress, because the major parties were numerically mutually stymied.　Therefore, in the last months of the generation, the labor lobby plus the Progressives got legislation that outlawed "yellow dog contracts" as bases for actions in federal courts, and defined the use of the injunction in labor disputes.　Part of a rounded program of legislation to deal with the problem of unemployment also hurdled the hazards of Congress and became law.　Progressives and Democrats together blocked a Senate confirmation of Judge Parker's appointment to the Supreme Court, and Judge Wilkerson's promotion in the federal courts.

While all of these accomplishments were decidedly pleasing to labor, they were a small grist compared to the favors received from the Wilson administration.　Moreover, Harding's Secretary of Labor, James J. Davis, could not be counted a tried and true labor man despite his early steel mill experiences; and Secretary Doaks' appointment by Hoover, although he was an officer of the Trainmen's Union, was a blow to the prestige and pride of the A. F. of L.; for of course the Trainmen were not affiliated with that body.   The Department of Labor certainly was not an annex of the A. F. of L. after 1920.

Railway Workers and Politics.—The special class of railroad workers became increasingly inclined toward political effort after 1910.   One reason was the rigid regulation of their industry by government, so that reforms by negotiation constantly were harder to secure; labor adjustments that added to costs no longer blithely could be passed on to shippers.   In addition, the railroads' amazing growth by decades ceased by 1910; and thereafter the railroads faced destructive competition from passenger automobiles, highway trucks, and airplanes.   In the earlier years of railway expansion, skilled engineers or conductors always were relatively scarce, but after 1910, when more tracks were abandoned than built, the supply of railroad labor tended to outrun demand.   With economic power withering, the railroad workers shifted attention to political power.

The ease with which the railroad men secured the Adamson Act from Congress in 1916 whetted their appetites for favors. These were forthcoming during the war when the rails were unified under government control and the whole railroad business of the United States was directed from Washington. Railway workers got a taste of what their political power might bring them.

Plumb Plan.—When the Armistice came, November 11, 1918, the railroad workers sought for a plan that would retain the industry under the government.   In 1919 they espoused the (Glenn E.) Plumb Plan, a kind of American syndicalism, which provided for government ownership with management shared between railroad executives and railroad labor.   The Plumb Plan was prepared in the form of a bill and submitted to Congress where it was buried under an avalanche of criticism.

When the Esch-Cummins Bill was introduced in Congress to provide the legal method of returning railroads to their owners, the railroad workers joined militant farmers in objection; but the bill became the Transportation Act of 1920.

Two years later the railway men joined the Conference for Progressive Political Action.   They also joined the Trade

Union Legislative Conference Committee, the enlarged successor in 1921 to the former A. F. of L. National Legislative Committee; in short, the A. F. of L. "lobby." After that time the former characteristic aloofness of the railroad brotherhoods to other labor organizations began to melt, so that by the end of the '20's the brotherhoods acted and counseled with the A. F. of L. upon many occasions. The members of the brotherhoods were much more inclined toward politics than their own or most of the leaders in the A. F. of L. unions.

Farmers in Politics.—Among farmers, the principal revolt during the war years had been that officered by the Non-partisan League, a 1915 North Dakota product. This body used the same political method as the A. F. of L. and Anti-Saloon League. Its program was socialistic. For a few years the Non-partisan League controlled North Dakota and put many of its measures into statutes. Spreading outward, it accumulated power but not control in states neighboring North Dakota and those in the Rockies and Cascade Mountains. Discredit of the leaders, mistakes in state-managed enterprises, the cost in taxes of government ownership, and the combined opposition of Republican and Democratic party machines together with their satellite judges, relaxed the grip of the Non-partisan League. The war years also gave some farmers the illusion of prosperity.

Farmers' Misery.—Peace brought years of misery to American farmers, especially in the Middle West. Farms and farm equipment had been purchased or extended at war prices and financed by mortgages or notes. The decline of farm product prices, together with a lesser fall or even increased price of commodities bought by farmers, made it constantly difficult to pay debts.

During all the "prosperity" of 1922-1928, farmers, save for exceptional cases, had no share in it. Farmers in the United States never have accepted adversity with resignation; so in the '20's they turned to state and federal governments for special legislation. For the most part, farmers kept their votes within the established parties; only the most restive broke away. As early as 1920, a group of these in Minnesota joined with labor to form a Farmer-Labor Party. The new organization had enough vitality to maintain itself in its own original area throughout the decade of the '20's. In that area it got its candidates into state office and even sent a nucleus to both branches of Congress.

Progressive Unionists.—To the railway workers and farmers should be added a considerable group of progressive unionists who desired a separate labor political party in the 1920's. The officers of some City Central Unions and State Federations, aware of their weakness in the A. F. of L. organization, visioned an increase in power if a labor party was formed; because, of course, city and state federations would be the natural centers of a political party. The example of the British Labor Party whetted the ambitions of many American unionists. Against the drift toward political action, most of the higher officers in nearly all the unions offered stiff resistance—the higher and longer in office the more against the scheme. To a labor party, they brought forth a formidable array of objections.

The Case Against a Labor Party.—They said that American unionists were craft, not class, conscious; that the unions enrolled only a minority of all workers; and that workers were divided into at least three antagonist groups. In refining this generalization, the opponents went on to say that the trade unionists belonged to a stratum of society that had possessed the vote (even when wage earners) for a generation before the national unions composing the A. F. of L. were organized; therefore, a tradition of old party loyalty was a generation older than fealty to a union. To be sure, party names had changed, but the nation nearly always had had two dominant parties, one representing wealth, the other appealing to the masses. Labor always had divided its loyalty between these two; for many workers supported the party that spoke and acted in the interest of wealth.

Any third party had before it a long struggle for recognition, and had scant favors to grant until recognition was won. Eventual success probably could come only by displacing one of the existing parties. However, unionists if they themselves got

converted to voting for a party of their own were nevertheless
only a minority of all wage earners.　In addition to the non-
union workers in positions that attached them to the party of
wealth, there was a great mass of alien workers who either were
not naturalized citizens or were already, by fair or foul means,
attached to one of the existing parties.　Then there were the
millions of Negro workers nearly all non-unionist and also
nearly all tied to the party of the Great Emancipator.　There
was no American working *class;* for wage earners not only were
widely separated between skilled and unskilled but segregated
into white Americans, immigrants, and Negroes.

Even if all wage earners did unite in one party they would
constitute less than a majority of all citizens eligible to the
franchise.　Moreover, half the population of the United States
lived under rural or village conditions and even when such citizens were wage earners they would have little understanding
of or sympathy with a party platform drawn by urban wage
earners.

Furthermore, if a labor party succeeded in the capture of the
federal government, it would be of small utility to them for
Congress had no power under the Constitution to enact labor
legislation except for workers employed by the federal government.　Herein was a vital difference in the British system of
government; for an act of Parliament applied throughout the
United Kingdom; but in the United States, the only possibility
of national labor laws lay in an interpretation of the taxing
powers or the powers over interstate commerce more liberal
than the U. S. Supreme Court had been inclined to construe as
valid.　Labor laws mostly were the creations of state legislatures, so a labor party would have to capture 48 governments,
not just one.

Finally, the opponents of a labor political party stressed the
historical evidence that showed the weakening effect upon
unions of the introduction of politics into the discussions of
union meetings.　One unacknowledged but real objection to a
labor party was that many highly placed union officers were
attached to one or the other old political machines; this meant
they got favors for unions and sometimes political prizes for

themselves.   To antagonize established parties would not only stop all boons but bring cunningly directed reprisals.

Case for a Labor Party.—The replies to these arguments were as follows: Craft consciousness was declining because the progress of the industrial revolution was eliminating craft at the same time that it wiped out the need for the lowest kinds of unskilled labor; therefore, labor was being crushed down or pulled up into one great common class of trained or semi-skilled people.   Since the economic desires of this ultimate class could be gained only by social and political means, class consciousness was sure to grow stronger as years passed.

Likewise, strict party loyalties of workers were being shattered by the close identity (in 1920's) of the aims or policies of the two leading parties, so that workers and others were forced to vote for candidates rather than measures.   Each of the two parties had similar right and left wings, so the time was ripe for the destruction of both old parties to make way for a new conservative and new radical party, the latter of which might well be a labor party.

As for the segregation of immigrants and Negroes, the restrictions on the one soon would produce a homogeneous American labor force and the progress of the other, together with its trek to the North, would free it from traditional ties, especially if a new conservative party took a new name.   Farmers were oppressed by the same forces that crushed labor, and both farmers and labor pinned their hopes on the same reforms; hence, they logically and emotionally belonged in the same political camp.

Capture of the federal government had much more to yield than Congressional legal grist; for the government not only conducted the greatest business enterprise of the nation but the party in power could direct the *administration* of laws so as to benefit labor as well as exercise considerable control (through appointments) over the judiciary.

Of course state governments had still more to offer to a labor party, and any such party naturally would try its strength in that field before aiming at Washington.   The appeal to history was misleading because no former unions turned to politics until failing as unions, so probably it was not politics that destroyed the unions so much as the internal weaknesses of the unions that made their political efforts futile. No American unions ever had given the political weapon a really fair trial.

The Tests.—Twice in the first half of the 1920's these conflicting ideas were put to test; first, in the Conference for Progressive Political Action, and secondly, in the LaFollette campaign.

Progressive unionists, officers of city and state federations, Socialists, the Non-partisan League, the Farmer-Labor Party, the National Catholic Welfare Council, and the Methodist Federation for Social Service came together in February (20-21) 1922 at Chicago. From their convention emerged the Conference for Progressive Political Action. The objects sought were an ultimate labor political party and an immediate nonpartisan support of measures that would socialize the electric-power industry and other key industries, curb the banking interests, and in general bring about a more equitable distribution of national income.

Weaknesses Revealed.—With this program the Conference entered the campaign of 1922 and at the second meeting, held in Cleveland December 11-12, professed satisfaction with the number of progressives elected. Nevertheless, the weakness of their heterogeneous group was manifested when the Farmer-Labor delegates introduced a resolution for immediate organization of an independent (Farmer-Labor) political party, a move for which the unionists and others were not ready. The ensuing debate shook the convention to its roots, and when the decision went against the Farmer-Labor faction it withdrew from the Conference.

In 1924 the Conference for Progressive Political Action endorsed the candidacy and platform of Robert Marion LaFollette, Sr., although, meanwhile, in 1923 there had been frictions within the Conference in states between those who wanted a speedy birth of a new labor party and those who used contraceptives on this idea.

The disappointment and disillusionment that came with the end of the LaFollette campaign were more than the loosely joined Conference could bear. The railroad members long since had lost enthusiasm for the Conference—they had been expectant of using the organization to promote the nationalization of railroads and the political fortunes of W. G. McAdoo, both of which hopes had evaporated. The chieftains of the A. F. of L. had sabotaged the Conference from its inception and after the defeat of LaFollette, remorselessly forced the city and state federations to withdraw from the Conference.

Fragments of the original Conference convened in Chicago on February 21-22, 1925. It was moved, but not voted, to continue as a non-partisan group; instead the convention adjourned without provision for further meeting or organization except as individuals or separate bodies. None of the fragments could discover an adhesive and consequently the whole collapsed.

"Labor" a Newspaper.—The principal survivor of the wreck of the Conference for Progressive Political Action was the means it had chosen for publicity, namely the newspaper, "Labor." This paper had existed prior to the Conference and was owned by the 21 standard railway unions; it obtained probably the largest circulation of any of the hundreds of labor journals. It owned its own building in Washington in the shadow of the Capitol, and at elections sometimes issued special editions running over a million copies for use in local and state politics. This continuing service made it likewise a power in national campaigns. Therefore, it not only survived but grew lusty as the largest weekly newspaper published by and in the interests of American labor.

LaFollette Campaign 1924.—In the foregoing there was unavoidable reference to the LaFollette campaign. The labor and radical support of this candidate extended beyond the Conference for Progressive Political Action; indeed the A. F. of L. itself, took the unusual step of endorsement of the LaFollette third party in the 1924 presidential campaign.

The A. F. of L., in tendering its endorsement, tried to make it clear that it was not forsaking its traditional policy for it deemed LaFollette one of its most notable friends; certainly he was a greater friend than Calvin Coolidge (whose national reputation was started by his supposed suppression of the 1919 Boston police strike) or the Democratic candidate, John W. Davis, whose closest associates were New York financiers. Nevertheless the A. F. of L. in giving its sanction to a third party candidate made many persons (including many of its own members) think that it had broken with tradition and at last was to enter politics as a separate contender for office.

Railroad workers joined LaFollette because he agreed with them that the Esch-Cummins Act should be drastically altered. Farmers were pinched by the post-war slump in farm product prices and believed in LaFollette's programs for social-economic reforms. The socialists claimed the Wisconsin Senator as one of their own and so gave him their pledge. They all agreed with his plank calling for popular control of courts and abrogation of the United States Supreme Court's assumption of power to declare laws unconstitutional.

As the campaign waxed, it began to appear that LaFollette's banners were upheld by too many varieties of progressives or radicals; indeed the candidate, himself, disavowed some of his ardent followers, but to no avail in shaking them loose. The more conservative unionists grew apprehensive as November approached, for most of LaFollette's platform was more radical than they liked, and in addition they feared and hated some of the trailers in LaFollette's army. This attitude was true of many individual unionists and found organized expression in the resolutions of a few city central unions. Hence, the only third party ever espoused by the A. F. of L. brought disorder and dissension in subordinate parts of that body.

When the votes were counted in November, it was found that Coolidge had nearly 16 million, Davis over 8 million, and LaFollette not quite 5 million. Although he made a strong showing in California, Minnesota, Iowa, Illinois, Ohio, and Pennsylvania, the only electoral votes captured by "Fighting Bob" were those 13 of his own state, Wisconsin.

After the campaign was lost, the A. F. of L. issued a statement which was a reiteration of its traditional non-partisan policy; pointed out that the recent support given LaFollette was in line with, not a departure from, its tradition; and pledged itself for the future to pursue non-partisanship, and not to enter any plans for the creation of a labor party nor permanently attach itself to any other third party.   So many wage earners ignored a candidate whose life had been devoted to their interests and whose platform promised them relief from oppression, that the experience undoubtedly gave strength to the conservatives in the A. F. of L. who wanted no traffic with party politics.

Communists.—Likewise, the exertions of the Workers' (Communist) Party after 1922 both within and outside the unions affiliated with the A. F. of L. enabled the latter's conservative leaders to maintain the policy of eschewal of party politics.   Indeed it was the attempt, early in the generation, of socialists to capture or wreck the A. F. of L., and the later identical strategy of the communists, that probably more than anything else kept the A. F. of L. from entrance into labor party politics.   At the same time, the conservative leaders maintained themselves in office in part by their real or simulated rôle as the defenders of pure and simple unionism against the attacks of radical "borers and smashers."

Here then was a double barrier against an independent labor party; members who advocated one could be branded as *agents provocateur,* and by resisting them the officers who were most hostile to the idea of a separate labor party kept their jobs.

Employers' Part in Politics.—That employers manipulated politics to their own advantage needs no extended demonstration.   Our government was founded by our most important property owners and the Constitution was their bulwark.   Before 1861 this rampart shielded the southern slavocracy; and, to the extent they needed it, the northern commercial and manufacturing interests.   The slavocracy possessed literally all political power in its home area, and formed an irresistible bloc in Congress.   Overthrown by the North's wealth, in materials, money, and men when the South precipitated a test by war, neither this nor any other agricultural group again wielded dictatorial political power in national affairs.   Big Business did.

Business was not firmly seated in the saddle of political power until Grangerism, Populism, and Bryanism were defeated. After 1896, the control of government by business was cumulative; it was quite open because the people were made to believe that what was good for business was equally good for them.

The two national parties after 1896 grew less and less separable with no great issues distinguishing one from the other. Business by its money contributions supported them both, although in states and cities it tended to give greater resources to the one whose machine enabled it to win the most elections. For the same reason, the Republicans got more but not exclusive support in national politics; if the Democrats had shown power to win as consistently as did the Republicans they undoubtedly would have received as much financial assistance.

It is axiomatic that the possessors of political power will employ it chiefly for their own advantage; and that they will use all the powers of the state—laws, courts, police, military and naval forces—to maintain and defend themselves in control. It is equally a truism that those who control whatever is considered wealth and income, also will control government. Therefore, it was in accord with world experience that in the United States, where the makers, buyers, sellers, distributors, and advertisers of things rose to the command of enormous wealth and primacy in social position, they should also constitute an oligarchy.

CHAPTER 11

"RED" FARMERS

The most consistent American radicals — that is, persons proposing fundamental changes in our socio-economic order— have not been urban wage earners but farmers. It was "embattled Farmers" who fired the shot heard 'round the world; it was the Grangers who first challenged the exploitations of railroads, and it was mostly farmers who gave strength to the Greenbackers and Populists. Later, the farmers' Non-partisan League of North Dakota came close to the creation of a cooperative commonwealth and the Farmer-Labor Party was the nearest to a proletarian political party achieved in this country before 1929. Therefore, an outline of American radical activities must begin with those fostered by farmers.

The Populists.—The Populists had about run their course in 1896, although they had been a potent force in the immediately preceding years. Their movement had started in 1890 with the formation of the Farmers' Alliance which, following the Granger tradition, elected in 1890 nine Representatives and two Senators. Prior to the elections in 1892, conventions of farmers and wage earners at St. Louis and Omaha organized the People's Party which demanded government ownership and operation of railroads, telephones, and telegraphs; recognition of unions together with a shorter work-day, and the abolition of child labor and Pinkerton spies; government currency instead of bank-notes; free and unlimited coinage of silver at the ratio 16 silver to 1 gold; a graduated income tax; postal savings banks; and the dispossession of speculators from the holding of public lands. The party captured a vote of over a million for its Presidential candidate, the former Greenbacker, James B. Weaver; the vote so distributed as to command 22 electoral votes. The vote was largest in Colorado, Kansas, Idaho, Nevada, North Dakota, Oregon and Nebraska from which the Populists sent 10 Representatives and 5 Senators to Washington. Candidates Cleveland and Harrison polled 5 million apiece.

The current depression (1892-1896) that sent wheat from 82 cents to 55 cents per bushel and reduced the population of Kansas by 100,000 persons—to say nothing of the miseries of unemployment — kept alive the interest in the Populist Party. The result at the polls in 1894 was a vote of 1½ million so concentrated in the former Democratic stronghold in the South as well as in the West that the Democrats were thoroughly alarmed.

Consequently, in 1896 the Democrats not only accepted most of the Populist platform but went beyond it in demanding that the U. S. Supreme Court be packed so as to reverse its decision that a federal income tax was unconstitutional. The party also protested government by injunctions, a plank that reflected the Pullman strike of 1894. This action made a predicament for the Populists; should they support the Democratic nominees, W. J. Bryan and Arthur Sewall, or put their own ticket in the field? Technically they did not wholly accept either alternative, for they accepted Bryan but gave him Thomas Watson, a Georgia Populist, for a running mate; practically they fused with the Democrats.

1896 Campaign.—The campaign that followed is famous as the last one before 1929 in which genuine issues separated the Democrats and Republicans. Seven million dollars of eastern money supported the Republican "educational campaign" while western silver-mine owners opened their purses to the Democrats. Of all the Populist-Democratic planks it was the free-silver issue that divided citizens into two groups,[1] sometimes hortative, sometimes surly and with "dirty work" under cover. McKinley polled over 7 million votes while Bryan got 6½ million; moreover, the Republican votes were so well placed

---

[1] In some states there were 7 different parties listed on the ballot and in Illinois there were 13.

that their candidate got nearly 100 more electoral votes than Bryan (271-176).

The Populists maintained their fusion not only in 1898 but also the two following elections.   By 1904 it seemed impossible to continue; for the Democrats by that time had lost their fervor for the West and for the lowly, a fact made plain by the nomination of the conservative New Yorker, Judge Alton B. Parker.   Besides, the country was prosperous and the scarcity of gold was relieved by a new metallurgical process.   Consequently the Populists put forward their own ticket, Thomas E. Watson and Thomas H. Tibbles; these nominees, however, got only 114,546 votes, the smallest, except for the Socialist Labor Party (33,490), of all the six parties then in the field.

This extraordinary shrinkage from the high vote of 1894 was due first to the fact that the most ardent former Populists had become Debsian Socialists, secondly, that the long years of marching at the rear of another party caused many to become outright members in order to move up in the line, and lastly because western farmers, at the time, were not suffering unusual distress.   Moreover, the Knights of Labor, the union that had supported the Populists, was dead; and its successor the A. F. of L. refused all overtures to cooperate.   The chief heirs to the Populists besides the Socialists of the Debs variety were the Progressive Republicans.

Non-partisan League.—The next politically "red" uprising of farmers did not come until 1915 when Arthur C. Townley in North Dakota started the Non-partisan League.

Except for Mississippi, there was no state more rural than North Dakota; 86.4% of her population lived outside of towns and villages and 58.2% lived on farms.   Moreover, the farmers of the state specialized in small grains—wheat, flaxseed, oats, barley, and rye — but more than 50% of crop land was devoted solely to wheat.   The state also was very young, for until after 1870 none but the Indian was in its area, and most of its growth came after 1890.   It was a mecca for farmers from the northern lands of Europe; predominant in its population were the blood-strains of Norway, Russia, Germany, Sweden, and Denmark. All of these countries had pronounced leanings toward cooperative business ventures. By 1915 about 80% of the people of North Dakota were born in this country, but they stood first among American states in the percentage of foreign-born or mixed parentage. Hence, the revolt that began in 1915 was primarily of second generation persons with an inherited inclination toward mutual benefit organizations.

North Dakota a Dependent.—Economically, North Dakota in 1915 was a satrapy of the Minneapolis Chamber of Commerce and similar grain exchanges in Duluth and Chicago. Since the Minneapolis Chamber originally had been the city's Millers' Association, the members as *buyers* of grain and chief figures of the market place—the Chamber had only 2 farmers among its 318 members and these farmers were the "gentlemen" not "dirt" variety — gave the grain growers' (*sellers'*) interest scant heed. Moreover, both the Chamber and the Millers were closely associated with the Great Northern, Northern-Pacific, and Chicago, Milwaukee, and St. Paul railroads. All of these in turn were investors in the terminal and country grain elevators joined together in chains. Finally the great banks of Minneapolis—and behind these the banks of Chicago and New York—sat in the center of the web of Exchanges, railroads, elevators, and country banks.

Dakota Farmers' Plight.—The North Dakota farmer's first contact with these interlocked businesses was at the time he purchased his farm, and thereafter each year when he purchased seed, farm animals, machinery, or supplies; the strand he touched was the local bank. There were 485 of these for the state's 600,000 population, a ratio of banks to population that was slightly more than six times that in New York State. The North Dakota country banks charged 14% interest on loans, and were known to add to this by pre-dating notes and by practicing other methods for forcing extra bank-income. Nearly two-thirds of the state's farms were mortgaged for an average of $5,284 and besides the banks held chattel mortgages, all at the high interest rates. The bankers gave the farmers strong hints as to which elevators to patronize.

The elevator bought the farmers' grain at the Minneapolis price, less freight from the point of purchase. Neither farmers nor their representatives shared in the price fixing process at Minneapolis. Local elevators sometimes misquoted the Minneapolis price, always in such instances, understating it. There were different prices for different grades of grain and the elevator determined the grade — it did the farmer no good to seek another elevator when he was certain his grain was being undergraded because the elevators acted in concert. The grain was weighed on the elevator's scales which later investigation proved were inaccurate in almost two-thirds of those tested. At some Minneapolis elevators the grain was weighed at the top after it had been pulled up through troughs where it was subjected to strong suction, presumably to remove dust — but these elevators sold many thousands of bushels of grain in excess of recorded purchases. The country elevator exacted a dockage for presumed dirt; here again investigation showed that the actual dirt content was one-fourth the amount charged. For wheat there were thousands of bushels of by-product screenings, bran, and shorts, all valuable animal foods; no allowance for these was made to the farmer but he had to pay for them if he needed them for his cattle and hogs.

If the farmer tried to circumvent his local elevators by shipping to Minneapolis commission-men these usually charged $1.50 per car for switching, although most railroads did not make this charge to the commission-men. Other novel trade practices prevented the farmer from getting advantages by shipment direct to the terminal market.

Farmers' Cooperatives.—To escape some of these tricks of the trade, farmers organized cooperative local elevators—there were 400 with this name in North Dakota in 1916. Competing elevators at once raised their local prices not only above those offered by the local cooperative but above the market—the loss being made up where there was no competition. If the cooperative survived, its share-stocks gradually accumulated in a few hands; sooner or later private offers, at irresistible prices, were made for the stock and the cooperative quietly became a chain elevator usually with no change of name. Of the 400 "cooperative" elevators in 1916 it was found that only 50 were genuine. The railroads sometimes hampered the real cooperatives by refusal of track side sites or inability to provide them with adequate car service.

By the medium of politics the farmers had been unable to get relief from the forces that bound them, because for years North Dakota had been ruled by "boss" Alexander McKenzie. His power, however, had been shaken by the Progressives three years before the Non-partisan League appeared; indeed Judge Andrew A. Bruce, a hostile critic of the League, said that McKenzie connived support for the League in order to break the political alliances that had loosened his grip on the state. In view of the ties of McKenzie, and the identity of the opponents of the League, it seems unlikely that McKenzie helped the League; nevertheless stranger situations have been known in politics.

Equity Association.—North Dakota farmers were restless for ten years before 1915; they constantly sought means to break their economic and political shackles. In the economic sphere their most conspicuous success was in the North Dakota Union of American Society of Equity, an organization originated by Kentucky tobacco growers and then spread to grain producers in Wisconsin, Minnesota, and North Dakota.

The Equity association, despite every handicap set up by elevators, banks, and railroads—the belt line (Minn. Transfer) railroad Minneapolis-St. Paul refused to move its grain cars—managed, under the able direction of George S. Loftus (d. 1916), not only to survive but to run after 1911 an Equity Cooperative Exchange. Fairly successful as a business body, Equity got no hearing at the North Dakota capitol. For example, in 1912 and 1914 the people of the state voted for a State Elevator but the state administrators retorted that it was inexpedient and unnecessary. It was at a midwinter 1915 convention of Equity where an attempt was made to influence politicians, one of whom was alleged to have advised the Equitists "to go home and slop your hogs," that the Non-partisan League was conceived.

Non-partisan League Starts.—The father of the idea was Arthur C. Townley, an American, born in Minnesota and in 1915 thirty-five years of age.   He had been wiped out as a dry-farming flax producer, then had been a "boomer," and finally an organizer for the state Socialist party.   Townley in February 1915 took his idea to F. B. Wood, a substantial farmer in Deering and a pioneer in Equity.   The idea was an old, much tested one; its application to farmers was new.   It was that farmers should organize so as to select candidates favorable to the farmers' political programs, and to vote for these picked candidates regardless of party labels.   This meant first thorough organization in each voting precinct then, from this base, building county and state committees.

Non-partisan League Grows.—Although F. B. Wood was skeptical he loaned transportation to Townley and sent along a son to give introductions to neighboring farmers.   On the first day Townley secured 9 recruits, and 79 in the first week.   By midsummer 10,000 had signed and 22,000 by early autumn. When time came for action in 1916 the League had 40,000 members in a voting population of about 105,000.

The method of organization was a political novelty; some 60 automobile-riding salesmen scurried among farmers selling them League memberships on a commission basis, the membership dues at first $2.50, then $6 and $9 after the first primary, $16 for two years (the legislature was biennial).   The dues, generally paid in advance-dated checks, covered also a subscription to the *"Non-partisan Leader"* on an "if, as, and when issued" basis; and in 1915 a year's subscription to *"Pearson's Magazine"* then carrying pertinent articles by Charles Edward Russell.   Nearly all learned societies included their *"Reviews"* in dues, and the *"National Geographic Magazine"* was sold to "members" of the National Geographic Society.   However, the Non-partisan League was the first known political organization to operate on dues that included a subscription to a periodical.

The *"Non-partisan Leader"* appeared on September 23, 1915; members were warned to rely on it for authentic Non-partisan news and were told that the state press was a "kept" press with consequent tainted news. (Heywood Broun has said "it is the little country newspaper that is most venal.") Townley had learned from the Socialists that the first principle of propaganda is "discredit the opposition." It was well for the Non-partisans that they were informed at the start that their opponents would, if they could, fill the state papers with damaging insinuations and outright lies. In fact the chief state papers did constantly attack "Townleyism," an opprobrious term they coined. The only state paper that changed from censure to support was the Grand Forks *Courier-News;* the League bought this paper on September 23, 1915.

First Campaign.—In 1916 the League very carefully entered its first campaign. From the smallest voting unit to the state organization every League representative was cautiously selected; likewise, the endorsed candidates were so prudently chosen that the state papers charged they were hand-picked by Townley, Wood, and the other three men on the executive committee. The League got Lynn J. Frazier to head their ticket; he was a real "dirt farmer" from Hoople, an ex-university footballer and graduate, and highly respected in his own community. His previous lack of political experience was a vote-getting advantage.

The 1916 platform included:

> State owned and operated terminal elevators, flour mills, stockyards, packing houses, and cold storage plants.
> State hail insurance.
> Exemption of farm improvements from taxation.
> State grain inspection and grading.
> Rural credit banks.
> Graduated corporation income tax.

With fresh candidates asking for votes on this platform, the League first swept the 1916 primaries—chiefly the Republican—and in November got control of the elective Supreme Court and

House of Representatives.   The Senate of 49 members was
only for half its membership up for re-election; the League got
18 of the 25 vacancies.   This, however, was insufficient to control the Senate for only 3 of the 24 holdovers were favorable to
the League; thus the Senate was anti-League by 28 to 21.   The
League held the House by 87 to 26.

The legislative session of 1917, like the campaign that preceded it, was a fierce clash of politico-economic ideas and per-
sonalities.   The Senate was the chief scene for the mutilation
or extermination of League bills.   Even so the session enacted
more progressive measures than any prior meeting of the legislature.   Among the most important was the requirement of a
state license for grain graders, an income tax on railroads and
other corporations, woman suffrage for national offices, reforms
in the administration of rural roads and rural schools, and reforms in state administration.   The Senate, however, killed
all the key socialistic bills of the League.

Second Campaign.—In 1918 a greatly strengthened Non-
partisan League again went before the electorate and this time,
by a majority of 17,000 votes, got complete control of the state.
Therefore, the 1919 legislative session was on the one hand one
of the most iconoclastic and on the other most constructive
(for believers in socialism) ever noted in American state history.   The League put through its whole program, the chief
features of which were:

> The Bank of North Dakota—for state deposits and redis-
> count.
> An industrial commission to operate state enterprises.
> North Dakota (Flour) Mill and Elevator Association.
> State inspector of weights, measures, and grain grades.
> Hail insurance—state operated.
> Workmen's Compensation—state monopoly insurance fund.
> 48-hour work week for women.
> Centralized control of education—state printing of public-
> school textbooks.
> State printing authorized in only one newspaper per county.
> Recall of all officials including judges.

Home-building assistance—a variety of Building and Loan
   Association.

Exemption of all buildings and improvements from taxation
   (Single Tax).

During the 1919 coal strike, Governor Frazier took over
and operated the state's lignite mines—two-thirds of the lignite
in the United States was in North Dakota.   The legislature also
enacted coal mine regulation.

Opposition to Non-partisan League.—This entire group
of statutes encroached upon a number of vested interests; it
hit banks, flour mills, elevators, grain exchanges, insurance companies, county newspapers, real estate promoters, railroads
(rates regulated and income taxed), publishers of school books,
and employers of wage earners.   Of course, such interests
would not accept dispossession without a struggle.   Their first
move, taken in the names of 42 taxpayers, was to halt by injunctions all the vital features of the new statutes.   Secondly,
they took advantage of constitutional and statutory changes
introduced by the League, to put before the people for vote the
1919 laws in regard to the state bank, railroad rates, state flour
mill and elevator, hail insurance, income tax, and state printing
of school books.

Meanwhile the League was threatened by internal schism;
and external attack on account of its alleged attitude toward
the World War.   The internal secessionists were William
Langer, Attorney General; Carl Kositzky, Auditor, and Thomas
Hall, Secretary of State.   This defection was serious because
the first officer, by statutory provision, was one of the three
members of the Industrial Commission that operated the state
enterprises; the Auditor of course could block state expenditures.
The League loyalists met this situation by cutting off the appropriations that supported the three offices.

Charges of Disloyalty.—The charge of obstructing the
prosecution of the World War had arisen in 1917.   The League
then was solidifying its position and was not attentive to national or world affairs and opinion.   Townley in his speeches

said what later was commonplace, namely that our entrance into the war was to protect our investments among the Allies— in 1917, however, this assertion could land its maker in jail as it did Townley in Minnesota. Governor Frazier was supposed to be strangely tender to the anti-war I. W. W. He, likewise, extended the hospitality of the state to a convention of the People's Council for Democracy, an organization suspected (later proved) of pro-Germanism. A Minnesota League meeting was addressed by Senator LaFollette, one of the "wilful 12," who voted against the war and representative of a German peopled state.

The enemies of the League clamored over these incidents while at the same time denying to the League all opportunities to appear before the public in any demonstration of loyalty. North Dakota, however, did its full share in subscriptions to the Liberty loans, raised its quota of war recruits and added to its wheat output although the federal fixed-price did not always cover North Dakota costs. Despite this exemplary conduct the odor of disloyalty clung to the League, and was used in endeavors to destroy it in 1919-20 when to be a "Red" was to be hounded.

League Wins.—To make matters worse for the League in 1920 its North Dakota innovations coincided with the peak of general prices but a slump in the price of wheat. Moreover, bankers in the East as well as the West boycotted the state bond issues by whose proceeds the state expected to finance its state-owned business ventures.

From all these blows the Non-partisan League ought to have been shattered; but the people of North Dakota believed in the League program even if they were not enthusiastic about every one of the leaders—Governor Frazier did receive their full confidence. Thus, in 1919, when the Opposition forced the referendum upon the principal League statutes, the voters gave them endorsement by 6,000 to 13,000 majorities. This year marked the peak for the Non-partisan League.

The 1920 election returned Governor Frazier to office, and sent Professor E. F. Ladd to the United States Senate. The

state Attorney General and Auditor were League men.   Nevertheless the Opposition, a combination of regular Republicans
and Democrats, put into state office their candidates for Treas-
urer, Secretary of State, Superintendent of Public Instruction,
and a Justice of the Supreme Court, and two members of Congress besides getting control of the North Dakota House of
Representatives.   They failed in the primaries to get William
Langer on the ticket as candidate for Governor.   [He held this
office in 1932].

Senator Ladd had been an invaluable staff man at the state
Agricultural College; it was his researches that convinced the
farmers as to how much they had been mulcted.   He held state
office under the auspices of the League in 1917 and 1919, and
in 1921 was further honored by the Senatorship.   Governor
Frazier, Senator Ladd, and Attorney William Lemke outshone
Townley although the latter did not aspire to state office.   William Lemke was Chairman of the N. D. Republican Committee
1916-20; and N. D. Attorney General 1921-23.   Ten years
later he entered the U. S. Congress as Representative At Large
for North Dakota.   [In 1936 he was the Social Justice Union
party candidate for the presidency].

League Wavers.—As a dues-paying association, the Non-
partisan League in North Dakota gradually disintegrated after
1921.   In that year, on October 28 in his third term, Governor
Frazier lost the office by a recall vote 107,332 to 111,434 for
the fusion candidate Ragnvald Anderson Nestos, a Rotarian
and lawyer of Minot.   Its accomplishments remained as did
also the habit of its members of examination of the principles of
candidates rather than their party labels.   The states' affec-
tionate respect for Lynn J. Frazier was shown in 1922, when
he went to the United States Senate on the votes of his North
Dakota admirers.   Nestos was re-elected in 1923 running
against Lemke.   In the 1924 campaign the state indicated its
inclination by giving La Follette almost as many votes as it
cast for the winner, Calvin Coolidge.

National Non-partisan League.—The *National* Non-partisan League was founded by Townley in January 1917, imme-

diately after the first success of the state league in North Dakota, although quiet penetration of neighboring states had occurred in 1916. Lemke was a member of the executive committee for this national organization. The national headquarters were established in St. Paul from which office not only the capture of Minnesota was planned but also South Dakota, Montana, Idaho, and Washington. In the two last named the League had early small successes that immediately were countered by old-guard political tricks; the alteration in the laws concerning the primary being the most wily. Thenceforth, in these states, the Non-partisan movement merged with other political progressives. South Dakota never had been as radical as its northern sister state but for awhile a minority of its voters dallied with the Non-partisan technique. This group in 1920 allied with the *National* Farmer-Labor party. Getting nowhere in a couple of campaigns, this variety of agitation subsided.

Minnesota.—It was Minnesota that was the real colleague of North Dakota. The state, despite its pre-eminence of agriculture, was by no means as rural as North Dakota and it had far more numerous and more deeply intrenched manufacturing, mining, lumbering, and commercial interests. It was also regional headquarters for railroads and banks. If North Dakota had been a satrapy then Minnesota was the castle of the satrap.

The Minnesota farmers, constituting a third of the state's population, suffered in the ways we have noticed in North Dakota; and besides the state's wage earners felt oppressed by the same interests that the farmers believed were exploiting them. Here then was a state three times as populous as North Dakota, with much more natural and money wealth, and yet with an accumulation of grievances among its farmers and workers; it seemed an excellent place to practice the Non-partisan tactics.

Non-partisan League of Minnesota.—The Minnesota League began its active bid for power in 1918. It endorsed a full state ticket for the primaries with Charles A. Lindbergh— father of the flier—former Congressman and Progressive Republican, as its selection for Governor. The "regulars," getting behind the incumbent Governor Burnquist up for re-election, garnered all the North Dakota newspaper criticisms of the League and its leaders, made the most of current attacks on the alleged disloyalty of the Non-partisans, and dug up plenty of slanders and epithets from their own ingeniousness. When a Congressman, Lindbergh had written a book entitled "Banking and Currency and the Money Trust" and currently he had issued another, "Why Is Your Country At War, and What Happens to You After the War, and Related Subjects." These two publications, furnished to the backers of Burnquist unequaled timely material for campaign attacks, no chance being overlooked or omitted. Of course the League had troubles in getting halls for meetings and some of its assemblies were dispersed.

Governor Burnquist won in the primary, 199,325 votes for Lindbergh's 150,626.

The League then dropped Lindbergh. In cooperation with union labor it nominated an independent candidate named David Evans, a hardware dealer of Tracy and hitherto a Democrat. This move netted no good to the League and much personal or business injury to Evans; as a candidate his vote was smaller than the one for Lindbergh in the primary. Burnquist went into office.

Farmer-Labor Party Conceived.—He called a special session of the legislature for September 9, 1919, which among other matters was to "revise the primary laws." The primary was a sine qua non for any kind of non-partisan voting because party conventions were too easily controlled to vent openings for insurgency. Therefore, it was believed that Burnquist and his backers intended to abolish not revise the primary. At any rate the legislature refused to change the existing law. On the other side of the political fence the state's union-labor organized a non-partisan political league of their own which tendered cooperation with the Townley-Lemke farmers' group. This was the germ of the Minnesota Farmer-Labor Party.

Farmer-Labor's First Campaign.—The 1920 elections saw the combination of farmers and wage earners promoting a vigorous campaign for Dr. Henrik Shipstead for Governor. Shipstead was a dentist who had been twice Mayor of his home town of Glenwood. In 1917 he had served in the Minnesota lower house. He made such an excellent candidate that he polled 41% of the total vote. His opponent, however, polled 44% and went into the Governor's office.

Results.—This campaign had three important results. It definitely established the Farmer-Labor Party (of Minn.). In turn this ended the *National* Non-partisan League; Townley would not cooperate with a rival catering to the same clients that he had nurtured for five years, so in 1922, he resigned. He declared he was against partisan politics and for non-partisan participation; but because the Republicans and Democrats fused against his Non-partisan League, it really, during most of its life, was an independent party. The *Non-partisan Leader* suspended publication in July 1923. The third result was the demonstration of the vote-getting proclivities of Henrik Shipstead. In 1922 the Farmer-Labor party was able to place him in the United States Senate defeating Thomas D. Schall, the regular Republican nominee. This was the Farmer-Labor party's first triumph.

The Minnesota Farmer-Labor Party had another and an unexpectedly early chance to try its mettle when Senator Knute Nelson died, thus causing a special election on July 16, 1923. The Republicans put up J. A. O. Preuss; the Democrats nominated James Carley; and the Farmer-Labor party tendered Magnus Johnson. The real fight did not involve the Democrat, but was a fierce contest between the other two. Magnus Johnson was a Swedish immigrant (1891) who became a citizen in 1899. Sixteen years later he served two years in the Minnesota House of Representatives and in 1917 entered the Minnesota Senate. In 1922, he ran on the Farmer-Labor ticket against Preuss for the governorship and lost. When proposed for the U. S. Senate the eastern press pictured him as uncouth but this was political slander. In Minnesota he was a power among farmers; he had been president of the State Union of American Society of Equity, and later became vice-president of that society's Cooperative Exchange; besides which he had been engaged in numerous cooperative associations outside of the Equity group. Consequently the farmers made a massed march to the polls to help one of their kind defeat a town lawyer; they succeeded by a margin of 95,000 votes.

Stabilization of Farmer-Labor Party.—In 1924 the tide shifted; the Governorship and Senatorship both went to regular Republicans. Theodore Christianson (R) beat Floyd B. Olson (F-L) to the governor's chair by 40,000 votes. The race for the Senatorial toga was very close between Magnus Johnson (F-L) and Thomas D. Schall (R); out of 600,000 votes for the two, Schall edged into victory by a scant 8,000. Nevertheless, this double defeat did not destroy the young Farmer-Labor Party. To be sure in 1926 Christianson (R) led Johnson (F-L) by 10,000 in a race for the Governorship and repeated in 1928 against Ernest Lundeen.[2] But Shipstead (F-L) stayed in the U. S. Senate, and was reelected in 1928 (and 1934); a third of the state delegation in the federal House of Representatives generally was sent there by the Farmer-Labor Party; and Floyd Bjerstjerne Olson took a long lease on the governor's chair in 1930.[3] Really, for most of the time after 1920, the Farmer-Labor Party was the "second" or "other" party in Minnesota. Its success was a constant refutation to those who said that farmers and workers never could form a party because "their economic interests were fundamentally opposed."

Case Against a Farmer-Labor Party.—The argument for the latter viewpoint first stressed that farmers were owners of land, buildings, cattle, and machinery and thus were capitalists;

---

[2] Ernest Lundeen, the son of a minister, served in the Spanish-American war and held a commission in the National guard. As a member of the war Congress, he voted against our entrance into the war and shortly thereafter voted against the universal conscription. This halted his political career. The 1928 effort was an attempted "come back"; he succeeded in re-election to Congress in 1932 where, among other things, he introduced a bill for social insurance that went far beyond the administration measure. He was re-elected in 1934 and 1936.

[3] He died in the midst of the 1936 campaign.

as such they viewed socio-economic problems in the same way as other capitalists. Secondly, farmers were employers; thousands of them depended on the kind of casual labor that turned "Red" with the consequence that farmers suspected all organized labor. In the third place, farmers wanted high prices for their products and low-priced manufactures; labor wanted just the opposite. Hence, only in periods of stress when both farmers and labor could pin their troubles to some common suspect, would these two groups cooperate. The history of past combinations of these two groups was said to verify this conclusion.

Case For a Farmer-Labor Party.—The short answer was " 'taint so." A longer rebuttal pointed out that all a farmer owned was the privilege of paying for taxes and repairs; his property was mortgaged to a bank, insurance company, or loan shark. (Posed against statistics this statement shrank a bit— about half our farms were free from mortgage and about a third of our farmers owed no debts.) If the question as to how much a farmer owns was passed over then it could be shown—statistically this time—that his income including homegrown food was the same or less than the income of skilled wage earners. His economic horizon had the same boundaries. A great many farmers who raised sugar-beets, tobacco, cotton, fruit, berries, and vegetables really operated open-air sweatshops; they themselves were exploited by refiners, manufacturers, and canners so in order to subsist must in turn exploit their own employes. These farmers certainly did not view matters with a capitalist's eye.

As employers those who were not "sweaters" often hired their own, their neighbors', and other farmers' sons. The master-servant relationship in such cases was not the same as prevailed in a factory or mill. A great many farmers hired only one or two "hands" and these often lived with the farm family in much the manner of medieval master-craftsmen and journeymen. Those that hired hoboes—itinerant *workers,* not "tramps," "bums," or criminals—learned that hoboes reacted as favorably to decent treatment as the rest of the human family to which they belonged. The ones that did not were either psychopathic cases, or, like bad-tempered horses, had been so badly abused as to bite and kick even a kindly approach.

It was true that both farmers and wage earners wanted the highest possible prices for their services. Some of each group realized that it was the *ultimate* price that caused distress; they saw that it was not the price received by the producers but the toll exacted by processors, middlemen, and distributors that forced the *ultimate price* to painful heights. If it was true, as Secretary Morrison (A. F. of L.) had said, "labor and farmers both have their pockets picked by the same interests," and if both realized it, they had a sufficient reason for joint action.

The appeal to history was misleading. Farmers in the past certainly did forget both bygone grievances and alliances whenever farm prices improved. However, the primary cause of past affluence among farmers was not the prices a farmer got for his products but the rise in the selling price of his land due to unusually rapid increases in population. In the future, if population depends on natural increase and not immigration, all existing gauges foretell but slight chance for *rapid* rises in farm land values. As for organized labor, its leaders since 1881 scuttled every natural rank-and-file political alliance with farmers. It can be concluded that in the past farmers did not have to live within the income of their own industry—their profit came from the real estate industry; and labor-leaders did not give a fair chance to any kind of labor-politics. The past history of American farmer-labor politics was a faulty guide to future possibilities.

These were the two verbal batteries turned loose by opponents and proponents of farmer-labor political alliances in the years that followed the Non-partisan League and Minnesota Farmer-Labor Party. A practical demonstration of one of the brakes put upon this kind of alliance came in 1920 with the formation of the *National* Farmer-Labor party.

National Farmer-Labor Party of 1920.—The *National* Farmer-Labor party grew from numerous state and city labor parties formed in 1918 and the two following years. Bridgeport and the state of Connecticut, Chicago and the state of

Illinois led a parade of cities and states whose unions militantly put forward independent labor parties. To weld these together a convention was held in Chicago, November 22, 1919, attended mostly by rank and file delegates; this body created the National Labor Party. In 1920 the name was changed to *National* Farmer-Labor Party as a bid to Townley's various Non-partisan Leagues and to the Minnesota Farmer-Labor party. Neither of these lent support; likewise, the Socialists and Communists disapproved of the rival in a field they had pre-empted. Nevertheless, individual farmers and local farmers' associations as well as Socialists and Communists did attach themselves to the *National* Farmer-Labor party. The core of the party was the Chicago Federation of Labor led by John Fitzpatrick and Ed N. Nockels.

The "redness" of the party may be surmised from its declaration, "We must smash to atoms the money power of the proprietors of the two old parties."

It was from another contemporary group, The Committee of 48, that the *National* Farmer-Labor Party picked its 1920 presidential candidate. The Committee of 48 was composed of intellectuals, professional men, and progressive business men picked from the 48 states. Since it was a strategy board of generals without an army, and looked upon the *National* Farmer-Labor party as an army without a staff, it seemed to the generals a wise move to merge. When it was attempted all that happened was the capture by the *National* Farmer-Labor party of all the generals' lieutenants and top sergeants. One of them, Perley Parker Christensen of Utah was the man chosen to head the 1920 ticket of the *National* Farmer-Labor party. His running mate was Max S. Hayes of Ohio, printer, trade-unionist, and war horse of the Socialist party.

The campaign and election need not detain us. In the year that Harding rolled up 16 million votes and Debs, while in jail, got nearly a million votes, the Christensen-Hayes ticket secured 272,000. Of these, 77,000 came from Washington, 49,000 from Illinois, and 34,000 from South Dakota, the rest from 17 other states. Utah contributed 4,000 votes; holding its prophet without honor. The same 17 states in 1922 again voted in about the same proportions but with somewhat fewer votes for *National* Farmer-Labor party congressional candidates.

National Farmer-Labor Party Dies.—The next year, in order to bolster itself, the party invited to its July 3, 1923 convention all manner of political protestants. The most enthusiastic and numerous response came from the Communists who captured the convention and rammed through their own program. The Chicago Federation of Labor, then (1924) submitting to great pressure from the A. F. of L., withdrew from the *National* Farmer-Labor party.

On the surface this was a record of futility; actually it was a prolonged fight against terrific odds. From the moment of its appearance the *National* Farmer-Labor party was combatted by the officers of the A. F. of L. and by the heads of national unions whose membership endorsed the party; e.g., John L. Lewis and the miners, John P. Frey and the molders. The A. F. of L. threatened to withdraw the charters of city central unions or state federations that worked in, for, or with the *National* Farmer-Labor party. In 1919 the union rank-and-file and local federations were eager for independent political action; if this had had official encouragement instead of caustic disparagement the outcome might have been less insignificant.

Socialists.—It was not farmer or labor political parties that the whole public recognized as "Reds" (1896-1929). Generally before 1920 the term would have been applied to the Socialists, and after that date to the Communists. Before 1929 the Communists were almost entirely urban in membership; on the contrary, the Socialists throughout the generation were hybrids of city workers and western farmers, miners, and small-scale business or professional men. Until the World War, the American Socialists were strongest where Populism, Progressive Republicanism, and Non-partisanism also were strongest. Hence it is logical to present the Socialists' story here, but to defer the tale of the Communists until the next chapter.

Socialist Labor Party.—In 1896-97 there were two groups that bore the name Socialist. The first, the Socialist Labor Party was an inheritance from earlier years, having been founded in 1876 and deriving its membership almost wholly from foreign-born workers and intellectuals. In 1890 the truculent, uncompromising, domineering Daniel DeLeon—born Loeb, island Curacao, December 14, 1852—plunged into the Socialist Labor Party, and with the assistance of Hugo Vogt and Lucien Sanial was its dictator until his death in 1914. Faced with two rival labor bodies, the Knights of Labor and the A. F. of L., DeLeon set out to capture them one after the other. He did get control of District Assembly 49 (K. of L.) of New York City; and in 1893, by means of this body, ousted Terence Vincent Powderly from the highest office in the K. of L. J. R. Sovereign, a Populist, was the new leader of the K. of L. DeLeon immediately quarrelled with this man whom he had helped to elect. In 1895, DeLeon was ejected from the K. of L. but took with him half the membership—31,000 total of which 13,000 seceded—of D. A. 49, an action which destroyed D. A. 49 and the last sizable remnant of the K. of L.

DeLeon next turned to the A. F. of L. trying to bore within it so as to make it declare for the Socialist Labor Party. There he met Gompers head-on; each man was intolerant of opposition and master of epithet, so the contest was bitter and scurrilous. Among the least turgid billingsgate they hurled at each other was DeLeon's charge that Gompers' A. F. of L. "was a cross between a windbag and rope of sand"; he called Gompers "a labor *mis*leader," a "labor fakir," a "capitalist's picket," and a "pure and simpleton." Gompers, in return, said that DeLeon "was a barnacle on organized labor," and "a sinister . . . infuser of vitriol into Socialist propaganda."

Failing to penetrate the A. F. of L., DeLeon in 1895 organized a rival and scabbing Socialist Trade and Labor Alliance. In its three years of existence this body contained 100 unions in New York City, Brooklyn, and Newark. None was large, and Jewish membership predominated. DeLeon demanded that every socialist trade-unionist member of an A. F. of L. union resign forthwith and join his Alliance; an order that was fiercely resented in the A. F. of L. and one that nearly broke wide-open the Socialist Labor Party. In 1898 the largest unit member of the Alliance in New York City withdrew, with the result that the Alliance immediately fell to pieces.

Socialist Labor Party Splinters.—Thwarted in his attacks on the two big labor organizations, DeLeon exercised his belligerency on his own organization; he expelled members, cancelled charters, and attempted to seize the Socialist press. The last move, July 8, 1899, culminated in a knock-down and drag-out fight quelled by the intervention of the city police. The DeLeon faction turned to the courts where they got sanction for the control of the party and its publicity organs. Although DeLeon captured the citadel, most of its garrison slipped away to the Socialist camp of Eugene Debs. The Socialist Labor Party after 1899 became a monastic political sect engaged in the study and propagation of Socialism—and the criticism of all other Socialists. It continued to submit tickets to the electorate but the only votes it got were from its own dwindling hundreds of members.

DeLeon himself was one of the founders of the I. W. W. and also the cause of its almost immediate split into two factions, each claiming to be official. The DeLeon "Detroit branch" did not outgrow its puny infancy and in effect was almost identical with his Socialist Labor Party; the other or "Chicago branch" flourished until the World War and was the one popularly associated with the title, I. W. W.

Importance of DeLeon.—From this brief sketch it is too easy to underrate the importance of DeLeon. He and Gompers individually, and by warring with each other, gave a fixed character to the later career of the A. F. of L. Gompers' latent distrust of Socialist politics was altered into active hostility to everything bearing the Socialist label. DeLeon's zeal for the goal and contempt for opportunistic palliatives influenced Gompers to reverse the ranking of these two aims. DeLeon versus Gompers was Utopia versus the next meal. Gompers unfortunately lacked DeLeon's vision, while DeLeon, even more unfortunately, lacked Gompers' horse-sense. Because men are prone to hate what they fail to understand, these men loathed each other.   On account of this personal relationship Gompers stamped out in his organization everything that reminded him of DeLeon.   Even if it is admitted that Gompers' views coincided with those of the minority of his membership, nevertheless, it is a fact that if he could have absorbed some of DeLeon's prophetic fervor Gompers might have steered the A. F. of L. toward some more idealistic destination than another 10 cents an hour—fully granting that extra dimes were also worth a fight.

Eugene V. Debs.—The Socialist leader that made a real impress on the generation after 1896 was Eugene Victor Debs. After serving six months in the Woodstock (Illinois) jail to purge himself of the contempt charge that arose from his defiance of a court order during the Pullman strike of 1894, Debs returned to his chosen work (November 22, 1895) filled with a newly found knowledge of Socialism.   Victor Berger and others, as well as books, had instructed Debs during his incarceration.   On June 15, 1897, Debs managed a convention of his associates in the American Railway Union, the organization that had conducted the Pullman strike.   The convention gave official obsequies to the union; and then and there re-organized with bolters from the Socialist Labor Party into the Social Democracy.   The next year the name was altered to the Social Democratic Party.

The Socialist Party.—The time was ripe for the venture. Many Populists who had sojourned in the Democratic party were aware of the subsidence of reformism in that organization after its defeat in 1896 and so were ready to swing to a party that promised to carry along the reform program.   The persons and organizations which DeLeon exiled from the Socialist Labor Party were searching for a new Socialist connection.   The trade unions in the A. F. of L. and Railway Brotherhoods—one of the latter, namely the Locomotive-Firemen's Union, Debs himself had nurtured—gave plain indications that their reforms were confined to wages, hours, and working conditions; therefore members of these unions who wanted broader reforms had to look for organized agencies outside the trade unions. Socialism itself was attracting interest among many young Americans.

In almost all of these Debs, the man, stirred warm human response. He was one of the most truly unselfish persons American public life ever had known; at the same time he had a marvelously magnetic personality. The Debs brand of Socialism was not full of foreign jargon nor rigidly doctrinaire; indeed he sometimes was criticized for his departures from what was supposed to be true Marxism. The flexibility of his Socialism appealed to Americans. Debs was a "grass-roots" American, born in Terre Haute, Indiana, November 5, 1855, where his parents, Alsatians, had been pioneers. Until Debs became its apostle, Socialism in the United States had been an alien idiosyncrasy, mostly an oddity of immigrant Germans. Debs gave it an American accent. Socialism had an international philosophy but it had to take on national traits in every country where it sprouted before it could gain in the voting booths.

Debs' function in public was that of the evangelist, while in party conferences he was a tranquilizer of heated opposing factions. Out of public sight there was a group, at first mostly either German or Jewish (or both), who did the unspectacular hard work of organization, formulation of policies, and the like. This situation is usual in most organizations. Throughout his public life Debs depended upon his brother Theodore to take care of all practical affairs and routine details; this brother also often was a cushion between Debs and the sturdy members of the party machine.

First Campaign of Socialist Party.—In the 1898 elections the new-born party got 12,411 votes; it was cheered, however, by its initial success in getting two of its candidates into the Massachusetts legislature and John C. Chase into the Mayor's office in Haverhill. Had they known it this was a portent; the Socialist Party before 1929 never polled more than a million votes in national elections but they got numerous candidates into legislatures and in several instances got control of city governments.

Second Campaign.—Just before the 1900 campaign the most militant anti-DeLeon faction of the Socialist Labor Party made overtures to the Debs organization for merger. The latter feared to introduce the virus inculcated by DeLeon even when borne by insurgents from his domination; consequently the proffer was not at once accepted. After considerable bickering the two groups got together, the insurgents bringing into the Social Democratic Party such zealous workers among others as Morris Hillquit, Max S. Hayes, Job Harriman, Dr. Halpern, and N. I. Stone. This faction already had nominated Harriman and Hayes so after the combination the Social Democrats offered to the nation the names of Debs and Harriman for U. S. President and Vice-President.

The 95,000 votes for these candidates were inconspicuous alongside the 7 million given McKinley or Bryan's 6 million; nevertheless, the Socialist vote was nearly 15,000 greater than the Socialist Labor Party had garnered in its record 1898 poll, and was the largest, to that time, ever cast for Socialists in the United States. Socialism presented with a twang enticed more ballots than when thrust forward in gutturals.

After the election the combination Debsians and anti-DeLeonites perfected their merger and thenceforward formed one united party under a new name adopted at the time of the fusion in 1901. The former title Social Democratic Party not only was a special distinction in contemporary German politics, but in this country easily was confused with the traditional Democratic Party. The new label, Socialist Party, escaped these pitfalls.

Success of Socialist Party.—In the three following national elections Debs was the Socialist Party candidate for President. In 1904 and 1908 Benjamin Hanford was his companion, and in 1912 that position went to Emil Seidel, Socialist Mayor of Milwaukee in 1910. The size of the vote in these campaigns was really astonishing in laissez-faire, individualistic America; in the first two the poll was over 400,000 and in 1912 reached

900,000 or 6% of the total national vote. Milwaukee in 1910 was the first large American city to yield to the Socialists; in that year the Socialists were put wholly in control. Victor Berger also in 1910 started the first of his six terms in the U. S. Congress as a representative of Milwaukee. In 1911 the cities of Berkeley, Butte, and Schenectady came under Socialist rule, and so did Barre, Vermont, in 1916. Elsewhere some 34 Socialists served as Mayors and over 200 Socialists were aldermen; in 1915 there were 38 Socialists in state legislatures and about 150 elected as school officials.

Where Socialist Party Was Strongest.—Careful analyses of Socialist polls indicated the sources of Socialist strength. Among farmers the region called by Stuart Rice "the mid-west culture area of political discontent"—the northern states from Michigan to the Pacific coast together with Kansas, Nebraska, and the southwest in sections wherever the soil was thin and rainfall light—gave many votes to Socialists. In 1912 Oklahoma gave the Socialists their highest percentage of the total local vote, 16.61%. The western metal miners usually were Socialists. In 1912 Nevada Socialists polled 16.47% of the total local vote and in Montana 13.66%. Industries in which there were immigrants from Teutonic and Scandinavian countries with strong Socialist parties showed tendencies to vote with the American Socialists. Railroad junction points, division terminals, or repair shop towns had strong Socialist inclinations. Temporary rises in Socialist columns often occurred where unions lost bitterly contested strikes. Teachers and preachers voted as Socialists for both economic and ethical reasons.

To get this record against its background it should be noticed that the years of Socialist progress 1901-1912 were ones in which the Republican party was arrogant in its control of Congress—the Aldrich-Cannon consulship for Big Business—while the Democrats had lost their Populist reformism. Hence, many Socialist votes were gathered as protests in the only available vehicle for registration of revolt. Also capitalism was taking on Brobdingnagian proportions and was believed by some people to be correspondingly insolent. This kind of capitalism bred an alternative Socialism. Octopus chain businesses drove many local small-scale business men into the arms of the Socialists.

Socialist Influence.—The true measure of the Socialists' program was not its reflection in votes but in mental patterns. The Socialists possessed a splendid corps of writers and speakers who worked tirelessly day and night. Their explanation of what capitalism meant and their suggestions as to measures to check capitalism's utmost ruthlessness were reiterated so often in so many guises, that even the dullest, most set mind caught glimpses of the Socialists' ideas. This changed America. In 1900 our tradition was that every man had untrammeled opportunity; hence complete individual liberty was his birthright and guarantee of success. By 1912 so many persons realized that these beliefs were not in accord with current facts that it was a commonplace remark "America is drifting rapidly into socialism."

Socialists and World War.—Whether or not that was true, the World War temporarily destroyed the Second International and nearly ruined the American Socialist Party. Before 1914 Socialism was so thoroughly international and pacifistic that Socialists boasted there could be no more war because the international brotherhood of man would not spill its blood for any nationalist cause. Even Germans said this. Up to the first mobilizations, Socialists tried to prevent conflict; however, when war was declared, the majority of Socialists everywhere forgot their declarations, donned uniforms, and proceeded to kill those in the uniforms of other nations. The few stalwart non-conformist Socialists who defied their national military machines were punished more harshly than interned enemies. Conventions of the Second International were halted by the war-time barriers to travel, churned hatreds, and jailed leaders.

Since Americans had forbears in all the nations at war, the Socialist committees here were disturbed by conflicting alignments of sympathies. Woodrow Wilson's encouragement of the A. F. of L. and the legislation passed by Congress seemed to validate the non-partisan tactic of organized labor. Besides, the false prosperity of a war-period made those who were piling profits intolerant of Socialist criticism, and those working steadily at high wage rates not susceptible to Socialist proselytism. Socialism began to smell like treason.

Pacifism and Internationalism of Socialists.—Nevertheless, the American Socialist Party did not compromise its principles. In August 1914 it issued a manifesto demanding that Congress place an embargo on the export of munitions or money. The next year it declared for peace, and said the terms of peace should not require indemnity or annexation of territory. It proposed a United States of the World empowered to administer all international affairs and to have domain over all seas and navigable waters. It demanded universal disarmament. To keep its own record clear and to do what it could to prevent American entrance into the war, the Socialist Party resolved (May 1915) that any member who voted for any expansion of the army or navy or voted for war should be expelled.

This consistency was rewarded by loss of membership and shrinkage at the polls everywhere except in cities with large foreign-born populations. In New York City, for example, the Socialists in 1914 elected 7 Assemblymen and sent Meyer London to Congress (re-elected constantly until 1921). The Socialist slogan was: "Every Socialist ballot is a vote against war." For the national campaign Debs, for the first time, was not at the top of the Socialist slate; his health just then was very poor partly on account of a sunstroke years before in West Virginia whose effects recurrently laid him low. In his place Allan L. Benson, a popular Socialist writer, was nominated for the Presidency, and George R. Kirkpatrick for the Vice-Presidency. Their platform was opposition to preparedness for war. The vote for them was large only in a few cities; the total vote was less than two-thirds of the vote for Debs four years before (590,415 against the Debs' 901,873).

Socialist Party Against American Entrance to World War.—In 1917 it appeared inevitable that the United States

would enter the war.   An emergency convention called by the
Socialist Party for April 7, 1917, in St. Louis to determine its
policy under the expected circumstance of war met, as it happened, the day after the United States declared war (April 6,
1917).   Three alternative resolutions were placed before the
delegates : the first was a stinging attack on all war and a special
diatribe against the existing one together with a ringing re-
dedication of the Socialist Party's position on war and peace;
the second and third resolutions softened the tone and shaded
the traditional policy.   The delegates chose the first.   Of 193
delegates, 140 voted for the first, 31 for the second, and 5 for
the third resolution; the rest not voting.   Upon referendum
to the membership, the action of the convention was sustained.
The accepted resolution was more than 2,000 words long, whose
import may be gathered from these excerpts :

> We brand the declaration of war by our government as a crime
> against the people of the United States and against the nations of the
> world . . . .
> We recommend to the workers and pledge ourselves to the following
> course of action,
>> 1. Continuous, active and public opposition to the war . . . .
>> 2. Unyielding opposition to . . . conscription.
>> 3-7. Resistance to censorship and any interference with free
>>   speech, press, assemblage, mails, and the right to strike.
>>   Propaganda promised on all these matters.

Resignations.—With war actually declared this defiance by
the convention came too close to treason to be accepted by some
hitherto prominent Socialists who in consequence resigned from
the party.   Among those who took this action were Allan L.
Benson, Charles Edward Russell, Upton Sinclair, A. M. Simons,
John Spargo, and William English Walling.   After Congress
on June 15, 1917 passed the Espionage Act the personal mail of
Socialists was tapped, Socialist periodicals were denied the use
of the mail, Socialist meeting places were raided, Socialist meetings were prohibited and if they managed to collect a gathering
this was broken up by the police.   Socialists were jammed in
jails, and those who refused to enlist or be drafted were sent to
federal penitentiaries where they had to endure torments as bad

as those met by front line soldiers.   What happened to Eugene Debs is told in Chapter 13 on "Martyrs."

Despite this official terrorism, the Socialist vote in the fall of 1917 showed an astonishing upturn in the largest cities. Morris Hillquit rolled up a large total of votes for the office of Mayor of New York City although he failed to be elected.   The city did elect 7 Socialist Party Aldermen and 7 Assemblymen, besides putting Jacob Panken in the judge's chair in a municipal court.   In 1920 Debs, at that time a federal political prisoner, got the largest vote of his long career—919,799.   This was a result of many motives on the part of voters: some were registering their protest at the martyrdom forced on Debs; others were swept by the revolt of the years 1919-1920; many were evincing approval of the Socialist stand on war; and the rest were members of the Socialist Party.

Schism.—Meanwhile, the Socialists of the whole world first had been exhilarated by the Kerensky Revolution of March 1917 in Russia, and then thrown into hissing factions by the Lenin November 7th Revolution.   The American Socialists did not escape schisms.   As a matter of fact the basis for a split always had existed.   On one side were impatient "revolutionists"— also dubbed "impossibilists," "lefts," and "Reds"—who argued for a violent working-class revolution without religious opiates, deterrent labor-parties, or other compromises on the fundamentals of Marx.   This faction had no regard for what was lawful but only for what was successful; the general strike was their avowedly favorite weapon.   On the other side were the "reformists"—termed by the other faction "opportunists," "rights," "yellows" and "slow-shulists"—who stood for peaceful evolution with emphasis on immediate demands in the spirit but not necessarily the formulae of Marx.   This faction appealed to all classes, all assistance to and from other groups, and all peaceful means to gain a Socialist state.   It believed the ballot more powerful than the strike.   Until 1917 it was this latter faction that swayed the American Socialist Party.

The lurking factionalism was increased after 1907 by the policy of the Socialist Party in encouraging affiliation of foreign national language federations with an interpreter at Socialist Party headquarters. The Finns were the first (1907) such group. By the end of the World War there were 14 affiliated language federations whose membership had jumped from 14% of the total Socialist Party in 1912 to 53% by 1919. The influence of Leon Trotsky and the action of a Boston cell as early as 1916 indicated a trend toward the extreme left wing ideas among these federations.

The Splits.—Since similar divisions existed among Socialists everywhere in the world they were made manifest by two conventions in 1919. The first, in February, was an attempt by the moderate Socialists at Berne, Switzerland to resuscitate the Second International. The other, March 2-6 was a meeting of the "left wingers" in Moscow where they organized the Third (Communist) International.

The long over-ruled "left wingers" in the American Socialist Party at once were uplifted by this Moscow recognition of their viewpoint. They got together in New York and Chicago and perfected a "left wing" alliance whereby they expected to take over the Socialist Party and convert it to Communism. The "right wing" in office, however, controlled the party machinery. They suspended seven language federations, two state branches (Massachusetts and Ohio), and several local units; this remedy was so drastic as to excommunicate a third of the party's membership. The remaining two-thirds, nevertheless, still contained a strong left wing faction.

Chicago Conventions in 1919.—The fight for control came to a head on August 30, 1919, at an emergency convention of the Socialist Party at Chicago. The "right wing" tried to be generous to their opponents but they did not yield power to them; whereupon the "left-wingers" bolted and held a rump convention of their own in the same building. From the rump gathering emerged the Communist Labor Party with a program that emphasized union organization more than politics. At the same time in another part of Chicago the seven expelled federations ran a rival convention at which was organized the Communist party which first, placed absolute reliance upon Moscow and secondly, made politics its select weapon.

Three-Way Split.—Thus there were three parties; the right wing Socialists, the moderate Communist Labor Party, and the revolutionary Communist Party. The second tried to merge with the third, but the latter would accept no compromise; both of these drew strength almost entirely from the language federations. Their later career is told in the following chapter.

Norman Thomas.—For the remainder of the time up to 1929 the Socialist Party had the task of re-filling its depleted ranks under a new standard bearer, Norman Thomas. Debs was a locomotive fireman, Thomas, a Presbyterian minister; both were editors and prolific authors. Debs was a rouser, Thomas a reasoner; Debs was most at home in a roundhouse, Thomas on a rostrum.

Among the recruits enlisted by Thomas were college students and professors, ministers, and other professional persons. The Intercollegiate Socialist Society—later re-named the League for Industrial Democracy—under the efficient guidance of Harry W. Laidler did effective work among college students in all the years after 1905. The contrasts of Thomas with Debs and the kind of new support gave rise to the Communist gibe; "the word Socialist is compounded from the two English words "social list." This sneer overlooked the fact that under Thomas the Socialists also enrolled many Negroes and made headway in interesting the white southern "share-croppers." More than half the Socialist Party's new membership came from wage earners in the manufacturing and mechanical industries. It was weakest among post-war farmers and farm workers, domestic servants, and clerks.

Norman Thomas was almost as frequently his party's candidate as Debs had been. In 1924 when the party supported LaFollette, the candidate for the Governorship of New York was Thomas. Twice thereafter he ran for the Mayoralty of New York City and in 1928 he campaigned with James H. Maurer for the Presidency and Vice-Presidency against Hoover-

Curtis and Afred E. Smith-J. T. Robinson. The Socialist Party never was able to put much of a dent in Tammany so Thomas did no better in New York City and State than Hillquit; and in the 1928 national campaign, at the peak of prosperity, the country was more interested in the repeal of prohibition or the chance for a Catholic to be President than it was in the Socialist program. Hoover, the "dry" Republican, got 21 million votes; Smith, the "wet" Catholic Democrat, got 15 million, while Thomas trailed with 267,835.

Until the 1929 depression began, the Communists attacked the Socialists as vigorously as they assailed Capitalism and the A. F. of L.; they had that bigotry which comes from complete faith in a cause and were not restrained by claims of manners, law, or ethics. Since Communists drew their ideas and orders from Russia and frequently spoke with a "dis and dat" accent, their aggressions against the Socialists had the result of making the latter appear American and respectable. The Communists were prone to the "either-or" type of argument—"either Communism or Fascism"—while the Socialists took a moderate middle ground; the Socialists wanted Capitalism out of the way, but were against violent revolution to accomplish the result. The middle position has been always the hardest to maintain; and also it has been the position of least movement. In 1929, therefore, the Socialist Party was one with slight vote-getting power although its ideas by absorption were constantly pushing the nation to the left. Its propaganda was as potent as its politics was neuter.

CHAPTER 12

"RED" INDUSTRIAL WORKERS

In the industrial field, before the World War, the spotlight picked out the Industrial Workers of the World (I. W. W.) as the chief "Reds." In the remaining dozen years before 1929 the Communists were the outstanding claimants of that ruddy rôle.

The I. W. W. was, itself, the foster child of the Western Federation of Miners, and the direct offspring of eastern radicals. The double function of midwife and wet nurse to the I. W. W. was performed by William D. Haywood, otherwise known as "Big Bill." It was he who brought together the miners of the canyons of the Rockies, the lumber-workers of the peaks of the Cascades, and the pinched textile workers of the tenements of Lawrence or Paterson. How he did it was the story first, of the Western Federation of Miners and secondly, that of the I. W. W.

Western Federation of Miners.—The Western Federation of Miners was proposed in the Ada County jail at Boise, Idaho in 1893, when a lawyer—but former miner—named James Hawley suggested organization to 14 miners held in confinement. On May 13, 1893, a convention at Butte, Montana formally organized this union comprised of miners in lead, zinc, copper, silver, and gold mines and smelters. Haywood, whose paternal ancestors had followed the frontier from Massachusetts Bay Colony to the early days of Salt Lake City where "Big Bill" himself was born in 1869, had, before the age of ten, begun his career as farm chore boy, hunter, cowboy, homesteader, and metal miner. With this behind him at 25 years of age, he was a skilled miner at Silver City, Idaho when, in 1894, he joined W. F. of M., and almost at once became one of its leaders.   He was ready for this step because wandering miners had taught him the history and purposes of the Knights of Labor and "Molly Maguires."

The W. F. of M., after absorbing remnants of the K. of L. left in the Rockies, began a struggle for betterment of the conditions of metal miners that marked the decade after 1894 as one of the most turbulent labor eras in American history.

Characteristics of the Industry.—Metal mining in the Rocky Mountains in the states of Colorado, Utah, Nevada, Idaho, Montana, and Arizona was done under rigorous natural conditions: high altitudes produced short, hot summers and long, cold, snowy winters; the location of ore put camps in narrow deep canyons subject to burial under landslides and snowslides; deep veins created hot working spots—one of the worst in a mine called the Never Sweat—dangerous from rock falls, fires, explosions, defects in haulage devices, and inadequate or interrupted ventilation; and usually miles across peaks and valleys from any large settled community.   In such mining only the most vigorous or most destitute workers were to be found, and lawlessness would be commonplace.   Employers and managers of mining enterprises subject to these conditions were not apt to brook interference with their own arbitrary conduct.   When a union was interjected into this situation there was the makings of tragedy.

Coeur d' Alene, Cripple Creek, Leadville, Telluride, Durango, Florence, Cañon City, Pueblo, Idaho Springs, Gold Field, and Tonapah were names that connoted brutality, violent death, and complete disregard of rights or law, in the acts of both workers and employers.

Demands.—On the side of the W. F. of M. in the above strikes, the demands were for a minimum wage, the abolition of wage-payment in company scrip, the right to trade in stores other than those operated by mining companies, the provision of decent housing, the right to a checkweighman, and the 8-hour day.   The two last demands were made matters of state law in Utah and Colorado but both were persistently ignored by

the mining companies.   To enforce these demands W. F. of M.
was on strike somewhere in the mountain states nearly all the
time for over ten years.   Men, reluctant to join the union,
were forcibly driven out of camps and on the other hand scabs,
brought to break strikes, were beaten and otherwise maltreated.

Opposition.—The mining companies, backed by the Mine
Owners' Association, the Citizens' Protective League, and the
Citizens' Alliance—bankers, storekeepers, and professional men
—on their side hired professional thugs and gunmen as scabs
and threw strikers by the scores into jails, often without warrants and with denial of every constitutional right.   The word
"jail" is a misnomer, for many strikers were confined in "bull-
pens," rough but strong wooden structures so crowded that
strikers, in several instances, were forced to stand most of the
time, and so primitive that no sanitary fixtures were present,
with the consequence that, after months of confinement, men
were covered with their own and each other's filth.   Disease
and vermin, of course, flourished.

County officers, including sheriffs and courts, were sum-
marily displaced by mine owners; and with slight legal warrant, whole areas were kept for months under the most ruthless
martial law.   The property of strikers, including union stores
and relief stations, was utterly destroyed and the strikers themselves, at the points of bayonets, were thrust beyond county or
state lines.   Resistance was answered with confinement in
"bull pens" or sudden violent death for which no soldier,
"guard," or mine-owner was held accountable.

Wherever there was a strike there was anarchy, sometimes
induced by the miners, but fully as often by the owners or their
representatives.   In this anarchy dynamite was freely used to
blow up smelters, mine shafts, railroad bridges or stations, and
human beings.   These crimes charged by each side to
the other.

The I. W. W. is Born.—It was in the midst of this Rocky
Mountain industrial war that in 1905 the Industrial Workers
of the World was organized, largely at the instigation of the

W. F. of M. Originally, the W. F. of M. had been affiliated with the A. F. of L. but withdrew in 1897; a union that looked upon bargaining as a peace forced by victorious belligerency was uncomfortable in a federation that exalted trade agreements drawn in conference rooms. In 1898 the W. F. of M. sponsored the Western Labor Union with headquarters at Butte in the expectation that it be a trans-Mississippi rival of the A. F. of L.

In 1902 the headquarters were moved to Chicago when a new name, the American Labor Union, was chosen. Both names and locations were equally ineffective in attracting much support outside the W. F. of M. except for a few organizations of cooks, lumbermen, teamsters, and waiters, mostly in the same places where the W. F. of M. had locals. It was virtual failure of American Labor Union that in part was the reason for the W. F. of M. making a new tender for broader organizations.

In 1904 six men met for a quiet planning of a new radical union to be based, at first, on certain existing organizations. The deliberations of this little group crystallized in a letter sent on November 29, 1904, to about 30 radicals, inviting them to a secret conference on January 2, 1905. Not all those invited accepted; but the majority did, among them "Mother Jones," the radical organizer of the United Mine Workers' Union. From this conference there was issued a Manifesto which, after first drawing a biting indictment of capitalism, set forth a plan to draw the international unions away from the A. F. of L. and to unionize unskilled workers. It also called a convention for June 27, 1905, to devise a constitution for the new federation that was expected to replace the A. F. of L.

To the convention held in Chicago came 203 delegates representing 60,000 workers in 40 occupations organized into 43 unions, 16 of which were in the A. F. of L. A number of delegates credited to unions really were spokesmen for the Socialist Party or its rival, the Socialist Labor Party. By far the most important voting group was that composed of delegates from the W. F. of M. and its satellite, American Labor Union; in addition the United Metal Workers—a foundling disowned by the A. F. of L.—the United Brotherhood of Railway Workers, and DeLeon's Socialist Trade and Labor Alliance possessed considerable blocs of votes.

However, it was not organizations so much as persons that determined the moulding of the I. W. W.   Charles H. Moyer, William D. Haywood (from the W. F. of M.), Daniel DeLeon (S. T. L. A.), A. M. Simons (Socialist Party), William E. Trautmann (Brewery Workers and Industrial Workers' Club), C. O. Sherman (Metal Workers), and T. J. Hagerty (ex Roman-Catholic priest) were the men whose ideas most dominated the 11-day convention.

Preamble and I. W. W. Constitution.—The accepted constitution began with a preamble that became both famous and a cause for internal schisms.   It read:

> The working class and the employing class have nothing in common.
>
> Between these two classes a struggle must go on until all the toilers come together on the political, as well as on the industrial field, and take hold of that which they produce by their labor through an economic organization of the working class without affiliation with any political party . . . .
>
> Instead of the conservative motto, 'A fair day's wage for a fair day's work' we must inscribe on our banners the revolutionary watchword, 'Abolition of the wage system' . . . .

The constitution provided for local industrial unions gathered into 13 international divisions or departments; and allowed individuals, in the absence of a proper local union, to become members of the parent organization.   C. O. Sherman was elected President and William E. Trautmann Secretary-Treasurer.   The presidency was tendered to Haywood; but he declined on account of his duties with the W. F. of M.   The two officers, with a General Executive Board, had what the revolutionary rank and file thought were highly centralized powers, subject, however—as were convention resolutions—to referendum and (the officers) to recall.

The infant I. W. W. was less united on a positive program than it was on hatred of capitalism and craft unionism; the western members also loathed politics and anything that pertained to state authority—their own experiences with official lawlessness made them despise officialdom. Hence, the membership was suspicious of the I. W. W.'s own officers, and skeptical of DeLeon's possible ulterior motives in the promotion of the new union.

Splinters.—The first three years, therefore, revealed the I. W. W. engaged in two struggles; one, the proselytization of the A. F. of L. unions, especially those of the brewers, and machinists; the other, the house-cleaning of its own constitution and General Headquarters. As to converts, the I. W. W. had slight success; instead it lost some of its own affiliates, e.g., the Amalgamated Society of Engineers, the American branch of the British union of machinists. The 24 strikes of the first 15 months scattered from Skowhegan, Maine to Goldfield, Nevada, nowhere were conspicuous for results. On the other hand, the internal dissension split the I. W. W. into two bodies and revamped its constitution. A partial split came in the second convention when a faction, led by President Sherman, tilted with another headed by DeLeon. The Sherman faction was ousted and the office of president abolished, but this faction hung around for a year or more before it acknowledged defeat.

Two I. W. W.'s.—The much more serious schism arose in the fourth convention September 21, 1908. The real issue was the Preamble phrase "the toilers come together on the political as well as on the industrial field." The western members wanted the constitution changed so as definitely to bar political action. The issue was made personal in respect to Daniel DeLeon for it was he who most insisted on the political phrase and also was the boss of the Socialist Labor Party. On the technicality that DeLeon presented credentials from the Office Workers' Union when he really should have been assigned to the Printing Workers, he was denied a seat in the convention. His followers left the convention with him; claiming to be the adherents of the original constitution, they announced themselves as the *real* I. W. W. Detroit was made the headquarters of this branch.

Meanwhile, the regular convention, packed by the Overall Brigade—a band of casual workers who had hoboed their way

from Portland, Oregon, and Spokane to the Chicago convention
—applied an eraser to the constitution. The troublesome
clause thereafter read:

> Between these two classes a struggle must go on until the workers
> of the world organize as a class, take possession of the earth and the
> machinery of production and abolish the wage system.

The I. W. W., after the operations of the three years, had a
dangerously low blood-count made worse by the (temporary)
loss of one of its bright red corpuscles, "Big Bill" Haywood.
He with Charles Moyer president of W. F. of M. and George
A. Pettibone in 1906 had been jailed in Idaho to stand trial
for the murder of ex-Governor Steunenberg. After the verdict
of "not guilty" on July 28, 1907, Haywood went on a long tour
in Europe and America, so that from the time of his "arrest"—
he was kidnapped—in Denver in 1906, until the close of his
tours the services and inspirations of Haywood were available
to the I. W. W. only at long distance.

I. W. W. Strikes.—At McKees Rocks, Pa., in 1909, the
pulse of the I. W. W. came back to fever count. There the
I. W. W. led a strike of 6,000 employes of the Pressed Steel
Car Co. During the two months that the strike lasted, the
I. W. W. startled the nation by its unusual tactics. It sent
no committees to the management to negotiate terms; instead
it posted its demands and kept the plants unproductive until the
management capitulated. The state constabulary, "called cossacks" by all radicals, was forced to soften its usual strike-
tactics because as soon as the police killed the first striker, the
I. W. W. gave notice it would kill a policeman for every striker
murdered. The ancient formula "an eye for an eye" was carried to its extremity, "a life for a life." As soon as the
I. W. W. made literal application of this formula, the constabulary curbed its brutality. The strike, in consequence, was
termed by the I. W. W. a double victory, one over the "steel
trust," the other over the "cossacks."

Bewildered Employers.—In addition to this strike, the
I. W. W. up to half its membership was involved in others.

To employers the I. W. W. strike tactics were either exasperating or bewildering, for the reason that the strikes always came without warning, proceeded without negotiation, and ended without trade agreements. The aim of an I. W. W. strike was not betterment for the workers but ruin for capitalism. This aim also explains the I. W. W. strike "on the job," an ages-old practice but at that time, recently by French syndicalists, labelled "sabotage." The countless tricks used by the I. W. W. in sabotage were said, by their perpetrators, to have been learned from the employers—where he adulterated his products a little the I. W. W. did a lot, where he limited output they made it impossible. Two of the most outrageous methods of sabotage were first, to tell customers the exact truth regarding products, and the other was to give literal obedience to employers' commands. In a restaurant, for example, the first quickly emptied the tables; while on a railroad or in a factory the second just as promptly produced chaos.

Free Speech Fights.—"Free speech" tactics of the I. W. W., 1909-12, were fully as startling as their innovations for strikes. Wherever an agitator was arrested for his public remarks, word by way of General Headquarters in Chicago, was relayed to all foot-loose I. W. W. to congregate as soon as possible at the place of arrest.

The "wobblies" poured into town and made inflammatory speeches so as purposely to get themselves arrested; the jails of course were jammed almost at once and yet the hoboes continued to arrive and to spout from soap boxes. Those behind bars sang brass-lunged revolutionary songs for hours on end, and no pleading nor commands could make them stop. The response in the towns was either to accept defeat and let the I. W. W. speak at will, or by mob frenzy try to put the I. W. W. into panic and retreat. The former method was carried out at Spokane, Fresno, Paterson, Denver, and Seattle, the latter most notoriously at San Diego and Everett. There were "free speech fights" also at Missoula, New Castle, Wenatchee, Walla Walla, and at least four other places.

In 1912 the I. W. W. frightened the East by its strike at Lawrence, Massachusetts, which was discussed in Chapter 4.

Paterson Strike.—Hardly was the Lawrence strike concluded when the I. W. W. were involved in another struggle, this time at Paterson, N. J. Founded by Alexander Hamilton and associates to lead America toward independence of Europe in manufactures, this city at first was noted for its cotton mills and then for its heavy metal output, chiefly locomotives. But after the Civil War its claim to fame rested in its production of silk braids, ribbons, and cloth.

At first the silk mills gave jobs to the feminine members of families whose males won their bread in the locomotive shops. When the growth of the silk business outran the original labor supply, the mills tapped the abundant stream of immigrants flowing into the country at nearby New York City. Gradually the least skilled operations in the preparation of silk yarn— called "throwing" but corresponding to spinning in other textile fibers—left Paterson for the scattered coal and iron towns of Pennsylvania seeking as employes the daughters, sisters, and wives of miners, cement makers, and steel workers. The more skilled operations of weaving and dyeing silk were concentrated in Paterson. Since these processes could be done on a small scale, competition among Paterson enterprises was sharp with a resultant constant whittling down of labor costs. On the other hand the labor, mostly foreign born, was amenable to collective action and susceptible to radical ideas.

Strike Tactics.—It was against this background that the I. W. W. in 1913 stepped in as leader of a labor revolt for more pay and fewer hours of work. In this strike the I. W. W. again showed its mastery of the technique of publicity. Massed pickets, sometimes numbering thousands, were taught to "boo-o-o" police after the manner of college cheering, a method tried out at Lawrence but magnified in Paterson. The funeral of a murdered striker was made into a dramatic episode with twofold effect of stiffening strikers' resistance and broadcasting their grievances. In offense at a teacher's remark that the strikers were "Anarchists and good-for-nothing foreigners," the children of strikers organized and carried out—not without aid from I. W. W. leaders—a school strike in which one of the demands was "No more homework." Another unusual feature was conducted at Madison Square, New York City where 1,200 selected strikers put on a five-act pageant telling the story of their conflict; this itself got marked attention from New York papers and opened their columns to further strike news for the duration of the struggle.

Employers' Acts.—For their part, the employers filled the city with law officers who harried picket lines, mass meetings, and leaders; and attempted to break morale by thrusting into jail some 1,800 men, women, and children. The American flag, so often used as a screen to hide distresses from the public, also was employed in Paterson where it decorated struck mills, stores, offices, and homes. This thrust was parried when the strikers held a flag parade with a placard stating:

> We weave the flag.
> We live under the flag.
> We die under the flag.
> But damn'd if we'll starve under the flag.

Just one "beau geste" came from the employers and that was an offer from the management of the Doherty mill to turn the property over to the strikers for a guarantee from them of a 5% return to stockholders, an offer that was rejected. But the owners of struck mills could do one thing that the strikers could not—they could wait. Their success in doing this for months finally broke the strike.

The Paterson workers got no return for their sacrifices; but the I. W. W. considered the strike a victory because it had supplied a sounding board for their *motifs*.

Other Strikes.—Concurrently, with the Paterson strike, the I. W. W. with 25 local members backed a strike of 7,000 workers in the rubber manufacturing plants of Akron. The strike, initiated by 60 organizers, began in one plant and flared quickly into violence over the whole city. Appeals to the Governor for militia were denied by that officer so the sheriff declared martial law which was enforced by 1,000 vigilantes who took command of the city streets.   The strike collapsed; it was followed by the introduction of company unions in the principal plants and the acceptance of the 8-hour day.

Immediately after the Lawrence strike, the I. W. W. led a textile strike at Little Falls, New York and furnished leaders in 1913 to strikes of hotel waiters and barbers in New York City.   Bitter strikes among copper miners, both in Utah and the Upper Peninsula of Michigan, were led by the I. W. W.   Of all their strikes between 1912 and 1914 the only other one of unusual importance was that in 1913 of the hop-pickers in Wheatland, California.

Wheatland, California, Strike.—Since California's agricultural products, fruits, nuts, vegetables, hops, and cotton required far larger forces at harvest than at any other season, it had become customary to rely upon migratory casual laborers of both sexes and all ages to do the work of gathering the crop. Because at any one ranch the maximum work-force was resident for a brief period, the equipment for housing, sanitation, drinking water, and the like often was inadequate or unfit; or both. Until the I. W. W. took up their problems, the casual laborers on California ranches, midwest grain fields, sheep folds, and northern forests had no aid in redressing their grievances; for the casuals were homeless, often womanless, and always voteless.

Conditions.—At Wheatland, California, the Durst Brothers had a hop ranch that illustrated the worst features of the system. The shelters were tents in not too good repair rented to pickers at 75 cents a week.   Since there were not nearly enough tents to house the 2,800 pickers, some of them slept in rude structures composed of waste lumber and gunny sacks.   The largest number slept in the open on straw or hop-vines.   For the great crowd of pickers there were only eight primitive toilets and these were filthy.   The excreta and camp garbage piles were not shielded from flies; so diarrhea, dysentery, malaria, and typhoid ran through the people in epidemic proportions.   The feature that was the direct cause of the August 3, 1913 strike was the absence of drinking water out in the baked fields where Califor-

nia's unclouded sun produced temperatures well above 100° F.
A relative of the Dursts did sell "lemonade" at 5 cents a glass
to pickers but even this beverage was made not of fruit but
citric acid.

Clashes.—Since interference with harvests threatened California's economic existence, the outbreak at Wheatland was
rigidly repressed by militia.   Clashes between soldiers and strikers were violent and mortal.   So the strike leaders, Richard
Ford and Hermann Suhr, were arrested and charged with being
accessories to murder.   Tried in a tense atmosphere they were
sent for life to Folsom Penitentiary, although many, including
members of the jury, thought a grave injustice was done them.

Aftermath.—Their arrest broke the strike; but enough Californians had been aroused to the conditions under which casuals
lived and worked that the state appointed a commission to investigate the facts in order to recommend corrective measures.
The commission found 876 labor camps in the state which, when
used to capacity, contained 60,813 persons; moreover, the conditions at the Durst ranch were found to be by no means unusual.   Facts thus revealed produced legislation aimed at
removal of the worst evils; so in the long run the strike did
bring some beneficial results to the casual laborers.

However, a law is as good only as its administration and
this in California has varied; consequently, on several occasions
after 1913, California was the scene of violent strikes of agricultural workers.   In fairness it should be said that California
protected her casual workers better than any other state.
Indeed in Maine, by a law enacted in 1907, the casual lumber
workers were actually reduced to a state of peonage, rebellion
against which brought stiff jail sentences.   The jail at Dover-
Foxcroft, Maine, often was crammed with lumbermen whose
offense was an attempt to void labor contracts made through
misrepresentations of operators; but if the operators made advances in supplies or materials the law held the befuddled lumberworkers to their contracts and jailed them for violations.
Other states in the West and Northwest countenanced peonage
while in parts of the South peonage was notorious.   In contrast

the California law and its administration before 1917 were benevolent.

Pariah.—The I. W. W. never had been popular even among other radicals and other labor unions; the A. F. of L. and railroad brotherhoods, representing the cautious skilled workers, fought the precipitate unskilled I. W. W. with a venom which was returned in kind.   As for employers, and the conservatives in general, the mercurial tactics and openly declared intention of the I. W. W. to seize all industries and run them for and by the workers raised an opposition sometimes as vicious as it was certain.

The pariahism of the I. W. W. before our prospective entrance into the World War was as adulation to the vindictive attempts at extermination the I. W. W. met with after 1916. If Eugene Victor Debs was the most prominent individual "martyr" to the war spirit 1917-1920, it is also true that the organization most harried in the name of patriotism was the Industrial Workers of the World. The I. W. W.'s own uncompromisingly hostile stand against all war save class-war was in itself at the time an invitation for persecution.   The fact that the membership of the I. W. W. contained many foreign born sheared them from the sympathies of Americans fired to frenzied patriotism.   Finally, as unskilled workers the I. W. W. were the undermost of underdogs.

War-Time Terrorism.—At first the animosity to the I. W. W. vented itself in isolated instances.   On November 5, 1916, some Seattle members chartered the steamer *Verona* and her sister-ship to carry them to Everett, the Olympic peninsular lumber-town where "a free speech fight" was in progress.   As the *Verona* approached the Everett wharf she was met by volleys from deputy sheriffs and volunteers hidden in ambush. Five of the *Verona* passengers were killed and many wounded; some of the rest returned the fire as the boat backed away from shore.   At Seattle the *Verona* was met by law officers who arrested the I. W. W. leaders on board and brought them to trial for the murder of some of the Everett ambuscade; found guilty, they were given long-term sentences. No one stood trial for the five dead I. W. W.

At Tulsa, Oklahoma, some members of the Commercial Club, assisted by police, seized a crowd of I. W. W. in their own hall, took them outside the city, beat them excoriatingly with blacksnake whips, tarred and feathered the fainting victims, and ordered them never to return to Tulsa.

Bisbee, Arizona, was the scene of another incident; there on July 12, 1917, the Vigilance Committee rounded up 1,162 I. W. W. miners, herded them into cattle cars whose floors were six inches deep with manure and shunted them to Hermanas where in a desert they were turned loose without water or food, later to be corralled by United States troops.

Within a month, at Butte, Montana, an I. W. W. organizer, named Frank Little, was caught by a gang who disregarded his leg and ribs broken in an earlier riot and dragged him, noosed by the neck, to a railroad bridge where they finished by hanging him.

Lawful Terrorism.—These were some of many individual cases. As early as January 1916, from 75 to 100 special agents, acting for the U. S. Department of Justice, trailed the I. W. W. On September 5, 1917, federal officers acting in concert from coast to coast raided I. W. W. meeting places, seized tons of property and hundreds of persons; a procedure which was repeated on September 28. The Espionage Act of 1917 furnished the legal ground for these raids. Similarly beginning with Idaho, March 4, 1917, 17 other states passed virtually identical Criminal Syndicalism laws which, on their face, were protections against conspiracies for the violent overthrow of government but were so drawn that they could be used as dragnets to catch, fine, and sequester almost anyone on the black lists of those in authority.

War-Time Trials.—From these federal and state sources, five principal groups of I. W. W. prisoners were jailed and held for trial during most of the time of America's participation in the World War. At San Diego and Omaha the groups were small, but at Wichita 39 were incarcerated, at Sacramento there were 39, while Chicago topped them all with 95 convicted.   The numbers refer to those finally sentenced from 1 to 25 years; those in Judge K. M. Landis's—afterwards the baseball "Tzar" —court in Chicago also got fines of from $20,000 to $30,000 apiece, the total amounting to $2,570,000, plus costs.   While waiting trial in county jails some of the I. W. W. died from the influenza epidemic, one was shot, and several went insane.

Post-War Terrorism.—The ending of the war did not stop the actions against the I. W. W.; rather it intensified them. One of the worst scenes of violence was Centralia, Washington.   In April 1918, a Red Cross parade turned aside to wreck the local I. W. W. hall; only two articles were saved, both auctioned on the spot for Red Cross funds; one was a victrola bought by a manufacturer, the other a desk that went to the Chamber of Commerce.   The persons inside the hall were beaten, threatened with lynching, but let off, some with jail sentences, others with deportation from the county.

The next year, when November 11 approached, plans for an Armistice Day parade included—among an inner ring of plotters—another assault on the I. W. W. hall.   A lawyer told the I. W. W. they had a right to protect their property.   So when the paraders swung aside to attack the hall with the concerted signal "Let's go-o-o! At 'em boys!" the front line of invaders were met with a fusillade of shots from within the hall.   Two parade-assailants were killed and several wounded. The paraders surrounded the hall and captured all its occupants save Wesley Everest.   He ran to the river in a fusillade of pursuing bullets and when unable to cross, turned and offered to surrender to any responsible officer.   The offer was met with more gun fire, so Everest raised his own weapon and in firing upon the advance pursuers killed Dale Hubbard, the nephew of the ringleader in the attack.   Everest was overpowered and his teeth were knocked out with a rifle butt on his way to the jail. Everest himself was an overseas veteran with a record for bravery under fire.

That night all the town lights went out.   In the darkness the jail door was smashed, Everest seized and piled into an automobile. During his ride he was castrated. Upon arrival at the Charles River, Everest was hanged from the bridge, but the rope proving incorrect in length so that life remained in him, he was hauled up, fitted with another rope, and hanged again. When dead, his body was riddled with shots and tossed into the river. Before dawn his body was recovered and taken back to the jail where his I. W. W. associates, themselves arrested, were forced to look upon it.

These associates were Eugene Barnett, John Lamb, Brett Smith, Bert Bland, Commodore Bland, Roy Becker, John McInerney, Mike Sheehan, Elmer Stewart Smith, and Loren Roberts. They were indicted for murder and tried at the town of Montesano where militia filled the streets and American Legionaires in uniform jammed the court room. All but the last three named above were convicted of second degree murder— Loren Roberts had gone insane from terror while in jail—and sentenced to 25 to 40 years in the Walla Walla Penitentiary. Later, six of the jury said their verdict was coerced. One juror said the preliminary ballot was unanimously for acquittal and after 22 hours and 20 minutes of balloting the first verdict rendered in court was conviction of third degree murder; the judge, however, refused to accept this verdict and sent the jury back to reconsider.

Their final verdict of second degree murder was accompanied by a plea for clemency, but the sentence was the full limit allowed by the law.

Red Drive.—Finally, in January 1920 there began the last concerted drive by Attorney General A. Mitchell Palmer against all "Reds" and other "undesirable citizens." Anarchists, socialists, and I. W. W. were arrested in batches at intervals during the year. Those who were both radical and foreign-born without citizenship papers were deported.

Haywood Passes.—"Big Bill" Haywood, the foremost I. W. W. leader, with the shadow of Leavenworth Penitentiary hanging over him and also suffering from diabetes, left the United States in 1920 on the *S. S. Oscar II*—once Henry Ford's "Peace Ship"—on an unlawful passport. He took up residence in Russia where he received acclaim and respect. A complication of alcoholism, diabetes, and paralytic shock caused his death May 18, 1928. Part of his ashes, at his own request, were sent to Waldheim Cemetery, Chicago, near the graves of the anarchists hanged November 11, 1887, for the Haymarket bomb case.

Haywood, who had been as much their idol as any I. W. W. would admit, was detested by the remnant left after 1920, because he had run out on his bail and escaped personal martyrdom; thus outraging cardinal principles of the I. W. W. He was suspected also of having the connivance of federal authorities in his escape, their purpose supposedly being to destroy the I. W. W. by the removal of its leader.

I. W. W. Survived.—The I. W. W. did not die. The De-Leon (Detroit) Branch had kept the significant letters for their title until 1916 or two years after DeLeon's death. At that time, announcing that the letters had been disgraced by the Chicago Branch, the former DeLeon faction numbering about 2,000 took the new name Workers' International Industrial Union. This feeble group, on the fringe of American radicalism, had just sufficient vitality to disband in 1924, principally in order that its members might join the Communists. The Chicago Branch, the one usually associated with the name I. W. W., did not quit its field.

Its energies, however, from 1917 to 1923, were devoted either to the release of its imprisoned members or to another internal revolt.

Amnesty.—At the close of the World War, President Wilson refused an amnesty to political prisoners. When the "Red Drive" of 1919-20 had quieted, many voices were added to those of the I. W. W. for a general amnesty. In Washington a Joint Amnesty Committee representing all the varieties of jailed radicals began a barrage of propaganda for their release. In 1923 the I. W. W. declared there must be "General Amnesty or General Strike"; they also started a general boycott and some special ones in California, Washington, and Idaho. Aside from the I. W. W. activities, the public pressure for amnesty was great enough to move the federal authorities to declare an amnesty at the end of 1923. The I. W. W. were released from all federal sentences; but the state convictions still held. Before 1930 all the I. W. W. were freed except those convicted in the Centralia case.

Dissension.—As soon as the leaders got out of jail, long smoldering dissensions within the I. W. W. burst into activity. Some of the jailed members were angry at others who had so much forgotten the I. W. W. principles, "no compromise with capitalism" and "solidarity," as to petition for individual clemency. Western members thought the organization had too much centralized power at Chicago headquarters; the same group also deplored the lukewarm militancy of the I. W. W. press. The lumberworkers' faction disagreed with the agricultural workers; likewise, the hoboes disdained the conservatism of members who had fixed jobs. Some members wanted to dally with the Communists while others thought the Communists' collectivism and centralized authority were odious to the I. W. W.'s anarcho-syndicalism.

These elements clashed in the 1924 convention, the lumberworkers, under James Rowan and M. Raddock, taking the lead in voicing the discontent. Rowan, Irish-born, was as inspiring a leader as Haywood, but far less constructive. Raddock was said to be an unscrupulous self-seeker. When this faction failed to win the convention to its views, it seceded, taking out of the I. W. W. some 200 Pacific Coast members. This nucleus gathered no adherents and subsequently dropped out of sight.

The squabble did have the result of weakening the central authority of the I. W. W. The offices of General Organizer and General Secretary were abolished; the General Executive Board was closed to administrative members and composed solely of representatives from constituent unions. The publications of the union were placed under the authority of the General Executive Board instead of the staff at General Headquarters. These changes reflected the desires of the western hoboes.

Meanwhile, the question of cooperation or affiliation with the Communists was a cause for discord.   One segment agreed with Haywood that Soviet Russia represented the fulfilment of I. W. W. dreams, and accordingly, should be aided in every possible endeavor.   Opposed viewpoints were two: first, that the Russian experiment was sure to fail because it did not follow Marx when it set Socialism upon an agricultural rather than an advanced capitalistic industrial nation; second, that the Communists' policy of state dictatorship was directly opposite to the I. W. W. philosophy of anarchism.   On their side, the Communists became members of the I. W. W. on account of its record for revolutionary activity and in order to amend what they considered its out-of-date philosophy and tactics of revolution.   In 1919 the General Executive Board voted to join the Moscow Third International, an action rescinded the next year by a new General Executive Board.   In 1921 the I. W. W. sent a delegate (George Williams) to the convention of the Red International of Labor Unions; nevertheless, before Williams got home to report, the I. W. W. had voted against any cooperation with the Communists.   In 1925 a resolution to alter this decision was lost.

When the Communists realized that boring within the I. W. W. was hopeless, they withdrew and took with them some 2,000 others, among them W. Z. Foster and Earl Browder, both later heads of the American Communists.   Thereafter the Communists hurled vituperation at the I. W. W.

Last Notice.—Only once again before 1929 did an I. W. W. strike command attention, namely in the 1927-28 "outlaw" coal mine strike in Colorado, running from October to February. The adjective "outlaw" refers to the fact that the strike did not comply with the Colorado "Investigation of Industrial Disputes" law.   The miners demanded wage increases, 6-hour day, 5-day week, checkweighmen, dead-work—timbering, cleaning, etc.—to be at company not labor expense, no increases in rent or charges for light, no physical examination or age discriminations, and no prohibition of union activity.   The strikers used the mass strategy of the I. W. W. and were repulsed by

massed militia—with resultant injuries and deaths. The direct
outcome of the strike was a wage increase. Indirectly, it caused
Josephine Roche to write an unusual trade-agreement with the
United Mine Workers' Union between whom and the I. W. W.
there was intense hatred.[1]

---

[1] The Rocky Mountain Fuel Company, engaged in mining coal in northern
Colorado, was controlled by Miss Roche's banker father whose shares made
her a director in 1923, the vice-president in 1927, and president in 1929. Miss
Roche's previous training—after graduation in 1908 from Vassar, and two
years later receiving her degree as Master of Arts from Columbia—had
been as a probation officer, clerk, and referee in Denver's Juvenile and Family
Court, followed by a war duty as Director of the Foreign Language Information Service in New York and Washington. The experiences prior to her
positions with the Rocky Mountain Fuel Company may have influenced Miss
Roche's policies in that company but whatever their origin they were astounding to Colorado. Her first act as president in 1929 was to write a working
agreement with her employes which fully recognized the United Mine Workers' Union. This was directly contrary to the policy of the Colorado Fuel
and Iron Company, the only operator in the state larger than Miss Roche's
company.

The Colorado Fuel and Iron Company, whose holdings mostly are in the
southern part of the state, had had a long record of opposition to unionism.
In the bitterly contested strike in 1913-14 a massacre of miners, their wives
and children at the Ludlow camp so incensed the miners that later they
erected a monument at the site and each year held memorial services for the
victims, not only in reverence for the dead but in defiance of industrial feudal-
ism. The famous strike of 1913-14 also was the direct cause of the first well
known "company union" or to give it the official name, "the Rockefeller Plan
of Employe Representation." Moreover, the strike was the reason for the
enactment, by the Colorado legislature, of "An Investigation of Industrial
Disputes Act" patterned directly after and written by the same man—W. L.
McKenzie King—as the famous Canadian law of the same title. Both acts
forbid strikes pending an official investigation of the causes of disputes.

In union headquarters the Colorado Fuel and Iron Company was listed as
among the worst enemies of regular unionism. Before Miss Roche's entrance
into coal mining, the Colorado Fuel and Iron Company had set the example
to the state for methods of meeting labor problems.

The five years after 1929 provided a severe test of the two theories, one
Miss Roche's complete acceptance of unionism, and the Colorado Fuel and
Iron Company's absolute negation of all unionism save their own "company
unions." The results were startling and are matters of public record. Miss
Roche's miners had higher wages—$5.25 a day minimum against $4.44 for
the Colorado Fuel and Iron Company—but her coal cost less per ton because
she obtained 3 tons more per miner than the Colorado Fuel and Iron
Company. Her men worked 191 days a year against a state average of 126.
The average annual earnings of her miners were $1,650, or two to three
times as much as many soft coal miners have gotten. While the tonnage of
coal mined in Colorado declined 50% during the 1929-36 depression, the output of the Rocky Mountain Fuel Company fell off less than 25%. Finally,
the Colorado Fuel and Iron Company—Miss Roche's rival—went into voluntary bankruptcy in August 1933; at the same time Miss Roche's company
was facing financial trouble, but her miners loaned her half their wages, went
out and helped sell her coal, and eventually pulled the company through without loss.

Appraisal.—The I. W. W. never really recovered from the blows it got during the World War.   No new leaders comparable to William Haywood and Vincent St. John came up from its ranks, and it was pushed and pulled by internal dissension. It engaged in only five "free speech fights" after 1916 and none after 1923.   Its strike technique lost its former mordacious humor and its press was an extremely faded "Red."   The recession of the frontier spirit made its anarchism an anachronism while the agricultural "combine" machine made hobo labor unnecessary.   Eastern members found more compatibility with the Communists than the I. W. W. and western members took to Fords.   The Communists became the headlined Revolutionaries.

The maximum paid-up membership of the I. W. W. probably never exceeded 100,000; the number that at some time or other belonged to the I. W. W. perhaps was close to 1 million. In 1929 the membership could not have been much over 5,000. Was, then, the I. W. W. a useless by-product of its generation? The answer decidedly is, "no!"   Its service was similar to that of flies; where there was intense buzzing attention was called to corruption.

When the Coal Code was formulated in 1933, Miss Roche was one of the employer representatives for the group that presented terms most acceptable to the United Mine Workers' Union.   When the Coal Code finally was signed Miss Roche, although she accepted, objected to it as being insufficiently liberal to the miners.   When the code in 1934 was amended to provide the 7-hour day, Miss Roche pressed other mine employers to accept this.

Not only all coal miners reverenced Josephine Roche but labor papers in many other crafts referred to her as the ideal type of employer.   Hence the action of organized labor in Colorado in proposing Josephine Roche for governor in 1934 had the sympathetic support of all union labor in the country. If she had become the Governor she would have had relentless opposition from all vested interests in Colorado, and these in the past had been potent in state politics.   The fact that Miss Roche was a woman would not have been much of a handicap in a state long noted for its woman suffrage; indeed its northern neighbor Wyoming already had seated one woman, Nellie Tayloe Ross, in the governor's chair, and across its southern boundary, Texas had been bossed by Ma Ferguson.

The 1934 Colorado labor political convention said it "based its support of Josephine Roche on her splendid fight made as president of the Rocky Mountain Fuel Company for union hours and working conditions, and her insistence that the Colorado state administration must more enthusiastically back President Roosevelt's recovery program."   When Miss Roche failed of election as Governor she was appointed, by President Roosevelt, as Assistant Secretary of the Treasury.

The Communists

The "Reds" of the most billiant hue after 1919 were the Communists.[2] In the decade that followed they had three problems: first, to establish their right to existence in this country; second, to formulate their fundamental doctrines, and third, adopt fitting tactics. For three years after 1919 the American Communists were outlaws, and kept alive only by secret organizations. In doctrine, the Communists had to alter from their prior Left-wing Socialism to Bolshevistic Communism according to Marx as interpreted by Lenin; a difficult task because the doctrine was not well understood, and furthermore, was subject to frequent variations sponsored in Moscow. Tactics depended on doctrine and consequently shifted considerably in the decade. Both doctrine and tactics gave rise to internal party factions that wasted energy which should have gone into national organization.

Right to Exist.—The two Communist parties organized at Chicago in August 1919, did not get out of their meeting halls before they were raided by the Chicago police. From then until A. Mitchell Palmer on March 3, 1921, retired from the Attorney-Generalship, the two parties plus three more that sprouted were spied upon, betrayed, arrested—with or without warrants—and deported. Their headquarters were seized and the materials in them destroyed. A clean up of over 200, held at Ellis Island on December 21, 1919, resulted in their sudden secret shipment to an unknown destination on the "Buford." On one later night, January 2, 1920, some 10,000 were apprehended by pre-arranged tips from secret agents and had a hard time getting recognition of their Constitutional rights; 3,000 were held for deportation and the rest freed after being subjected to various kinds of abuse.

So perilous was the life of known Communists that the parties were forced to hold secret meetings; for Secretary of Labor, W. B. Wilson, agreed with Attorney General Palmer that the Communists parties were illegal and that mere membership in

---

[2] The *outline* for the material on the Communists was furnished by Donald H. Miller, Jr.

them was sufficient ground for deportation.   As an aside, it may
be mentioned that Commissioner Edward Corsi has said that
a number of homesick Scots claimed to be Communists or
Anarchists in order to be deported, thus getting a free ride to
Scotland.

When they were still under cover the five different Communist factions strove for unity.   The two Chicago-born parties
did come together in May 1921 in the United Communist Party,
and maintained this secret conspiracy until April 1923.   From
the former Communist Labor Party the new unified party gained
John Reed and Ben Gitlow; from the original Communist Party
there came Louis Fraina and Charles Ruthenberg.   In 1922
Earl Browder and Wm. Z. Foster, one time members of the
I. W. W. joined the Workers' Party of America.

Palmer's "Red Terror," however, was too bold, lawless, and
sweeping to avoid criticism from American citizens who were
far from being Communists; Palmer was forced to be more
discreet and to abide by the letter of legal procedure.   Nevertheless, the Communists did not dare venture in the open until
after Harding had been in office for nine months.

Temporary Unity.—In December 1921 most of the Communist segments, with the direct assistance of the Communist
International, coalesced in the Workers' Party of America, an
official legal organization.   This was a periscope for the underground United Communist Party and after April 1923 was the
sole American section recognized at Moscow.   In 1925 the
official title was changed to Workers' (Communist) Party of
the United States.   Once more in 1929 the name was altered,
this time to the Communist Party.

Doctrinal Uncertainty.—The frequent change of name was
outward sign of internal doctrinal uncertainty.   At the beginning, the first groups to call themselves Communists were secessionists from the Socialist Party or recruits from the Socialist
Labor Party.   Their association with the Socialists and adherence to social democracy had prevented them from knowledge or
full acceptance of the Bolshevist doctrine.   Moreover, other
fledgling Communists were former I. W. W. whose doctrines

had sounded like Communism before that word was popularized but who in reality by belief in syndicalist anarchy, were at farthest pole from centralized dictatorship of the proleteriat. According to Bolshevist standards, the former Socialists were right-wing and the former I. W. W. were left-wing. In the process of Bolshevization some of the membership moved too slowly, or offered downright resistance; these were "liquidated" by expulsion. The struggle for purity and unity of doctrine was complicated by individuals' ambitions for power.

The most serious doctrinal division was between on the one side W. Z. Foster, A. Bittleman, Earl Browder, Wm. F. Dunne, and others who proposed belief in "practical" doctrines and an immediate future revolution in the United States; and on the other side J. Lovestone, C. Ruthenberg, B. Gitlow, R. Minor, and others who stood for theoretical formulas and believed that in the United States the proletarian revolution lay in the distant future. The internal strife was so bitter that in 1927 the matter was transferred to Moscow where the decision was made in favor of the Lovestone-Ruthenberg group. This faction dominated the American Communists until the Wall Street crash in 1929. With the prospect that the United States was not going to have—as Lovestone had claimed—a long period of industrial prosperity, the Foster-Browder faction was favored by Moscow and the rival faction ousted. This drastic surgery produced doctrinal unity in 1929.

Structure.—Meanwhile, 1925, the organization structure inherited from the Socialists, namely, units based on language was abolished; instead the units were based on territories and work places; that is, street and shop nuclei. This move was indicative of a two-front tactic; one, the street nuclei were strategic for political efforts whereas the shop nuclei were favorably situated for economic (union) organization.

Partisan Politics.—The Workers' Party of America entered the 1924 campaign with William Z. Foster and Benjamin Gitlow as its nominees for the highest federal offices; and got 33,361 votes out of a grand total of 29 million. In the 1926 local and state elections the Workers' (Communist) Party was active chiefly in New York where the bulk of its membership lived; its voting power, because of factionalism, was at its lowest ebb.   In 1928 the party again placed William Z. Foster in nomination for the Presidency; and he secured votes in 35 states, the exceptions being mostly in the South and Far West. His total vote was 48,770 out of 36,800,000 cast.   The conclusion is inescapable that before 1929 the Communists in the United States were scarcely a threat to the longer intrenched parties.

Union Factions.—In the economic (union) field the Communists at first operated through the Trade Union Educational League formed in 1922.   The connection of the T. U. E. L. to the Communists was kept secret for many months.   Under William Z. Foster's guidance, the policy of the T. U. E. L. was to cooperate with radicals or progressives in the A. F. of L. and independent unions.   This effort met with surprising success, probably because progressive unionists were disappointed with the conservatism of the officials in the A. F. of L. and also because the T. U. E. L. was an advocate of industrial or "labor" structure in place of the outmoded craft basis for unions.

However, the Worker's Party officers could not wait for the evolutionary process of the T. U. E. L. and not only exposed the Communist basis of the League but became dictatorial and rabidly opposed to compromises in Communist doctrines necessary for the continuance of the influence of the T. U. E. L. Nevertheless, at this stage Communists had secured offices in and won over large blocks of members in the International Ladies Garment Workers' Union and the Fur Workers International besides enrolling quite a number of supporters in the Amalgamated Clothing Workers' Union, the Machinists, and United Mine Workers.

Their success was their undoing; for on the one hand it made them show their uncompromising nature and political aims in the two unions in which they held offices while on the other it aroused the penetrated unions and all others as yet untouched into vigorous defensive warfare against Communism.   When the A. F. of L. turned its full batteries upon the Communists it fairly blasted them out of the regular trade unions. The first shot in a long campaign was fired in October 1923 when the A. F. of L. convention sitting in Portland, Oregon, refused delegate credentials to W. F. Dunne on the ground of his Communist affiliations despite the fact that he held properly accredited papers as delegate from a regularly constituted central labor union.

Dual Unionism.—Having failed "to bore within" existing unions, the Communists in 1928 turned to dual unionism setting up as rivals to older bodies the Needle Trades Workers' Industrial Union, the National Miners' Union, and National Textile Workers' Union. The first was composed largely of Communists expelled from the International Ladies Garment Workers' Union and Fur Workers' International; the second, at times, gave considerable trouble to the United Mine Workers, especially when used by employers as a club over the older union; the third gained notoriety at strikes in New Bedford, Mass., Paterson, N. J., and Gastonia, N. C.

There were local Communist unions among marine workers, office workers, and wage earners in sugar beet fields. Under compulsion from the Workers' Party, all of these Communist unions were joined together in the Trade Union Educational League, which in June 1929—again by direction of the Workers' Party—was renamed the Trade Union Unity League. This was intended to signify abandonment of "cooperative boring" in favor of outright federation of its own unions. In the strikes, especially those of textile workers, the tactics of Communist leaders plainly showed a greater intention to advance Communism politically than to improve the economic position of the strikers.

Dualism Abandoned.—The policy of dual unionism was abandoned soon after the Lovestone faction was dispossessed. The Communists were ordered to return to the A. F. of L. unions in order to build within them a left-wing rank-and-file in opposition to the ultra-conservative officers. The A. F. of L. officials resented the tactics of the Communists, and used every device to purge the unions of Communist members or influence.

The A. F. of L. did not altogether suffer from the Communists' depredations; within itself the danger of Communist invasion was an aid to conservatives in holding themselves in office; in the eyes of sections of the public the A. F. of L. gained esteem by contrast with the Communist "Reds."

Appraisal.—Doubtless the Communists themselves would agree that their first ten years of history in the United States was a discordant, groping ineffectuality. They would label it their "formative period" and therefore disclaim its fumbles; they probably would assert that their really constructive program *began,* not ended, in 1929. If this be true there is an injustice in closing the Communist story with our terminal date of 1929.

CHAPTER 13

"MARTYRS"

Nearly every institution has had its "martyrs" and the American labor movement was no exception. Early in the generation, Eugene Debs acquired a halo of martyrdom in the injunction suits and jail sentence that followed the Pullman strike; and again in the World War period Debs endured, in the Atlanta Penitentiary, a martyrdom for his principles. Messrs. Gompers, Mitchell, and Morrison were sacrifices in the cause of labor during the years that the Buck's Stove and Range Company cases dragged through the courts. Moreover, the individual members of the Hatters' Union of Danbury as well as hundreds of other union officers and members at times were victims of damage suits, injunctions, and jailings for boycott and strike activities. Well nigh the entire membership of the I. W. W. at some time or other suffered for their cause. Individual Anarchists such as Alexander Berkman or Emma Goldman learned well what political prisoners had to endure.

Nevertheless, there were five conspicuous instances other than those mentioned in which individual union officers suffered vicariously for groups. Haywood, Moyer, and Pettibone in 1906 were the men selected for punishment for the murder of Frank Steunenberg, former governor of Idaho; the McNamara brothers, for months in 1911, were deemed the martyrs picked for vengeance by capitalists for the dynamiting of the building of the *Los Angeles Times;* 33 officers of the International Association of Bridge and Structural Iron Workers in 1912 were considered victims of the wrath of the employers' National Erectors' Association; and Mooney and Billings, particularly the first named, were believed by workers, for almost a score of years after 1917, to be the persecuted prey of malicious capitalists. The Sacco-Vanzetti case gave radicals all over the world new photographs to frame in the niche of martyrs and gave to radical speakers two names to rouse the wrath of the lowest group of labor against the "tyranny" of industrial titans.

The stories of these "martyrdoms" are part of the folklore of underprivileged persons in the United States and therefore warrant inclusion in any work that seeks to describe and explain the actions of wage earners.

Steunenberg Murder Case

Background.—In 1905, five days after Christmas, as Frank Steunenberg opened the gate to his home in Caldwell, Idaho he was blown to bits by a bomb attached to the gate. This atrocity was the culmination of a series of outrages in the mountain mining states during the previous ten to fifteen years. Mining in Idaho, Colorado, and Montana had been a lawless, turbulent industry from its inception; but after 1890 when miners began to organize, there were constant disruptions that amounted almost to civil war. The acts of both employers and workers frequently were so far outside the law that the names Coeur d'Alene,[1] Cripple Creek, and Telluride carried the connotation of Monmouth or Gettysburg. Employers on July 13, 1904 kidnaped 33 union strikers at Cripple Creek and dumped them—with the aid of Colorado soldiers and without legal arrest or indictment—in the desert of New Mexico; they locked strikers in cattle stockades—"bull pens" —and treated them as if they were locoed steers; they hired gunmen as guards and used local peace officers as instruments of brutality. On the other hand, strikers dynamited mine shafts or smelters, shot scabs from ambush, and brawled with mine bosses; the leader of the miners, President Boyce, in 1897 urged every local organization of miners to set up and train a rifle club.

---

[1] This town today (1936) is one of shaded, paved streets, comfortable, well-kept homes and impresses visitors by its clipped lawns and cherished flower beds.

For these titanic, not sullen, outrages by both parties, Idaho was a focus during the decade after 1896. The union concerned was the Western Federation of Miners created as a result of the bloody strike at Coeur d' Alene in 1892. When in 1905 this union affiliated with the Industrial Workers of the World it engaged in a terroristic campaign in the mountain states.

Frank Steunenberg, a printer, was swept into the Governor's chair on the last wave of "Populism" in 1897. Despite his labor background and backing he asked for federal troops to quell a strike at Coeur d' Alene in 1899. The troops sent by President McKinley were companies of Negroes from Brownsville, Texas. Steunenberg embittered his former labor friends both by his request for troops and by the kind of soldiers used, although he was not responsible for the latter. Moreover, the workers of Idaho did not like the fact that this printer left the Governor's office as a prosperous citizen with the financial ability to engage in extensive sheep ranching.

Arrests.—In February and March 1906, three [2] arrests for the murder of Governor Steunenberg were made. William Haywood—"Big Bill"—secretary of the Western Federation of Miners, Charles H. Moyer, president of the same body, and George A. Pettibone, former member, were seized in Denver and without legal warrant or legal extradition were whisked in a special train across the state line to Idaho where they were indicted for the murder of Steunenberg, the first two as principals and Pettibone as the alleged maker and seller of the fatal bomb. The three were held in an Idaho jail for more than a year before being brought to trial.

The Trial.—The trial began May 9, 1907, amidst demonstrations by labor groups in many of the larger American cities. Because Theodore Roosevelt had dubbed the defendants and Eugene Debs as undesirable citizens, many workers who were engaged in the demonstrations threatened, on May Day (1907),

---

[2] More than three were first arrested, but the others were released.

to wear lapel buttons inscribed "I am an undesirable citizen." The evidence against the accused was secured by the Pinkerton detective agency in the person of the same McParland who had been conspicuous in the "Molly Maguire case" (1876). The detective, himself, did not take the stand in this Idaho case as he had in the trials of the "Molly Maguires"; instead Harry Orchard, a self-avowed agent of the terroristic ring of union officers, was the principal witness for the state. On the witness stand he poured forth an almost incredible story drawn forth by William Edgar Borah, attorney for the state.

Harry Orchard.—Orchard confessed that he had murdered 26 persons upon order from the Western Federation of Miners; had in 1904 blown up the railroad station at Independence, Colorado in which explosion he had killed 13 scabs arriving by train; and had dynamited a mine shaft upon union order. Orchard went on to say that he was a bigamist, a drunkard, an inveterate gambler, a burglar, thief, kidnaper, and a spy in the employ of the mine owners, the state, and the union. The newspapers suggested that Orchard had lost mental balance when, as a striker, he was driven out of Coeur d' Alene in 1892 and in his flight sold mine stock for $600 later worth $6 million. He himself said on the stand he was making this clean breast of his anti-social activities because "he feared to face death a sinner."

The Defense.—The defense put forward by the attorneys for the accused—E. F. Richardson, Denver's ablest criminal lawyer, and Clarence Darrow—was first, the alibi that none of the defendants were in Idaho at the time of the crime; secondly, that the defendants were victims of a conspiracy of the Mine Owners' Association aided by Pinkerton to exterminate the Western Federation of Miners; and lastly, that the state's witness, Orchard, was either utterly untrustworthy or his entire confession had been put in his mouth by the Pinkertons. Evidence was adduced also of the condition of civil war in the mine areas and the unlawful acts committed by mine owners and state officials.

Acquittal.—In the closing speeches of the trial in July, Borah held the floor for nearly the whole of a Saturday afternoon and evening, the gist of his speech being that the state was not fighting organized labor but conducting a mere murder trial, and that the evidence, as presented, called for Haywood's conviction. The defending lawyers spoke for 20 hours, of which Darrow consumed 11, to say that the arrests were unlawfully made; the indictments improperly drawn; the prisoners unjustly held in jail and made the victims of a "frame up" in which unionism, not the three individuals, were the real targets of the prosecution; that detectives had joined the union and themselves committed the outrages so as to manufacture evidence against the union; and finally, that there was no shadow of evidence to connect Haywood with the death of Governor Steunenberg. On July 28 the jury, mostly poor farmers, acquitted Haywood whose trial was the first of the three and this decision was in accord with the instructions of the trial judge. Later Moyer and Pettibone were freed.

After leaving the court room, Haywood forsook the Western Federation of Miners and until the World War was the principal agitator, strike leader, and spokesman for the I.W.W. Moyer, when liberated, went back to his job with the W.F.M. which disassociated itself from the I.W.W. to affiliate with the A. F. of L. Pettibone went to California where he died of tuberculosis contracted in the Idaho prisons. Borah in 1906 was elected to his first term as Idaho's representative in the United States Senate. Harry Orchard was sentenced to life imprisonment.[3]

The trial of Haywood not only made him a "martyr" but was used by labor leaders as conclusive proof of the injustice of the law; it also was taken as an example of the alleged practice of vindictive employers in "framing" the active spokesmen for labor.

---

[3] He appeared in the news again on January 27, 1934 when the warden of the penitentiary and the Idaho Pardon Board permitted him to occupy the pulpit (Feb. 1, 1934) of the First Methodist Church of Boise to speak on the subject, "What Christianity Has Done For Me"; for in custody, Orchard had turned from the rôle of all around "bad man" to that of a convert to religion. Later in that year he was released.

Los Angeles Times Explosion (McNamara Case)

At 1 o'clock in the morning of October 1, 1910 a terrific explosion completely destroyed the building of the *Los Angeles Times;* and of 100 people in the structure at that hour 20 were killed and 60 injured. The same night, unexploded bombs were found at the homes of the newspaper proprietor and the Secretary of the local Merchants' and Manufacturers' Association.

At once inquiries were started by the police, grand jury, Mayor's committee, civic bodies, the City Council, and by the Labor Council. All but the last investigators declared that the type of explosion indicated that dynamite was the cause of the disaster; the Labor Council announced that the damage was due to a gas explosion; basing their belief upon the continued annoyance from gas suffered by inmates of the building during the previous month of September. On Christmas night 1910, another explosion greatly damaged the Llewellyn Iron Works of Los Angeles.

Search For Culprits.—General Harrison Gray Otis, proprietor and editor of the *Los Angeles Times,* offered a reward of $300,000 for the culprits responsible for the outrages; and three groups of detectives began the search, one the local officials, and the other two the agencies under Pinkerton and William J. Burns. At an expense of about $1,000 a day, these groups of detectives searched for more than half a year for evidence that would lead to a conviction.

Arrests.—On April 14, 1911, William J. Burns arrested at Detroit James B. McNamara and Ortie McManigal. The latter made a confession which led to the arrest of John J. McNamara, brother of James B., at Indianapolis where with a hurriedly procured warrant and extradition proceedings he was transferred along with the first two by a round-about confused route to the Los Angeles jail. There they were joined by O. A. Tveitmoe and Anton Johannsen, labor-political leaders of San Francisco. M. A. Schmidt and David Kaplan also were implicated but these two were not then found;

and the two San Francisco suspects were released. The McNamara brothers were held as the principal culprits, as was McManigal as witness for the prosecution.

"Frame Up."—John J. McNamara was Secretary of the International Association of Bridge and Structural Iron Workers' Union and had employed his brother as assistant in the organizing work of that union. McManigal also was an employe of the union. Therefore, the American Federation of Labor—although it never had heard of James B. McNamara nor McManigal but did know the reputation of John J. as an active, efficient union leader—with the cry "frame up" sprang to the defense of these men. In the months that followed, the A.F. of L. raised a $¼ million defense fund. Clarence Darrow was retained as defense counsel and he took as local associate the famous Socialist, Job Harriman.

Motive: Personal.—The strands that connected these facts were woven in newspaper stories in the summer of 1911. General Harrison Gray Otis had come to Los Angeles in the early 1880's, and by his newspaper had come to the front not only as the city's leading promoter but as the champion of all the anti-union forces in southern California. In 1890 he strangled the unions in his own print shop and then kept up a continuously virulent campaign against unions throughout the territory served by his news sheets. His personal militancy was indicated by his naming his home "The Bivouac" and by his mounting a small cannon on the hood of his automobile at the time of the McNamara trial. Theodore Roosevelt, writing in *The Outlook* in May 1911, characterized Otis as the "violent opponent of organized labor and a consistent enemy of every movement for social and economic betterment." Otis, therefore, was the kind of man who invited attack, especially by organized labor.

Motive: Economic.—The second strand had its end in San Francisco. This city, after the earthquake and fire in 1906, had been in the hands of a combination of politicians and labor union officials with the result that unions dominated

every skilled activity in that city.   Although this alliance was
loosened in 1909, San Franciscans believed that it had caused
the loss of business, population, and prestige to its "open-
shop" rival in southern California.   Therefore, according to
William J. Burns, a secret combination of capitalists and unionists sent emissaries from the Golden Gate to the City of the
Angels to organize the workers of the latter place.   Olaf
Tveitmoe, Johannsen, and others were said to have been
selected for this missionary work and in 1910-11 they were
supposed to have operated through Job Harriman's Socialist
party in Los Angeles.   Tveitmoe and Gompers, in later years,
denied the existence of any such "plot" or actions.   At the
time many persons believed it.

Why Burns Entered Case.—A third strand led to the National Erectors' Association, a combination of steel makers and
fabricators who were hostile to all unions and particularly opposed to the Association of Bridge and Structural Iron
Workers' Union.   A series of "accidents"—25 in 1910 alone,
as well as 88 others in the five previous years—on buildings·
and bridges constructed by the members of the National
Erectors' Association caused that body, on September 4, 1910,
to enlist the services of Detective William J. Burns.   He was
hired in order to ferret the cause for damages on the Erectors'
contracts.   Burns, on this mission, was in Los Angeles on
October 2, 1910, the day after the *Times* building was
destroyed.

Deductions By Burns.—From the method of construction
of the unexploded bombs as well as from the identity of clocks
and batteries found in these mechanisms to other unexploded
bombs found earlier in the year on construction jobs by Burns'
agents while running down clues for the National Erectors'
Association, Burns felt certain that the perpetrators of the
Times tragedy belonged to the same group whose actions he
had been tracing for some weeks.   He approached the Los
Angeles authorities and they, after considerable hesitation, enlisted his services.   The hesitation was caused—so Burns has

said—by his former efforts to bring to justice certain capitalists in San Francisco involved in the political graft scandals of that city as well as his investigations of certain timber transactions in the state of Washington.

Search By Burns.—Agents of Burns penetrated an anarchists' colony near San Francisco and although they failed to trap the men they sought—Schmidt and Kaplan—they did learn there, and in San Francisco, the source of the dynamite used to destroy the *Times* building; in addition they got good descriptions of the purchasers and located the place where the dynamite had been stored.

A watch kept by Burns' agents on suspects in the Middle West led them, towards the end of the winter 1910-11, to a hunter's camp in Wisconsin where two suspects became chummy with detectives who were disguised as mining engineers. From words and other hints dropped unknowingly by the suspects together with snapshots taken on hunters' picnics the detectives learned that these "hunters" were men the detectives wanted. Shortly afterwards the "hunters" left the woods, and—according to Burns—just as they were about to do another job of dynamiting, they secretly were arrested at Detroit by Burns.

State Witness Ortie McManigal.—Until extradition papers arrived from California, the prisoners were kept under guard in a suburban residence of a Chicago police officer. This delay enabled Burns to "work" on the more promising of the two prisoners until he succeeded in getting a written confession from the man. Ortie McManigal was the one who confessed and then became the state's witness. His fellow prisoner was James B. McNamara. Since the confession directly implicated John J. McNamara in the Los Angeles crimes, Burns went to the union headquarters in Indianapolis and made a surprise arrest and extradition of the elder brother. The circuitous journey by which Burns took his prisoners to Los Angeles was to prevent friends of the accused bringing legal detaining actions in states crossed by the travelers.

Labor's Reactions.—These strands weaving together looped the McNamaras and McManigal into the Los Angeles jail. All unionists and many others believed the brothers had been "framed." Dynamite as a means of coercion was not in union tradition. The similarity of method of the detectives in this case to that in the Haywood-Moyer case tended to confirm the accusation of "frame up" by the detectives. Moyer himself made this claim. Private detective agencies, especially those engaged in affairs that involved industrial relations, had an unsavory reputation. The secrecy of the arrests and extraditions lent color to the labor charge that the prisoners were "kidnaped" without legal warrants. Workers everywhere in the nation accepted the explanation of the Los Angeles group that the explosion was due to gas. The iron workers could have no conceivable grudge against the *Times;* and the printers were believed to be too intelligent to use dynamite. The well-known bitterness of General Otis against unions made unionists believe that he was capable of any plot to discredit unionism. Many thought that Otis himself had destroyed his own plant in order to accuse unions—these suspicious persons pointed out that no important executive of the newspaper was in the building at the time of the explosion, and that the other two bombs at homes failed to fire.

Labor Crusade.—For all these reasons, union defense of the McNamaras became a nationwide crusade, reaching its peaks on "May Day" and Labor Day 1911. As part of this uprising of labor during the summer, the Socialist, Job Harriman, in May 1911 was nominated for Mayor of Los Angeles. This candidate, as we have said, was one of the defense lawyers. At the primary in October the vote for Harriman exceeded that of all other candidates; so that as the campaign rumbled on into December it appeared certain that Harriman would win. As another apparent indication of the emotional condition of people was the fact that when the trial opened on October 11 it took until the middle of November to impanel a jury. Many years later, from the autobiographies of Darrow and of Lincoln Steffens, it was learned that Darrow deliberately delayed the choice of a jury in order to gain time for Steffens to drive a "bargain" with the authorities.

Negotiations.—Behind the scenes, secret matters bearing on the case were going forward. Darrow was certain that the state had an unbreakable case; and his only hope was in making a deal with the authorities and for this purpose Lincoln Steffens was emissary. If the state convicted the men there would likely be a dangerous revolt from all organized labor as well as from other sections of the population. None of them ever would believe that the men really had been guilty. If the conviction was made, the local labor resentment probably would result in a Socialist sweep in the contemporary political campaign. Darrow and Steffens offered to get a confession from the prisoners, if there could be an understanding that the sentences would be lighter than for first degree murder.

The Los Angeles "big wigs" and court officers were won to this compromise; the McNamaras stubbornly resisted until finally persuaded by Darrow, Steffens, and others.

Confession.—According to the carefully guarded plan, the prisoners on December 1, 1911 were conducted into the court room and the judge, instead of proceeding with the trial, recognized Attorney Darrow who stated that his clients wished to change their plea to "Guilty as charged." Unbelief, consternation, and hysteria among workers everywhere in the United States followed this confession.

Why Confess.—Why did they confess? This question was on every one's lips. Various answers were made. It was said that John J. had declared it was because his brother James B. could not sleep. Another report was that if the men had been tried and convicted the workers of the nation, convinced that an injustice was done, would have gone out on a nationwide general strike; the confession was intended to forestall this calamity. Friends of the prosecution said that the defense attorneys had been caught bribing a talesman and juror and to save Darrow from arrest Darrow was forced to urge his clients to confess. It was reported also that the brothers made a bargain that they would confess if promised that punishment would fall short of hanging. Another story that gained credence was that the confession was to save "men higher up." Burns himself many times repeated this explanation with the insinuation that one of the men higher up was Samuel Gompers.

Guilty.—The real reason for the confession was that the men *were* guilty. An insurmountable mountain of detailed evidence impossible to overturn had been secured against them. This evidence would have shown that John Joseph McNamara was the directing head of the plot. His brother James Barnabas McNamara was "J.J.'s" tool. At the suggestion of persons on the Pacific Coast, John J. was to furnish experts to blow up buildings in anti-union centers. The first blow was to be aimed at the arch enemy, General Otis. If this did not bring him and Los Angeles to terms, the city was to be terrorized by wholesale explosions. Since Otis in fact was not humbled but became more militant, the second bombing on Christmas night 1910 was intended to destroy three buildings, namely the auxiliary plant of the *Times,* the Baker Iron Company, and the Llewellyn Iron Company. This second blast also was planned to convince detectives that local "bad men" were responsible for the explosions in Los Angeles and others that had occurred in cities further north. Ortie McManigal was the actual bomber on the Christmas night case but he did not obey orders; for when he found two of the three structures well guarded he bombed only one, the Llewellyn works. John J. ordered this job and paid McManigal for it just as he had paid his brother for the *Times* job—$200 apiece and expenses in each case. The prosecution could prove this story by Ortie McManigal as state's witness backed up with detailed corroboratory evidence.

Sentence.—On December 5, just four days after the confession, James B. McNamara was sentenced to life imprisonment and John J. to a term of 15 years (he served 10 and then was released becoming again an officer in his union). The sentences were more severe than the "bargain" had arranged.

A Sunday had intervened between the pleas of Guilty and the pronouncement of sentence; sermons all over the United States had so harshly criticized the McNamaras that the judge felt it unwise to impose light sentences.

Results.—The outcome of the case was a severe blow to organized labor. Public sympathy had been with the Mc-Namaras and unions; but the confessions tended to confirm the most intemperate accusations brought by the most belligerent employers against unions. The public could not separate the deeds of individual criminal unionists from the law-abiding rank and file; nor distinguish between one union and other unions. Because unionists had defended J. J. McNamara as a martyred union leader, his confession besmirched all unions and union members. Gompers was an especial target for abuse, particularly under Burns' hints of "men higher up." The news of the confession reached Gompers as he was journeying from Washington to Albany to sit as a Commissioner of the New York State Factory Commission. Throughout the journey, during the session—at which Gompers had to preside due to the absence of Robert Wagner and Alfred Smith—throughout the return journey, and after his arrival in Washington Gompers was bombarded incessantly by reporters. Gompers later wrote that abhorrence to the McNamaras as traitors, grief over the great injury done the labor movement, and indignation for the unwarranted innuendoes by Burns regarding Gompers' own character made the week of the confession one of the most miserable in his career. Incidentally, Job Harriman lost the election as Socialist Mayor of Los Angeles; for the election took place immediately after the sentencing of the two brothers.

Further Results.—To Burns the confession of the Mc-Namaras was only a prelude to greater disclosures. McManigal, during the months of his incarceration in Los Angeles, had continued to pour out to Burns information concerning the headquarter's activities of the International Association of Structural Iron and Bridge Workers. Enough of this was disclosed to President Taft upon a visit of his to California in 1911 to cause him to order the federal government to take action against the heads of the union.

Consequently, as soon as matters were settled in Los Angeles, Burns took McManigal to Indianapolis where the union's principal office was located. There over 50 of the executive council, former officers, and members, were placed under arrest.

Nitroglycerin, dynamite clocks, and some other devices were found in the union vaults, in barns, and other caches; and union records kept by J. J. McNamara revealed that these destructive agencies had been used by his order and under knowledge and authority of the executive council to destroy non-union jobs. Charged technically with a conspiracy to transport dynamite and nitroglycerin in a manner harmful to the public, 38 of the defendants were convicted and sentenced on December 31, 1912 to from 1 to 7 years in Leavenworth Penitentiary.

This wholesale conviction brought still further shame to unionism. Without seeking to excuse the lawlessness of the union officers, it is well to remember that the structural steel business was one unattractive to meek men and that dynamite was a tool of the trade. Moreover, it should be recognized that the National Erectors' Association (employers) was ruthless against unionism and used the power given by its capitalistic strength to crush mercilessly every attempt at labor organization. It directed its enmity not only to unions in its own industry but seized every opportunity to destroy or discredit unionism wherever it appeared.

Gompers in his autobiography stated that Tveitmoe told him that Burns had induced the Prosecuting Attorney of Los Angeles to offer Tveitmoe a bribe to implicate Gompers in the McNamara case.

Darrow in the meantime was indicted and tried (twice) on a charge of attempted bribery of a McNamara juror; these trials vindicated Darrow and implicated Burns and the interests behind that detective.

Mooney-Billings Case

Background.—In 1916 various bodies of citizens in San Francisco including some of those most eminent in commercial, business and financial affairs planned a mammoth parade of the city's people in demonstration of their support of the possible entrance of the United States into the World War. The proposal for this Preparedness Day Parade did not command universal support; conscientious pacifists, radical labor groups, and capitalists of Germanic origin wrote and spoke against such a deliberate incitement of the war spirit, and a large mass meeting denounced the scheme.

Moreover, at that time American soldiers—among whom were companies from California — were mobilized on and across the Mexican border on a punitive expedition against Villa; and the California Hearst papers were screaming for a war of conquest against Mexico. Resentment of Mexicans in California was expressed by fuse bombs, one exploded in a southern Pacific train and another at a temporary ammunition arsenal at Nogales. The public announcement that Spanish War veterans were to carry in the Parade a prized battle flag scarred with Latin American bullets fanned the fires of Mexican hatred against the bulldozing northern republic. Under these circumstances a great war parade was foolhardy.

The Bomb.—Nevertheless, on July 22 at 1:30 P. M., the greatest parade in San Francisco's history started at the Embarcadero for the long march south-westward on Market Street. Twenty-six minutes after the head of the parade had passed Steuart Street, and while the Spanish War Veteran contingent was filing out of that street to take its place in the rear of the procession, a violent explosion at 2:06 P. M. near the corner of the two streets resulted in the death of 10 persons [4] and the critical injury of 40 others among them women and children. The parade lines were re-formed by the quick resourceful actions of Police Captain Matheson who thus averted what might have been a disastrous panic; so the parade went on as planned,

---

[4] Six were killed outright and four others died during the next week.

the police roping off and then cleaning the spot where the catastrophe took place.

Public Reaction.—The newspapers, accurately reflecting popular opinion, shrieked demands for the arrest and conviction of the perpetrators of the horrible deed. A Bomb Squad organized among the city police working in presumable cooperation with the office of the District Attorney was given the task of investigation of all clues.

Arrests.—Four days later (July 26), three men were arrested in connection with the crime. These were Warren K. Billings, a 22-year-old machinist, Israel Weinberg, a taxi[5] driver, and Edward Nolan, local head of the Machinists' Union.

At the same time the police announced they were searching for Thomas J. Mooney, a moulder by trade and labor leader, and Mrs. Rena Mooney, a music teacher and the wife of Thomas J. These two who were on a camping excursion on the Russian River at Montesano saw the notice of the police and telegraphed their whereabouts and intention of immediate return to San Francisco. The police, thus informed, took the two on July 27 off a train at Guerneville on the outskirts of the city and placed them in separate jails. All five prisoners were kept incommunicado for days while the police without search warrants, ransacked the homes of the accused in search of incriminating evidence.

Clues Neglected.—No attention was paid by the police to clues to the crime that led away from the five suspects. For example, only casual investigation was made at the spot of the disaster to determine what kind of explosive was used. Several witnesses who reported they had seen a falling object just before the blast were ignored. Some 200 others reported having received postal cards from the "Employes' Liberty League"

---

[5] At that time individual automobile owners in many cities competed with street railways in carrying passengers on regular routes. The auto fares were low—usually a nickel—and the cars were called "jitneys." Weinberg operated one of these "jitneys" and also was an officer in the S. F. Jitney Owners' Union. Street car companies hated the jitneys and ultimately ruled them off the streets on the grounds of "menacing public safety."

prior to the parade; on the cards was a crudely printed warning to stay away from the parade.   Although many of the cards were turned over to the police, nothing was done to unravel this clue or to question the recipients of the cards.   The United States postal authorities did keep watch for years for clues to these cards, but with no discovery of the identity of the "Employes' Liberty League."

At least seven reputable persons reported having seen two men with a suitcase at the fatal corner just before the explosion; but since the description of these two men tallied with none of the suspects the authorities did nothing about the clue.   The descriptions pointed plainly to Mexicans whose coloring, weights, heights, and ages in no way resembled the persons under detention.

Another line of search that was ignored was the possible complicity of German or German agents despite the fact that these already had been proven guilty of bomb outrages along the Pacific Coast, and at that very time the Consul in San Francisco was under arrest.

Finally, San Francisco had been the scene of a prolonged capital-labor "war" in which capital had been proved to have "framed" dynamite charges against labor leaders, and the latter to have used dynamite against capital as in the (then) recent *Los Angeles Times* case.

Despite these many leads, the whole effort of the police under the direction of the District Attorney was to discover evidence that would convict the prisoners already in custody; therefore, all bits of information that led in other directions were ignored.

Prosecution Theory.—The theory that the prosecution followed was as follows: Nolan had manufactured the bomb, a timed automatic dynamite arrangement enclosed in a suitcase. This was carried by the other four to 721 Market Street with the bomb timed to explode as employes of the Pacific Gas and Electric Company passed that spot.   However, a delay of half an hour in the starting of the parade upset the conspirators' calculations, so they taxied east on Market Street to the junction of Steuart Street where Billings, with the suitcase, got out of the car and placed the bomb on the sidewalk next to the wall of a saloon, Mooney acting as lookout. After the "plant," Weinberg drove away with Mrs. Mooney while Billings and Mooney separated and walked away in opposite directions from the death corner. Witnesses were found whose testimony substantiated this theory.

Witnesses.—When these witnesses were taken to the jails to identify the prisoners, the latter were not placed in line with others as is the usual and fair method of identification; instead with each suspect the witnesses were given a tip as to the proper person to point out as the supposed criminal.

The principal witnesses for the events at 721 Market Street were Estelle Smith, Mrs. Mellie Edeau, and the latter's daughter, Sadie. For the placement of the suitcase and bomb at Steuart and Market Street, the chief witnesses were Frank Oxman and John McDonald. Among the corroboratory witnesses were John M. Crowley and Peter Vidovitch.

Estelle Smith, a morphine addict, had a police record of convictions in Los Angeles as a prostitute, and she had been indicted in that city along with her "uncle" James L. Murphy for the murder of one Irene Smith; of the latter charge the "uncle" was convicted when Estelle turned state's witness. Estelle's step-father, Daniel Kidwell, was serving sentence in Folsom penitentiary as a forger at the time of the Mooney-Billings trials; Estelle's mother, Alice Kidwell, was mistress of Louis Rominger, who served as a corroboratory witness in the Billings trial.

Mrs. Mellie Edeau, a dressmaker's assistant in Oakland, was known to the police in that city to suffer from hallucinations. When confronted with her claims to have been both at 221 Market Street and at the Steuart Street corner at the same moment she said her physical body was at one spot and her astral body at the other.

Frank Oxman at the time of the Mooney trial was known as a "wealthy cattleman from Oregon," but a few weeks later was arrested and tried on a charge of subornation to perjury.

John McDonald was an unemployed penniless waiter with an advanced case of syphilis and later was called a "psychopathic liar" by the California Supreme Court.   John Crowley had a police record of conviction for wife desertion and earlier had figured in two suits, one brought by his 17-year-old bride for separation on the grounds that she had contracted syphilis from him while his counter claim was that the bride was the original syphilitic.   Peter Vidovitch, a miser, once a money lender in Alaska, was an inmate of charity lodging houses, although at his death he was found to be possessed of $83,000.

Indictments.—On August 1, 1916, the Grand Jury indicted each of the five defendants for first degree murder on eight counts, one for each death that had occurred up to that time.

Billings Tried.—Warren K. Billings was tried September 11, 1916, before Judge Frank H. Dunne.   Because Billings already had served a sentence for unlawful possession and transportation of dynamite he was a second offender.   Although this prior conviction bore all the signs of a "frame up," this was unknown to the public.   Hence, the state should have an easier task in getting a second conviction; besides if he were convicted first the state would pave the way for a conviction of Mooney. Against Billings, too, the state used the charge of murder of the victim who was a mother of young children.

Billings relied upon an alibi—he was sabotaging automobiles on the day of the parade by injuring their paint—and although car owners and saloon patrons verified his actions and alleged movements the alibi carried no credence with the jury.   James Brennan, in charge of the prosecution, so doubted the credibility of the state's own witnesses that he asked the jury not for a verdict of hanging but of life imprisonment.   To the astounded public it was said that this plea was based on Billings' extreme youth.   On September 23rd the jury declared him guilty of first degree murder but asked for a life sentence.   He was 22 years old at that time.   He made no move for liberty until 1929 (November 7) and public sympathy never was as much extended to him as to Mooney because that first conviction loomed in the public mind.

Mooney Trial.—Thomas J. Mooney went to trial on January 3, 1917, before Judge Franklin A. Griffin. An alibi figured also in this trial. The Mooneys had lived in the eight-story Eilers Building at 875 Market Street, 6,088 feet, or well over a mile from the corner at Steuart Street. Twenty people —sixteen of whom testified for Mooney—from the flats at the Eilers Building gathered on the roof to view the parade, and among these was an amateur photographer, Wade Hamilton, who with a Brownie camera took three $2\frac{1}{4}$x$4\frac{1}{4}$ pictures of the parade. When the films were developed the prints showed Mr. and Mrs. Mooney in the crowd on the roof. Wade Hamilton, who had no love for a radical, such as Mooney, turned the films over to the District Attorney, Charles M. Fickert, who, not until a court order compelled him, let the defense have enlarged prints. These were so blurred as to be nearly useless, but were used in the Mooney trial. After the trial another court order compelled Fickert to let the defense enlarge prints direct from the negatives and these not only clearly revealed the two Mooneys but also a jeweler's clock indicating times just before and just after 2 P. M., the explosion having occurred at 2:06 P. M.

These facts were used in a petition for retrial of Mooney. At the original trial the jury on February 9, 1917, declared Mooney to be guilty, and he was sentenced to be hanged. Judge Griffin later wrote that it was Oxman's testimony that was most convincing of Mooney's guilt. Oxman was a large, naïve, countryman of apparent simple honesty who, with no previous warning whatever, was sprung as a surprise witness on the defense.

Oxman Discredited.—Shortly after Mooney's condemnation, letters written by Oxman to Ed. Rigall in Grayville, Illinois, came into the hands of the defense and were published in the *San Francisco Bulletin.* These letters were ungrammatical and filled with misspellings. They urged Rigall to come to San Francisco at state expense to give certain testimony. This testimony, it appeared at Oxman's trial, was that Rigall was with Oxman at the corner of Steuart and Market at the time of the explosion; that is, Rigall was to corroborate Oxman.

On their face, without the explanation of what the "testimony" was to be, the letters were a subornation to perjury. The Grand Jury refused to indict Oxman, yet he was brought to trial on a judge's order.   Although he was not convicted in this court of law, he was in the court of public opinion.   This feeling later was made certain by affidavits confirmed by hotel registers that Oxman himself was at Woodland, near Sacramento, 90 miles away from Steuart and Market Streets at 2:06 P. M. on July 22, 1916.   He had spent the morning, luncheon period, and time up to train departure at 2:15 P. M. with Earl Hatcher of that town; to these facts Hatcher and his wife gave sworn statements.

Mrs. Mooney.—In the cases against Rena Mooney and Israel Weinberg, Oxman was not a witness.   His place was filled by John McDonald, the syphilitic, unemployed waiter. Mrs. Mooney was tried before Judge Emmet Seawell, the trial beginning May 21, 1917.   She was acquitted on July 25.   In all the cases there were eight counts in the indictment, one for each death that had occurred at the time the indictments were drawn.   The District Attorney, Fickert, declared Mrs. Mooney acquitted of only the first indictment and so held her in jail on the other seven counts until March 30, 1918, when a court order secured her release—but on a bail of $5,000.   Since all the counts were for the same basic crime and since the prosecution relied on the same evidence and witnesses for all the counts, this long retention of Mrs. Mooney in jail after acquittal amounted to persecution.   In addition her acquittal was a refutation of the guilt of her husband.

Weinberg Case.—Israel Weinberg was tried before Judge Emmet Seawell beginning on October 10, 1917.   For six weeks District Attorney Fickert fenced for a conviction, but Weinberg was declared not guilty in less than 30 minutes by the jury on November 27.   Yet he, too, was held in jail until March 22, 1918, and then released only by the compulsion of a court order, but upon a $15,000 bail.

Nolan Not Tried.—Edward Nolan never was tried.   He was released April 17, 1917, on a bail of $2,000 shortly after the revelations concerning Oxman. The materials seized by the police in Nolan's cellar—the basis for the charge that he had manufactured the bomb—were declared by the city chemist to be harmless flash powder, some clay, and a large quantity of Epsom salts. No other evidence of any kind could be found to connect Nolan with the crime. Yet he had to stay more than nine months in jail before Fickert decided that Nolan was innocent.

Witnesses Discredited.—The destruction of the value of the Oxman testimony was followed in 1917 by Estelle Smith in a series of recantations extending over 12 years. In 1921 John McDonald declared that his entire testimony had been false. Hence, as early as 1917, many persons began to believe that Mooney's guilt had not been proven. This feeling eventually rose so high, especially among workers in the United States and abroad, that it threatened to have a bearing upon the World War. President Wilson intervened after hearing from a Mediation Commission he had appointed to investigate the case; Wilson asked Governor Stephens either to pardon Mooney or arrange a new trial on one of the remaining counts in the indictment. But the governor increased the legal snarl by commuting Mooney's sentence on November 29, 1918, to life imprisonment.

Appeals for the retrial of Mooney were denied on the basis of legal technicalities. Appeals to each successive Governor of California for a pardon were denied. Governors Stephens (1917), Richardson (1926), Young (1928), and Rolfe (1932) all were unable to discover reasons for pardoning Mooney. An appeal for the intervention of the United States Supreme Court was denied on the ground that there had been no contravention of the constitution. Mooney thus became the most world-famous inmate of San Quentin Penitentiary. He also became organized labor's outstanding martyr.

Another Theory.—Behind the legal story as sketched there was another story. The five defendants all were associates of the well-known anarchist, Alexander Berkman, who in 1916 in San Francisco was the publisher of a newspaper called the

Blast, in which revolution by force was advocated. Mooney, furthermore, had endeavored to unionize the platform men of the San Francisco street railways and had in 1913 and 1916 led unsuccessful strikes of these men. During the 1916 strike the San Bruno towers carrying the railway power cables were dynamited.

Martin Swanson, formerly a Pinkerton agent who had been hired by the Pacific Gas & Electric Company as a private detective, tried to bribe Billings and Weinberg to swear that Mooney bombed the San Bruno towers. Upon their refusal Swanson swore "to get them." The head of the Pacific Gas and Electric Company had been indicted for graft and other charges by an attorney who ran against Fickert for the office of District Attorney. When Fickert won he dropped the charges against the public utility magnate.

Only July 22, 1916, immediately after the explosion, Swanson secretly was attached to Fickert's staff, and Swanson suggested the arrest of the five defendants. Swanson led the search parties over the defendants' premises, Swanson was with witnesses when they identified the defendants in jail; Swanson and Detective Draper Hand also coached the witnesses in their testimony before the courts. It was the employes of the Pacific Gas and Electric Company that the defendants were accused of intending to blow up instead of the Spanish War Veterans who were the actual victims. The above statements are not hearsay but were presented under oath by various persons.

Real Reasons Why Mooney "Martyred."—An interview with Assistant District Attorney Edward A. Cunha, reported in the July 1917 *Survey* by John Fitch, quoted Cunha as follows: "They are a bunch of dirty anarchists, every one of them, and they ought to be in jail on general principles." Before the California Supreme Court in 1930 Cunha said: "So far as I was concerned I was not worrying about direct witnesses at all. I was satisfied that Mr. Mooney should be convicted upon his activities alone. . . . I was satisfied to have Mooney even hung upon that theory; that is, without direct connection with the crime." The elected judges did not rebuke this statement. Again Cunha is reported as having said, "If I knew that every single witness that testified against Mooney perjured himself in his testimony I wouldn't lift a finger to get him a new trial."

Investigations.—The Mooney-Billings cases were investigated three times by Federal authorities. In 1917 President Wilson, as we have said, appointed a Mediation Commission headed by the Secretary of Labor to inquire into the conduct of the trials, and in 1918 a secret investigation was made for the Department of Labor by John B. Densmore, then Director General of Employment. The Mediation Commission reporting on January 16, 1918, declared that although it was beyond its province to make a finding concerning the guilt or innocence of Mooney it did declare that "a solid basis exists for the feeling that an injustice was done, or may have been done, in the convictions that were obtained, and that an irreparable injustice would be committed to allow such conviction to proceed to execution."

It was on the basis of this report that President Wilson wrote three letters to Governor Stephens of California urging a stay of Mooney's execution so that he might be retried. Governor Stephens, November 29, 1918, commuted Mooney's sentence to life imprisonment, but Mooney was denied retrial.

The Densmore Report never officially was made public but was printed as House Document No. 157—66th Congress, 1st Session, and also was printed by the *San Francisco Call* a week prior to Mooney's commutation of sentence. The Densmore Report was derogatory to District Attorney Charles M. Fickert's prosecution of the Billings and Mooney cases.

In 1930 President Hoover appointed a National Commission on Law Observance and Enforcement which, by the name of its chairman, was known as the Wickersham Commission. A subcommittee made a particular study of "lawlessness in law enforcement" and it was this body, headed by Judge W. S. Kenyon of Iowa, that contained a detailed analysis of the

Mooney-Billings' trials. The actual authors of this subsection report were Dr. Zachariah Chafee of the Harvard Law School, Carl Stern, and Walter Pollack, assisted by Thomas A. Halleran. When in August 1932 the Wickersham Commission's report was published, the Mooney-Billings sub-section of the sub-committee's report was suppressed. However, due to the insistence of Senator Burton K. Wheeler and others a *single copy* was secured by the U. S. Senate and in November 1932 a transcription of this was published in book form by Gotham House, Inc., of New York City.

What Other Side Got.—On the other hand, Estelle Smith's "uncle," serving sentence for a capital offense, was released from jail after a term of three years; her stepfather was promised a parole.

Fickert endeavored to involve Alexander Berkman in the toils of this case but was foiled when Governor Whitman of New York—whence Berkman had fled—refused to grant extradition papers without examination of Fickert's evidence. Fickert never gave the evidence.

By 1929 Swanson and Oxman were dead. Fickert, upon the expiration of his term of office, had difficulty in earning a living. When Governor Rolfe—who as Mayor of San Francisco had led the Preparedness Day Parade—came into office he appointed Fickert to a state sinecure.

Recruits for Mooney's Defense.—Judge Griffin who tried the original Mooney case joined the group that endeavored to secure a retrial or pardon. So did Captain Matheson, the police officer in charge of the Preparedness Day Parade and also in charge of the police investigation of the blast, until drawn off by District Attorney Fickert. Assistant District Attorney Brennan and District Attorney Brady who succeeded Fickert in office joined the forces for a retrial or pardon. So also did 9 of the 10 living jurors who had convicted Mooney.

Not only in labor circles but wherever the law and its enforcement were vital subjects, the Mooney case became a celebrated affair "akin"—said the Wickersham Report—"to the Dreyfus case in France." [6]

The Eugene V. Debs Case of 1918

Socialists and War.—In April 1917, on the day after the declaration of war by the United States against Germany, the American Socialists met in convention in St. Louis to determine the attitude of Socialists to war. The "Declaration" ultimately adopted by the convention was unflinchingly condemnatory of all war, and all measures contributory to war. Although this bold statement caused many hitherto active Socialists to resign, it was in accord with the long-held principles of Eugene Victor Debs, then the American Socialist Chieftain; so Debs, by speech and writing, advocated the rightness of the Declaration despite shrill cries against his "treason."

Espionage Acts.—On June 15 Congress enacted the Espionage Law which made it a penal offense to thwart, or to incite others to thwart, in any manner, the means taken by the United States to conduct the war. In 1918 the Espionage Act was broadened to cover obstructions to the Draft or spreading disaffection among soldiers, sailors, or marines.

Debs Speaks Out.—When in the fall of 1917 the Bolshevik Revolution in Russia occurred, many American Socialists thought the St. Louis Declaration should be recast. Statements were made by both Socialists and capitalists that Debs had changed his views on war. Meanwhile scores of persons, mostly I. W. W.'s or Socialists, had been arrested for violations of the Espionage Acts. So Debs felt he should make his position so plain that none could doubt his stand.

For his purpose he chose a state convention of Socialists held at Canton, Ohio. There on June 16, 1918, in a two-hour speech, Debs set forth his sympathy with those already arrested for violation of the Espionage Acts, specifically mentioning

---

[6] The Mooney case did not end at the point we have closed the story. This book does not go beyond 1929; the Mooney case extended onward into the 1930's. At the time of publication Mooney was still in San Quentin Penitentiary.

Wagenknecht, Baker, and Ruthenberg, convicted of aiding and abetting one another in failing to register for the draft; also Kate Richards O'Hare and Rose Pastor Stokes, convicted of obstructing the enlistment service and attempting to provoke insubordination in the military forces. After commending these and saying if they were guilty so was he, he then launched into a vigorous denunciation of all war, and praise for the pacifism of Socialists.

Debs Arrested.—Two weeks later, Debs was arrested under indictment as a violator of the Espionage Acts. His trial took place at Cleveland, September 9, and was remarkable for Debs' own conduct; for after making no denial of an incomplete shorthand account of his Canton speech as given by a youthful witness for the government and another digest of it by a newspaper reporter, Debs took the stand himself and made a long speech to the jury. Not only was this an unusual court procedure but the address itself was remarkable, because it was aimed less at the farmer jury than at posterity; Debs wanted future Socialists to know how one leader stood in the midst of a great World War.

Debs' Speech at Trial.—The speech traced the record of revolutionists in America's history showing that statements, deemed treasonable when they were uttered, later became the treasured parts of folklore. Debs then turned to the subject of war, and first putting Woodrow Wilson's "The New Freedom" into the evidence read from that work the President's earlier condemnation of war. Finally Debs tore aside the veil of patriotism and revealed the economic motives of war and pointed out that although the common man made most of the sacrifices to war he got almost none of the gains if war yielded any gains at all!. One passage stands out, "I have been accused of obstructing the war. I admit it. Gentlemen, I abhor war. I would oppose the war if I stood alone." This court speech itself was as much a violation of the Espionage Act as the Canton speech for which he was brought into court; so of course the jury found Debs guilty. He was sentenced (September

14, 1918) to 10 years in the Moundsville, West Virginia Penitentiary.

Appeal.—An appeal was taken to the United States Supreme Court chiefly on the grounds that the Espionage Act violated the Bill of Rights. On March 10, 1919, the Supreme Court unanimously upheld the U. S. District Court, Northern District of Ohio, and found that "Debs had obstructed and attempted to obstruct the recruiting service of the United States, and thus violated provisions of the Espionage Act." The validity of that law the Supreme Court already had sustained in *Schenck v. United States* in which case also the Bill of Rights had been an issue. Thereupon the marshal, April 12, 1919, took Debs to the Moundsville, West Virginia Penitentiary.

Transfer to Atlanta.—At Moundsville, Debs was given many privileges, including unlimited receipt and dispatch of mail, frequent callers, considerable freedom of movement, and a virtually private jail apartment. Suddenly on June 13, 1919, all these favors ceased, for Debs was transferred to the Atlanta Federal Penitentiary where he was placed in an ordinary cell block, in a cell with five other prisoners, put at hard work, limited to one letter a week, and allowed no callers.

It took some time for Debs' friends to learn what had happened and when they did they immediately suspected that Debs was being officially persecuted. However, it was learned that the transfer had been brought about by the accident that West Virginia and the federal government were in dispute over the number and payment to the state of federal prisoners cared for at Moundsville. Debs was the sole federal prisoner and the state wanted either more prisoners and more pay for their care or none. The need for the farming-out arose from the overcrowding of federal penitentiaries by offenders against war measures and the scores dragged behind bars as the result of the "Red Drive." The Moundsville dispute was settled by the removal of its single federal case who happened to be Debs.

Protests.—Yet the harsh treatment of Debs at Atlanta drew protests, among them that of Clarence Darrow who threatened

action if Debs was not less rigorously punished. Debs was
transferred to the hospital ward but still denied favors in regard
to mail and visitors. Debs' friends sent a petition to Wilson
for a pardon, but it was denied by the President on January 30,
1921. Joseph Tumulty, Wilson's secretary, in a newspaper
series reported Wilson as having said, "This man was a traitor
to his country and he will never be pardoned during my
administration."

Debs Candidate for Presidency.—Meanwhile the presidential nominations and campaigns of 1920 were under way.
The Socialist convention would endorse no candidate over Debs
for the office of President so their campaign poster showed
their candidate, clad in jail garb, standing before a cell door.
Debs had run for the same office at every election since 1900,
save 1916, but as Convict Number 9653 he polled more votes
than he or anybody else ever did on an American Socialist ticket.
His popular vote was 919,799, and there is no doubt that many
non-Socialists voted for him as the most conspicuous "martyr"
to war hysteria; from this emotion many had recovered as early
as 1920.

Debs Pardoned.—Perhaps this large popular approval of
Debs had an effect on President Harding and at any rate it was
good politics to remove the crown of martyrdom from a political
rival; whatever the motive it was the fact that Harding pardoned Debs on Christmas Day, 1921.

At Terre Haute, Indiana, birthplace and residence of Debs,
his homecoming train had to be stopped a full quarter-mile from
the station so great was the press of people gathered to welcome
him. This was Debs' last triumph; for his energy-consuming
life as an agitator, a sunstroke, while speaking in Virginia prior
to 1908, and the hardships of jail, which had accentuated breath-
less heart attacks took their toll in his 71st year. He died at
a hospital in Elmhurst, a suburb of Chicago, October 20, 1926.

Among radical labor groups and by most who knew him,
Debs was loved while alive, and after his death he was well-nigh
canonized.

CHAPTER 14

"MARTYRS" EXTRAORDINARY—SACCO AND VANZETTI

The Sacco-Vanzetti case outranked all others of recent years in the book of American labor martyrs. For seven years Nicola Sacco and Bartolomeo Vanzetti knew the mental anguish of uncertainty as to their fates, and the bodily suffering of close confinement in Massachusetts prisons. To radicals of the entire western world these men were the symbols of capitalist injustice. To those who honored law and the courts, the case involving these men was a distressing test of these means for the preservation of order. To extreme conservatives these men and the ideas they upheld were menaces to the foundations of American government.

In short, the Sacco-Vanzetti case was carried to its conclusion in an atmosphere of passion. On the one side were persons whose warm emotions enfolded these men as victims of a vicious system; on the other were equally vehement partisans who considered the courts too lenient and slow in infliction of merited punishment. Only a few cool minds tried to weigh the evidence in order to reach a reasoned decision; and these unfortunately were not in the court rooms nor in newspaper offices. Were Sacco and Vanzetti guilty of atrocious murder; or were they unfortunate sacrifices to the unpopularity of their beliefs? Let the case itself supply the answers.

On Pearl Street, South Braintree, Massachusetts, at a few minutes after three o'clock in the afternoon of Thursday, April 15, 1920, there was enacted a crime for which Nicola Sacco and Bartolomeo Vanzetti were held responsible.

Geography of Case.—To visualize Pearl Street, South Braintree, think of a line drawn from left to right across the middle of this page with a slope that would tilt the line on the left and depress it on the right.   Near the center of the page, then think of six tracks of the New York New Haven and Hartford Railroad that crossed Pearl Street, not quite at right angles but with a slight northeast-southwest inclination.   The South Braintree railroad station would be near the upper left center of the page.   Between the station and Pearl Street, and to the west of the roadway from Pearl Street to the station, place a wooden shoe factory and label it Slater and Morrill Co. # 1.   This building should be thought of as to the west of the railroad crossing and some 80 feet north of Pearl Street. Next, in about the center of the lower right-hand page thus about 150 feet *east* of the crossing, and on the *south* side of Pearl Street, place a larger shoe factory and call it Rice and Hutchins.   In front of this put an iron pipe fence and across the street an excavation for a cellar.   Much further east or near the right-hand edge of the page, think of a third shoe factory, Slater and Morrill # 2; this, too, place on the south side of Pearl street which is the same side as the R. & H. factory.

Hold-Up and Murder.—On the morning of April 15, 1920, about 9:15, money for the payrolls of the two Slater and Morrill shoe factories arrived by express at the South Braintree station.   Expressman Neal placed the money box on his horse-drawn wagon, took it to the express office on Pearl Street some distance west of the railway crossing, and in so doing he noticed a 7-passenger Buick car with engine running in front of the express office.   Breaking the express seals and unlocking the box, Neal carted it to S & M factory # 1; that is, the one near the station west of the crossing of Pearl Street.   At the factory entrance Neal noticed two strange, dark, short men who aroused Neal's apprehension.   In the factory office, the money ($15,776.51) was distributed into pay envelopes, these inserted into special rack boxes, and the whole enclosed in locked cases resembling small suit cases. The paymaster, Frederick A. Parmenter, about 3 o'clock took one of the cases while his guard, Allessandro Bernardelli, took another and together they started from S & M #1 to walk across the railroad tracks downhill to S & M plant #2.

At the fence, in front of the Rice & Hutchins shoe factory, two loungers stepped up to Parmenter and Bernardelli, firing into their bodies. As Bernardelli sank to the gutter more lead was pumped into him; Parmenter meanwhile had dropped his box and scurried across the street toward the excavation, but shots in the back felled him. The two gunmen were joined by a third who came from behind a pile of bricks west of the excavation. A 7-passenger Buick car came slowly upgrade from the east-end of Pearl Street and the killers, with their booty, piled into this car. A rifle or shotgun poked through the rear window held back would-be pursuers while revolver shots intimidated observers at the sides of the car. At the crossing an approaching train had caused the gateman to lower the gates, but menaces and directions from a revolver made him raise them enough to let the car pass. After the crossing, the car picked up speed and disappeared toward the west.

Because the car attracted attention by its size, its flapping down-pulled curtains, and its broken-out rear window, it was observed by enough people to enable a subsequent tracing of the first part of its route. It was last seen by a gate tender, Austin T. Reed at Matfield Crossing, who stopped it on account of an approaching train. When allowed to proceed, a man on the front seat brandished a revolver at the gate tender and yelled, "What the hell are you holding us up for." Reed saw the car return across the tracks a few minutes later. A school girl, Julia Kelliher, reported seeing a similar car on the outskirts of Brockton.

Car Found.—On Saturday of that week (April 17) two horseback riders jogging through a wooded lane not far from Brockton saw an abandoned 7-passenger Buick car. Reporting their find to the Brockton police, they aided officers in getting the car out of the lane. The police then drove the car to the police garage in Brockton.

Arrests.—Less than a month later (May 5, 1920), late in the evening, Sacco and Vanzetti were arrested on a street car coming into Brockton from West Bridgewater. Upon removal from the street car to a police automobile, it was said by Officer

Michael J. Connolly that, during the ride, Sacco twice reached inside his coat and Vanzetti once toward his hip. At the station, searches revealed a Colt revolver stuck in Sacco's waistband and a Harrington and Richardson .38 pistol in Vanzetti's hip pocket. Both guns were fully loaded. Besides, Sacco had loosely in his pants pocket 22 cartridges, while Vanzetti had four shotgun shells. These arsenals were the basis for holding the two men in jail for the next four months.

Vanzetti in Another Case.—In the interval, a more serious charge than carrying an unlicensed gun was brought against Vanzetti. After a hearing May 12 at the Brockton police court, Vanzetti was bound over to the Superior Court. On June 11, 1920, he was indicted for alleged participation in a payroll hold-up that had occurred at Bridgewater on December 24, 1919. On June 23, 1920, he pleaded *Not Guilty* and was immediately brought to trial on a charge of assault with intent to kill. Because the *Boston American* on Sunday, June 20, 1920, printed a lurid story of the crime and the alleged connection of Vanzetti with it, Vanzetti pleaded that the case be postponed until the next term of the Superior Court, the claim being that public indignation, already much aroused by a series of hold-up and other crimes, had been fanned into such heat by the newspaper story that no jury could be unprejudiced. The petition was denied. The case turned on identification and the jury believed the stories of several witnesses that identified Vanzetti, so on July 1, 1920, a verdict of guilty was returned. Judge Webster Thayer sitting in the case sentenced Vanzetti (August 16, 1920) to 12-15 years in the state prison at Charlestown. The Prosecuting Attorney in the case was Frederick G. Katzmann.

Sacco-Vanzetti Trial.—On September 11, 1920, both Sacco and Vanzetti were indicted for the murder of Bernardelli-Parmenter in South Braintree. Both men pleaded *Not Guilty,* so both were held for trial. The case was heard at the Dedham Court House beginning on May 31, 1921, and continued for 37 court days, or more than six weeks, concluding on July 14, 1921.

The atmosphere of the trial was one of extraordinary tensity for not only was Massachusetts incensed by the South Braintree crime as the most cold-blooded, openly defiant, of a long series of outrages, but the United States Attorney General A. Mitchell Palmer in 1919-1920 had conducted an hysterical campaign of seizure and deportation of "Reds." During their year in jail prior to trial, the Massachusetts newspapers had pilloried Sacco and Vanzetti as the perpetrators of the South Braintree slaughter and as draft dodgers, anarchists, and foreigners who spoke in broken English. On the other hand, radicals in America and abroad with the cry of "frame up" had organized a Sacco-Vanzetti Defense Committee. An I. W. W. lawyer from San Francisco, Fred Moore, had hurried to Massachusetts—where after the Lawrence strike of 1912 he had appeared for Ettor—and placed himself, without invitation, at the head of Sacco's defense. From the start, therefore, the trial aroused such passionate partisanship as to make it one of the most noticed cases in the history of the state's criminal sessions of courts.

Jury Chosen.—In view of this situation, Chief Justice Aiker ordered the calling of 500 citizens for jury duty. Of this number only 7 were qualified. Thereupon Judge Webster Thayer ordered the sheriff to go through the county and bring in 200 more citizens. From these the 5 remaining jurors were selected. The 12 sifted out of 700 were a fair cross-section of the population; 2 were real estate operators, 2 were machinists, 1 each was a driver, stockkeeper, clothing salesman, shoemaker, photographer, farmer, grocer, and stone mason.

The Judge and Attorneys.—The judge presiding in the case was Webster Thayer, a name bespeaking Puritan lineage and a man who, in the opinion of one of his friends, was "narrow-minded, intensely patriotic, and with simple clearcut mental images of Right and Wrong," a man, too, who in the course of the case was indiscreet in expressing his opinions concerning it when off the bench. The District Attorney was Frederick G. Katzmann, incisive, alert, and determined to punish. Besides Fred Moore as attorney for Sacco, he was represented by Wil-

liam J. Callahan. For Vanzetti there appeared Jeremiah J. Mc-
Anarney and the latter's brother Thomas T. McAnarney.

Neither brother—according to the record in the case—was
capable of such thorough logical presentation as the opposing
District Attorney. Moore although indefatigable in running
down clues for his clients was a distinct handicap to Sacco.
Moore had the unfortunate quality of irritating every one with
whom he came in contact, while his reputation as a "long-
haired radical," together with the fact that as a Californian he
was an outlander in a Massachusetts court and in the laws of
the state, did his client no good. Indeed, Sacco and his wife
begged Moore to retire from the case, a plea which was seconded
by the McAnarney brothers; but Moore stuck. Sacco did not
know he had the right to dismiss Moore. Judge Thayer was
openly hostile to Moore; in the court room the judge's manner
inimical to the attorney was well understandable by the jury and
off the bench the judge frequently, to his associates, castigated
Moore.

No Separation of Trials.—Each of the defendants was a
burden to the other. Vanzetti's prior conviction although not
openly brought into this case was an influence in it, and thus
harmed Sacco. On the other hand, Sacco was much more implicated by witnesses than Vanzetti and so Vanzetti was injured
by his association with Sacco. The defense lawyers were well
aware of these possibilities and attempted to secure separate
trials but Judge Thayer denied their plea.

Prosecution's Case.—The trial developed three arguments
to fasten the South Braintree murder on the defendants. One
was the identification by eye witnesses; the second was the actions of the men at, and after, arrest that showed consciousness
of guilt; and the third was to trace the fatal bullet to the Sacco
revolver. Besides these there was certain circumstantial evidence that especially implicated Sacco.

Witnesses.—Of eye witnesses there was no lack, for the
crime took place in daylight on a busy street in front of a factory filled with workpeople; besides, there were two other fac-

tories giving partial views of the scene. A gang of laborers was in an excavation directly opposite the site of the shooting, another gang was working on the railroad tracks close to the crossing, pedestrians and car drivers had parts of the crime or flight in their lines of vision, the gateman was actually threatened by the fleeing criminals, and still other people viewed the car and its occupants at points along the route of escape.

From this host the prosecution put seven on the stand who positively identified Sacco and six who could not identify him.

Lewis Pelser, a shoe cutter for Rice & Hutchins, was the first witness to make a positive identification; that is, he said the gunman was "the dead image of Sacco." His observation on April 15, 1920 was taken in the time necessary to open a first-floor window and then slam it shut. His testimony was combated by three defense witnesses who were at the same place at the same time and declared that Pelser ducked under the cutting table during the shooting.

Mrs. Lola Andrews, a practical nurse and formerly a shoe operative, testified she had spoken to a man who was partly under a 7-passenger Buick car who, to give her directions in answer to her inquiry, rose and faced her. That man she said was Sacco. This incident in time was just prior to the murder.

Miss Frances J. Devlin, bookkeeper for Slater and Morrill, from a second-story window in factory # 1, eighty feet from Pearl Street saw the "bandit" car go over the railroad crossing and a man lean from the car waving a pistol. Her vision was a matter of seconds but her identification of Sacco was positive. Miss Mary E. Splaine with the same opportunity and view as Miss Devlin also identified Sacco.

Carlos Goodridge, a salesman playing pool in a store on Pearl Street at the time of the crime, dashed to the sidewalk as the bandit car went by and saw in the car a man he said was Sacco.

Lewis L. Wade, gas pump man for Rice & Hutchins had said before the trial that Sacco was one of the gunmen but on the stand in court he said he wasn't sure because in a barber shop weeks after the crime he had seen a man who so closely resembled the gunman that he was frightened. This incident made his mind uncertain of his ability to identify any man as the gunman.

Michael Levangie, gate tender at the South Braintree crossing, identified Vanzetti as the driver of the bandit car. (In the trial and even by Judge Thayer, the Buick was called the "bandit car.") Inasmuch as the overwhelming evidence of eyewitnesses was that the driver was young, smooth-faced, cadaverous, and light-haired while Vanzetti was in his thirties, brown-haired and had a conspicuous flowing brown mustache, the District Attorney himself rejected Levangie's testimony. The only other witness to identify Vanzetti was Austin T. Reed, crossing tender at Matfield, who said that Vanzetti was the man who shouted from the bandit car "What the hell are you holding us up for."

Two other witnesses identified as Sacco a man they had seen in South Braintree before the hour of the crime. William S. Tracy, real estate operator had seen him and another alien leaning against a drug store window on the west end of Pearl Street about noon on April 15. Harry Doebeare, a repairman for pianos, had seen him drive through the station square in the morning of that day. John W. Faulkner, wooden pattern maker, had seen on April 15 a man on the train from Plymouth to South Braintree who he said was Vanzetti. William J. Heron, railroad police officer, saw two excited Italians—of whom one he identified as Sacco—in the South Braintree station about 12:30. Austin C. Cole, the conductor of the street car on which the defendants were riding when arrested testified that the two men had ridden on the same car line from the same car stop on the night of April 14 or April 15.

The Defense: Credibility of Witnesses.—The defense, in cross-examination of the above witnesses, brought out that most of them a few minutes, hours, or days after the shooting were much less positive of their identification than they were at the trial more than a year after the crime. Time had sharpened not blurred their mental image of the criminals.

Defense Witnesses.—Besides thus attacking the credibility of the prosecution witnesses, the defense put on the stand 22 witnesses of its own.   Of these, 14 were Italians and 8 Americans.   These persons were drawn from those in the work gangs in the excavation and railroad tracks, from persons on the street or at the crossing, and from shoe workers at windows comparable to those at which stood Pelser and the Misses Splaine and Devlin.   These witnesses were positive that Sacco was not the man who shot on the street or from the car.   None saw any one who remotely resembled Vanzetti.   Examination of witnesses also brought out the fact that when witnesses before the trial were asked by police officers for identification of the defendants it was either from photographs, or by seeing the defendants by themselves in the jail.   In no case was a witness obliged to select a suspect from a group of men.

Prosecution: Consciousness of Guilt.—To establish the fact that the conduct of Sacco and Vanzetti proved consciousness of guilt, the Commonwealth put several witnesses on the stand.   The first were Ruth Corinne Johnson and her husband Simon E. Johnson, a garage man.   This couple lived not far from Elm Square, West Bridgewater.   On the night of May 5 (the night of the arrests) an Italian Mike Boda (Mario Buda) called upon Mr. Johnson to get an Overland car of Boda's that was in Johnson's shop for repairs.   (The police had arranged with the Johnsons that when Boda called for the car the police were to be notified; for Boda was sought by federal agents for deportation as a "Red.")   Upon Boda's arrival, Mrs. Johnson walked some distance down the road to a neighbor's (Horace Bartlett) house to telephone.   She said there was a motorcycle on the road with three men about it.   Two in the beam of the headlight followed Mrs. Johnson to the Bartlett house, waited for her reappearance, then stalked her back to her own home.   These men so apprehensive of her movements, Mrs. Johnson said, were Sacco and Vanzetti.

When arrested, the attempts to pull guns on the officers— according to the officers' testimony—was an indication of a feeling of guilt.   (When Officer Connolly with a beaming smile told of the attempt to draw guns, Vanzetti from the cage shouted, "You're a liar.")   Later in the police station the

discovery of the heavy armament of the two men was conducive to the belief that they walked in fear—of something,
perhaps arrest.   When questioned by police on the night of
May 5, and later by the District Attorney, the two men told an
extraordinary series of lies.   To falsify and to go to unnecessary lengths in fabrication seemed more a confession of something to hide than actions of fearless honesty.

Reply by Defense.—The defense offered the explanation,
made principally by Sacco and Vanzetti as witnesses in their
own behalf, that the men were conscious—acutely so—not of
guilt but of danger.   They had been draft evaders, having gone
to Mexico to avoid bearing arms; for as philosophical anarchists
they disbelieved in war and nationalism: they were pacifists,
internationalists, and believers in universal free individualism.
More than fear of arrest as draft dodgers—"slackers" in the
terminology of the day—they feared arrest and deportation for
their radicalism.   Friends of theirs had had this fate, and one
in New York, in the month prior to May 5, had been found
crushed to death by a fall from a high window after interview
by police.   Vanzetti had gone to New York in the latter case
and had been advised to return to Massachusetts and collect
from all his radical friends whatever radical literature they had
on their premises.   To find a place of deposit and then to collect
the literature, Vanzetti needed a car.   Conference with Sacco
and another friend, Riccardo Orciani led to the attempt to
secure Boda's Overland car.   Finding from Mr. Johnson they
could not drive it due to lack of 1920 number plates they decided
to return home—Orciani and Boda on the former's motorcycle
while Sacco and Vanzetti went by street car.

When arrested both men were certain it was on account of
their radicalism.   The first question asked them by the police,
"Are you an anarchist, a communist, the member of any society
or organization" intensified their belief in the reason for the
arrest; so they lied not just to save themselves but to prevent
revealing the names and addresses of their radical associates.
They were not told for weeks that they were being held for
murder, nor were they indicted on that charge for months

(September 11, 1920).   As for their armament, they said that
was due to the troubled times, crime rampant in the state, and
that their radical missions required them to be on lonely ways
late at night.   The shotgun shells had been given to Vanzetti
that day (May 5, 1920) by Sacco who was cleaning house and
packing in preparation for a visit to his father in Italy.

Prosecution: Ballistics.—Besides identification by eye-wit-
nesses, and acts indicative of consciousness of guilt, the District
Attorney relied upon the evidence of ballistic experts to convict
Sacco and incidentally Vanzetti.   The testimony of the experts
on guns and ammunition ran through several court sessions and
was of course highly technical.   The gist of it from the prosecution's side was that the bullet which killed Bernardelli was
fired through Sacco's Colt .32 and that Vanzetti's pistol, the
.38 Harrington and Richardson, was one that had belonged to
Bernardelli and taken from him after his murder.

The defense experts said the fatal bullet could have been
fired through a Colt .32 or Austrian Steyr or a Bayard, Savage
or Walther, but were emphatic that it had *not* been fired through
Sacco's gun.   As for Bernardelli's pistol, it had been taken for
repair to the Iver Johnson Company in Boston, with no record
of its return to its owner.   Moreover, Vanzetti's gun was traced
to its prior owners, Orciani, Eldridge Atwater, and the latter's
brother-in-law.   The gun originally had belonged to Atwater's
father-in-law of Dexter, Maine, and had been brought to Massachusetts by the mother-in-law who gave it to Rexford Slater,
another son-in-law by whom it was sold to his shop mate,
Orciani.   The ballistic testimony of the prosecution made an
undoubted impression on the jury.

Prosecution: Circumstantial Evidence.—The circumstantial evidence was slight in amount but it weighed heavily with the
jury and the public.   First, the only day for months that Sacco
was absent from his job as shoe worker in the 3K factory of
Stoughton was April 15, 1920.   Then a cap picked from the
ground beside the dead Bernardelli (who himself had worn a
soft felt hat) fitted Sacco's head, was like one worn by him to
the shoe factory and had holes in the lining as if torn by the

nail on which Sacco habitually had hung his work cap. Four shells found at the murder scene were identical in make and size with shells found on Vanzetti when arrested.

The defense of course cross-examined all the prosecution's witnesses and in most cases showed that they had told stories differing from their court testimony at the inquest, at the earlier Vanzetti trial, or in conferences with the defense attorneys. Moreover, witnesses for the defense nearly all of whom were in better positions to view the crime than the opposing witnesses testified either flatly in denial of the presence of Sacco and Vanzetti or in ability to identify anybody on account of the brevity of their vision of the outrage.

Among the most important of these witnesses were Frank J. Burke, an itinerant exhibitor of glass-blowing, who was close to the crossing when the bandit car passed; Mrs. Barbara Liscomb, a Rice & Hutchins employe, whose window directly overlooked the crime, was shot at, fainted, and was sure that "the face of the gunman she would see always" but that face was not the face of either of the defendants; Mrs. Jennie (Pierce) Novelli, a nurse who in passing the bandit car prior to the shooting on the journey down Pearl Street noticed the driver with particular care because at first she thought he was some one she knew; she also noticed the driver's companion, but neither man was either of the prisoners.

Witnesses drawn from work gangs in the excavation and railroad tracks probably did not aid the defense because they were mostly Italians, told conflicting stories and were rebutted by the District Attorney's witnesses to the effect that the excavation gang ran and hid while the foreman of the railroad gang barred his men from near approach to the scene of tragedy.

We have seen that the defense explained the actions of the defendants after the arrest as fear of exposure of their own and their friends' radicalism; and the ballistic testimony resolved itself into credibility of conflicting experts. The remainder of the defendants' case consisted in building alibis for both men.

Alibis.—For Vanzetti it was shown that he was in his home town of Plymouth for the entire day of April 15, 1920. The principal corroborants of this contention were first a Jewish peddler named Joseph Rosen who about noon sold Vanzetti a suit cutting of blue woolen cloth. This witness was highly amusing especially under cross-examination by District Attorney Katzmann but Rosen's story stood the test. The other principal witness was Melvin Carl, a fisherman of Plymouth, who on the fateful day was painting his boat and in the early afternoon had a long conversation with Vanzetti. The ticket agents at Plymouth and nearby stations testified that no ticket was sold to South Braintree on April 15; the train conductor said he had received no cash fare; the railroad trainmaster said that no such car—combination baggage and smoker—as Faulkner described was on that train on which Faulkner rode, and the station master of South Braintree said that a man similar to Faulkner's "Italian" got off at the South Braintree Station frequently on days following April 15. Eleven witnesses in all, six Italian and five American, contributed to the Vanzetti alibi.

For Sacco it was shown that his absence from work on April 15 was due to a visit in Boston to the Italian consul to secure passports. Sacco's mother had died and his father was ill and wished to see him before the father, too, came to his grave. Sacco's employer had been informed of his intentions and the date for leaving work was not a certain fixed one but dependent upon Sacco's catching up with his work and training a substitute. Witnesses testified to seeing or being with Sacco in Boston on April 15. Sacco's employers said he was a highly skilled, faithful employe, paid $45 to $85 a week and at times night watchman in addition to his regular day work. A savings bank book revealed that Sacco had saved from his earnings about $1,500. Sacco and his wife denied his ownership of the cap placed in evidence by the District Attorney. Ten witnesses, five Italian and five American, built the Sacco alibi.

No Character Witnesses.—The defense was withheld from putting witnesses on the stand to testify to the excellent character of the two men. A start was made in this direcion as regards Sacco but the Court wiped the stories from the record. The two sets of counsel struck a bargain whereby the prosecution was to refrain from reference to Vanzetti's prior conviction and sentence, while the defense was to make no effort in respect to "character" witnesses.

This turned out to be a sorry bargain particularly so for Sacco, for not only was Vanzetti's earlier case a matter of common knowledge—thus presumably known to the jury—but indirect references to it crept into the testimony on the stand. On the other hand no one but their intimates had any knowledge of the high regard in which Sacco and Vanzetti were held in their own communities. This was even more true of Sacco than of Vanzetti for while Sacco was a married man with a fixed job at a skilled task and a home, Vanzetti was without ties and worked at all sorts of common labor jobs of which fish peddling was only one.

Both men came from families considerably above the ordinary levels in Italy and, of the two, Vanzetti's relatives stood the higher in social position. If he had remained in Italy, Vanzetti's life could have been one of easy gentility but he felt a call for evangelization and so deliberately chose the life of a common laborer, and, like a priest, considered celibacy a requisite of his mission. In mentality Vanzetti was far above Sacco; with opportunity and training he easily might have been a professor of philosophy.

Alibi Cross-Examined.—District Attorney Katzmann's cross-examination of Vanzetti and Sacco was concerned less with the South Braintree crime than with the defendant's draft dodging and anarchistic beliefs. The first question to Vanzetti was, "So you left Plymouth May 1917 to dodge the draft did you?" and to Sacco the first questions were, "Did you say you love a free country? Did you love this country in the month of May 1917?" Later Katzmann said, "The extent of your love of this country is measured in dollars and cents, isn't it?" Vanzetti quite well withstood the baiting of the cross-examination except that his refusal to implicate his friends in radicalism cast some doubt upon his claim that his association on May 5 with Sacco, Boda, and Orciani was for the purpose of the

collection and storage of radical literature. But with Sacco
the District Attorney's skilful questions produced a torrent of
radical statements that, regardless of their truth or misconception,
damaged him gravely with the jury.

Summing By Attorneys.—Again after the defense attorneys
in summing the case had consumed 4½ hours Katzmann,
the D. A., spent even longer on the prosecution's case; curiously,
much of this time was consumed in rehearsing the draft evasion
and radicalism of the defendants rather than exhaustive argument
of the evidence in the Commonwealth's case.

His honor, Judge Thayer began his charge to the jury on
the theme of "Loyalty to country" and ended it with the words,
"Gentlemen be just and *fear not*. 'Let all the *end* thou *aimest*
at be *thy country's,* thy God's, and Truth's.' "   [The italics
in this quotation are the author's.]

The jury came to a quick decision on the evening of the same
day (37th day of trial July 14, 1921) as Judge Thayer's
charge. The verdict was *"Guilty"* against both Sacco and
Vanzetti. When this was announced by Foreman Ripley,
Sacco cried "They kill an innocent men. [sic] They kill two
innocent men."

But it took six years to do it. For after the verdict there
began a series of remarkable legal appeals. Some were based
on alleged errors in the conduct of the trial, some on the alleged
perjury of key witnesses for the Commonwealth, and some on
new evidence. (This is not the actual order of the presentation
of appeals, but is thus classified here to save space.)

Appeals Ripley Affidavits.—Aside from the ordinary appeals
that the court had erred in the admission or denial of
evidence, there was an especial appeal made upon the acknowledgment
that Jury Foreman Walter R. Ripley had in his pocket
during the trial shells very much like those discovered on Vanzetti
at the time of his arrest; and that Ripley had discussed with
other jurors, shown to them, and compared in their presence,
his own and Vanzetti's shells. The illegality of these actions
lay in the fact that nothing should be shown or discussed in the

juryroom save that which had been admitted as evidence in open court.

Moreover, it was shown that Ripley was not just a stock-keeper as he declared but formerly had been Chief of Police in Quincy, Massachusetts. He was quoted as having said before the trial "Damn them, they ought to hang them any-way." If true, this prior conviction of guilt of the defendants should have disqualified Ripley as a juror. Ripley died on October 21, 1921, before the motions in his case came before Judge Thayer. The latter refused to grant a new trial on the Ripley affidavits because he said the "petition was not based upon established facts."

Appeals Perjury Charges.—The perjury of key witnesses was alleged by affidavits in the cases of Lewis Pelser, Mrs. Lola R. Andrews, Carlos Goodridge, and Captain Proctor. Pelser, in an affidavit to the defense, declared he could not identify Sacco and did not know how he came to say the gunman "was the dead image of Sacco." Immediately after signing this confession, Pelser denied its truth in a confession to Katz-mann and said he had been trapped, while drunk, into making the former confession. Judge Thayer denied a new trial as based on Pelser's retraction of testimony.

Mrs. Lola R. Andrews was led to recant her identification. Defense lawyer Moore had unearthed a mass of data concern-ing Mrs. Andrews' early life in Maine which was of such a nature that a Maine court had removed her son, John Andrew Hassam, from her custody. Confronted with this in the pres-ence of her son, Mrs. Andrews signed an interview in which she denied any ability to identify Sacco. At the trial Mrs. Andrews had been flatly contradicted by a mentally alert old lady from Maine who had been Mrs. Andrews' companion on April 15, 1920. Other witnesses had testified that Mrs. An-drews' reputation for veracity was very poor and she had been involved in devious transactions concerning insurance. Now on top of her own confession she appeared before Katzmann and swore that her "confession" was obtained by duress while hysterical in the presence of her son. In denial of petition for a new trial on this "confession," Judge Thayer went into a lengthy castigation of Counsel Fred Moore for unprofessional conduct designed to take away the rights of the Commonwealth and prevent the establishment of Justice between the Commonwealth and the defendants.

The affidavits concerning Carlos Goodridge were numerous, tracing his whole life. His real name was Erastus Corning Whitney. As a boy in New York state he was convicted of grand larceny (2nd degree) and sentenced to the Elmira Reformatory. As a young man he had served 1½ years in Auburn Penitentiary for grand larceny (2nd degree) and was indicted for another but escaped the state by fleeing to Vermont where he lived under the assumed name Edward C. Willis. He was joined there by a woman with whom he lived without benefit of clergy. Together with two others they burned a house whose furniture they had insured for far more than its value.

Coming into Massachusetts, Whitney (or Goodridge) was married and divorced by two different women. In getting the marriage licenses he swore to falsehoods as to name, residence, and prior marital status. One woman, who discovered his aliases and previous career, made him go through two marriage ceremonies—one in Rhode Island, the other at White River Junction, Vt. In Massachusetts on September 11, 1920, he was under two indictments for grand larceny. In the court, where Katzmann was the District Attorney, Goodridge (Whitney) pleaded guilty, made restitution for the full amount of the theft, and was allowed by Katzmann to go free on probation. It was in the court room that he saw Sacco and made the identification of him to which he later testified in the Sacco trial.

The affidavits hinted that such a witness was incapable of honest testimony and insinuated a "deal" between Goodridge and Katzmann. Goodridge's counter affidavit showed that Moore had approached him with all this record and actually had Goodridge jailed for two days under threat of returning him to New York to face the untried indictment. Moore tried to get Goodridge to reveal a "deal" with Katzmann but Goodridge refused all leads.

Upon these affidavits Judge Thayer refused to grant a new trial on the grounds that the untried indictment of Goodridge was outlawed by time; and that Goodridge's testimony had been successfully impeached during the Sacco-Vanzetti trial. Judge Thayer also severely criticized Counsel Moore for the methods he used in securing the Goodridge affidavits and the signed interview with Goodridge.

Captain Proctor at the trial had been the police ballistic expert. He had not directly affirmed that the fatal bullet had been fired through the Sacco revolver but had said "My opinion is that it is consistent with being fired by that pistol." The new affidavit sworn by Proctor's friend Hamilton was, that Proctor had told Hamilton that the above statement had been pre-arranged with District Attorney Katzmann because Proctor's private opinion was that the bullet had *not* passed through Sacco's gun. If this affidavit were true then Proctor had committed perjury, not overtly, but in intention to deceive the jury. Unfortunately, Proctor had died before the Hamilton affidavit was filed, and Hamilton had been a defense ballistic expert. The two men were friends.

Thayer dismissed a motion for new trial on account of this affidavit because he deemed it was not based on established facts and therefore was immaterial.

Appeal New Evidence.—An appeal for a new trial based upon the discovery of new evidence was made when the defense attorneys found one Roy E. Gould and took his affidavits. Gould, a wandering salesman of a preparation for sharpening razors, had gone to South Braintree on April 15, and upon descent from the train inquired at what time the local shoe shops paid off their employes. He was told "There goes the paymaster, Parmenter, now," so Gould followed Parmenter and Bernardelli down Pearl Street toward Slater and Morrill plant number 2. He was so close to these men that when the shooting commenced a shot went through Gould's coat. He got a better view of the criminals than any other witness and at a unique angle. He reported his facts, his name, and address to officer John J. Heaney and then departed on a selling trip through New Brunswick, Nova Scotia, and Prince Edward Isle in Canada. Thus he read no newspaper account of the arrests and trial of Sacco and Vanzetti.

The defense not knowing Gould's address could not produce him at the trial; but by constant inquiry finally after the trial located him in Maine. The District Attorney who had Gould's address had made no attempt to secure him as a trial witness. The *Boston Post* story of the crime had named Gould as a witness so the prosecution had ample notice of his proximity to the scene of the murders. Shown by the defense lawyers various pictures including those of the defendants Gould stated that none of the photographs was of the man or men he saw at the crime. Shown pictures of Sacco and Vanzetti the witness Gould was emphatic in saying neither man was seen by him at the shooting.

Judge Thayer denied the motion for a new trial based on the Gould affidavits. The judge said that not only was Gould's evidence merely cumulative of what had been told by other witnesses on the stand during the trial but that the probabilities were against Gould's accuracy in memory of faces 18 months after Gould's encounter with the bandits.

Madeiros Affidavits.—Far more striking than the Gould affidavit was a series of affidavits procured after an original one sworn to by Celestino F. Madeiros. On November 18, 1925, Madeiros, himself confined in the Charlestown jail on a murder charge, smuggled to Sacco's cell this message. "I hear by confess to being in the South Braintree shoe company crime, and Sacco and Vanzetti was not in said crime." Madeiros, several times before he succeeded, had tried to get this message to Sacco.

The defense lawyers—at this time William Goodrich Thompson, a leader of the Massachusetts bar, and an associate, Herbert B. Ehrmann, a lawyer noted for his investigation of the criminal court of Cleveland, questioned Madeiros. His story sent Ehrmann post haste to Providence, Rhode Island, to check the leads given by Madeiros. At first the defense attorneys were skeptical; for Madeiros was subject to epilepsy, came of parents both subject to the same ailment, and although still a young man had had a long career in petty and major crime culminating on November 11, 1924, in the murder of a Mr. Carpenter, Cashier of the Wrentham, Massachusetts Bank which Madeiros was attempting to rob.

Morelli Gang.—Confirmation of the Madeiros story seemed clearer the longer the attorneys investigated its clues. The story implicated the "Morelli gang" of Providence, a "mob" of five Morelli brothers and others who by reason of character, habits, previous career, and disposition were capable of committing the South Braintree murders.

Closer than these predispositions was the fact that the Morellis were desperately in need of funds on April 15, 1920, to fight their own federal indictments for robbing freight cars in the Providence yards, crimes for which they afterwards were convicted. In the Morelli indictments five counts were for stealing shoes from shipments made by Rice and Hutchins and Slater and Morrill of South Braintree. The gang's method was to place a "spotter" at the point of shipment to tip the gang which cars to open. Hence it may be reasoned that the spotter was familiar with the payroll procedure at South Braintree. On April 15 all the gang—save one incarcerated brother—were at liberty.

It is noteworthy that against Sacco and Vanzetti the state never proved a motive for the crime save an inference that they wanted the money for the "Red Cause." Orciani, after deportation, had his baggage sequestered and returned to the United States where it was searched for the missing money; none was found.

In the Morelli gang was one Steve Benkosky whose picture was identified by both government and defense witnesses as the "light-haired, thin, driver of the murder car." Tony Mancini, a member of the Morelli "mob" was likewise identified as one of the gunman on Pearl Street, and as the man seen climbing from the back to the front seat of the get-away-Buick. Joe Morelli, the leader, looked so much like Sacco that witnesses who did not at once say of his picture "That's the man," said the picture was one of Sacco. Joe Morelli owned a Colt .32 and Mancini a Steyr .765, found on him after he was caught in a murder in New York City.

The South Braintree murder party then may have comprised Joe and Mike Morelli, Steve Benkosky, Tony Mancini and Madeiros, thus accounting for the full car, not just two members. Madeiros had the job of manning the rifle through the rear window to hold back any pursuers. These men were American-born, which would account for the fact witnesses who heard the talk of the men leaning on the Rice & Hutchins fence reported it was in plain English and not Italian or broken English; it accounts for the Matfield crossing expression—"What the hell are you holding us up for." The Providence police had suspected the Morelli gang of participation in the Braintree affair before news of the arrest of Sacco and Vanzetti.

Madeiros said that the Buick car was hidden in woods just outside of Braintree whereupon the bandits got into a Hudson car concealed there; after the exchange the party drove by back roads to Providence. An incident first reported by Madeiros as happening on Oak Street West Bridgewater near the hideaway was confirmed by two witnesses.

In his analysis of this story Judge Thayer attacked the credibility of Madeiros. The judge said of him that he "was a crook, liar, rum runner, bouncer for a house of ill fame, smuggler, and man convicted of murder." The judge further said that Madeiros was unable to identify any conspicuous landmark in South Braintree (he was on the rear seat with curtains drawn, half drunk and greatly excited by his first "big job") and could not remember important dates and names. After 55 pages of analysis Judge Thayer said "To set aside a verdict of a jury affirmed by the Supreme Judicial Court of this Commonwealth on such an affidavit would be a mockery upon truth and justice. Motion denied."

To Supreme Judicial Court.—Exceptions to Judge Thayer's rulings in the trial itself and on all these motions for re-trial twice went to the Supreme Judicial Court of Massachusetts.

This body twice found no error in law in the Judge's conduct of proceedings.

On April 9, 1927, Judge Thayer sentenced Sacco and Vanzetti to be electrocuted in the week beginning Sunday the 10th of July, 1927. At this court-session Vanzetti made a temperate but eloquent statement that has become a classic in radical circles. It even moved the District Attorney to tears.

Last Defense Activities.—The defense lawyers, defeated in the courts, turned on May 3, 1927, to Governor Alvan Tufts Fuller for executive clemency. The governor himself held hearings; he also appointed an Advisory Committee consisting of Judge Robert Grant (a retired Probate Judge), President Abbott Lawrence Lowell of Harvard, and President Samuel W. Stratton of Massachusetts Institute of Technology, which committee in turn held hearings. In these hearings, beside all the foregoing there was testimony of the prejudice of Judge Thayer and the close connection between former District Attorney Katzmann and the federal agents in Boston of the U. S. Attorney General's office.

As to the judge's prejudice there were many reports of his conversations before, during, and after the trials in which his vehement hostility to the defendants was expressed in gutter terms. It was shown that the federal agents had been trailing Sacco and Vanzetti in order to get evidence upon which to deport them; the agents, it was asserted, offered to dig the murder evidence against these two men if Katzmann in his cross-examination would endeavor to get the defendants to admit their own extreme radicalism and to implicate their friends. During the trial, the agents were convinced that these two men were too amateurish to have done the job in South Braintree and the agents felt sure the murder and robbery was the work of professionals. This also was the conclusion of Pinkerton detectives concerning the Bridgewater hold-up for which Vanzetti was convicted. But said one of the federal agents, Feri Felix Weiss, "Maybe they (S-V) are not the right men but they are bad actors and would get what they deserved anyway." It was shown that Mr. Wadsworth, a prosecution trial witness giving his occupation as an employe of Iver-Johnson, once had been a federal agent.

About midnight August 3, 1927, Governor Fuller made public his decision to let the sentence of death stand. The full statement of the Advisory Committee dated July 27, 1927, was released for publication in the newspapers of Sunday, August 7, 1927. The Committee had found no reason to urge executive clemency.

On August 6, 1927, defense counsel (Arthur D. Hill, Charles Field, and Richard C. Evarts) moved before the Supreme Court of Norfolk County of Massachusetts for revocation of sentence. They asked for a new trial on the basis of Judge Thayer's prejudice. Chief Justice Hall of the Superior Court ruled that this motion must come before Judge Thayer. Oral argument was heard by Judge Thayer on August 8, 1927. On the same day he denied the part of the motion asking for new trial and the next day he denied the remainder of the motion. On August 6, also, a petition for a writ of error was taken to Judge Sanderson of the Supreme Judicial Court of Suffolk County. The Judge disallowed the petition on August 8. To these decisions the defendants excepted. They presented their Bill of Exceptions to the Supreme Judicial Court of Massachusetts on August 16, 1927. This body over-ruled the exceptions on August 19, 1927.

Thereupon the defense counsel sought the intervention of the United States Supreme Court. This court not being in session during the summer the petitions were to separate justices for a stay of sentence until the court convened and could hear the case. Justices Holmes and Stone were approached on August 20, 1927. Neither justice could see any grounds for federal intervention. Three petitions for habeas corpus to three United States judges—Holmes, Anderson, and Morton—all were denied.

Shortly after midnight on August 22, 1927, the sentence was carried out. As his last words Sacco shouted "Long live anarchy"; Vanzetti thanked his jailer for many favors and asked the spectators to remember that he "forgave some of his enemies."

Aftermath.—On August 23, radicals all over the western world engaged in violent demonstrations; on the day of the funeral, American police broke up the procession. Five years later Mrs. Lincoln Steffens reported that the children's primers of Soviet Russia printed after the letter D this statement: "D is for death, the legal lynching by a dried-up old New England judge of brave class-war prisoners—Sacco and Vanzetti. M is for Mooney still a class-war prisoner in a California prison."

On the other hand W. G. Thompson,[1] a leader of the Massa-

---

[1] Obituary *New York Times,* Sept. 12, 1935.

"William Goodrich Thompson, defense counsel in the Sacco-Vanzetti case in 1927 and senior partner of the law firm of Thompson, Spring, & Mears, died today at his home, 545 Hammond Street, Chestnut Hill. He was in his 71st year.

A Vice-President of the Boston Bar Association and for many years chairman of its grievance committee, Mr. Thompson was one of the most widely known lawyers in the State. He was graduated from Harvard Law School in 1891. He began his Boston practice 44 years ago.

Mr. Thompson, who took over the defense in the Sacco-Vanzetti case three years after the two radicals had been convicted in 1921 of the murder of a paymaster and a guard at South Braintree, Mass., won the admiration of his colleagues at the bar for his courageous and tenacious conduct of the *cause celebre.*

Professor John Dewey, who was one of the most fervent of the many who claimed that Sacco and Vanzetti were innocent, paid the following tribute to the chief defense lawyer of the two doomed men:

"Mr. Thompson was convinced of their innocence. He was conservative in his social and political views. At great sacrifice of time and of social and professional standing, he made a gallant fight for the accused out of jealous zeal for the repute of his own State for even-handed justice . . . ."

A man of considerable social standing and a prominent lawyer who had little experience in criminal cases, Mr. Thompson was much criticized by the so-called "upper ten" in the fashionable Chestnut Hill section when he took up the defense of the two anarchists after Fred H. Moore, the California lawyer, had resigned.

His fees were small compared with those of his predecessor but his zeal was never-wavering, although he was a nervous wreck when the case ended in August 1927. Motion after motion was denied by Judge Webster Thayer and by the judges of the Supreme Court of Massachusetts but Mr. Thompson returned to the attack against odds that eventually proved insurmountable.

Personal abuse and misrepresentation of motives were heaped upon Mr. Thompson at various times, but he refused steadfastly to abandon his clients.

In 1926 he presented 61 affidavits purporting to show the innocence of Sacco and Vanzetti, as well as the confession of Celestine Madeiros, convicted murderer, but to no avail. Mr. Thompson charged tyranny and gross unfairness, and the case dragged on into 1927, when he made his last great appeal for a new trial before the full bench of the Supreme Court of Massachusetts. The motion was denied on April 5. Judge Thayer sentenced

chusetts bar published in New England's principal literary periodical, *the Atlantic Monthly,* in its issue of February 1928 the last statement of Vanzetti given by him to Mr. Thompson a few hours before the execution.   In Massachusetts and New England there were and are a great many citizens who, although they are far from radicals of the anarchist or any other variety, deeply grieve at what to them was the serious miscarriage of justice in the Sacco-Vanzetti case.

The question endlessly is debated, "Were Sacco and Vanzetti guilty?"

Sacco and Vanzetti to death on April 9, and on August 23, 1927, they were executed.

William Goodrich Thompson was born at Peacham, Vermont, on November 16, 1864, the son of Charles Oliver and Maria Goodrich Thompson.   He was graduated from Harvard College in 1888 and from Harvard Law School in 1891.

From 1893 to 1895 he was Assistant United States Attorney for the District of Massachusetts, and then returned to private practice in Boston. Since 1925 he had been a member of the firm of Thompson, Spring & Mears.

Mr. Thompson had lectured on brief-making, practice and preparation of cases at Harvard Law School since 1912, with few intervals.   He was second Vice-president of the Bar Association of the City of Boston and 1930 his name was mentioned as Republican candidate for the United States Senate.

He was a member of Phi Beta Kappa and of Union Club, Boston, as well as of Harvard Club in Boston and New York.   Mr. Thompson contributed to the *Harvard Law Review.*   In 1896 he married Mary Hinckley Huntington of New York."

CHAPTER 15

SOUTHERN FARM, MINE AND LUMBER
WORKERS

Introduction.—If American Capital had been fully awake to its own advantage, it would not have wasted its resources in imperialism after 1896 until it had exploited the empire within its national boundaries. Sixteen southern states, with an area about twice the combined areas of the United Kingdom, France, and Germany, and with a population of 18 million people, the most truly native of all Americans, were ready for a quickening by Capital. Few empires ever had greater natural resources; farm lands, forests, minerals, water-power, some in record quantities or qualities awaited development. The potential greatness was there; the actual accomplishment in 1896 was meager.

Southern agriculture, with cotton still King, was as a Dean of a southern university has said, "a set of inherited motions." The forest and mineral wealth had been only tapped. As for manufacturing, cotton mills had just begun to prove the latent productivity of the millions of southern whites. Railway transportation partly had been linked into systems but the process was incomplete. The southern people as a whole either dwelt in the myth of a by-gone Golden Age, or were provincially conservative, sensitive to criticism, and woefully poor. The South in 1896 was an economic frontier.

By 1929, the South was startlingly altered. In agriculture the South kept its world leadership in cotton culture, but had added extensive vegetable, berry, and fruit crops, and had made a start toward hog, beef, and dairy production. The South had topped the nation in the manufacture of cotton textiles and was active in the associate fields of knitting and rayon. Nevertheless, more wage earners were engaged in southern enterprises other than textile manufacture. Aside from the manufacture

412

of tobacco—the other traditional product of the South—there arose a great furniture industry as well as other wood-working enterprises based, of course, on the South's great lumber activities. In the "heavy trades" the South had become notable for its iron and steel, shipbuilding, coal, copper, and phosphate mining, for all of which it had rich resources. Petroleum and natural gas were other natural products whose exploitation was advantageous. Besides these the South was a considerable manufacturer of clothing, straw hats, shoes, paper, glass, pottery, sugar, cotton-seed by-products and canning.

As for land transportation there were some 15,000 miles of railway track laid in the South during the '80's more than doubling existing trackage. In the '90's over 6,000 miles were added, while in the decade after 1900 there were 12,000 miles of track laid. A map of the 48 railways of Georgia in 1929 showed almost as dense and complex a network of railways as a similar map of the 59 railways of Illinois, the state that held the record for railway net.

In short, the South by 1929 had considerably diversified its agriculture, set up basic manufacturing industries, and unified its transportation.

To change a backward agricultural empire into a modernized society was profitable to those who promoted the revolution; to the white and black people whose labor accomplished the transformation there was an accompaniment of both comfort and pain. The comfort came from greater cash income, improved housing, better schools, rain-proof roads, and all the social advantages of village life in place of the loneliness of an isolated small farm. The pain was caused by exploitation; despite richness of resources it was cheap labor that gave the South competitive superiority.

The exploitation was rooted in the fact that the South had two superabundant labor supplies, one white, the other black. The numbers of either were sufficient to depress labor standards and, by playing upon racial prejudice, employers kept both groups under subjection. Racial prejudices, tradition, and mutual scabbing made it difficult to unionize separately either race of workers and almost impossible to join them together in one union.   Wage earners were far more race conscious than class conscious.   Both races were unprepared by their former modes of living to assert the rights of labor against the power of capital.   A slave was a kept person with no experience in work-contracts nor in self-protection.   A "poor white" was a self-sufficing farmer who knew nothing of wage-work, nor little of cooperative undertakings for mutual benefit, and had only the slightest acquaintance with the use of money.   Both races were accustomed to domination by a small class of whites in positions of authority.   In the South the industrial revolution was thrust into a feudal society; therefore the industrial work force was, without effective protest, painfully exploited by industrial lords and landlords.

The impact of the changes is best understood by separate descriptions for the leading industries.

Southern Agriculture

Agriculture by all measurements—capital invested, numbers of people employed, value of output—continued after 1896 to be the greatest single industry in the South with cotton, of course, the greatest single crop.   Originally imposed by necessity after the Civil War, the share-cropper system persisted as the characteristic method of southern cotton farming.   The share-cropper furnished nothing but labor; he was staked by the landlord or some one else to a supply of seed, tools, fertilizer, and a house.   He was paid by a share in the crop.

In favor of share-cropping it could be said that it gave men, without capital, access to the best soil, a feature especially beneficial to the "poor whites" formerly exiled to the least productive land.   When honest landlords happened to coincide with favorable weather and market prices, the croppers had a chance to accumulate enough capital to become cash tenants or even independent farmers.   In the years immediately after 1896, the Negroes more often than the "poor whites" improved their status; and during the World War, numerous members of both races either got out of debt or became owners.

Share-Croppers Are White.—Between 1920 and 1925 there was a decline of about 120,000 in the number of southern

Negro farmers and a decrease of 80,000 in the colored farm
tenant class.   The whites increased by 90,000.   Of the 2½
million tenant farmers in 1925 only one-fourth were Negroes;
of those in the South (1½ million) a third were share-croppers
and half of these were white.   The share-cropper class rapidly
was bleaching.

Exploitation of Share-Croppers.—Of course thousands of
share-croppers of both races never rose out of peonage.   They
were always in debt and that condition by local law or gentlemen's agreement—landlords would not rent to a person until
a debt-release was displayed—kept families attached to the soil.
Because the croppers usually were illiterate all accounts were
kept by the landlords, storekeepers, or other stakers; these were
known to refuse to give any written accounting to the croppers.
The credit sales to croppers also were all too often at exorbitant prices.   The lenders sold the mortgaged crop and pocketed
half the proceeds.   Most share-croppers owned literally nothing
except the ragged clothes they stood in and a few pots, pans, or
blankets.

Share-Croppers' Miseries.—The shelters rented to share-
croppers for about $50 a year were shacks, without paint, plas-
ter, window glass, or cellars.   Two-thirds had no privy or any
other convenience.   Water came from dug wells, and there
was no sink or pump.   For food, the mainstays were corn
meal, molasses, and the cheapest cuts of hog-meat with a rare
variant of wild greens and wild berries.   The croppers' staples
were said to be the 3 M's—meat, meal, and molasses.   Pellagra,
malaria, and rickets were commonplace.   To this life the chief
releases were found in fornication, feuds, and religious fanati-
cism.   The whites had the added satisfaction of stressing racial
superiority over the Negroes.   Of the million and a half 100%
Americans of both colors who belonged to the tenant class, the
half-million plus share-croppers were the most miserable of
American workers.

Southern people of the higher economic ranks called the
share-croppers "shiftless," "listless," "no-account," and implied
that the croppers' plight was innate.   To this exculpating

charge the observation might be submitted that maybe a barren existence begot a barbarous people.

Tenants.—Tenants who paid a cash rent possessed a modicum of property, usually one to three mules, a few farm implements, and some personal belongings. They farmed more acres than share-croppers and by getting a larger crop lived on a more elevated plane. Their relation to the croppers strongly resembled that of the manorial villeins to the cotters. The quarter-million cash tenants both white and Negro, at worst skirted the edge of debt and descent into the cropper class; at best they might aspire to ownership.

Effects of Cotton Prices.—For croppers and tenants alike, if landlords were honest the market price of cotton was the determinant of the fullness of life. From 1890 when cotton at the plantation averaged for the year was 11 cents a pound, the price steadily dropped until 1899 when it averaged 6 cents. Prices turned in 1900 but not appreciably until 1905 when 10.9 cents was reached; thereafter until 1913 prices swung between averages of 9 cents and 14 cents. During these years the absolute minimum of existence even for share-cropper standards required 5-cent cotton at which price the ordinary share-cropper family had to live on the equivalent of $135 a year.

In 1915 cotton began its war climb, reaching 35 cents in 1919 and 40 cents the next year. Cost of living also advanced so that existence required 12- to 16-cent cotton. The actual margin above these figures was translated into freedom from debt, "second-hand" cars—$10 variety, enlarged wardrobes, more varied diet, and visiting among kinsfolk.

After 1920, cotton prices fell back to about 22 cents, and the standard of living likewise was shorn of "extras"; because it was the boll weevil and bad weather that kept the price above the pre-war level. Even at a high price the short crops meant a relapse to subsistence living. Some share-croppers had a gross income of only $76.80 per year and a high gross income was $250 a year. Nearly two-thirds (60% in 10 states) of all persons engaged in cotton farming had gross incomes of less than $500 per year. This condition continued until the end of

and beyond the period covered by this book (1929).   The lowest prices in each year after 1890 ran from 3 cents to 30 cents
below the average with consequent misery to those who sold on
the days such prices were touched.

Corporate Farming.—Meanwhile, large-scale production by
absentee corporate ownership had invaded cotton production.
Cut-over timber lands as in Tennessee, rich bottom lands as in
Alabama or Arkansas, and "delta" lands in Mississippi were
acquired in tracts of thousands of acres.   The façade of the old
plantation system was restored, but without the beneficent presence of the "master."   Corporate agriculture not only in the
South, but in Ohio onion fields, Utah sugar beets, and California fruits and vegetables frequently rivaled the worst sweatshops in inhumane exploitation of workers.   Southern share-
croppers, tenants, and managers who drifted to some of the
corporate plantations hit the lowest level of degradation.

The "Plantation" Disappears.—Each of the cotton states
had a few plantations on which the traditional ways of work and
living were maintained.   A resident owner in his pillared, high-
ceilinged mansion gave careful attention to the human and crop
details of his domain.   Out of sight from the "big house" were
clusters of neat cabins, the homes of the plantation's workers.
An air of comfort and slow-moving accomplishment pervaded
the place.   Probably some number less than 1,000 would account
for all such plantations in 1929, and of these a goodly proportion
were bolstered by income derived from some source other than
the land.

The larger number that had existed in 1896 mostly had been
sold piecemeal in small parcels to private owners, or in single
tracts to corporations.   The younger people of the planters'
families forsook the land for the professions or, more rarely,
entered business; the daughters married into these groups because the supply of eligible young planters was limited.   The
former field workers in less than 10% of the cases became small-
scale owners; a few more became cash tenants, while the rest
merged with the share-cropper class.   As a system, the plantation of the historic type disappeared between 1896 and 1929;

the very large plantation even under slavery never had been as prevalent as tradition implied.

Needs for Labor.—Regardless of size or ownership, all cotton farms had two peak periods in need for labor. One was after the plants had grown a few inches above the ground. At that time the plants had to be thinned in the rows by hoeing, and for 8 to 10 weeks afterwards in May-June the spaces between rows from 1 to 3 times had to be freed from weeds with the help of 1, 2 or 4 mule plows. For this work the families on the farm usually had enough members and mules to do the job.

The other peak, September-November, was at the picking season prolonged throughout the late summer and fall because no one plant ripened all its bolls at one time; flowers and ripe bolls were visible on the same plant for weeks. Picking gave work to all the members of farm families from tots at the walking age to grandsires and granddams. When every one had turned out for the picking and yet more laborers were needed the supply came from the villages and towns.

The pay ranged from 50 cents to $1.50 per hundredweight of seed cotton picked. Most persons picked from 100 to 200 pounds per day although records of 1,000 pounds per day were known. The length of the work day was limited only by the ability of the scale-man to read its dial. Upon an hourly basis for this hot, painstaking, job the rate might be as low as $3\frac{1}{2}$ cents or as high as 15 cents. The day that picking was started was one of jubilation, for it marked the realization of a whole year's labor; likewise the last picking day was welcomed as the end of a long, laborious, poorly rewarded task.

Machinery.—After the World War the situation in some places was altered. The plantations owned and operated by corporations and those at that time being extended in the high plains of western Texas turned to machinery for the cultivation peak. Machine cultivators extending over 3 or more rows at once and drawn by tractors, reduced work of weeks to hours. Likewise, at the picking season in western Texas, although transient Mexican labor was used in most years, a mechanical substitute was employed in those years when prices were lowest.

The device was a V-shaped sled drawn open-ended down the rows snapping off the bolls as it went.   Cotton thus gathered fetched a lower price than that hand-picked.   Therefore the perennial search for a machine-picker was quickened and several models were in experiment before 1929.

In Georgia, Alabama, Mississippi, and Louisiana the post-war cotton growers found a less ready response to the call for pickers among town-dwellers.   The North had lured away thousands of Negroes to replace immigrants.   New jobs in southern towns and cities made pickers' wages and work conditions seem unattractive and cotton growers could not raise pickers' wages very much over $1 per hundredweight.   The sight of unpicked crops spoiled by rain aroused considerable interest in machine-pickers, but no satisfactory machine appeared before 1929.   [The Rust Brothers machine was demonstrated in 1936.]

Cotton Production Made Many Jobs

Recognition should be given to the fact that the cotton crops gave jobs to thousands of people who had no direct connection with cotton fields.

First were the bankers and storekeepers who financed the landlords and tenants.   Next was the cotton gin crew.   When and where plantations were large they often had their own gins; but most seed-cotton (1896-1929) passed through one of the 19,000 public gins.   These were cheaply constructed buildings usually of wood into which the cotton was air-sucked from farmers' wagons and through which it passed either by gravity or air currents.   The machines separated lint from seed, the former going to a baler, the latter either to the farmer's wagon or a storage bin; in either case the farmer got the value of the seed. Gin crews generally were Negroes.

The loosely compressed bale was carried by rail or water to another compresser.   The transportation and handling furnished more jobs to and from the compresser.   Besides reducing the size and increasing the density of the bale so that 75 bales could go into a railway car instead of the 35 gin-bales, the compresser workers fully covered the bales and repaired holes made by samplers.   At ports the bales sometimes were re-compressed into still smaller size and greater density.   The port cotton handlers were Negro and immigrant longshoremen who, in the South, were called stevedores.

Marketing.—The market mechanism for moving the crop consisted of local spot buyers, agents, factors, and brokers whose functions were to get the cotton started to export markets, consuming markets, spot markets, or warehouses at each of which were other agents, etc.   Cotton in a warehouse might give rise to warehouse receipts which being negotiable could be used as money—which brought bankers again into the picture although behind the scenes they had financed each of the preceding movements.   The top market was the future-market where speculative buying and selling set cotton prices.   All together the marketing supplied thousands of jobs, many of them unnecessary.

Cotton-Seed Oil.—The cotton seed, likewise, was moved from the gins to oil mills, the journey and each of its terminals giving rise to jobs.   At the seed oil mill Negro workmen operated machines that first removed the fuzz from the seeds.   This short fiber, trade-named "linters," was the raw material for more than two-score products; as absorbent cotton dentists put it in tooth cavities or as nitro-cellulose it could blow off a head; as an adulterant it could take the itch out of wool drawers; as a pyroxylin it gave lustre to new automobiles; as a plastic it served as a "new skin," celluloid receptacle for old skin or preserved the appearance of the whole skin on a photographic film; it could be stepped on in carpets; slept on in mattresses; or wept on in writing paper.   In all these and other transformations there were jobs.

When the "linters" had been removed, the hull of the seed was cracked off to become part of a fertilizer.   The kernel was pressed for oil which, like linters, had scores of uses.   The final "cake" became one of the most nutritious cattle foods.   And in this short paragraph thousands of jobs were hidden.

No one has traced all the employment to which our annual cotton crop gave rise but the total must have been amazing.   It probably was true also that most of the jobs based on the cotton

crop paid greater annual incomes than were received by the
share-cropper whose work started all the others.   Moreover
all these job holders resisted diversification of southern crops:
although dependence upon a one-crop system was uneconomic.

Tobacco Farming

What has been said of cotton culture has considerable application to tobacco growers, especially those who raised cigarette
tobaccos.   Tobacco, to be sure, was not and never had been
produced on the extensive scale associated with cotton; at all
times the largest tobacco "plantation" would have made a small
cotton plantation.   The reason was two-fold: a single tobacco
plant was much more valuable than a single cotton plant; and
secondly, tobacco culture required much more constant and
meticulous care than cotton.   Moreover, the tobacco plant exhausted soil fertility far more rapidly than cotton; one year's
American crop removed 65½ million pounds of phosphorus,
nitrogen, and potassium from the soil.   These characteristics
made tobacco farming an intensive variety of agriculture; much
labor on a small area resulted in large crop values averaging
about five times as much per acre as cotton.   Therefore tobacco
farmers were more often small-scale owners rather than renters
or croppers.

Warehouse System.—Tobacco was sold by farmers at public auction warehouses, a system that was supposed to benefit
the producer by the competition of buyers.   For some varieties
of tobacco this result was accomplished.   Not so for the growers of cigarette tobaccos after 1900.   The manufacture of cigarettes was by a few large-scale companies once combined in
one "trust" and later operating much in harmony.   When buyers for these corporations appeared in tobacco warehouses there
was usually a remarkable uniformity in their bids on a particular farmer's lot of tobacco.   Actually a large number of producers competed for the orders of a half-dozen purchasers; the
warehouses were not a sellers' but a buyers' market.

Subsistence Living for Tobacco Farmers.—Taking one
year with another the prices of cigarette tobaccos at auction

warehouses were just high enough to keep growers from turning to alternative crops.   The price was one that allowed subsistence at southern standards.   Once in a while a bad season brought high prices, a boon to those few fortunate in having undamaged crops.   During the World War the unusually high prices (of about 2½ times the 1913 prices) produced a temporary prosperity; only to be shattered in 1920.

Since the tobacco industry was highly concentrated at the point of manufacture whereas the production of the leaf lagged within the sphere of free competition, the southern growers were forced down to a subsistence level.   The southern tobacco grower's family was only slightly less miserable than that of a cotton tenant farmer.

Truck Crops

A type of farming new to the South became important after 1900 when fast railroad service first connected Florida with New York and New England.   The whole of the southern Coastal Plain was a potential area for the production of vegetables, berries, and fruits.

Since the two thousand miles of coastline extended north and south there was a marked difference in the advent of spring. Hence, beginning with Florida in January there was a succession of crop seasons northward to New Jersey and Cape Cod. Refrigerator cars on express schedules rushed oranges, peaches, strawberries, cabbages, lettuce, and other products to markets at Baltimore, Philadelphia, New York, and Boston.

A similar development took place in the lower Mississippi Valley to furnish the markets in the cities around the Great Lakes and westward to St. Paul, Minneapolis, St. Louis, and Kansas City.   Each southern area in normal weather had its turn at the northern consumers' top prices.   If the weather did not behave, two areas were likely to overlap causing glut and prices ruinous to producers.

As is usual with truck crops the southern farms generally were small scale; there were great yields if intensive labor was applied to small areas.   As a rule the routine planting and cultivating were done by the owner with the aid of his family. Although these owners were both whites and Negroes, the whites predominated.

Casual Harvest Labor.—On all farms of the truck-fruit variety the peak season for work was the harvest.   For products such as lettuce, cabbage, fruits, and many vegetables, judgment in picking was necessary and this meant human labor.   The demand for labor was temporarily acute in one spot and then moved northward with the weeks.   The solution of this labor problem was the same in the South as elsewhere—dependence on migratory casual workers supplemented by local hired hands drawn temporarily from other pursuits.

The southern migratory workers differed from western casual labor in that the southern groups were composed largely of family units.   While a few southern "poor whites" were to be found among the migrants, it was exceptional because "poor whites" as a rule did not like to wander far from kith and hearths.   Negroes joined the procession for part of the route but not often for the entire journey.   That is, Negroes moved across their own and the next state; it was customary to find Virginia and Maryland Negroes in the summer fields of New Jersey, but Florida and Georgia Negroes seldom ventured north of the Carolinas and the latter states' blackfolk did not get much beyond Norfolk.   Similarly in the Mississippi Valley.   The people who made the whole trek were foreign-born whites, mostly Italians.

Rush Job.—Everywhere the job was rushed.   The peach that was tardy in leaving Georgia was competitive with one starting from Delaware.   Therefore at each crop place, workers were in the fields from faint dawn to deep dusk; in emergencies they worked into the night in the glare of automobile headlights. Living quarters were for temporary use, and sanitation usually was primitive.

These conditions were not unbearable if they had to be endured only two weeks.   The local temporary help sometimes felt exhilaration in their fatigue—the glow of a hard, worthy task accomplished and the pocketing of a few extra dollars. With those who followed the crops continuously, the rush and long hours were severe strains.

The matter was made worse by reason that the most numerous perpetual migrants were children. Prolonged back-breaking toil under a hot sun, no real home life, improper diet, and complete absence of schooling balked all normal childish activities. These children were headed toward perpetual pauperism and premature old age—or crime. Public officials did not reach them because the children did not have residence long enough anywhere to arouse officialdom.

Canneries.—After truck farming was established, surplus crops began to cause farm losses. The potential capacity of the Atlantic lands alone far surpassed any possible effective demand. To offset these crop gluts, as well as to reach other markets, canneries dotted the coastal region, with a high concentration around Chesapeake Bay. Most of the canneries were small, planned for one product and operated solely during harvest.

The same kind—often the same persons—worked in field and cannery. The pace in the canneries was the limit of endurance and the hours of work had the same limit. Women and children who predominated in the work-force were unprotected by state laws because cannery owners most vehemently protested any application to their business of protective legislation. The plea that the canneries not only must run with the harvest period but were limited to it was valid; the error lay in the fact that the employes of the one cannery moved to another, thus always working at top pressure.

Some canneries expanded to care for different crops; some canned chicken, oysters, and other non-field products; some made soup or other prepared food. These were regular manufacturing businesses with peak seasons well leveled. White and Negro women made up most of the personnel. Wage rates were low and decreased southward because the jobs were simple and done by women; the few skilled jobs were held by men.

Generalizations Concerning Southern Agriculture

The picture of southern agricultural labor has been painted in sombre colors; in fact the majority of southern farm families had drab lives. This condition for so many millions was a serious matter even when its effects were viewed solely from the economic and not the human aspect. The South could not consume its own products, and its purchasing power was so low that it could not command much of the production of other regions. In Great Britain it used to be said that 'British cotton factories would thrive if an inch could be added to the Chinese shirt tails." If southern farm labor could have had an added dollar a week in spending power there would have been a marked improvement in health, housing, and clothing; if the addition could have been a dollar a day the South could have stepped up with the rest of the country and the nation as a whole could have operated at a higher economic level.

To have produced this change it would have been necessary to encourage the industrialization well begun in the South and to have increased the diversification of the occupations of its people. This would not have meant a mere exchange of location for certain industries; there would have been national gain first from the production of goods at the most economical point, and second, by the increase in southern purchasing power the South could have bought more of its own and the North's products. The cure for low wages was more jobs.

That the industrialization obtained by the South was mostly by reason of its low wages does not vitiate the above argument; the industrialization before 1929 did not go far enough to absorb the labor supply.

Promising Changes.—Upon farming the mill villages did produce one desirable diversification; the farmers nearby found in milk, butter, eggs, and green crops a few commodities that villagers could buy.

Much more promising were the tentative experiments of a few southern farmers toward an animal culture. Before the Revolutionary War much of the Piedmont section was operated as a cattle range with cowboys, "round ups," branding, and other features associated with the wild West; after Whitney's gin the Piedmont forsook cattle for cotton. Before 1929 a few bold venturers went back to the original activity. The climate of most of the South was better adapted to cattle farming than were the places where most of the nation's beef was on the hoof Blizzards, sand-storms, and drought were not hazards in the South, and the winters were so mild that expensive barns were not needed. With more than 40 inches of rainfall, grass, hay, and legumes easily were produced; and corn, the most essential animal food, was luxuriant.

Although hog products were the only meat used by millions of southern workers, the region had little specialized hog-raising; instead its considerable hog production was usually a side line in connection with other farming. Nevertheless, a few farmers did realize that the South was as logical a place for a corn-hog economy as it was for a beef-animal culture. These farmers were the ones freed from tradition, and guided by enlightened self-interest; their experiments were guides to the future in southern agriculture. That a farm organization based on animal production had potentiality for high-grade rural citizenship had been proved in Iowa.

Other Extractive Industries

Cotton and tobacco farming existed long before railways were known; the other extractive industries of the South were dormant until railroads stimulated them into activity.

Railroad Influence.—The southern railroad construction and merger into east-west north-south systems that was completed shortly after 1900 was of inestimable benefit to the South because by the railway net a set of six geographic provinces were bound together. The Coastal Plain and Piedmont always had been intimately related although generally hostile to each other, but the Blue Ridge had barred easy access from the east to the Great Valley, and this latter natural north-south highway was walled on the west by the face of the Alleghenies. Except for the easy path around the southern edge of the Alleghenies through Alabama and Louisiana, the south Atlantic coast states

were barricaded from the Mississippi Valley by the Blue Ridge
and Alleghenies.   These two mountain territories themselves
were isolated from all contacts.   The railway net penetrated
and joined all these areas which nature had separated.

Coal Mining.—The first result of the improved railway net
was the opening of the great coal resources of the South.   The
Coastal Plain and eastern Piedmont were barren of coal except
for two small areas west of Richmond—the oldest continuously
worked deposits in the United States—and two equally small
seams in North Carolina.   But the Allegheny region was under-
lain with coal through parts of West Virginia, Kentucky, and
Tennessee to Alabama.   Lower-grade coal in the Gulf Fields
was found in sections of Mississippi, Louisiana, Arkansas, and
Texas.   Hence only two southern states—South Carolina and
Florida—lacked workable coal deposits.

The Allegheny coal field as a whole was not only the largest
in the United States but held also the world record for size.   Its
highest grade coal (highest in heat units) was found in West
Virginia and the adjoining western segment of Virginia.   The
coal of Alabama near Birmingham was likewise of excellent
quality.   In the whole United States only the Cambria and
Clearfield coal areas of Pennsylvania approached the heat value
of the West Virginia-Virginia coals.

Besides the Allegheny and Gulf coals, the South possessed
the southern portion of the western segment of the great Central
Coal Field which stretched from Iowa on the north to Oklahoma, Arkansas, and Texas on the south.   All together there
were as vast deposits of coal in the South as were found in the
whole British Empire.

Of the South's immense coal resource it was the portions in
West Virginia, western Virginia, and Alabama that were most
diligently exploited after the railways made it possible to bring
it out of the highlands and lowlands where it was hidden.   The
Alabama coal was used, to a considerable extent, in local enterprises so that it was primarily the West Virginia and Kentucky
coal that entered the national market.   The railways carried the
West Virginia and Kentucky coal to the Atlantic seaboard at

Newport News and Baltimore at which ports it was transferred
to barges for distribution along the north coast to Boston and
the south coast to Jacksonville.   Rail-borne westward from the
mines, it competed at lake ports or inland places with Pennsylvania and Illinois coal.   From these principal mining areas and
from the lesser ones in Tennessee, Arkansas, and Oklahoma to
say nothing of the small mines in the Carolinas and Georgia,
there was hardly a southern community in which bituminous
coal was not a cheap commodity both for industrial and domestic use.

Coal Miners.—The opening and expansion of the coal industry provided employment in and near the mines for thousands of white and black citizens of the South.   The relative
proportions of the two races varied between regions and mines,
the northern Appalachian areas tending toward an excess of
whites (20% blacks) while in Alabama the reverse was true
(over 50% blacks).

In West Virginia there was an inclusion of foreign-born
workers about as numerous as the Negroes and drawn mostly
from eastern and central Europe.   The mixture of races and
nationalities was a deliberate policy on the part of mine operators to prevent cohesion of labor.   The whites were largely of
the mountain type and of all the "poor whites" these had the
most implacable racial prejudices against blacks.   Furthermore,
the whites' feudist traditions divided them from each other.
To the whites any outlander was an object of suspicion so that
foreign-born, alien-speaking persons were especially to be
avoided.

The blacks were scattered among all mine areas but were
most concentrated in the southern counties of West Virginia
and in Alabama; they were bound by the southern tradition of
racial segregation and so far as possible avoided the whites.
Whenever the Negroes came in contact with the foreign whites,
the Negroes were suspicious of the alien's lack of racial prejudice, and as 100% Americans the Negroes felt contempt for
the immigrants.   Allegiance to the boss inherited from slavery

attached the Negroes to the operators notwithstanding the exploitation practiced by operators.

Hard to Unionize.—The southern coal fields, thus, were the worst possible areas for labor union sentiment and organization. Grievances were not lacking because wage rates were below those in Pennsylvania, Ohio, and Illinois, periods between pay days were unusually long, pay was often in scrip or other non-negotiable tokens, and the company store and house were unalloyed evils.

Under the banner of the Knights of Labor, the southern miners had made their first united efforts, but this had been thwarted by racial animosity. Later, after 1900, organizers of the United Mine Workers' Union strove valiantly to bring together all the labor groups so as to exert united resistance to operator oppressions. The official attitude of the union was racial tolerance; but this was a rule that many white miners below the Mason-Dixon line found hard to follow. They preferred non-unionism to recognition of Negroes as equals. Hence, every early drive toward unionization despite some temporary successes was thrust aside.

Negroes Allied With Bosses.—A few bitter experiences in the union convinced Negroes that the boss, not their fellow white-worker, was their best friend, and the operators took advantage of the feeling to break white organizations by Negro scabs or temporarily increasing the proportion of Negro miners and mine laborers.

Beginning in the '80's, southern Negro miners were carried north to mines in Pennsylvania and Ohio and even as far as Kansas to break strikes or relieve labor shortage. Because the Negroes frustrated the efforts of the whites south and north, the whites felt that their hostile opinion of blacks was justified. In southern West Virginia the Negro miners were attached to the boss by the Negroes' own leaders in churches and politics. Most of the black leaders really believed that racial economic deliverance and eventual social recognition would come by a close alliance with capitalists; the leaders who wavered from this belief were won to it by employer gifts and other aids to

Negro churches, schools, or fraternities and by white capitalistic support for Negro politicians. In Alabama, any union that proposed to gather in one body both white and black miners was bitterly denounced not only by whites in pulpits, offices, and businesses but by white mechanics.

For all these reasons the United Mine Workers' Union had a heavy task in penetration of the South. The key battles were in West Virginia, Kentucky, and Alabama. To get these southern struggles into proper perspective it is necessary to examine the national position of the soft coal industry.

The National Situation in Respect to Soft Coal.—In the years immediately after 1896, coal mining kept pace with industrial expansion for which coal was the chief source of mechanical power. The leading producers of the coal were mines from western Pennsylvania to Illinois called the Central Competitive Field. The union was able to keep a strong organization in this area for the reason that most of the operations were small scale, fiercely competitive, and with labor charges their principal (60% to 65%) cost. It was good strategy to recognize the union whereby labor costs could be kept uniform and thus removed as a factor in competition. Hence, the organization of operators signed biennial trade agreements with the United Mine Workers from 1900 to 1924 but not without strikes in 1906, 1908, 1910, 1912, 1919, and 1922.

Unfortunately for the cause of industrial peace, bituminous coal was present in 32 of our states and in all of them capable of being mined on a small scale. The Central Competitive Field had no monopoly on supply. Only as long as it was the chief production area could the trade agreements there guide labor conditions in other mining areas.

Captive Mines.—Between 1905 and 1914 several of the largest northern manufacturing corporations sought coal mines of their own. Since the best steam coals were to be found in West Virginia, a corporation with sufficient capital to enable it to select the best, naturally entered West Virginia with a subsidiary coal mining company. In the coal trade these were called "captive mines." For mid-West manufacturing corporations, Kentucky and Tennessee coal areas were the goal. With these examples of corporate interest in southern coal, other local capitalists became operators; indeed some Central Field operators (e.g., Pittsburgh Consolidation Coal Company) entered the new areas.

In 1907 the United States Steel Corporation became the dominant steel producer in Alabama and, as the greatest single user of local coal, became also the leading Alabama coal operator. The Corporation extended its labor policies to the new Alabama enterprises, and, as elsewhere, induced other Alabama businesses to adopt its own anti-union policies.

The United Mine Workers' Union was not blind to the trends nor unaware of the danger to unionism. The union made no headway in Alabama; it did get a foothold in northern West Virginia and toe-grip in Kentucky and Arkansas.

War Stimulus.—The World War quickened the shifts in the coal industry by stimulating every coal-bearing region to unprecedented mining. The number of operators kept increasing until it reached a peak at 9,000 (1923); likewise, mine capacity mounted to 970 million tons. To do the work in this gigantic industry there were needed 700,000 men. The largest increase in mines and men was in the South; for during the war-years and immediately afterwards the center of bulk production slid southward. The result was national over-capacity; even in the war period in the record year for coal consumption only 579 million tons were used.

Chaos.—From 1919 until the end of our period the coal industry was in chaos. Overcapacity alone was not responsible. Among other causes were inequitable freight rates that favored southern over mid-western coal fields. Technological improvements in mining so increased output per man that 200,000 men were thrown out of the industry; from 1923 to 1929 this increase per man was 30%, and over the longer period from 1900 to 1929 it was 60%. At the same time, coal users were changing their boiler equipment and prime movers so that a given amount of coal did far more work; once it took 4 pounds of coal to deliver 1 horsepower-hour of energy but after 1919 the best devices used only a part of an ounce.   In 1920 locomotives consumed 172 pounds of coal per 1,000 gross ton miles; in 1929 from 75 to 121 pounds did the same work.   These changes meant lowered tonnage demand.   Other competing products— hydro-electricity, oil, natural gas—made deep inroads upon coal markets.

Price Cuts.—The operators' method of meeting the conditions of the time was to cut prices, one cut leading to another because nearly all operators tried to meet each other's prices. Some captive mines, that had coal in excess of the needs of their parent-companies, sold the excess for considerably less than $1 a ton.   The price wars inevitably led to wage-cuts in non-union mines and attempts to cancel agreements in union mines.

United Mine Workers' Strategy.—The United Mine Workers' strategy was to impose a high wage rate which (it was hoped) would eliminate the excess mine capacity by removal of the marginal high-cost mines.   The strike of 1919 was over a demand for a 60% wage raise; the miners got a two-year 27% increase by arbitration decision of President Wilson's Bituminous Coal Commission.   Another strike in 1922 (April 1-August 30) prevented the union operators from cutting the old rate.   This strike, too, led to the appointment of the United States Coal Commission which on January 4, 1923, urged that the coal industry continue under the old rates for another year. So from April 1, 1923, to April 1, 1924, the wage was $7.50 for a basic 8-hour day, and $1.08 per ton for piece workers. The Coal Commission report, issued in the fall of 1923, advocated that the Interstate Commerce Commission, through a specially created Coal Division, collect facts and exercise whatever regulatory powers over the coal industry were necessary to the public interest.   The Commission did not favor nationalization of the coal mines but did approve removal of legal restraints upon private consolidation.   In getting either public or private action, the Commission's voluminous report was a dud.

Jacksonville Agreement.—On April 1, 1924, at a conference in Jacksonville, Fla., the *union* coal operators and the

United Mine Workers agreed to extend the existing union wage scales to April 1, 1927. The "Jacksonville Agreement" was a term so liberally sprinkled all through labor prints that it became famous. In itself the agreement was notable by reason of its proclamation of the success of the United Mine Workers' wage strategy; that is, success in retention of war-won wage rates.

The flaw in the union's theory that the rates in the Central Competitive Field would control mine labor prices was the non-unionism of the southern coal mines. To triumph, the union had to clamp its wage rates on *all* mines competing with each other. If the union failed to do this, its high rates would destroy the operators who signed union agreements. Therefore in West Virginia, Kentucky, and Alabama unionization was imperative; to fail in these localities would wreck the national organization. That was the reason why these states were truthfully battlegrounds after 1920.

Organizing the Southern Miners.—The campaign began in West Virginia in the spring of 1920, when counties Mingo, Logan, and McDowell were invaded by union organizers. In Mingo County the operators promptly locked out their miners and called in the strike-breakers of the Baldwin-Felts "Detective" Agency. On May 19, 1920, Albert C. Felts killed Mayor Testeman of Matewan who was friendly to the union. Immediately the miners massed into a riotous mob and smashed their way to Felts and his men, killing Felts, 7 of his detectives and 3 others. Town Marshal, Sid Hatfield, and 15 strikers were indicted for these murders but were acquitted on March 21, 1921. Hatfield, however, was later murdered.

From the day of Felts' death until December 1920, there were constant, open clashes between the strikers (locked out at first, the miners declared a strike on July 1, 1920) and the operators or their hired guards. Both sides appealed to the federal government, the miners asking President Wilson to intervene, while the operators, through Governor John J. Cornwell, begged for U. S. Army assistance. Neither bid for aid was granted, so the Governor called out the state militia.

Virtual War in West Virginia.—In the spring of 1921, ambush, assault, murder, and riot were preliminary to the summer's organized, armed, battle forces. Tent colonies of the strikers were raided by the militia; and on the other side 2,500 gun-toting miners threatened Logan County. Conditions were so alarming that the U. S. Senate, on June 24, 1921 ordered an investigation, on July 6 named the committee, and July 14 began hearings. President Harding on August 30 ordered the miners to disperse to their homes by September 1 or else he would send federal troops into the state. Most of the strikers had no homes save company houses from which they had been ejected; besides they refused to disband in advance of appearance of regular Army soldiers for fear of personal assaults from company thugs. Thus, 2,000 soldiers were dispatched to the state on September 1, arriving in position on September 5.

Companies Win.—The struggle in West Virginia during the next three years was less overt although in 1922 the local strike merged with the national strike of that year. With the militancy subdued in this three-year period, the coal companies got the upper hand. The political power in the state was subject to the operators; for instance, the sheriffs of Logan County got $32,500 a year from the mine owners. As for the courts, they certainly stroye to protect property. The companies insisted upon the "yellow dog contract" and it was a West Virginia court that first declared these to be lawful documents. The courts granted hundreds of injunctions not only against attempts at interference with the signers of "yellow dog contracts" but against every normal union activity. Unions practically were outlawed.

Second "War" in West Virginia.—On April 1, 1925, the United Mine Workers again became militant in West Virginia by calling an organizing strike. The operators retaliated by lockouts and evictions at critical points or by wholesale injunctions and arrests. About 6,000 miners were locked out in April; 1,200 families evicted in July; 2,000 strikers were arrested in one day; and 5,000 suits were brought against the union: West Virginia was just as non-union in December as it had been in January. In no year before 1929 was the union able to batter down the resistance it met in West Virginia.

Also "Wars" in Other States.—A similar story could be told in regard to Harlan County, Kentucky. In Jefferson County, Ala., the union made less impression than in Mingo, Logan, and McDowell Counties of West Virginia. The second Ku Klux Klan so thoroughly supported southern mine operators against unionists that the U. M. W. expelled any of its members who anywhere joined the KKK. These union failures in the South were typical; the United Mine Workers' Union could not make or hold gains in that region.

Results.—What difference did the absence of a strong union make? At no time, except during the British coal strike of 1926, did the southern operators pay wages equal to the union rate. Some companies paid in scrip, tokens, or other non-negotiable instruments. Check weighmen were conspicuously absent. Mine safety devices were neglected. Deadwork (timbering, etc.) was at miners' expense. The U. S. Coal Commission reported that out of 713 company houses examined in the South, only 23 passed the Commission's moderate standards. The same authority declared that only two houses were furnished with drinkable water and had adequate sewage disposal. The worst housing among miners was to be found among southern gully coal camps. In some instances the company houses had electric lighting supplied by the company power plant usually, however, at exorbitant rates per kilowatt hour. Company stores almost universally overcharged the miners who were forced to patronize them. It is possible that a powerful union might have modified some of these conditions.

The sole advantage of non-union southern workers was a somewhat more regular work year than that of union miners.

Repercussions in Central West.—The failure to capture the South caused the United Mine Workers to lose strength in the Central Competitive Field. Several of the largest operators broke the Jacksonville Agreement or closed their northern mines. By July 1925, the output of the central Pennsylvania district had shifted from 95% union to 70% non-union. The shrinkage in membership and prestige caused general predictions in 1928 that the United Mine Workers' Union shortly would disappear. Weakened, the union was further assailed by internal factionalism causing early in the 1920's the split-off, the Illinois Progressive Miners' Union; and in 1928 the National (Communist) Miners' Union. The Illinois organization, for a time, was set up in two unions each claiming official right to the title and property of the state U. M. W. The national organization, sinking in defeat, grasped at government ownership of coal mines as a rescue measure.

Defeat in the South, therefore, was well nigh fatal to this largest single member of the American Federation of Labor. [After 1932 the union so revived as to become the leading union in the United States.]

Wood Industries

Just as railways made available the South's great resources in coal so, too, they penetrated the enormous forest resources. When by 1900 the timber of the Great Lakes forests followed into oblivion that of New England, New York, and Pennsylvania, the lumbermen turned to the only remaining extensive forests east of the Mississippi, namely those of the South. The South had three great forest areas, one along the Atlantic Coastal Plain, one in the lower Mississippi Valley, and one in the southern Appalachians. Each of these differed from the other two, and all of them introduced novelties in logging methods and arrangements for labor.

Yellow Pine.—In the yellow pine forests of the Coastal Plain the absence of snow prohibited horse-drawn sledloads of logs and the presence of deep sand militated against horse-drawn wagons. On the other hand the generally level topography made easy the building of railroads and since there was no seasonal bar to year-around operation, a logging railroad could be made to pay. As there were few streams fit for log-driving the forest railroad was connected with trunk railroads along whose rights of way log "yards" were constructed.

Logging, therefore, was a normal job carried on the whole year. The labor force was not recruited for a few winter months and then disbanded; the forest camp was not exclusively male. Instead, little villages of shacks blossomed at the end of the railroad; indeed the shacks often were built on flat-cars so that after months or years when cutting was finished in one location the whole town could be rolled to another.

Caste Among Forest Workers.—The workers in the Atlantic forests were 80% Negroes, and the rest included scarcely any foreigners. In the East-Gulf region a few Mexicans were sprinkled through the camps. Within the camps there were several social castes based on income, race, and marital condition. The white bosses and railroad men were the best paid and lived somewhat apart from the main camp. The married Negroes had half a flat-car shack with a partition separating it from another family; or else each Negro family lived in one of a row of one-room shacks set on stilts. Single men lived in dormitory car-shacks shunted on sidings by themselves. Hogs, as camp scavengers, rooted underneath the cars and shacks.

The cleanliness of the "village," the order within it, and the normality of life varied with the lumber companies and the kinds of persons they employed. Some camps were decent and respectable; some were filled with rented convicts in chain gangs and were at times roisterous, at others ominously quiet. All of the camps were so remote from public gaze that anything could happen in them without public knowledge. In the convict camps this sometimes led to outrageous brutalities of which floggings, resulting in deaths, were the least cruel.

Lower Mississippi Forests.—The forests of the lower Mississippi had two divisions, due to topography. Since the valley was a vast delta the center was higher than the ground east or west of the river. On the slopes near the river were the local farms. At the bottom of the slopes were great swamps covered with cypress and hardwoods. East or west of the swamps the ground gradually sloped upward into sandy ridges. There the yellow pine predominated and the lumbering connected with it was akin in every respect to that of the Atlantic Coastal Plain.

The swamps, however, presented a new characteristic. Sleds, horses, and railroads were all alike impossibilities for logging; resort, therefore, was had to canals and boats. The logging crews, with their families, lived on house-boats. Except for this change for the worse the swamp camp life was much the same as that in the Coastal Plain forest.

Hours of Work and Wages.—The hours of work in all the southern lumber camps were ruled by the sun and the amount of humanity possessed by the bosses. The *reported* hours were 65 per week in 1896; 60 in 1906; 66 during the World War; and 60 in 1929. However, in 1929 some southern lumber-workers had a 12-hour day and 7-day week.

Choppers in 1896 got 13 cents an hour as against 19 cents in the North and West; in 1906 the rate was 17 cents as against 29 cents. Since these were average figures, the actual rates by states were more enlightening.

Alabama in 1915 paid 3 cents an hour to choppers; Florida and Georgia 10 cents, Mississippi and North Carolina, 14 cents an hour. Washington paid 31½ cents an hour. In 1928 the Louisiana rate was 31 cents, at a time when Washington paid 74½ cents an hour.

The *highest* wages paid in 1929 to cutters were: Louisiana, 41 cents; Mississippi, 36 cents; North Carolina, 35 cents; West Virginia, 55 cents; California, $1.19; and Washington, $1.28. These figures should be interpreted in the knowledge that the chopper or faller was a *skilled* worker. The unskilled water-boys and "whistle punks" in the West got 35 to 62 cents an hour while in the South their wages were 10 to 30 cents.

Hardwoods.—Lumbering in the southern Appalachians was quite different from that described. It was in the highlands, comprised hardwoods instead of softwoods, and the labor force was 85% native white Americans, the "poor whites."

This hardwood forest was nowhere established in pure stands of one species but mixed oak, chestnut, walnut, cherry, hickory, basswood, and the like, and even some soft woods such as white pine and hemlock.   Most of these hardwoods were used for furniture, vehicles, implements, and posts, ties, or fencing. Some of them, chiefly oak, chestnut, and hemlock, having a bark high in tannin were utilized in the leather industry.

For the most part the hardwoods had been distributed among a large number of owners so that small-scale logging operations were more general than in the other regions.   The methods used were as various as the owners, and call for no special comment.   Moonshine whiskey and hardwood logs were the two chief money crops of the mountain whites.

In the lowlands, Louisiana and Mississippi produced a half-billion or more board feet each of oak and red gum hardwoods.

Wood Manufactures

Manufacture of the soft woods of the Atlantic Plain and lower Mississippi did not progress beyond saw mills and planing mills for lumber, or for shingles, sash, doors, and blinds.   The principal mill centers were Bogalusa and Shreveport, La., Crossett, Ark., Meridian and Laurel, Miss.   In these and smaller mills the usual long hours and low wages of the South contrasted unfavorably with the West.   Sawyers using band saws in 1928 in Alabama and Georgia for a 61-hour week got 82 cents an hour; in Louisiana, the rate was 87 cents and in Mississippi, 88 cents.   At the same time in California the rate was $1.02 and in Washington was $1.17½ for a 54- and 48-hour week respectively.   Sawyers using circular saws in all states were paid less; that is from 51 cents an hour in Georgia to $1.09 in Washington.   Putting two averages together, one that of all sawmill workers and the other of all years from 1914 to 1929 the average yearly earnings per state were as follows: North Carolina, $703; Mississippi, $798; Arkansas, $824; Louisiana, $850; California, $1,379; and Washington, $1,422.   There was no I. W. W. in the South.

Furniture Manufacture.—The Appalachian hardwood forest brought to the South several wood-working industries of which the chief were wagon factories and furniture plants.   In the wagon factories producing work vehicles for farms and city haulage the southern factories specialized in the cheaper grades for which the best market was in the South itself.

Likewise, when the furniture factories began business in 1888 their products were chairs and tables designed for use in kitchens. Soon a few factories tried to make articles for the front rooms of the house, and succeeding in this experiment, went on into the still better grades of furniture. The town of High Point, in the Piedmont of North Carolina where in 1888 the first southern furniture factory had been built, became the exemplar for five other small plants in North Carolina before 1900.

Clustered in High Point after 1900 were more than three-score furniture and wood working plants. So many were gathered there that the manufacturers developed the Southern Furniture Exposition meeting twice a year and placing High Point in the trade along with Grand Rapids, Michigan and Jamestown, New York. The local interest in furniture manufacture was evidenced furthermore by the publication at High Point of two furniture trade journals.

Tennessee, second to North Carolina in the south's furniture industry, trailed North Carolina by a wide margin and in turn was trailed by Virginia and Georgia.

White Labor.—Except for jobs around the lumber yards, drying kilns, and shipping rooms the labor in the wagon and furniture factories was white, drawn from the Piedmont farmer class. The actual manufacturing jobs were done by both men and women in variable proportions. The males were dominant in the machine room and polishing department. On the other hand, females did most of the sewing and were in large numbers in the whole upholstery division. But there were no jobs in which some members of both sexes were not employed. The hours of work in most factories were 10 per day, but a few ran 2 hours longer; however, night work and Sunday work was not an evil in southern furniture plants.

Wage Rates.—A consideration of wage rates is complicated by the fact that every job carried two rates, one for men, the other for women.   As between men and women for the same job, the differential in favor of men was about 50% ; that is, a man got $18 a week for a job that paid women only $12 a week.   The lowest rates for women yielded no higher weekly earnings than in a textile mill or cigarette factory, but the female carvers, cabinet makers, and similar skilled craftswomen got a weekly income about twice that of their sisters in the other mills.   For the men the furniture making jobs did not pay very much better than the best textile job; however, the textile mill offered high opportunity to a scant few whereas the furniture factory employed many at the top scales.

For comparison in wages between southern and northern furniture factories it is necessary to rule out those factories near New York City where the rates were highest, partly because nearly all wages were higher there but mostly for the reason that the making of furniture to special order required the most expert craftsmanship whose high wages pulled up the averages for the vicinity.   Massachusetts, Michigan, and Indiana offered fairer contrasts with North Carolina, Tennessee, and Virginia.   The 3 northern states averaged not quite 100% more per week to their *male* furniture makers and 66⅔% more for their females.   The average yearly earnings for all furniture workers for 1929 was: Massachusetts, $1,387; Michigan, $1,333; Indiana, $1,088; North Carolina, $822; Tennessee, $799; and Virginia, $845.   If hourly rates are considered then the 8- and 9-hour day outside the South was much higher compensated than the 10- to 12-hour day in the South.

South's Labor Is Cheap.—It was this labor price advantage, added to large cheap resources in raw materials and excellent railway facilities, that gave southern furniture manufacturers their competitive edge especially in the cheaper grades of furniture where selling price was a principal sales argument.   The southern furniture workers did not organize and rebel for the same reasons that their cousins engaged in other southern industries did not offer organized protest to their low pay and long hours.   There were not enough jobs to go around, and the furniture factory jobs were better than others. They paid higher wages; and despite subdivision of labor and mechanization of process there was a higher appeal to craftsmanship even in machine-carving the rung of a kitchen chair than in watching the breaks on four spinning frames producing standard No. 40 yarn.

CHAPTER 16

SOUTHERN FACTORY WORKERS

Cotton Manufacture

The manufacturing industry which, normally, is the easiest to start in an agricultural community is the making of cotton yarn. This was true of England, New England, India, China, and Japan; likewise, it was the first type of manufacturing to become prominent after the Civil War in our southern states. Machine produced cotton yarn was not difficult to inaugurate because by 1830 the mechanisms for its output had been so perfected that the human actions in connection with manufacture had been reduced to a few quickly learned motions. Green hands thus soon became expert. Because there was no advantage in giant yarn mills, the contrary being true, an adequate plant could be built and equipped for $150,000. Since the machinery although bulky was light, not much power was needed. For these reasons cotton yarn mills have been early entrants in industrialization nearly everywhere.

Before 1880.—The South had a yarn mill at Statesburg, South Carolina, on the Santee River as early as 1790, the same year that saw the first successful (Slater) mill in New England at Pawtucket, R. I. Until 1810 the South produced as much textiles as New England; after that date the South was gripped by the slavocracy that purposely stifled all attempts to add cotton manufacture to cotton agriculture. Only a few tiny custom mills—producing customers' yarn to order from customers' cotton—operated before the Civil War, despite southern promoters who urged the economy of manufacture in the South of its principal crop.

After 1880.—By 1880 several factors coincided to start yarn mills in the South. The Reconstruction chaos was over, gold (low) prices were restored so that yarn mills could be built for $20 a spindle instead of the greenback $40, the misery of millions of "poor whites" called for some form of relief, machinery manufacturers were eager for new markets, an English-born Confederate editor of the Charleston, S. C. *"News and Courier"* instigated a newspaper campaign for mills, and chauvinistic southerners were eager to beat the "damnyankees" at their own game.

As a result, the seven southern states that in 1880 had 500,-000 spindles (when New England had over 8½ million) so enlarged the number of mills that by 1892 the South had 1½ million spindles to New England's 11 million. The southern states had increased 100% to 300%; New England, 26%.

In New England in 1896 there was more amusement than alarm at this rise of southern manufacturing; the humor was caused by the sale of some of New England's obsolete machinery to a few gullible southerners. Moreover, the South for the most part was making yarn not cloth; the yarn was coarse and sold mostly to Baltimore and Philadelphia machine knitters.

South Leads.—As the years went on the New Englanders stopped smiling, became worried, and finally were panic-stricken. The statistics explain why. While the United States increased its spindles by 1½ times between 1890 and 1925, the cotton-growing states multiplied theirs by 11 times. New England increased its spindles much more slowly up to 1923 and after that date steadily *lost*. In 1925 there were 15 million spindles in the North and 17 million in the South; by 1929 the South's spindles were very close to 20 million. In consumption of cotton the southern mills in 1910 passed the North.

The South had not been laggard in the manufacture of cloth; beginning in 1880 with 11,000 looms there were 358,000 in 1929. The ratio of looms to spindles in the North was 1 to 40; in the South it was 1 to 56 indicating that the North still had a slight advantage in production of cloth.

Both in yarns and cloth the southern mills constantly advanced in the production of finer grades so that, for many varieties, the South was on a par with the North. Only in bleaching, dyeing, and printing—called "converting"—did the

North in 1929 still have a decided superiority to the South; even this last branch of cotton textiles had begun to move southward before 1929 and by that date there were 40 "converting" plants in the South of which 26 were in the two Carolinas.

Why South Led.—The reasons for this revolution in the manufacture of cotton textiles were many. Nearness to raw material, the most modern mill buildings and machinery, cheap power and individually electrically powered machines, and low taxes all have been advanced as explanations. Without doubt they contributed, but their importance has been over-rated. Cheap labor was the principal advantage of the South.

Labor Supply.—There was no problem of labor supply for the first southern cotton mills. As soon as a mill opened, families moved to it from the surrounding country. These people were the descendants of the farmers forced on to the poorer soils by the slave system. Although abjectly poor, these people were not degenerates; they had been isolated and their development arrested, but they had no higher percentage of perversion than is found in any social order. They had lived at a subsistence level and few of them had known a cash income as high as $25 a year. Moreover, on their farms for most of the year there had been insufficient outlet for the work-energy of the women and children.

To several hundred thousands of these people a wage of 30 cents to 40 cents a day for men, women, and children seemed munificent. The confinement and rigid mill routine at first were irksome; for relief the people either "laid off" for a day or two, or packed their belongings into a farm wagon and moved on to another mill.

No Localization.—The factories dotted the whole Piedmont from Virginia to Georgia. "Poor whites" were everywhere and mechanical power was no confining factor. Although the Piedmont was rich in water power the factories, unlike those of early New England, were by no means limited to water-power sites. Steam and electric power had been applied to cotton manufacture before the southern mills were built. Before

1900 coal and wood were available for fuel at cheap prices, and afterwards hydro-electric power lines gridded the South.

Consequently, the South had no textile cities comparable to the concentrations of the industry in Lowell, Fall River, and New Bedford. The nearest approach to localization was a region, 200 miles around Charlotte, N. C., in which by 1929 there were 542 cotton mills. With the years, the mills spread beyond this center, some being built on the Coastal Plain and others in the lower Mississippi Valley, especially in Alabama and Texas.

Mill Villages.—Scarcely any mills were erected within city limits; even those associated with cities or towns were set outside the corporate limits to escape high tax rates. Most of the mills were in tiny villages and many were placed in open fields. Therefore, nearly every southern cotton mill had a mill village built and owned by the same capital that constructed and operated the mill. As a matter of fact, about a quarter of the capital of a southern mill corporation was invested in houses, schools, churches, stores, streets, and other village appurtenances.

It is impossible to generalize about these villages. Some of them provided the best living conditions that southern wage earners knew; others were as unkempt as the coal camps tucked in mountain coves. In the best villages the houses were somewhat individualized and were painted and plastered. They had electric lights, running water, and connections to sewers; and their dooryards were neat, as also were the streets and sidewalks. Such housing rented for 75 cents per room per week.

The worst villages had rows of box-houses all exactly alike and none with paint or plaster. Common water pumps or hydrants for a whole group of houses matched the common privies (or none). Some of these houses might have electric lights attached to company current but often oil lamps were the sole illuminants. Streets were pitted with holes and covered with litter just as yards were the repositories of tin cans and garbage. Since the houses were placed on wooden or brick stilts and since these were in disrepair the houses tilted at crazy angles.   The rent for these places was 25 cents per room per week.

At best or worst the mill villages made the mill boss also the landlord, and directly or indirectly, the official village father. They opened the way for the unscrupulous to fleece the workers of their pitiable incomes.   Socially they kept mill people in a segregated class, the butt of ridicule, and the object of disdain by southerners in other walks of life.

A "White" Industry.—The southern cotton textile industry (1896-1929) was mostly reserved to whites; it was started in part to relieve their distress, and in the generation under discussion there always was enough white labor to meet the needs of the mills.   The process of spinning was in the hands of white women and girls, a fourth of them in their childhood years; weaving was done by both women and men.   White boys and men filled the auxiliary jobs in the spinning and weaving departments.   Until about 1910 the women and girls were more preponderant than was customory in northern mills; "pappy" and the older boys stayed home to run the farm when cotton prices were high, or else the fathers were too old and muscle-bound to do the mill work.   After 1910 the new generation that had grown up in the mills as child-workers became men and so stayed with the job in maturity.

A Few Negro Jobs.—The Negroes connected with cotton mills worked in the yards and shipping departments, and also in the "picker" room where bales were opened and cleaned, a job so dirty and dusty that whites were happy to relegate it to Negroes.   It was said that Negroes were unfitted by physique and temperament for the jobs in spinning and weave rooms. That such assertions were nonsense was proved by the Negroes who performed all cotton mill operations under slavery; and by a few modern mills in which the entire work-force was black. Social caste rules barred Negroes from spinning and weaving, and not incompetence.

Exploitation of Labor.—Everywhere in the world cotton mills got their start by the exploitation of labor, a rule to which the South was no exception. In 1880 the southern unskilled doffers got 30 cents a day, trained drawers-in got 45 cents, spinners got 30 cents to 50 cents, weavers 60 cents to 90 cents and skilled loom fixers $1.25. At that time the standard week in the South was 66 hours. In 1896 the corresponding rates were: doffers 20 cents to 90 cents, drawers-in 40 cents to 75 cents, spinners 30 cents to $1.00, weavers 50 cents to $1.43, and loom fixers 50 cents to $1.25. Hours had lengthened to 69.

Even persons unacquainted with textile occupations can notice the wide diversities in pay for the same job, and the hourly rates tended to decline as the new industry gathered momentum. To save the tedium of extended comparisons with cotton mill wages in the North it can be stated that they ran 33⅓% to 50% higher and hours 6 to 9 less; i.e., a 60-hour week.

The southern differential with the years did not change much although the wage rates in both regions were considerably boosted. For illustration, it will suffice to show the rates for the two extremes, unskilled doffers and skilled loom fixers. In 1928 doffers were paid as follows: North Carolina and Georgia, 28 cents an hour; South Carolina, 27 cents an hour; Massachusetts, 39 cents an hour; Rhode Island and New Hampshire, 40 cents an hour. For loom fixers the 1928 rates were: North Carolina, .418 per hour; Georgia, .379; South Carolina, .377; Massachusetts, .592; Rhode Island, .615; and New Hampshire, .647.

A Low Wage Industry.—It is easy to get the impression from the foregoing that New England mill hands were well paid; as a matter of fact there were few factory enterprises that had so low a wage structure as these northern cotton mills. Their *highest* paid workers, the loom fixers, both in 1896 and 1929 were 10% below the *average* wages for all American factory workers. New England cotton textile workers, at all times after 1896, got piteously low wages; for women $20 a week was an unusually high average and for men a $25 average, likewise, was received only in most booming periods.

But Southern Mill Wages Lowest.—Southern cotton mill hands had only one-half to two-thirds as much in their pay envelopes as the New England textilers.   In 1925 when New Hampshire cotton mill women were paid $20.90 those in Alabama had to be content with $11.43 per week.

It has been said that southern mill help did not need as high earnings as those in New England; their clothes, food, housing, and recreations all were cheaper.   Competent investigations disclosed that the differences in *prices* between the two regions were negligible.   The differences in *expenditures* were due to purchases of different commodities or lower qualities of the same articles.   The southern workers spent less because they had less to spend; this had no relation to their needs and wants.

Not only were southern mill hands paid less than those in New England, but they worked longer hours.   By using night shifts the mills operated on a 24-hour basis.   In the absence of a strong union, the hours of work were fixed by custom or law. It has been universal experience that an agricultural society accustomed to daylight working hours is reluctant to set legal limits on factory operation when these industrial ventures are novel.   In England the industrial revolution commenced in 1733 with Kay's flying shuttle, but it was 1802 before Parliament made its first feeble regulation, and then only for children. New England dated its industrial revolution from Slater's factory of 1790; its first regulation, again for children, was not enacted until 1842.   Likewise, the South for many years ignored factory regulation.

Opposition to Regulation.—The industrialization brought such obvious economic advantages—profits at first were as high as 50% per year—that nearly all southern leaders hesitated to discourage its advance.   The cotton mill folks most affected were either inarticulate or voiced no grievances where they could be heard.   Suggestions that mills be brought under legislative control were looked upon as disloyal to the South when advocated by southerners, and as a new kind of interfering "abolitionism" when raised by outsiders.   In the latter case it was suspected—in some cases rightly—that the pleas were in

the interest of northern competitors. Therefore, for some
years, southern mills without legal restraints ran day and night,
with women on both shifts, employed children under 10 years
of age, and paid wages at subsistence levels.

Hours of Work (For Women).—Nevertheless, all save
three of the southern states after 1900 enacted some kind of
legal restraint upon the employment of women. Alabama
along with Florida and West Virginia were the exceptions.
Virginia allowed her women wage earners to work for 70 hours
per week. North Carolina, Georgia, Mississippi and Louisiana
set 60 hours as the limit; Tennessee put her limit at 57 hours;
while South Carolina had the lowest at 55 hours.

These weekly standards were supplemented by limits per day.
The same three laggards had no daily limits. North Carolina
allowed 11 hours in one day, Tennessee 10½, South Carolina
10 (12 in emergencies), and Delaware, Georgia, Kentucky,
Louisiana (9 in 1936), Maryland, Mississippi, and Virginia
each set 10 hours. Only Texas and Arkansas put the limit at
9 hours, and none had either an 8-hour law or prohibited night
work although Maryland allowed only 8 hours of night work.

By way of comparison Connecticut had a 55-hour law;
Maine, Rhode Island, and New Hampshire, 54; and Massachusetts, 48. Besides Massachusetts prohibited night work.
New England's longest legal limit, 55 hours, was identical with
the South's shortest.

Ages of Child Workers.—Every southern state fixed an
age below which children might not legally go to work in factories or stores. Except for Texas where 15 years was the
standard all the others set 14 years. In Virginia the younger
children could work in factories in non-school hours. In Arkansas and North Carolina a 14-year-old child could get a work-
permit if it had passed only the 4th grade in school. In Louisiana, Mississippi, South Carolina, and Virginia no educational
test was required for a work-permit.

In the North 15 states required that 14-year-old applicants
for work must have passed the 8th grade; and 5 states required
the child to be 16 years of age. No southern state allowed

children under 14 to work at night, but some permitted exceptions up to 7, 8, or 9 P. M.

Enforcement of Laws.—No law is better than its enforcement. This depends upon the legislative appropriations for inspectors, the degree to which inspectors or their superiors can be "influenced," and the extent to which public opinion sanctions the law. Child labor was flagrant in southern cotton mills, and many a woman, many a day and week, labored beyond the legal hour limits. Both federal child-labor laws were held unconstitutional by Judge Boyd of the U. S. District Court for the western district of North Carolina; both cases, thus arising in the South, were carried to the U. S. Supreme Court by money and counsel furnished mostly by southern manufacturers.

Unionism.—In fixing wages and hours of work, unions in many industries have been more effective than laws. Why did not the southern textile workers join a northern textile union or form one of their own?

Among northern textile unions the only one with a long record was that of the Mule Spinners. A "mule" was a particular variety of spinning machine requiring skilled male labor. Mule spinners were either English-born or English-trained and in both cases were militant trade-unionists. Their power was narrowed to small compass by two facts: mule spinning in America was used almost entirely for fine yarns of which American production was small; secondly, the great bulk of American yarns was produced by ring spinning for which trained girls not skilled men were employed. The South did scarcely any mule spinning so even if the union had been dominant in the North there would have been no membership for it in the South.

Other textile unions in the North after 1880 were short-lived. This was true of the Knights of Labor, the (1890) National Union of Textile Workers sired by the A. F. of L., and the I. W. W., the Amalgamated Textile Workers 1919, child of the Amalgamated Clothing Workers, the National (Communist) Textile Workers' Union, and 21 local or regional independent unions. Only two textile unions had longevity in the North: the first was the independent American Federation of Textile Operatives formed in 1916 with a membership of skilled workers—among them the mule spinners—in New Bedford and Fall River; the other was the United Textile Workers' Union promoted in 1901 by the American Federation of Labor.

In the textile industry whose cotton branch alone employed 400,000 persons the United Textile Workers at its maximum strength in 1919-20 claimed 125,000 members in all varieties of textiles which was more than twice its normal strength between 1901 and 1929. That is, this largest textile union only once had much over 12% of the possible membership in the cotton industry; until 1917 it never had a full 10% enrolled.

Weakness of Unions Explained.—The United Textile Workers was weak because its field was so full of competitors. This condition, in turn, was due to northern employers who used the principle of division to conquer. Moreover, the northern textile mills were sieves for immigrants; each new lower standard alien group was inveigled into the mills and stayed until its standards rose above the wage levels maintained in the mills. As many as 30 nationalities were employed in the mills at the same time. The diversity and fluidity of the streams of immigrants imposed an extraordinary difficulty for permanent unionization. Employers fought the union with every legal or expedient weapon that came to hand. Not until late in the 1920's did some employers realize that they could use the union to frustrate their southern competitors' chief advantage, namely cheap labor working long hours.

United Textile Workers Invade South.—Despite its northern weakness and small treasury—its members were too close to pauperism to pay high dues—the United Textile Workers realized the menace of unorganized, exploited, southern, cotton-mill wage earners. Three times it put forth great efforts to bring the southerners into the union fold. The first was in 1914.

Prior to 1914 the union had made several gestures toward organization of southern textile workers but had been unable to keep organizers constantly in that field. In 1914 the union secured the aid of the A. F. of L., the Georgia Federation of

Labor, and the Atlanta Federation of Trades and set forth on a determined drive among southern mill workers.

The first step was to help 1,200 strikers of the Fulton Bag and Carpet Company of Atlanta to secure union recognition and a 54-hour work-week.   The company evicted the strikers from company houses and met all attempts at negotiation with "there is nothing to arbitrate."   Notwithstanding that the union could not point to victory in this case, its efforts advertised it in Georgia.   The remainder of the 1914-15 drive in Georgia and the Carolinas was without drama or the formation of permanent locals; its chief accomplishment was in getting a few mill hands interested in unions.

Desultory visits in the South by union organizers occurred between 1915 and 1919.   From these agitational forays there resulted just one closed shop agreement; this was with a Chattanooga company, signed in September 1919, and provided for a 54-hour week with the prevailing union scale of wages.   Upon the heels of this agreement unorganized strikes broke out in the Carolinas which brought the union's second large-scale invasion of the South.

World War Influences.—During the World War, when the cotton business was booming, the southern mills for the first time experienced a relative scarcity of labor.   The war price of raw cotton made cotton culture so attractive that the people on farms could not be lured into factories and some of those already in mills went back to the land.   Coal mines, lumber camps, steel mills, and clothing factories competed for labor.   The army took away thousands of white and black youths, and the absence of immigration in the North created a demand for thousands more of the southern reserves of both races.   The southern cotton mills were forced to grant successive increases of wages which gave mill workers their first taste of an economic margin above bare costs of existence.

Post-War Strikes.—After the Armistice the mill managers tried to deflate labor by wage cuts ranging from 37½% to 65%; it was this snatching away of tasted fruits that precipitated a wave of strikes from Columbus, Georgia, northward through Charlotte in northern North Carolina

Most of the strikes were unplanned walk-outs. Once on strike the United Textile Workers' organizers were called in, or went in, as mentors. Quickly some 50,000 southern mill hands were enrolled as union members. The strikes soon collapsed. The employers brought a furious counter attack against them, not the least effective of their blasts being that the strikes were not due to the mill help's ingratitude or discontent but to outside agitators sent into the South by competitors. The depression of 1921 quieted the last traces of strike fever.

The 50,000 southern members stayed in the union only a year. The union which in 1920 had a national membership of 104,000 was reduced to 30,000 in 1922; much of the gain and loss was in southern membership. The southern mill managers thereupon cut the workers' pay, began the "stretch out" system, and sugared the dose by an expansion of Welfare Work.

Beginning in 1922 the United Textile Workers (along with the Amalgamated Textile Workers) were fully occupied with a great strike of 60,000 to 80,000 workers in the Pawtuxet and Blackstone Valleys, R. I., which spread to Massachusetts and New Hampshire. Since the northern strike lasted 10 months and cost the U. T. W. about a million dollars the union had no time, money, or organizers to spare for the South.

Third Campaign By U. T. W.—The third organization campaign by the union was based upon plain evidences of southern unrest in 1927-30. The workers had the positive grievances of the hasty, amateurish manner in which the "stretch-out" was applied, and exploitation in the company villages and stores; negatively they were aggrieved by their growing disparity in wages and hours as compared with northern mill workers. On its side the union was dismayed at the southward non-union trend of its hitherto strongest division, the Full-Fashioned Hosiery Industry. The union in this branch dispatched to the South its most able organizer, Alfred Hoffman. For the United Textile Workers' headquarters staff, Frank Gorman spent increasing amounts of time and energy in the South.

The first break came on August 4, 1927, when about 800 unorganized textile employes in Henderson, N. C., struck for a wage increase of 12½%. Although this strike was lost, other small strikes in different villages flared up only to be quenched by mill owners. Then in 1928, and the two following years came the wave of strikes of which the most famous were those at Elizabethton, Gastonia, Marion, and Danville. These and their results were described in Chapter 5.

Why Unions Failed.—Southern textile unionism before 1929 was impotent and impermanent for two chief reasons: There was a superabundant supply of labor so that any strike could be defeated by scabs. The mill owners belonged to the First Families and so were backed by social and political power in addition to their economic advantage over poverty-bleached workers. Literally, as at Marion, N. C., a mill owner "could get away with murder."

Intra-South Competition.—Brief mention should be made of two other facts concerning southern textiles. The first is that the old mill centers in the Carolinas and Georgia have been put under the same kind of economic pressure—low wages, long hours, child labor—from Alabama that the Carolinas exerted against New England. The other states in the lower Mississippi valley have followed the lead of Alabama. In truth then, southern cotton textiles have had two centers of which the older in the Carolinas developed the higher standards in respect to hours and wages. Alabama by 1929 had 98 cotton mills with about 2 million spindles and 34,000 looms (ratio 1-56); three of the mills employed 1,500 hands, and 18 had from 500 to 1,200. The products were coarse yarns and heavy cloths, the identical ones which the Carolinas at first manufactured. Is Alabama going to do to North Carolina what the latter did to Massachusetts? Alabama is nearer the center of cotton growing, is possessed of valuable coal lands, and snuggles against the Tennessee River Valley electrical power development in a region full of "hill billies." For a market the Alabama products already have entered the large cotton-goods distributing city, St. Louis.

The second fact is that many other textiles have followed cotton manufacture to the South. Knit goods, especially hosiery manufacture, by 1929 was represented by 367 mills containing 60,000 knitting machines. Most of these mills were in North Carolina (178) or Tennessee (77) but the largest, that of the Interwoven Mills, Inc., with 3,000 knitting machines, was in Martinsburg, West Virginia. Rayon mills, braiding, mattress, felt and batting, woolen, and silk mills all were numerous in the South with scarcely a one that was not lured there by the bait—in the words of the power companies—of "cheap and docile labor."

Tobacco Manufacture

One of the South's oldest resources was tobacco. In the colonial period the maximum output was 130 million pounds. Between 1896 and 1929 the American output, most of it in the South, ranged from a half-billion to a billion and a half pounds with values from $53 million to $211 million. The manufacture of tobacco into mixtures for pipe smokers and plugs for chewers had started in Virginia as early as 1732.

A distinctive peculiarity of the tobacco plant was that seed from one flower, if planted in different soils and grown under different climates, produced markedly distinctive products. Therefore, as tobacco culture spread around the world special types were utilized for various products manufactured from tobacco. This behavior of tobacco had economic effects which among other places influenced the tobacco manufacturing of the South.

Pipe, Chewing, and Snuff Products.—In point of time the oldest tobacco manufacturing in the South was the production of cheap mixtures for pipes, plugs for chewing, and snuff. For these purposes the leaf tobacco was not highly selected; as a consequence the manufacture of it was not confined to the South but appeared also in the North and Mid-West near tobacco-producing regions. In the South the earliest "factories" for these products had been in kitchens and the later manufacturing premises resembled barns—rather dirty ones. The work was dusty, and tobacco dust, when dampened, makes nasty brown

smears, so the buildings were unsightly.   The same kind of dry
dust covered and was inhaled by the workers to the detriment
of their health.

Stripping.—The first job, as in all tobacco manufacturing,
was the removal of the stem of the leaf; technically called "stripping" or "stemming."   "Stripping" was not hard work and
called for only enough skill to avoid waste of the valuable leaf.
Hence it was done by the very old, very young, or very hopeless.
In the South it was a Negro job, mostly in the hands of women.
Immigrants did the work in the North.   In 1896 "strippers"
in Virginia got 1 cent per hour and 2 cents per hour in Florida.
In the 1900's the rate rose to 7 cents or 11 cents per hour and
in the 1920's was 18 cents or 19 cents.

The other jobs required more strength and skill, although
not much of either.   The dust, odor, and (in some processes)
heat repelled white workers, with the result that Negro men had
a monopoly of the jobs.   Their wages in the early '90's were
$5 to $6 per week; in the 1900's a wage of $12 a week was a
prize seldom reached as was $15 a week in the 1920's.   More-
over their jobs tended to disappear because chewing and taking
snuff were waning in popularity; each decade saw less production and sale of plug tobacco, twisted tobacco, and snuff.   Even
pipe tobacco production failed to keep pace with the increase in
population.

Cigar Manufacture.—With cigar manufacture it was market, not raw materials, that determined location.   Cigars really
were an assembled product and the raw materials varied in
accordance with the quality of the cigars.   The three parts of
the cigar, filler or bunch, binder, and wrapper, usually were
made of different kinds of tobacco.   These might come from
either the West Indies or East Indies and if entirely of domestic origin might draw supplies from Ohio, Wisconsin, Tennessee, Florida, Pennsylvania, or Connecticut.   Hence there was
no economic advantage in getting close to the source of any
one kind of tobacco.

In addition, cigars were essentially hand products until well
after 1920.   Cigar manufacture, thus, was strewn all over the

nation from Florida to Maine and from Norfolk to Los Angeles. In the South, because hand-made cigars were the result of highly skilled labor, they were made almost exclusively by white men. As long as cigars were produced by hand the industry was controlled by the Cigarmakers' International Union organized in 1864 and in its day, one of the most vigorous unions in America. It was the union in which Samuel Gompers held his membership card. Hence this union had a 44-hour week as early as 1888 and kept wages at times as high as $7 a day and with $2 a fair average for all times and places in the nation. The union also insured its members against the hazards of unemployment, sickness, or death. Southern members shared the short hours, high wage rates, and insurance.

Unfortunately for hand cigarmakers the conditions did not endure; they were assailed by machinery and a falling demand. The technological difficulties of forming a bunch, winding a diagonal binder, and then applying a smooth wrapper—all with unstandardized materials—delayed machinery for nearly two generations. The first tentative move toward mechanization—the mould for gathering the bunch filler—had appeared as early as 1869. The union fight against each technical advance also delayed a complete machine. The technicians, however, would not be denied; after 1910 they had machines good enough for cheap cigars. In the 1920's the last technical barriers were leveled and fine cigars, 500 or more per hour, increasingly poured from machines rather than taking slower form in human fingers. Moreover, the new machines could be operated by trained girls.

Union and Cigar Industry Both Decline.—The union reduced its hand rates and lowered its entrance requirements to include every wage earner—even janitors—in cigar factories; women also were invited into membership. A rival union frankly industrial and based on low dues and no insurance was started. These acts were vain endeavors; membership dropped from 39,000 in 1920 to 17,500 in 1928. Most of the new large mechanized cigar factories were run as "open shops," i.e. closed to unions; their employes, largely women, were paid 25

cents or less per hour with the tendency downward. Thousands of male cigar rollers were unemployed—increasingly so
each year—from 1915 to 1929.

Mechanization followed by lower selling prices for cigars
did not save the industry from the falling popularity of its
product. The young men from 1900 onward did not smoke
cigars to the extent that their fathers and grandfathers had.
In 1900 over 8 million cigars were produced; in 1929 the output
dropped to 6 million; this meant that in 1900 there was 1 cigar
to 11 Americans but in 1929 there was only 1 to 17. Young
men refused cigars because they were too heavy to smoke while
men were working, took too long to smoke at odd snatches, and
were too expensive to throw away partly consumed. The cigarette was the popular smoke.

Cigarette Industry.—Cigarettes made their first commercial
appearance about 1860. In 1869 internal revenue tax was paid
upon only a million cigarettes. By 1896 the number had expanded to 4 billion. Large as that figure seemed, it was insignificant beside the 122 billions produced in 1929. The latter
figure was an allowance per capita of a little over 13 packages
a day—a figure that of course includes the packages that were
exported.

The cigarette branch of the tobacco industry not only ushered in a novel product but brought entirely fresh practices. The
tobacco of which it was made usually was a blend of domestic
and foreign leaves, but domestic leaf constituted 80% more or
less of the mixture, and of the domestic leaves the bright, lemon-
shaded, flue-cured tobacco of North Carolina, South Carolina,
Georgia, and southern Virginia predominated. This kind of
leaf could not be used for cigars or snuff but was extraordinarily
popular for cigarettes and pipe-smoking mixtures. North
Carolina specialized in its cultivation. Therefore, cigarettes
were unlike cigars in that the raw material outstandingly was
domestic in origin and highly localized in one state. The
greater use of Kentucky burley leaf, heat-processed, came later;
this kind of tobacco was about 4 cents a pound cheaper and more

widely grown than the other cigarette varieties. Without special treatment it was too strong for use in cigarettes.

A Machine Industry.—Another striking difference between cigarette and cigar manufacture was that virtually from the start cigarettes were made by well-nigh automatic machinery. Thus the business lent itself easily to the large-scale factory method of production. Since the machinery needed only cursory supervision, women and children could be hired as machine attendants. The work was tedious and unhealthful but light; so white women and children were taken into the factories. A work force of these people was something hitherto unheard of in the southern tobacco industry.

Cigarette manufacture became highly concentrated in North Carolina, the communities most notable as cigarette makers being Winston-Salem, Reidsville, Durham, and Statesville. After North Carolina, whose output was about half the total, came New York, Virginia, and New Jersey. The two northern leaders indicate the influence of market in factory location, but the manufacture there of cigarettes contained an unusual proportion of unusual kinds of imported leaf, a factor that had had a bearing on location. The plants were placed in an excellent market that also was the port of arrival for foreign tobacco. North Carolina plants had branches in or near New York City in order to be near a large consuming market. Louisville, after the World War, became the most important new center for the manufacture of cigarettes.

The "Trust."—In the '80's there were several different machines for making cigarettes and the owners or lessees of these conducted an aggressive commercial war to defeat each other and capture the consumers' markets. Extensive advertising and price cutting featured the conflict for supremacy. The most adroit commander of one of the leading contenders was James B. Duke. With his father and brother, he was the owner of large works at Durham, North Carolina, and had in 1884 set up a branch factory in New York. He ended the cut-throat competition in 1890 when he drew into one organization—The American Tobacco Company—the five principal cigarette manufacturers. These were Allen and Ginter of Richmond; W. S. Kimball of Rochester; Goodwin and Company of New York City; Kinney Tobacco Company of New York and Richmond; and the Dukes. By this move The American Tobacco Company owned the best equipped and most favorably located cigarette factories, became possessed of the most popular brands of 1890, and controlled about 85% of the entire cigarette output.

The "trust" intrenched in the cigarette field set out to acquire all the rest of the tobacco manufacturing industry, and by 1900 had about accomplished its purpose. The Continental Tobacco Company, a consolidation of makers of plug tobacco, was bought in 1898, and the next year P. Lorillard Company, Liggett and Myers, and the R. J. Reynolds Tobacco Company were absorbed.

Only the cigar branch for a long time proved impregnable. The latter's small-scale, potential one-man competition, together with its lack of machinery and slight need for capital investment, gave nothing upon which the "trust" could grip. Hence for all its endeavors in this market the best the American Cigar Company—subsidiary of American Tobacco Company formed in 1901—could accomplish was control of one-quarter of the output of cigars. Not until the complete cigar-making machine of the 1920's was perfected did large capital capture much of the cigar production. In all other branches, including the raw material market, the manufacture of boxes, tin foil, licorice, and the export market besides straight tobacco manufacturing, the American Tobacco Company and its affiliates dominated.

The Government's monopoly suit of 1907 and dissolution order of 1911 restored the forms of competition by division of the "trust" into 9 separate companies but disturbed very little the power of the principal stockholders in the "Big Four"—The American Tobacco Company, R. J. Reynolds Tobacco Company, Liggett and Myers Company, and P. Lorillard Company. (The Little Five made cigars, stogies, and snuff).

Exploited Labor.—The money for the campaigns toward monopoly, and for the distribution of lucrative dividends—23 to 65 million a year by the Big Four—was derived from the operating economies of large-scale production. A goodly share of these "economies" came from labor worked long hours and at subsistence wages. An unusually high percentage of the wage earners in cigarette factories were children. The number up to 1905 never was less than 9% and at times (the '80's) was as much as 21%. To the children, wages of less than 50 cents a day were a normal scale in the cigarette factories. Even the women got barely this wage and seldom before the World War were paid as much as one dollar a day. In 1905 the average annual wage for men was $272 per year; for women $183, and for children $119.

In 1929 the average annual wage for all workers was $813. Women and children were docile workers and unorganizable into unions. The only alternative wage-paying jobs open to them in textile factories were as poorly remunerated and had as lengthy a day's work. The sole means of protest was to quit. So many did this that the labor turnover was unusually high; but this did not trouble the employers because the work largely was unskilled and there were scores of women and children willing for a time to rush into vacancies.

Improved · Machines.—Exploited labor, however, did not account for the entire profits of tobacco companies. Technological improvements were other levers that pressed costs into smaller units. Since the manufacture of cigarettes was a machine industry, it lent itself easily to the genius of engineers. How astonishingly they applied themselves may be best realized by their own favorite yardstick-figures. With output per worker in 1919 expressed as 100, the outputs of other years were:

1899	1914	1921	1923	1925
53.5	65.7	102.0	120.4	155.7

The Liggett and Myers Tobacco Company (Chesterfields) and the R. J. Reynolds Tobacco Company (Camels)—both pieces of the old "Trust"—belonged among the 50 American corporations that, according to the Standard Statistics, Inc., stood first in total assets, current assets, invested capital, working capital, cash on hand, net profits and largest payments to holders of their stocks and bonds. The American Tobacco Company (Lucky Strikes) was not far behind the two named. The R. J. Reynolds Company was the prize performer; an investment in 1914 of 100 shares in this company would have cost $25,000. In 10 years the dividends would have been $39,000 and the value of the stock $254,000. Low wage labor plus amazing mechanisms procured these large profits for the companies.

What these tobacco companies did with their money was brought out in court early in 1933. The American Tobacco Company paid its president $2 million a year in salary and bonus. If to this is added the $750,000 to $1,000,000 received by each of 5 vice-presidents of the same company then these 6 individuals were paid one-tenth as much as all the 106,000 wage earners in the entire cigar and cigarette industry. That is, the 6 together were paid as much as 9,840 of their employes; each executive was rated as worth 1,640 factory workers in the same industry.

None of the 6 who got a million or more a year could possibly spend it all on goods for their own or their families' satisfactions; they had to re-invest most of their income. On the contrary the 106,000 wage earners who got $813 per year did not have enough to spend for anything beyond the bare means of keeping alive. This condition in this industry contributed to the crash in 1929 when national under-consumption produced national over-production—and depression.

Unions in Cigarette Industry.—When the tobacco "Trust" was still in infancy the Tobacco Workers' International Union was organized (1895) with an initial membership of 25,000 and accepted at once by the A. F. of L. Since it was not also accepted by the "Trust," the latter's growth in control of the industry was accompanied by a decline in the union. The dissolution of the physical "Trust" in 1911 did not alter the tactics and policies of its parts. Never again before 1929 did the union have as many members as in its first year; from 3,000 to 4,000 members was its usual roll. A spurt in 1920 brought

12,300 members, all but 1,500 of whom were lost by 1924.
And 100 more dropped out in 1925, so that in the next two
years the membership stood at 1,400.

Inasmuch as the union found sanctuary in the little independent tobacco plants, and because these always were threatened by the maw of the Big Bad Wolf, the union never engaged
in any spectacular struggle to improve the wages, hours, or
working conditions of its members.   The only asset of the
union was its label, and this had value only on tobacco products
sold to workingmen.

In 1928 the dreary history of this union suddenly was en-
livened by the meteoric rise of the Axton-Fisher Tobacco Company of Louisville, Ky.   This company, completely independent,
swept the market with two products; one was a 10-cent package
of good cigarettes (20 Grand), the other, a mentholated cigarette (Spuds), sold at a slightly higher price than the most popular "Trust" brands.   Each of these new cigarettes, in its own
field, so captured buyers that the Louisville plant had need constantly of more workers, and soon of more plant.   It became
the largest independent cigarette and tobacco manufacturing
company in the world, doing a $40 million business.   The com-
pany had had a trade agreement with the union for 33 years.
In the 1922 shopmen's strike, the company had furnished the
strikers with tons of cigarettes and smoking mixtures.

The "Trust" moved to restrict the abrupt loss of business to
the upstart independent, by putting out 10-cent packages under
new brand-names.   The production of a mentholated cigarette
(Kools) at Louisville by the Brown and Williamson Tobacco
Corporation was pushed by national advertising and the inclusion in packages of gift coupons.   The latter company also accepted unionization and in its national advertising conspicuously displayed the union label.   The B-W Company had been
started in 1894, incorporated in 1906, and was noted for its
production of snuff at its Winston-Salem, N. C., plant.

Woodford F. Axton, the president of the Axton-Fisher Company, refused to accept from the leading stockholders a salary
in excess of $10,000, remarking that "If there is going to be any
pay raising in this factory it will start at the bottom and not at

the top. One of the greatest troubles with the country is that business executives are taking too much for themselves . . . people must have enough to buy back the products of their labor."

Iron and Steel Industry

Jones' Valley in 1870 was a cotton field creased by two railway lines; a real estate promotion company connected with these founded the boom town that became the South's premier industrial community. The basis for the fortunes of Birmingham was a unique proximity of coal, iron ore, and limestone, the three essentials for the manufacture of pig-iron. Nowhere else in the world were these found in the same locality.

At Birmingham, Alabama.—Until 1896 the Birmingham iron works were confined to the production of pig-iron and foundry iron, the former marketed abroad and the latter distributed to foundries in the North and West. The Alabama iron ore had too high a phosphorus content to be used for making steel by the methods then in vogue. Only a fourth of the smelted iron was fabricated in Alabama; this was in the manufacture of stoves, radiators, farm tools, car wheels, and cotton gin machinery. The panic of 1893 crippled the entire southern iron industry and at the same time the Alabama ores were discredited by the newly exploited Mesabi Range ores of Minnesota. The consequent distress in Birmingham led to notable reorganizations of companies and a concentration upon open hearth steel instead of stopping with the prior stage, pig-iron.

These changes made Birmingham the logical center for any southern combination of iron and steel companies, or for alliances with northern combinations. The Republic Iron and Steel Company of Ohio and Indiana in 1899 had a hold in the Birmingham district. However, the combination that gave the greatest promise was that collected by the Tennessee Coal, Iron, and Railroad Company. In the panic of 1907 this company got into a financial tangle from which it was rescued by the United States Steel Corporation when the latter bought the southern company for $35 million.   By multiplying by 6 the capital investment in or near Birmingham, the Steel Corporation made the city one of the principal steel centers of the United States.

At Baltimore, Maryland.—Besides the Birmingham steel works another founded on rail-borne coal was started at Sparrows Point (Baltimore) Md., in 1887 as a subsidiary (The Maryland Steel Company) of the Pennsylvania Steel Company (1886) whose principal works were at Steelton (near Harrisburg), Pa.   Later, (1904) and (1917), these companies were absorbed by Schwab's Bethlehem Steel Corporation.   At Sparrows Point, ore imported from Cuba was changed into pig-iron and this into cast-iron and steel by coal from Pennsylvania and West Virginia.   While the products of the plant were carried by rail and water to American markets the location of the mills on tidewater gave to the Maryland Steel Company the primary purpose of reaching export markets.

The Alabama and Maryland iron and steel industries were by far the most important in this kind of manufacturing in the South.   Nevertheless, smaller producers were scattered through Virginia, Tennessee, West Virginia, and Kentucky.   The aggregate production of coal, iron ore, and pig-iron in the South by 1896 was equal to the total output for the United States twenty years earlier.

Labor in Steel Industry.—The iron and steel industry (1896-1929) was one that relied increasingly upon machines. To control the machines a relatively small number of highly skilled men were necessary; in service to both the machines and the skilled group there was a large body of unskilled laborers. In the South as in the North the skilled positions were held by native-white Americans.   The larger mass of unskilled labor was composed in the North of burly immigrants; in the South it was made up of Negroes.

The hours of work per week in 1896 were shorter (60) in the South than at Pittsburgh (72), but in 1903 the southern plants increased the work period; after that date the southern work-week always was as long as the North and remained high even after the northern mills cut hours on some jobs.

Wages Low in Southern Steel Mills.—In respect to wages, both for skilled and unskilled workers, the southern mills at no time on any job paid as high hourly rates as the northern plants. Here are a few sample comparisons: Blast furnace keepers in 1896 got 21½ cents an hour at Pittsburgh and 13 4/10 cents at Birmingham; in 1903 the rates were 22 cents and 14 cents and in 1926 were 63 cents and 41 cents. Rollers in the North in 1896 got 93 cents an hour, in the South the rate was 54 cents; in 1903 there was the similar discrepancy of $1.06 and 62 cents; and in 1926 of $1.75 and $1.58. Catchers in 1926 in northern rolling mills got 49 cents an hour, while the same job in Alabama paid 13½ cents an hour; in 1903 the rates were 68 cents and 14 cents; and in 1926 were 90 cents and 61½ cents. Skip-hoist operators in 1926 worked 55 hours a week at Pittsburgh for 58 cents an hour; while in Birmingham the week was 68 hours and the rate 35 cents an hour.

Union Weak.—There was no union except the Amalgamated Association of Iron, Steel, and Tin Workers in the iron and steel industry after the Homestead strike in 1892. This one union had a membership ranging from 10,000 to 20,000 in an industry employing 400,000 and was limited first to very highly skilled men earning $5 to $20 or more per day and secondly, to the sheet and tinplate division of the industry in the North. The union's efforts were directed mostly to exclusive tactics to preserve the highly favored position of its own little coterie.

In the South the whites kept their grip on the best jobs; nevertheless, once in a while a Negro climbed into the skilled group, and even into foremanship over his own race. There is no information as to the motives of the southern steel companies in promoting an occasional Negro; it was a fact, however, that a strike in steel mills could not succeed if the small skilled group did not go out with the mass of unskilled. In the famous 1919 steel strike, southern Negro steel workers were shipped by train-loads in sealed cars into the Pittsburgh district. Thousands remained there; in 1923 in 23 Pittsburgh steel plants the 16,000 Negroes constituted 21% of the entire force. Of these Negroes 90% were unskilled common laborers. In the succeeding years until 1929 the number and percentage of Negroes in Pittsburgh plants increased on account of the shortage of immigrants. The southern mills may have served as preparatory schools for the Pittsburgh and Gary plants.

Welfare Work.—The steel companies carried into the South the Welfare Work used in the North as an antidote to unionism; in the South it was an antidote to labor turnover. Regardless of the motive and also in spite of the charges that unions have brought against Welfare Work, it must be admitted that it introduced to southern workers standards of safety, health, cleanliness, and housing to which they were not accustomed. Even the wages, low as they were in comparison with those at Pittsburgh or Gary, were higher than those paid in any other southern industry except railroading.

Birmingham was the only large southern city with no nostalgic tradition, because it did not exist in the days of jasmine-scented belles; it was as modern as bobbed-haired bandits. There has been nothing softer about Birmingham than the steel it made; for Birmingham worshipped the same gods as Pittsburgh, but with less apostasy.

Summary of Southern Work-Conditions

Enough samples taken from southern extractive and manufacturing industries have been presented to drive home by repetition the economic and human facts of that region. Between 1896 and 1929 the South was an economic frontier. As such it searched for investors of capital and gave them a free hand in the development of the South's resources. In material resources the South was exceptionally endowed; these, however, were not the principal attractions for investors. The magnet that drew capital to the South was its superabundance of white and black labor.

For the precise reason that it was over-abundant the southern supply of labor could be hired for low wages. Likewise, it could be exploited in other ways such as long hours, or poor housing. In the South there was almost complete lack of all those facilities, comforts, and even gadgets that made skilled workers elsewhere in the nation demand and enjoy a high standard of living. The South, in all the 33 years before 1929, was undergoing the painful readjustment of living and making a living. Compared with the prior condition of the South's two working classes and especially its white workers the process of adjustment itself wrought improvements. On the other hand, compared with contemporary workers elsewhere, those in the South least enjoyed the fruits of an advanced economic system.

To raise southern workers no more than abreast of other Americans, two things were needed. The first was a change of mind on the part of those who ruled the South—a change from obstruction of social controls of capitalistic enterprise to insistence upon them. A region that was noted for support of the Democratic Party had the greatest need for real democracy in its everyday affairs.

Secondly, the South needed to take the second step in industrial revolution. It had taken the first step of establishment of the fundamental extractive and manufacturing enterprises. The next, logically, should be the inauguration of complementary enterprises. To steel mills should be added foundries and machine shops; to textile mills join converting plants and then the manufacture of textile machinery. Similarly, with other primary industries, there should be attached their supplements.

Under capitalism there is so much interdependence that it is the truth that an "injury to one is an injury to all." Likewise, the converse is true "the benefit of one, benefits all." Southern white and black workers too long have been injured; and with them the rest of us. They must begin to enjoy benefits if any are to have long-time benefits.

CHAPTER 17

THE NEGRO WORKERS

The story of Negro labor has had one theme with two variations. Migration was the theme, one variant of which was the shift from traditional occupations to new ones, the other was a geographic change first within the South and then from the South to the North.

From slave days onward most Negroes were engaged in field labor, household, and personal service, transportation and mechanic arts. From the field labor the recruits for the others were drawn. This process continued after 1896 and led to the formation first, of a middle class distinguished from Negroes engaged in common labor, and eventually to an aristocratic class composed of Negro capitalists, artists, and professional persons.

Before 1890 the majority of Negroes were engaged in farming. In the later years the number in agriculture decreased by actual numerical count and also proportionally to the whole Negro population. Two streams of Negroes flowed from the plantations, one toward manufacturing, lumbering, mining, and other jobs as laborious as farm work but of different kinds; the other stream toward domestic and personal service. In turn the domestic servant group furnished most of the fledglings in the mechanic arts, trade, and professions.

Negro Farm Workers.—Despite the occupational migration from agriculture to other pursuits, the farm Negro remained the typical representative of his race if numbers were the criterion. Most plantation Negroes were unskilled field hands, working for hire. About half as many were share-croppers or tenants. The economic standing of field laborers and croppers was almost identical; as we have seen they both were among

the most exploited workers in the South.   This fact, of course,
in large measure explained the eagerness of the most intelligent
or best informed to try some other occupation.

Negro Land Owners.—The cash tenants as owners of a
small amount of property—mules, tools—were enough better
off to keep them on farms with the hope of becoming land-
owners.   That this rise in status was not impossible was proved
by a quarter-million or thereabouts who actually became owners.
Negro land owners were superior persons respected alike by
their own race and by whites of the ruling class.

However, the "poor whites" hated the successful Negro for
the Negro had attained an economic status that the "poor
white" had not reached and thus had flouted the theory of white
superiority.   The land-owning Negro, therefore, had to be
wary to avoid the venomous reprisals of the envious whites.

Besides this danger the landed Negro knew that transfers
occurred in both directions; bad crops and heavy debts reduced
owners to tenants, the latter to cropper, and these in turn to
hired laborers.   It seldom happened that Negroes made the
whole upward leap in one generation although a series of bad
years such as in the 1920's could cause a precipitate fall from
ownership to common labor.

Types of Farming.—The traditional types of farming for
Negroes were tobacco and cotton culture, so naturally these two
claimed the largest armies.   Nevertheless, several hundred
thousand Negroes broke with tradition to engage in dairying,
stockraising—beef and hogs, truck farming, and the growing
of peaches or apples.   For the most part in these newer varieties
of agriculture the Negroes were either one extreme or the other,
namely laborers or owners.   That is, there were scarcely any
tenants or share-croppers.   The reasons were plain; cotton and
tobacco were salable only in large lots at definite places so there
was no point in hiding or "losing" part of the crop, nor could
either of them be eaten.   Cotton and tobacco crops thus could
be grown by tenants or croppers without much loss to the landlord, storekeeper, or bank.   Not so with cattle, vegetables, or
fruits.   Hence, the Negro tenant and cropper was scarcely

known in these branches of farming.   The Negro laborers in these activities were indistinguishable from other hired men of the race; the Negro owner, on the other hand, was apt to be an outstanding man because he had broken two traditions by being not only a proprietor but a pioneer into new kinds of farming.

Domestic or Personal Service.—Negroes engaged in domestic or personal service ranked numerically second to those in agriculture (until 1910; after that ranked third).   Within the group itself the women outnumbered the men by about 3 to 1. For that matter about twice as many Negro women proportionally were engaged in gainful pursuits as other women in the United States; that is, from two-fifths to one-half of all Negro females over 10 years of age had some kind of job whereas only one-fifth of other women worked for wages.   Although of 10 American women only 1 was a Negress, out of 10 working women 2 were colored, and out of 10 Negro women 4 or 5 had wage-work.   Poverty was the principal reason for this high percentage of working Negro women, but other causes were first the large demand for the kind of services Negro women could render; second, the less demand for male Negroes; and third, Negro females outnumbered the males 100 to 97.

One pronounced characteristic of most Negroes engaged in domestic or personal service was their lighter pigmentation than the black Negroes "who could get any job under the sun." In slavery, light-skinned Negroes were household servants or mechanics, a favoritism due to the understanding that these people were blood-relatives of the masters or overseers.   A similar explanation of their light complexions accounted in later years for the preference for them; they had a considerable mixture of white blood, were more like the whites, and got along better with them.

The phrase, "domestic or personal service," covered a wide variety of occupations.   It included servants, washerwomen, household occasional helpers, cooks, waiters, and waitresses, doormen, porters, barbers, bootblacks, stablemen, coachmen, chauffeurs, janitors, sextons, and several others among them the "beauticians" who served their own race.

Working Conditions.—This whole category of Negroes met with varied treatment from employers. Some were treated with as much consideration as if members of the families for whom they worked; others were regarded as scarcely human and therefore immune to pain, fatigue, or feelings. In the South the tradition of Negro quarters separate from the plantation house carried over to modern times so that it was not customary for colored domestics to live in the homes where they worked; instead they retired to their own cabins on the premises or to the houses in the part of the city reserved for Negroes. To this extent they had private lives. Those who did "live in" had the varied experiences of servants in respect to rooms and privacy; too often they were relegated to attics, cubby nooks off the kitchen, or cellar holes.

Low Wages.—The pay of Negro domestic servants as a rule was less—often considerably less—than a dollar a day for 12 or more hours of work: wages of a dollar a *week* plus food were not unknown. Southern whites justified the low wages by the statement, "Nigras are just like children; they work only when you are looking at them and it takes at least two to do what one Yankee white 'help' would do."

The real reason for the low pay was the abundance of Negroes and the lack of other jobs for them. When for any reason the supply of local Negroes declined, the pay for domestic service rose. Besides their money wages the Negroes had the benefit of many forms of petty graft; it was expected that a colored cook would feed her own family from her employer's larder. The cast-off wardrobe of the employer's whole family found its way by one means or another to the Negro quarters. Personal servitors such as bootblacks, waiters, or barbers got tips; they developed an effective technique in making whites glow at their own generosity. Despite its welcome as addition to low wages the necessity to accept graft demeaned Negroes by the tacit acknowledgment of their inferiority.

Competition from Immigrants.—In the domestic and personal service occupations the Negroes outside of the South, for some time after 1896, met disastrous competition from immigrants.   Italians and Greeks drove them out of the bootblack-ing business, several nationalities excluded the Negroes from jobs as head-waiters and table waiters.   Negro stable men were replaced by white garage mechanics and the prideful colored coachmen were superseded by white native and alien chauffeurs. Personal maids and valets were drawn from Europe rather than the South.   Negro barbers in the North disappeared.   Even in those sections of the South where northern tourists congre-gated there was a tendency to employ foreign-born servitors. The percentage of Negroes in domestic and personal service de-clined after 1900; the World War and successive exclusion acts against aliens again gave Negroes opportunities; they then (1925-1929) constituted a third instead of a fifth (1910) of this occupational group.

Negroes in Civil Service.—Somewhat related to the fore-going group was the large number of Negroes employed in the civil service of cities, states, and the federal government.   A considerable portion of the civil servants were engaged in the same kinds of work as those in domestic and personal service. Quite above these in prestige, income, and character of jobs were the colored letter-carriers and policemen.   A still higher group was the one in government offices mostly doing clerical work but with a few in supervisory positions.   Among Negroes those in the civil service, the Pullman service, and a few highly skilled craftsmen made up a colored lower middle class; above them were the Negro professional and business people, below them were the masses of unskilled Negroes engaged in common labor.   Therefore, most Negroes were eager to get into some kind of civil service.   Besides the prestige attached to these positions the jobs were steady and often carried a pension, precious boons to unskilled Negroes afflicted with irregularity of work and dependent old age.

Negroes in Manufacturing.—It was in the manufacturing industries that the Negroes found their newest opportunities after 1896.   How great a giver of jobs manufacturing was may be measured by the fact that more Negroes by 1910 were em-ployed in or around mills, factories, or workshops than in any other occupation save agriculture.　Under slavery, Negroes in a few instances had been engaged in textile or iron mills and in more cases had done handicraft manufacturing on and for the plantations.　However, only a tiny minority ever had had these jobs.　Until the South began its industrial career after 1880, Negroes rarely saw the inside of any kind of factory.　Consequently Negro mill workers, as a large class of employes, was a phenomenon of the generation after 1896.　The percentage that Negroes bore to the total of all factory help more than doubled between 1896 and 1929.

Heavy Industries.—Where did they work?　In steel mills, foundries, lumber mills, and furniture factories; in shipyards, meat-packing plants (at first in southern branch packing plants), and distilleries.　In short, all the southern "heavy industries" used Negroes for common labor.　The raw material enterprises connected with these also were large employers of Negro labor; this was true of iron and coal mining, and logging camps.

Surprisingly, not all the Negroes in these "heavy industries" were men.　In 1920 there were 1,000 Negro women in iron and steel mills, 3,000 in lumber and furniture (2,000 in saw mills alone), 81 miners in 1910 and 337 in 1920.　They were not all cooks and washerwomen; in the iron and steel industry 700 Negro women in 1920 were classed as semi-skilled operatives, a number a third that of the Negro men similarly classified.

Light Industries.—In the "light industries" the Negro women outnumbered the men.　Canneries and tobacco factories were not such particularly new sources of wages as were the clothing factories.　In all of these the women were badly exploited.　In clothing manufacture at last the powerful arm of organized labor in northern plants reached into the South, and lifted the workers there to higher levels of wages, hours, and working conditions.　A few Negro printers of both sexes were in like manner protected.　Negro men had a few jobs connected with textile plants and a few Negroes were highly skilled tool makers, engravers, and jewellers.

Nearly all of the manufactures mentioned that possessed their own boiler and engine rooms had these manned by Negro firemen and most of their stationary engineers also were Negroes.

Migration.—Every one of the heavy and light manufactures that in the South gave employment to Negroes became labor reserves for similar northern enterprises. Generally the Negroes got their first chances to go North when strikes there produced labor shortages. Northern employers thus had an ever-ready supply of trained scabs. Negroes have been bitterly denounced for their ready acceptance of jobs as strike breakers. The partisanship of the castigators made them blind to the Negroes' side of the case.

A great many Negroes were completely uninformed about unionism; on the other hand many had been debarred from unions. Regardless of the union aspect, it should be expected in a competitive system that the most lowly class of workers would seize every opportunity to get some of its members out of the cellar of society. Viewed in this light it was a generous gesture made by many Negroes who, when lured North without being told of strikes, resolutely refused to scab as soon as they learned why they were given such glittering inducements to migrate. Those that did not refuse merely followed the laissez-faire rule of self-preservation: "when your competitor is helpless, grab his business." The rule often enough was used *against* Negroes to warrant their application of it *for* Negroes when the situation permitted.

Negroes in Transportation.—Negro workers have been used in the transportation industry almost as long as the race has been in America. They drove the mules hitched to rolling tobacco hogsheads; they dragged, poled, or rowed boats through creeks and bayous. On land and water they did both the laborious and skilled tasks connected with commerce. As years passed the means of transportation changed but the Negroes went along as workers.

Until the Civil War all the jobs except the captains' and first mates' on river and coastwise steamboats in the South were in the hands of colored folks. The deck-hands and roustabouts of course were black; so also were the firemen and engineers

below deck, while in the galley and staterooms still other blacks
served the public.   On southern ante-bellum railroads the entire train crew, except the conductor, often were Negroes;
engineers, firemen, brakemen, and porters all belonged to the
African race.   The longshoremen at wharves and the baggage
handlers at stations naturally were blacks.

Whites Seize Negro Jobs.—After the scene at Appomattox
Court House on April 9, 1865, the Negroes' grip on the transportation industry was a cause of envy to the southern whites.
Slowly at first and then more speedily the whites "horned in"
on the blacks' jobs.   The attack began at the topmost tasks,
those of the colored marine and locomotive engineers; then
the Negro railway firemen and finally the brakemen were subjected to pressure to yield their jobs to whites.   In the railway shops white machinists and mechanics elbowed aside their
Negro competitors; even the Negro longshoremen had to divide
work with white immigrants.

The railway unions, especially the "Big Four" Brotherhoods
of train employes, rigidly barred Negroes from membership;
on several occasions the Negro train crews organized into unions
by crafts and petitioned the proper Brotherhoods for charters
only to be refused.   Instead, whenever the black train workers
got into disagreements with the railway managers the Brotherhoods assisted southern whites to scab the Negroes.   Moreover,
the state legislatures were petitioned to set up license systems for
train workers and to put administration in Boards composed of
white unionists, a scheme to eliminate Negroes by the Boards'
refusal to license.

The result of inter-racial competition was neither victory nor
defeat for either race; it was the managers who won by playing
one race against the other.   Southern train crews sometimes
were all blacks (save the conductors), sometimes all whites, but
most often mixed.   Wherever both races worked on the same
train there were Jim Crow rules; Negro brakemen had the cars
next the engine, the whites those in the rear, while in the locomotive cab a white engineer sat at the throttle watching a Negro
fireman keep up steam-pressures.   Black engineers rarely had

white firemen.   One factor alone preserved train jobs for southern Negroes; for the same job on the same run they could be gotten to work for less wages than whites.

Similarly among longshoremen, the top deck and side next the wharf belonged to the whites.

Pullman Car Workers.—After 1867 when George Pullman constructed his "palace cars" and got railways to use them, a great new field of employment was opened to Negroes drawn from the South but eventually stationed wherever railways contracted for Pullman service.

The Negroes for many years were so grateful to the Pullman Company that they did not rebel at long hours, scant sleep, hasty and improperly balanced meals (except for dining car workers) and very low pay.   Although tips added an uncertain amount to wages, the two together did not average $1.50 a day.   The Pullman Company did provide dormitories at the most frequent layover spots and paid small pensions for a lifetime service; otherwise it took full advantage of the Negroes' good will toward the Company for providing the race with respected jobs.

The first porters who in 1915 suggested the formation of a union among Pullman car employes were incontinently fired. These actions apparently halted the agitation for a while, but during federal control of railroads during the War unionism kept seeping to the surface.   In defense, the Pullman Company in 1920 turned to a company union and discreet Welfare Work.

Nevertheless, in August 1925 under the leadership of A. Phillip Randolph, A. L. Totten, and S. M. Grain, the Brotherhood of Sleeping Car Porters and Maids was organized.   The two last-named organizers together with Roy Lancaster the Secy.-Treas. of the union were fired in November by the Pullman Company.   Randolph never had been an employe of the Pullman Company and so continued in his office.

Grievances of Pullman Car Workers.—The union's chief grievances were low wages and irregular hours of work.   The average wages then prevailing for porters were $67.50 a month plus tips.   Hours of work in preparing cars for runs were not counted in computing wages and neither was overtime unless the month's runs exceeded the abnormal high of 11,000 miles or 400 hours. All other train workers had a standard month of 240 hours. On duty, porters were not allowed to sleep more than two or three hours and even this might be broken by station stops; at the end of such a run a porter might have to start another because for some reason the supply of porters at the terminal was inadequate to the demand for Pullman cars.

Since the union besides organizing within its own field tried to stimulate other Negroes to organize and to break the barriers to colored entrance into white unions it was not chartered as a national union under the A. F. of L.; it did have the encouragement of the highest officers in the A. F. of L.

Pullman porters, from the time their trade began, always had been recipients of the highest regard from other Negroes; the porters' union, therefore, was endorsed by the National Association For the Advancement of Colored People, the National Urban League, and the National Federation of Colored Women's Clubs.

Pullman Co. Anti-union.—The Brotherhood of Sleeping Car Porters and Maids like the Order of (White) Sleeping Car Conductors—organized in 1918—got no endorsement from the Pullman Company. Every means was used by the company to break these unions of its employes and to gain acceptance of its own company union. Even Negro politicians were induced by the company to discredit the union. Not the least of the resistances to the porters' union was the company's tactic in hiring Filipino porters for some of its cars. For some time the company had employed Negro maids on some of its de luxe equipment; while this move by itself was admirable in every way for the colored race it had in it a concealed possibility of replacement of male porters by women. After all most of a porter's job was housekeeping; for his movement of heavy baggage was limited to the length of the car. Not the least weapon of the Company was the set of seniority privileges that went with long service. The highest silver stripers—one stripe for 5 years' service—for example had first choice of runs, free uniforms, as well as slightly higher wage rates to say nothing of expected pensions.

Men long in service, therefore, ran great risks if they joined the union.

The Union Shrinks.—Notwithstanding the malignant opposition of the company the union within a year (1926) had signed 51% of all the porters. In the same year but through the *company* union, wage rates were advanced to about $78 a month. Added to this sum was an average of $58 a month in tips and a deduction of $33 for uniforms (men with less than 10 years' service), shoe polish, lodgings on duty, and food. The average net wage of porters was $102 per month. In 1928 the union with blaring publicity tried to get a case under the Watson-Parker Act before a Mediation Board and backed its demands with a strike order. The Mediation Board recognized the union as spokesman for the porters but did not deem Pullman service an essential one. The Pullman Company refused to recognize the union and dared it to pull a strike by filling terminals with Negroes willing to become strike-breakers. The union backed down. The loss of the fight, together with loss of prestige, brought a decided loss in membership.

Become Affiliated with A. F. of L.—Enough members and initiative remained for the union to press its petition to the A. F. of L. for a charter which had been asked for prior to the "strike." No charter was issued because the Hotel and Restaurant Employees' International Alliance claimed jurisdiction over Pullman workers. The Executive Council of the A. F. of L. used its power to issue federal union charters to grant charters to 13 local unions of the Porters' Brotherhood and thus made them direct affiliates of the A. F. of L.

This most interesting and temporarily largest Negro union seemed in 1929 on the verge of collapse. Its fatal weaknesses were that Pullman cars easily could be dispensed with by the public and that a porters' strike unlike one of engineers, firemen, or conductors was not a calamity to a railroad; porters' jobs could be done by thousands of people eager to replace porters on strike.

Negroes in Mechanic Trades.—Before the Civil War, Negroes in the southern mechanic trades by a ratio of 5 to 1 were more numerous than whites. The Civil War emancipated the "poor whites" by removal of the masters' economic motive to back Negro artisans and the whites crowded into the trades that before the war had been virtually monopolized by Negroes. The whites also tried to restrict Negro artisans by local ordinances. During the '70's and '80's, therefore, the Negroes were being shouldered out of the most skilled and best paid of the trades; Negroes could hold on only by undercutting the white craftsmen's wages.

Negroes in Mechanic Unions.—After 1896 the most powerful white unions in the United States were to be found in the mechanic trades, namely the large group of building trades, the printers, and the machinists. These unions in the South did not face in southern Negroes a new set of persons aspiring to enter the trades; rather it was the other way about, the unions were enrolling southern whites who had pushed into Negro trades. The unions could not obliterate the skill of Negro carpenters, masons, printers, and the like; if the possessors of this skill were not conciliated they could scab upon and wreck southern white unions in these trades. Therefore the unions faced things as they were, and opened their southern locals to Negro members. This policy led to a division of locals into white and black sections with separate meetings but common purposes.

What happened next depended upon particular unions; some used the admission of Negroes as means of keeping the Negroes forever in the lowest strata ("helpers") of the trade, others fined any member or local that practiced any kind of racial discrimination, a rule that often was circumvented or ignored. As a matter of fact a great many Negroes remained outside the unions especially those unions that doomed the black workers to lifetime positions at the bottom of the trades; as independent undercutters of union wage rates the Negro could rise higher outside than inside such unions.

From 1896 to 1929 the real number of Negro mechanics increased parallel to the growth of population; the *relative* number of the Negroes in each trade continued as a constant. Of all craftsmen among the building trades, machine and printing trades, the Negroes never constituted as much as 10% of the total except the plasterers (the latter only after 1920). In no mechanic trade were there more than a handful of Negro mechanics at work in the trade anywhere outside the South.

Negro Business Class.—From the Negro viewpoint, the story of the workers in transportation and mechanic arts was one of defense against inroads of whites. The rise of a new Negro business class was far more encouraging to the black-folk. The very discriminations against Negroes were largely responsible for the emergence and growth of their own trading places. Beginning as tiny corner shops in Negro neighbor-hoods, the Negro retail stores swelled into an important part of the American economic system. As early as 1900, under the stimulation of Booker T. Washington there was formed the National Negro Business League.

Retail stores were the largest single group of Negro businesses, there being as many as 21,000 after 1920. Some of these were connected in chains, wholly owned and operated by Negroes. Grocery stores bulked high in the total although there were many dry goods, drug, and shoe stores; in addition there were 7,000 Negro eating places ranging from "dog wagons" to elite restaurants. Curiously, of the more than 100,000 persons attached to these enterprises, not all the employes were Negroes although Negroes were in the majority. For young Negro girls, these establishments opened careers that none of their ancestors had enjoyed.

With a flourishing Negro retail industry the need arose for Negro banks. To be sure in the Reconstruction period there had been the Freedmen's Saving Bank, but this had failed in the panic of 1873. The next Negro bank was started in Washington in 1888 from which date there was a constant growth of these institutions, until in 1928 there were 137 of them. Some 82 others had been started and failed. American banks as a whole have left a wide trail of destructive failures so it was not unique that Negro bankers so often lacked sagacity; nevertheless their percentage of misfortune was high. Nearly all the Negro banks whether of savings, commercial or investment types were small as befitted the financial standing of their variety of customers. The really large-scale Negro business men readily could get accommodations at non-Negro banks inasmuch as capital was color-blind; this left to Negro banks mostly the small accounts.

Another financial institution wholly in Negro hands was the insurance company. For a long time local Burial Societies, Building and Loan, or Sick Insurance Mutuals had been organized and operated by and for Negroes, and these never ceased to be popular. The first attempt to form a more inclusive insurance company was in 1880; yet it was 1913 before there was any Negro old line legal reserve insurance company. By 1928 the Negroes had no less than 12 fair-sized insurance companies of their own.

Negro Capitalists.—Business men, bankers, and insurance officials constituted a Negro capitalist class. Even wealthier were a few Negroes who manufactured Negro patent medicines or Negro beauty preparations. The Negro capitalists drew their ideas from the white capitalists; by their very great influence in their own race the Negro capitalists did a thorough job of indoctrination of the mass of Negroes with beliefs that bulwarked the capitalistic system. Communists asserted that white capitalism encouraged Negro capitalists in order that the latter's authority would keep the millions of Negroes from joining any kind of revolt against capitalism. Whether or not there was some such conscious motive the result was the same; the Negro capitalist had little fault to find with a system that elevated themselves, and this contentment, by filtration to the Negro masses, tended to counteract the radical propaganda that poured over Negroes after 1920.

Negro Professionals.—Rather more than less united to the Negro capitalists were the colored professional people. In point of time the Negro professions far preceded the business groups. Between 1773-1800 Negro preachers had congregations in Savannah, Augusta, Petersburg, Richmond, Lexington,

Philadelphia and New York City. The African Methodist Episcopal Church was founded in 1791. At no time before 1929 did Negro preachers cease to hold sway over the Negro race; the actual church members never fell below half the total Negroes. Not even the Roman Catholic Church was so successful in maintenance of authority over a working class as the Negro churches. Therefore in every plan concerning Negroes, the preachers first had to be won.

The new profession of Negro teachers (1896-1929) came to outnumber the preachers. Before the Civil War when it was unlawful to teach Negroes to read and write there could be no organized Negro education. Some masters provided for the education of favorite slaves; and there was some surreptitious instruction in reading and writing; the bulk of the Negroes were taught *ideas* rather than the 3 R's by their own wise men and women. Before the Civil War there were only 34 Negro college graduates, the first from Bowdoin, Middlebury, Wilberforce University and Oberlin—the last named accounting for two-thirds of the whole. In our period there were over 1,000 Negro High Schools and 80 colleges as well as schools of manual arts. From these and the northern colleges came the Negro teachers who were more numerous than any other Negro profession.

The need for Negro teachers was great inasmuch as Negro illiteracy as late as 1920 was 23% as compared with 4% for native whites and 13% for foreign-born whites. How little the need was met in the South may be gauged by the facts that whereas in the whole United States the expenditures per school-age child were $60 to $100, in the South the amounts were for whites $25 to $30 and for Negroes $2 to $5. Before 1920 the educational facilities for southern Negroes were provided in large measure by white philanthropists, not by the states or counties; not until extensive migrations occurred did some southern states accept responsibilities for the education of Negroes. Of course the salaries of Negro teachers were tiny.

Besides the preachers and teachers the Negroes had their own doctors. The first one was James Derham, born in Philadelphia in 1767; the first one admitted to the Massachusetts Medical Society was John V. DeGrasse in 1854. Besides Negro doctors there were colored lawyers, dentists, trained nurses, musicians, actors, artists, and authors (prose and poetry). Also there was a flourishing Negro press. If the proportion of professional whites to the total white population is used as a yardstick, then by similar calculation for Negroes their race had only half enough professional people; on the same standard the only adequate profession was the preachers. Furthermore, these statistics included all American Negroes; the showing was less favorable for the South, for the professional Negro class like their white co-professionals and artists tended to export their best brains and talents from the South. The professions and arts flourish most where there is the most freedom of expression and incidentally where there is the most wealth.

Migration to North.—Nothing since Lincoln's Proclamation so influenced American Negroes as the northern common labor shortage caused by the World War and the laws that excluded immigrants.

A small amount of migration among southern Negroes had been noticeable ever since the Civil War. Country Negroes had moved into southern cities, and from one city to another. Negroes from the border states regularly had gone into adjoining northern states and there was a constant seepage from the South to New York City, Philadelphia and St. Louis with smaller dribbles to Pittsburgh, Indianapolis, and Cincinnati. The total Negro populations of these cities stood in size in the order named. By far the largest drift of colored people was from the southern Atlantic coastal states toward the southwest.

Urban League.—Enough Negroes had arrived in northern cities by 1910 to cause the formation of the National League on Urban Conditions of Negroes, a title soon shortened to National Urban League. The backers of this organization were both whites and Negroes. The original function of the League was the placement in jobs of Negroes who wandered into urban centers. The function was so well fulfilled that individual employers and Chambers of Commerce contributed so much support to the League that it became the principal Negro employment office.   This financial influence in League affairs may have accounted for the fact that in many cities it became a reactionary influence in the Negro labor field even furnishing scabs for struck plants; and in some cities becoming notorious for its anti-unionism.   On the other hand, the national officers of the League particularly after 1919 tried to pursue a policy of mutual friendliness with the A. F. of L.   Nevertheless, except in Greater New York, the local branches of the League did not adopt tactics that favored unions; "he who pays the piper calls the tune."

During the World War, immigration greatly was reduced and emigration increased at the very time when northern industries and farms were clamoring for unskilled labor.   In smallest part this was satisfied by an inflow of Porto Ricans, Mexicans, and Filipinos; the attempt to breach the barriers against Orientals was defeated.   The vacancies remaining were either offset by machinery or filled by Negroes.   The small trickle of Negroes to the North noticed in 1906 and considerably commented upon in 1910 became a stream 1914-1919 and a torrent in 1922-23.

Northern Jobs for Negroes.—The Chicago packing houses took the most Negroes; in 1910 out of 10,840 employes only 67 were black but in 1920 and 1929 the colored folk in this industry constituted over 20% of the total work force.   Chicago in 1910 had 44,000 Negroes; in 1920 there were 109,000 living in the city.

The steel industry was another Mecca for migrants especially in Cleveland which city's Negro population in a decade jumped from 8,000 to 34,000.   During the steel strike of 1919, the chief strikebreakers were Negroes and they not only remained but increased in the industry in the later years.

The first Negroes entered the automobile industry in 1916 with the result that Detroit led all cities in the percentage increase of its Negro population; the figures were 5,741 in 1910 and 40,838 in 1920 or an increase of 611%.   Flint, Buffalo, Gary and Milwaukee, each between 1920-30 had an increase in Negro population of over 200%.

A large number of Negroes were employed on northern road-construction and other building projects including shipbuilding. The women of the migrant Negro families entered the various branches of the food industry, went into commercial laundries, and into clothing factories. Northern states, just above the border, used a large number of colored farm laborers. The years after 1922-23, the peak torrent of Negro migrants, showed only a partial slackening, and indeed in some cases, such as the Negro flow to Detroit, the migration did not subside at all.

Race Riots.—The immediate effect of the unprecedented rise of Negro populations of northern cities was such frightful overcrowding in former colored neighborhoods as to cause overflow into white areas. This, together with frictions in work places and the supposition that all Negro workers scabbed strikes and tended always to lower wage and work standards, produced several terrible race riots and many minor violent race collisions.

In July 1917 the simmering troubles in East St. Louis broke out into a riot that left dead 38 Negroes and 8 whites. Within a few weeks (September 1917) a riot at Chester, Pa.—a ship-yard town south of Philadelphia—had five fatal Negro casualties. In 1919 at Chicago and near Elaine, Okla., there were extremely violent outbursts. The Elaine case was brought about by the southern farm system, the immediate incitement being a request by a tenant union for an honest accounting by landlords. Over 100 Negroes and 5 whites were slaughtered in this riot. The worst outbreak of all took place May 31 to June 1, 1921 in the boom oil city of Tulsa, Okla., where Negro oil workers were accused of being "too uppity." In this brief civil war 150 Negroes and 10 or more whites were killed; besides the entire Negro quarter was destroyed by fire with a loss to Negroes of $1½ million.

Negro Political Power.—The more remote effect of the migration was the increase in Negro political power in the northern cities. In Chicago the Negro vote, in return for favors, was given in support of William Boyce Thompson; the Negro voters of this city also sent a representative to the United States

Congress and to the Illinois legislature. Political power, as always, meant more government and private jobs, better pay in public service and from civic contractors, improved streets and schools in the voters' wards, and similar rewards. The Negro vote may have been reflected in the Coolidge Message to Congress on December 8, 1925 in which violence against Negroes was deplored. Victor Berger, Socialist from Milwaukee, introduced in Congress in 1926 an Anti-Lynching Bill. The demand by Negroes that they serve on juries in cases involving Negroes was another indicator of larger political power.

Negro Economic Power.—The American Federation of Labor was forced to give more attention to discrimination against Negroes in national unions. In 1920 the convention voted an unprecedented interference with national union autonomy when it passed a resolution that the Brotherhood of Railway Clerks cease the erection of barriers against Negro membership. In 1922 the convention was faced with similar problems in the Railway Carmen's, and Boilermakers' Unions. Each following convention had the issue raised in some form.

Effects in South of Migration.—In the South the migration had the effects of a labor shortage. For example, in 1923, the 32,000 Negroes who left Georgia constituted 13% of the total farm hands; in the same year Alabama and Arkansas lost 3½%, South Carolina 3%, Florida 2%, and Louisiana 1%. The total migration of that one year was 478,000. The South tried to stop the flood by requiring labor agents to take out licenses and then charging from $500 to $2,500 for license fees. These were futile; for the best labor agents were Negroes already in the North who reported high wages, better housing, and no formal Jim Crowism. Southern people were forced to raise the wages of colored domestic servants, improve Negro dwellings, and to pay more attention to Negro schools.

An effect not so pleasing to Negroes was the stiffening of the laws of vagrancy in Georgia, Florida, Mississippi, and Texas. Negroes called vagrants by judges could be forced to labor on farms, in forests, on roads, and in mines, a power that often was grossly prostituted.

Finally an unlooked for effect was a corresponding migration to the North of many thousand southern "poor whites."

Nothing in the long run would have been better for the South and the nation than the withdrawal to northern jobs of a million or more Negroes and whites. The pressure of two working classes, one Negro and the other white, and both more numerous than the economic demand for either kept the South in a condition of economic and social backwardness; in turn this condition directly affecting 8% of the nation, indirectly retarded the whole nation. It has been an economic law that in an inter-dependent society such as ours an economic weakness at any point causes unfavorable reactions throughout the whole social order.

The United States could not be strong if the South was weak; to make the South strong more jobs for southerners were needed preferably in the South but in the North if the South could not expand fast enough to absorb its own super-abundant supply of labor.

AFTER WORD

On October 23, 1929 a drastic drop in prices on the New York Stock Exchange marked the end of an era. For 41 months thereafter, all news was bleak despite occasional chirrups heralding return of normalcy. Our productive capacity was ample for our needs; our consumption demands could use all we produced; but our economic system was maladjusted.

Factors in Collapse.—Of the many factors that brought about the 1929 collapse, one was the simultaneous but diverse economic principles operative in different branches of enterprise. Farmers and four out of five laborers functioned by a system of free competition, whereas most of our manufacturers, and banks protected by high tariffs, conducted their affairs as semi-monopolies. Two price systems ran at the same time; those groups working under free competition had the prices of their products or services fixed by the higgling of the market while those within the control of semi-monopoly more or less fixed and controlled their own prices—of course at the point of highest net income. Since there was no relative scarcity of farm products or of labor-power the competition in these fields tended toward relatively low prices and certainly toward low purchasing power. On the contrary the prices of manufactures and of credit (interest) were pegged at highly profitable levels despite a large increase in productive capacity for manufactures and an abundance of loanable credit in banks.

Use Made of Profits.—As a result, profits of manufacturing and banking were extraordinarily high. It was the use made of these profits that finally was most influential in bringing about catastrophe. The profits went into reserves, dividends, munificent salaries, and bonuses to executives, foreign investments, and speculation.

Out of the reserves, dividends sometimes at the 1929 or higher rates were paid for two or more years after 1929. The practice of reserves was excellent but the amount thus segregated was mountainous; corporations "saved" too much and spent too little in wages or other means of immediate consumption. The receivers of dividends who were most generously endowed with stocks, could not spend the dividends and thereby sustain production. Instead they invested in still more productive equipment, whose output the farmers and laborers could not purchase. Some of the excess dividends went into foreign investments at the rate after 1922 of a billion dollars a year. At the same time a high tariff blocked the foreigners from paying back either interest or principal in the only sensible forms, namely in goods—the other alternative, gold, we did not need and they did not possess. Another portion of the dividends was poured into speculation, the corporate profits themselves pushing up stock prices and making further speculation alluring. The average price of 351 industrial stocks in 1924 was 69.7; the same stocks in September 1929 averaged 216.1, a plain sign of abnormal stock gambling.

Unbalance.—This unbalanced economic system could have succeeded only if there were free trade, and if our surplus output were sold abroad. Trade was not free and was made less so on our side by the Hawley-Smoot Tariff, and by various retaliatory restrictions imposed by our customers. The postwar world disturbances, likewise, prevented large expansion of foreign trade.

Our system cracked warningly in 1924 and swayed badly in the autumn of 1927. Yet we were heedless of these symptoms of malady until the plunge of stock prices in 1929 gave clear demonstration of deep rooted economic disease. Even then and until June 1930 there was slight recognition that our troubles were fundamental, not temporary.

Contributory Factors.—After the crash other contributory factors added to our economic sickness. We had over-invested in certain varieties of buildings which we could not finance after business confidence was destroyed. Our working class after 1925 when ordinary demand slackened had been cajoled into instalment purchasing and therefore, after 1929, were saddled with debts. Our public and private investments in Germany were imperiled in 1931 followed at once by the abandonment of the gold standard by the United Kingdom and 24 other countries. Our banks were bogged down with frozen or valueless notes or collateral. Drought in 1931 and again in 1933 and 1934 heightened the miseries of our farmers some of whom by 1932 were in open revolt against their oppressions.

Unemployment.—Most ominous of all, long before 1929 the level of unemployment had begun to rise. From 1925 onward displaced workers were not quickly re-absorbed. After October 1929 unemployment rose in a year to 3½ millions and by 1931 was over 6 million. The loss in purchasing power from this unemployment by 1931 was 15 times the loss of all business failures—these at a 36-year peak—and 2 times the value of our entire foreign trade. In another two years unemployment touched 13 million, the highest recorded in the world.

Where competition prevailed—among farmers, soft coal mining and non-unionized workers—the depression at once brought slashed prices. Among the protected semi-monopolies and highly unionized laborers the ability to peg prices prevented a correlation between prices and demand—that is, prices slipped somewhat but did not plunge downward. The theoretical self-correction of depression under a competitive economics did not operate.

Prognosis.—Enough of diagnosis; what of prognosis? We cannot succeed with an economic system that is half freely competitive and half price-controlled. Compulsory universal free competition is as impossible as it would be unwise. If capitalism is to work at all it must be brought under social control. Its fruits must be distributed by one means or another—mostly high wages, high taxes, and lower prices—to the whole people not just a few favored fortunates.

We no longer need to offer glittering rewards to those who control production; we do need a more widespread distribution of the good things of life so that the whole people can have what Gompers long ago said union workers wanted, namely, "More."

Conclusion

SELECTED REFERENCES

A. Bibliographies

Sources of:
- International Labor Office.
- National Bureau of Economic Research.
- National Industrial Conference Board.
- United States Bureau of the Census.
- United States Department of Labor.
- Russell Sage Foundation.
  - Labor in Industry, 1925.
  - Negro in Industry, 1924.

B. Special Studies

Commission on Industrial Relations, created by Act of Congress on August 23, 1912. *Report:* 11 volumes, published 1916.

Hoover Commission.
- *Recent Social Trends.*
- *Recent Economic Trends.*

Information Service of the Federal Council of Churches. United States Department of Labor: Womens' and Childrens' Bureaus; Bureau Labor Statistics.

C. Periodicals

Daily:
- Files of New York Times; Christian Science Monitor.

Weekly:
- Independent; Labor; Nation; Outlook; World Tomorrow; Weekly Newsletter (A.F.L.)

Monthly:
- Atlantic, Contemporary Review, Current History, Federationist, Forum, Harpers, Living Age, Monthly Labor Review (Bureau Labor), Monthly Survey of Business (A.F.L.), Review of Reviews, World's Work, Yale Review.

Journals:
- Annals American Academy Social and Political Science, Journal of Political Economy, The American Economic Review, History, Encyclopedia Reference Book (A.F.L. Proceedings analysed) Volume 1, 1919; Volume 2, 1924.

Annuals:
    American Labor Yearbook—Rand School.
    American Yearbook—New York Times Publishing Company.

D. Biography and Autobiography

Bailey, Thomas A. *Theodore Roosevelt and the Japanese-American Crisis.* Stanford University Press, 1934.

Barron, C. W. *They Told Barron.* New York, Harpers, 1930.

—— *More They Told Barron.* New York. Harpers, 1931.

Beers, Thomas. *Mark Hanna.* New York, A. A. Knopf, 1929.

Berkman, Alexander. *Prison Memoirs of an Anarchist.* New York, Mother Earth Pub. Association, 1912.

Bishop, Joseph Bucklin. *Theodore Roosevelt and His Time.* New York, Scribner's, 1920.

Bowers, Claude G. *Beveridge and the Progressive Era.* New York, Literary Guild, 1932.

Browne, Waldo Ralph. *Altgeld of Illinois.* New York, Huebsch, 1924.

Carnegie, Andrew *Autobiography.* Boston, Houghton Mifflin, 1920.

Coleman, McAlister. *Eugene V. Debs.* New York, Greenberg, 1930.

Corey, Lewis. *The House of Morgan.* G. Howard Watt, 1930.

Corsi, Edward. *In the Shadow of Liberty.—The Chronicle of Ellis Island.* New York, Macmillan, 1935.

Croly, H. A. *Marcus Alonzo Hanna.* New York, Macmillan, 1912.

Flynn, J. T. *God's Gold: John D. Rockefeller and His Times.* Harcourt Brace, 1932.

Glück, Elsie. *John Mitchell, Miner.* New York, John Day Co., 1929.

Goldman, Emma. *Living My Life.* 2 volumes. New York, A. A. Knopf, Inc., 1931.

Gompers, Samuel. *Seventy Years of Life and Labor.* New York, Dutton, 1925.

Harvey, Rowland Hill. *Samuel Gompers.* Stanford University Press, 1935.

Haywood, W. D. *Bill Haywood's Book.* International Publishers, 1929.

Hillquit, Morris. *Loose Leaves From a Busy Life.* New York, Macmillan, 1934.

Howe, Frederick. *Confessions of a Reformer.* New York, Scribner's, 1925.

Jones, "Mother." *The Autobiography of Mother Jones.* Chicago, Kerr & Co., 1925.

Josephson, Matthew. *The Robber Barons.* New York, Harcourt Brace, 1934.

Karsner, David. *Debs, His Authorized Life and Letters.* New York, Boni & Liveright, 1919.

LaFollette, Robert M. (Sr.). *Autobiography*. LaFollette Co., Madison, Wis., 1913.

Lewisohn, Ludwig. *Upstream*. New York, Boni & Liveright, 1922.

Longworth, Alice Roosevelt. *Crowded Hours*. New York, Scribner's, 1933.

O'Conner, Harvey. *Mellon's Millions*. New York, John Day Co., 1933.

—— *Steel Dictator*. New York, Reynal Hitchcock, 1935.

Russell, Charles Edward. *Bare Hands and Stone Walls*. New York, Scribner's, 1933.

Tarbell, Ida. *Life of Elbert H. Gary*. Houghton Mifflin, 1924.

E. Books other than Biography or Autobiography

Abbott, Edith. *Women in Industry*. New York, Appleton, 1910.

—— *Immigration*. Chicago, University of Chicago Press, 1924.

Adamic, Louis. *Dynamite*. New York, Viking, 1931.

Allen, Frederick Lewis. *Only Yesterday*. New York, Harpers, 1931.

—— *Lords of Creation*. New York, Harpers, 1935.

Allen, Henry Justin. *The Party of the Third Part*. New York, Harpers, 1921.

Anderson, Nels. *The Hobo*. Chicago, University of Chicago Press, 1923.

Andrews, John Bertram. *Labor Problems and Labor Legislation*. New York, American Association for Labor Legislation, 1922.

Andrews, Irene Osgood. *Minimum Wage Legislation*. Albany, New York State Factory Investigation Comm., 1914.

Anthracite Coal Strike Commission. *Report to the President*. Washington, Government Printing Office, 1903.

Asbury, Herbert. *The Barbary Coast*. New York, Knopf, 1933.

Atkeson, Mary Meek. *The Woman On the Farm*. New York, Century, 1924.

Baer, Willis N. *Economic Development of Cigar Industry in United States*. Lancaster, Pennsylvania, Art Printing Company, 1933.

Baker, Elizabeth Faulkner. *Protective Labor Legislation with Special Reference to Women in the State of New York*. New York, Longmans.

—— *Protective Labor Legislation*. New York, Longmans, 1925.

—— *Displacement of Men By Machines*. New York, Col. Univ. Press, 1933.

Barnett, George E. *Chapters on Machinery and Labor*. Cambridge, Harvard University Press, 1926.

Beard, C. A. and M. *Rise of American Civilization*. New York, Macmillan, 1927.

Beard, Mary R. *America Through Women's Eyes* (anthology). New York, Macmillan, 1934.

—— *On Understanding Women.* New York, Longmans, 1931.

—— *Short History of the American Labor Movement.* New York, Doran, revised edition, 1924.

Benson, Mary Sumner. *Women in 18th Century America.* New York, Columbia University Press, 1935.

Berglund, A. Starines and DeVyver. *Labor in Industrial South.* University of Virginia, 1930.

Bernheim, Alfred and Bernheim, Dorothy Van Doren. *Labor and the Government.* Published for 20 C. Fund by New York, McGraw-Hill.

Berman, E. *Labor and the Sherman Act.* New York, Harpers, 1930.

Berman, Edward. *Labor Disputes and The President of the United States.* New York, Columbia University, 1924 (Studies in History, Economics and Public Law No. 249.)

—— *Labor Disputes and The President of the United States.* New York, Longmans, 1924.

Bernhardt, Joshua. *The Railroad Labor Board.* Baltimore, Johns Hopkins Press, 1923.

Bimba, Anthony. *History of American Working Class.* International.

Bittelman, Alexander. *15 Years of the Communist Party.* Pamphlet. New York, Workers' Library, 1934.

Blanchard, P. *Labor in Southern Cotton Mills.* New York, New Republic, 1927.

Boeckel, Richard. *Labor's Money.* New York, Harcourt, 1923.

Bonnett, Clarence Elmore. *Employers' Association in the United States.* New York, Macmillan, 1922.

Borchard, Edwin M. *Convicting the Innocent.* Yale University Press, 1932.

Boyle, James. *The Minimum Wage and Syndicalism.* Cincinnati, Stewart & Kidd Co., 1913.

Brandeis, L. O. *Other People's Money.* New York, Stokes, 1932.

Brawley, Benjamin Griffith. *A Social History of the American Negro.* New York, Macmillan, 1921.

Briffault, R. *The Mothers.* New York, Macmillan, 1927.

Brissenden, Paul F. *The I. W. W.* New York, Columbia University Press, 1920.

Brooks, John Graham. *The Social Unrest.* New York, Macmillan, 1903.

—— *American Syndicalism—The I. W. W.* New York, Macmillan, 1913.

Brookings, Robert S. *Industrial Ownership.* New York, Macmillan, 1925.

Browder, Earl. *Communism in the United States.* New York, International Publishers, 1935.

Bruce, Harold R. *American Parties and Politics.* New York, Holt, 1927.

Burns, William J. *The Masked War.* New York, Doran, 1913.

Burton, E. R. *Employe Representation.* Baltimore, Williams & Wilkins, 1926.

Butler, Elizabeth Beardsley. *Women and the Trades.* (Pittsburgh Survey). New York Charities Publishing Committee, 1919.

Carroll, Mollie Ray. *Labor and Politics.* Boston, Houghton Mifflin, 1923.

Chadbourn, J. H. *Lynching and the Law.* Chapel Hill, University of North Carolina Press, 1933.

Chase, Stuart. *The Tragedy of Waste.* New York, Macmillan, 1925.

Childs, H. L. *Labor and Capital in National Politics.* Columbus, Ohio State University Press, 1930.

Clark, Jane. *Deportation of Aliens.* New York, Columbia University Press, 1931.

Commission of Inquiry, Interchurch World Movement: *Report on the Steel Strike of 1919.* New York, Harcourt, Brace and Howe, 1920.
—— *Public Opinion and the Steel Strike.* New York, Harcourt, Brace and Howe, 1921.

Commons, John R. and Andrews, John Bertram. *Principles of Labor Legislation.* New York, Harpers, 1920, 1927, and 1936.

Commons, John R. *Races and Immigrants in America.* New York, Macmillan, 1907, revised edition 1920.

Commons, John R. and Associates. *History of Labor in the United States.* Volume 1, New York, 1918 and 1921. Volume 2, New York, 1918 and 1921. Volume 3, New York, 1935. Volume 4, New York, 1935.

Consumer's League, National. *The Supreme Court and Minimum Wage Legislation.* C. L. New York, 1925.

Coombs, Whitney. *The Wages of Unskilled Labor in the Manufacturing Industries in the United States, 1890-1924.* New York, Columbia University Press, 1926.

Couch, W. T., editor. *Culture in the South.* Chapel Hill, University of North Carolina Press, 1933.

Coulter, E. M. *A History of Georgia.* Chapel Hill, University of North Carolina Press, 1933.

Crook, Wilfrid Harris. *The General Strike.* Chapel Hill, University of North Carolina Press, 1931.

Cross, Ira B. *The Essentials of Socialism.* New York, Macmillan.

Day, Edmund E. and Thomas, Woodlief. *The Growth of Manufactures, 1899-1923.* Census Monograph VIII, Washington.

Davis, Watson. *The Story of Copper.* New York, Century, 1924.

Debs vs. United States. United States S. C. No. 714 October Term 1918 (March 10, 1919).

Densmore, J. B. *Report on Mooney-Billings Trials*. Doc. 157, 66th Congress 1st Session.

Devine, Edward T. *Winnipeg and Seattle*. The "Survey" October 4, 1919.

Douglas, P. H. *Real Wages in United States*, 1890-1926. Boston, Houghton Mifflin, 1930.

Douglas, Paul H. *The Coming of A New Party*. New York, Whittlesey House, McGraw-Hill, 1932.

DuBois, W. E. B. *Black Reconstruction*. New York, Harcourt Brace, 1935.

Duncan, H. G. *Immigration and Assimilation*. New York, Heath, 1933.

Dunn, Robert W. *The Americanization of Labor*. New York, International Publishers, 1929.

—— *Company Unions*. New York, Int. Publishers, 1927.

Dunn, Robert W. and Hardy, Jack. *Labor and Textiles*. New York, International, 1931.

Eastman, Crystal. *Work Accidents and the Law*. Pittsburgh, Survey, Russell Sage Foundation New York Charities Pub. Comm., 1910.

Ehrmann, Herbert B. *The Untried Case, The Madeiros-Morelli evidence, in re Sacco-Vanzetti case*. New York, Vanguard Press, 1933.

Ellingwood, Albert R. and Coombs, Whitney. *The Government and Labor*. Chicago, A. W. Shaw, 1926.

Epstein, Abraham. *Facing Old Age*. New York, Knopf, 1922.

—— *Insecurity*. New York, Smith-Haas, 1933.

Evans, Chris. *History of United Mine Workers of America*.

Federated American Engineering Societies Committee on Elimination of Waste in Industry. *Waste in Industry*. New York, McGraw-Hill, 1921.

—— *The 12 Hour Shift in Industry*. New York, Dutton, 1922.

Feldman, H. *The Regularization of Employment*. New York, Harpers, 1925.

—— *Racial Factors in American Industry*. Harpers, 1931.

Fine, N. *Labor and Farmer Parties in United States, 1828-1928*. New York, Rand School of Social Science, 1928.

Fitch, John Andrews. *The Causes of Industrial Unrest*. New York, Harpers, 1924.

—— *The Steel Worker*.

Foster, W. J. *The Great Steel Strike and Its Lessons*. New York, B. W. Huebsch, 1920.

Fraenkel, Osmond Kessler. *The Sacco-Vanzetti Case*. New York, A. A. Knopf, 1931.

Frankfurter, Felix and Greene, Nathan. *The Labor Injunction*. New York, Macmillan, 1930.

Frey, John Philip. *The Labor Injunction*. Cincinnati, Equity Publishing Co., 1922.

Gaines, Frances Pendleton. *The Southern Plantation.* New York, Columbia University Press, 1924.

Gambs, John S. *The Decline of the I. W. W.* New York, Columbia University Press, 1932.

Gaston, Herbert E. *The Non Partisan League.* New York, Harcourt, Brace & Howe, 1920.

Glocker, T. W. *Government of American Trade Unions.* Baltimore, 1913.

Gulick, C. A. *Labor Policy of United States Steel Corporation.* New York, Longmans, 1924.

Haber, William. *Industrial Relations in the Building Industry.* Cambridge, Harvard Univ. Press, 1930.

Hansen, O. C. *Americanism and Bolshevism.* Garden City, New York, Doubleday, Doran, 1920.

Hapgood, Norman, editor. *Professional Patriots.* A & C Boni, 1927.

Hardman, J. B. S., editor. *American Labor Dynamics.* New York, Harcourt Brace, 1928.

Heer, Clarence. *Income and Wages in the South.* 1930.

Helbing, A. T. *The Departments of the A. F. of L.* Baltimore, Johns Hopkins, 1931.

Henry, Alice. *Women and the Labor Movement.* New York, Macmillan, 1923 and 1927.

Herring, E. Pendleton. *Group Representation Before Congress.* Institute for Government Research. Baltimore, Johns Hopkins, 1929.

Hiller, E. T. *The Strike.* Chicago University Press, 1928.

Hillquit, Morris. *History of Socialism in the United States.* New York, Funk and Wagnalls, 1910.

Henrichs, A. F. *The United Mine Workers of America and Non-Union Coal Fields.* New York, Longmans Green & Co., 1923.

History Committee of the General Strike Committee; *The Seattle General Strike.*

Holcombe, Arthur Norman. *The Political Parties of Today.* New York, Harpers, 1924.

Hollander, J. H. and Barnett, G. E. *Studies in American Trade Unionism, 2 volumes.* New York, Holt & Co., 1905.

Hopkins, Ernest Jerome. *What Happened in the Mooney Case.* New York, Brewer, Warren and Putnam, 1932.

Howard, Sidney. *The Labor Spy.* New York, New Republic, 1924.

Hoxie, R. F. *Trade Unionism in the United States, 2nd edition.* New York, Appleton, 1923.

Huggins, W. L. *Labor and Democracy (Kansas Court).* New York, Macmillan, 1922.

Hunt, Edward Eyre and Tryon, F. G. and Willits, Joseph H. *What the Coal Commission Found.* Baltimore, Williams & Wilkins, 1925.

Hunter, Robert. *Labor in Politics.*

—— *Violence and the Labor Movement.* New York, Macmillan, 1914.

International Labour Office. *An International Enquiry into Costs Of Living, Series N., Number 19.* Geneva, 1931.

Jacobstein, Meyer. *The Tobacco Industry in the United States.* New York, Columbia University, 1907.

James, G. M. *American Trade Unionism.* Chicago, M. Clurg, 1922.

Kennedy, F. A. *Bibliography of Negro Migration.* New York, Columbia University Press.

Kennedy, Louise V. *The Negro Peasant Turns Cityward.* New York, Col. Univ. Press, 1930.

Laidler, Harry W. *Concentration of Control in American Industry.* New York, Thos. Y. Crowell Co., 1931.

—— *History of Socialist Thought.* New York, Crowell, 1927.

Langdon, Davies. *Short History of Women.* Viking, 1921.

Lemerson, W. L. *Adjusting the Immigrant to Industry.*

Lemert, Ben F. *The Cotton Textile Industry of the Southern Appalachian Piedmont.* Chapel Hill, University of North Carolina Press, 1933.

Lescohier, Don D. *The Labor Market.* New York, Macmillan, 1919.

Levine, Louis. *A History of International Ladies Garment Workers Union.* New York, B. W. Huebsch, 1924.

Levinson, Edward. *"I Break Strikes! The Technique of Pearl L. Bergoff."* Robert McBride & Company, 1935.

Lewis, E. E. *The Mobility of the Negro.* New York, Col. Univ. Press, 1931.

Lobsenz, J. *The Older Woman in Industry.* New York, Scribners, 1929.

Lorwin, L. I. *The American Federation of Labor.* Washington, Brookings Inst., 1933.

Lubin, Isidor. *Miner's Wages and The Cost of Coal.* New York, McGraw-Hill, 1924.

McCabe, David A. *National Collective Bargaining in the Pottery Industry.* Johns Hopkins Press, 1932.

McIsaac, Archibald M. *The Order of Railroad Telegraphers.* Princeton University Press.

McLean, D. A. *The Morality of the Strike.* New York, P. J. Kennedy, 1921.

McMahon, T. H. *The United Textile Workers of America.* New York, Workers Educational Bureau, 1926.

McNeill, Georg E. *The Labor Movement.* Boston, A. M. Bridgman & Co., 1886.

Mack, R. H. *The Cigar Manufacturing Industry.* Philadelphia, University of Pennsylvania Press, 1933.

Masters, Edgar Lee. *The Tale of Chicago.* New York, G. P. Putnam's Sons, 1933.

Merriam, Charles E. *The American Party System.* New York, Macmillan, 1922.

Merritt, W. Gordon. *History of the League for Industrial Rights (pamphlet)*. New York, L. I. R., 1925.

Mitchell, John. *Organized Labor*. Philadelphia, American Book & Bible House, 1903.

Morris, H. L. *The Plight of the Bituminous Coal Miner*. Philadelphia, University of Pennsylvania Press, 1934.

Morris, Victor P. *Oregon's Experience with Minimum Wage Legislation*. Columbia University Press, 1930.

Mumford, Lewis. *The Story of Utopias*. New York, Boni & Liveright, 1922.

Myers, Gustavus. *History of Great American Fortunes*. Chicago, Charles H. Kerr & Co., 1910.

Nathan, Maud. *The Story of an Epoch Making Movement (Labor Legislation)*. New York, Doubleday, Page, 1926.

Nickerson, Hoffman. *The American Rich*. Garden City, New York, Doubleday Doran, 1930.

Norton, T. L. *Trade Union Policies in the Massachusetts Shoe Industry, 1919-20*. New York, Columbia University Press, 1932.

Nyman, Richard C. and Smith, Elliott D. *Union Management Cooperation in the Stretch-Out*. Yale University Press, 1934.

Olds, Marshall. *"Analysis of the Interchurch World Movement Report on the Steel Strike."* New York, G. P. Putnam's Sons, 1923.

Oneal, James. *The Workers in American History*. New York, Rand School of Social Science, 1921.

Orth, Samuel P. *The Armies of Labor*. New Haven, Yale University Press, 1921.

Page, Thomas Nelson. *The Negro: the Southerner's Problem*. New York, 1904.

Parker, Carleton H. *The Casual Laborer and Other Essays*. New York, Harcourt, Brace & Howe., 1920.

—— *The I. W. W.* Atlantic Monthly, 1917.

Parker, Cornelia Stratton. *Working With the Working Women*. New York, Harpers, 1922.

Parsons, Alice Beal. *Woman's Dilemma*. New York, Crowell, 1926.

Perlman, Selig. *A History of Trade Unionism in the United States*. New York 1922, Macmillan.

—— *A Theory of the Labor Movement*. New York, Macmillan, 1928.

Plumb, Glenn E. and Roylance, William G. *Industrial Democracy*. New York, Huebsch, 1923.

Pound, Arthur. *The Iron Man in Industry*. New York, Atlantic, 1922.

Powell, L. M. *History of United Typothetae of America*. Chicago, University Press, 1920.

Pruette, Lorine. *Women and Leisure*. New York, Dutton, 1924.

Rand School of Social Science. *American Labor Yearbook, Annual*. New York, 7 East 15th Street.

Raper, Arthur. *The Tragedy of Lynching.* Chapel Hill, University of North Carolina Press, 1933.

Reed, L. S. *Labor Philosophy of Samuel Gompers.* New York, Columbia University Press, 1930.

Rhodes, J. E. *Workmen's Compensation.* New York, Macmillan, 1917.

Rhyne, J. J. *Some Southern Cotton Mill Workers and their Villages.* Chapel Hill, University of North Carolina, 1930.

Rice, Stuart. *Farmers and Workers in American Politics. Studies in History, Economics and Public Law, Volume C XIII, Number 253.* Columbia University, 1924.

Rice, Stuart Arthur. *Farmers and Workers in American Politics.* New York, Longmans, 1924.

Ringel, Fred J. (editor). *America as Americans See It.* New York, Harcourt Brace, 1932.

Robbins, Hayes. *The Labor Movement and the Farmer.* New York, Harcourt, 1922.

Rockefeller, John D. Jr. *The Personal Relation in Industry.* New York, Boni & Liveright, 1924.

Ross, Edward Alsworth. *Roads to Social Peace.* Chapel Hill, North Carolina, University of North Carolina Press, 1924.

Rubinow, I. M. *Social Insurance.* New York, Holt, 1913.

Russell, Bertrand. *Proposed Roads to Freedom.* New York, Holt, 1919.

Russell, Charles Edward. *The Story of the Non-Partisan League.* New York, Harpers, 1920.

Ryan, Frederick L. *Industrial Relations in the San Francisco Building Trades.* University of Oklahoma Press, 1935.

Ryan, J. A. and Husslein, J. *The Church and Labor.* New York, Macmillan, 1920.

Saposs, David J. *Left Wing Unionism.* New York, International Publishers, 1926.

—— *Readings in Trade Unionism.* New York, Macmillan, 1926.

Savage, Marion Dutton. *Industrial Unionism in America.* New York, Ronald Press, 1922.

Sayre, Francis Bower. *Selection of Cases and Other Authorities on Labor Law.* Cambridge, Harvard University Press, 1922.

Schlossberg, Joseph. *The Workers and Their World.* A.L.P. Committee, 1935.

Schneider, D. M. *The Workers Party and American Trade Unions.* Baltimore, J. Hopkins Press, 1928.

Seidman, J. L. *The Yellow Dog Contract.* Johns Hopkins Press, 1932.

Selekman, Ben M. *Employees' Representation in Steel Works.* New York, Russell Sage Foundation, 1925.

—— *Sharing Management With Workers.* New York, Russell Sage Foundation, 1924.

Selekman, Ben M. and Van Kleeck, Mary. *Employees' Representation in Coal Mines.* New York, Russell Sage Foundation, 1925.

Shadwell, A. S. *Breakdown of Socialism.* Boston, Little, Brown, 1927.

Smith, Bruce. *The State Police.* New York, Macmillan, 1925.

Smith, Darrel H. *The United States Employment Service.* Baltimore, Johns Hopkins Press, 1923.

Soule, George. *The Coming American Revolution.* New York, Macmillan, 1934.

Spargo, John. *Applied Socialism.* New York, B. W. Huebsch.

Spero, Sterling D. and Harris, Abram L. *The Black Worker.* New York, Columbia University Press, 1931.

Spielman, Jean E. *The Stool Pigeon.* Minneapolis, American Publishing Company, 1923.

St. John, Vincent. *The I. W. W.—Its History, Structure and Methods (pamphlet).*

Starnes, George Talmadge and Hamm, John E. *Some Phases of Labor Relations in Virginia.* New York, D. Appleton-Century Co., 1935.

Stecker, Margaret L. *National Founders Association.* R. J. Econ. Volume 30.

Steffens, Lincoln. *Autobiography, 2 Volumes.* New York, Harcourt Brace, 1931.

Stevens, A. C. *Cyclopaedia of Fraternities.*

Sullivan, Mark. *Our Times, 6 volumes.* Charles Scribners Sons.

Tannenbaum, Frank J. *Darker Phases of the South.* New York, Putnam, 1924.

Tarbell, Ida. *History of Standard Oil Company.* Macmillan, 1904.
—— *The Business of Being a Woman.* Macmillan, 1912.

Thomas, Norman. *The Conscientious Objector in America.* New York, Huebsch, 1923.
—— *Human Exploitation.* Stokes, 1935.

Thornthwaite, C. Warren. *Internal Migration in the United States.* Philadelphia, University of Pennsylvania Press, 1934.

Tippett, Tom. *When Southern Labor Stirs.* New York, Jonathan Cape & Harrison Smith, 1931.
—— *Horse Shoe Bottoms* (Fictionalized History).

Tolman, W. H. *Safety.* New York, Harpers, 1913.

Tostlebe, Alvin Samuel. *The Bank of North Dakota.* New York, Longmans, 1924.

Trachtenberg, Alexander. *American Socialism and the War, pamphlet.*

Tracy, G. A. *History of the Typographical Union.* Indianapolis, 1913.

Transcript of the Record of the Trial of Niccola Sacco and Bartolomeo Vanzetti, 5 volumes, 1 supplement. New York, Henry Holt, 1928.

Tryon, F. F., Mann, L., Rogers, H. O. *Coal in 1930.* United States Department of Commerce, Bureau of Mines, 1932.

Turner, Frederick Jackson. *The United States 1830-1850.* New York, Henry Holt, 1935.

United States Bureau Labor Statistics. *Condition of Woman and Child Wage Earners in United States.* Investigations in 1907-8, Report 19 volumes published 1910-1913. Summary of above—Bulletin No. 175-1916.

United States Bureau of Labor Statistics. *Collective Bargaining the Anthracite Coal Industry.* No. 191 March, 1916.

Van Doren, Durand H. *Workmen's Compensation.* New York, Moffat Yard & Co., 1918.

Walling, William English. *American Labor and American Democracy.* New York, Harpers, 1926.

Walker, Stanley. *The City Editor.* New York, Stokes, 1934.

Ware, Norman. *The Industrial Worker, 1840-60.* Boston, Houghton Mifflin, 1924.

—— *The Labor Movement in the United States, 1860-1895.* New York, Appleton, 1929.

Warren, Charles. *Congress, the Constitution and Supreme Court.* 1925.

Wedge, F. R. *Inside the I. W. W.* Redwood City, California, 3rd edition, 1924.

Wesley, Charles H. *Negro Labor in the United States.* New York, Vanguard Press, 1927.

Whipple, Leon. *The Story of Civil Liberty in the United States.* New York, Vanguard Press.

Wickersham Commission. *(Suppressed) Report on Mooney-Billings Cases.* New York, Gorham House, Inc., 1932.

Williams, Whiting. *Mainsprings of Men.* New York, Scribner, 1925.

Willoughby, W. F. *Employers Associations for Dealing with Labor in the United States.* R. J. Economics 20.

Withers, Hartley. The Case for Capitalism.

Wolf, H. D. *The Railroad Labor Board.* Chicago, University of Chicago Press, 1927.

Wolfson, Theresa. *The Woman Worker and the Trade Unions.* New York, International Publishers, 1926.

Wolman, Leo. *Growth of Trade Unions, 1880-1923.* New York, National Bureau Economic Research Publishers No. 6, 1924.

—— *Hardman American Labor Dynamics,* Chapter—"Recent Economic Changes." New York, Harcourt Brace.

—— *Women and Child Wage Earners, Volumes 9 and 10.* Senate Doc. Volumes 94 and 95.

Wood, Louis A. *Union Management Cooperation on Railroads.* New Haven, 1931.

Woodson, C. G. *A Century of Negro Migration.* Washington, 1918.

Wright, Carroll D. *Battles of Labor.*

Wyman, A. L. *The Employers Association.* Little Falls, 1920.

INDEX